Architectural Programming and Predesign Manager

Robert Hershberger, Ph.D., FAIA

McGraw-Hill

New York San Francisco Washington, D.C. Auckland Bogotá
Caracas Lisbon London Madrid Mexico City Milan
Montreal New Delhi San Juan Singapore
Sydney Tokyo Toronto

Library of Congress Cataloging-in-Publication Data

Hershberger, Robert G.
   Architectural programming and predesign manager / Robert G.
Hershberger.
     p.   cm.
   Includes bibliographical references and index.
   ISBN 0-07-134749-6
   1. Architectural design—Data processing. 2. Computer-aided
design. I. Title.
NA2728.H47   1999
720—dc21   99-14447
                                       CIP

McGraw-Hill

A Division of The McGraw·Hill Companies

1 2 3 4 5 6 7 8 9 0   DOC/DOC   9 0 4 3 2 1 0 9

P/N 135218-X
PART OF
ISBN 0-07-134749-6

The sponsoring editor for this book was Wendy Lochner, the editing supervisor
was Andrew Yoder, copy editing was by Audrey Brichetto Morris of the
Herberger Center for Design Excellence of Arizona State University, and the
production supervisor was Pamela A. Pelton. It was set in MattAntique by Lisa
M. Mellott through the services of Barry E. Brown (Broker—Editing, Design
and Production).

Printed and bound by R.R. Donnelley & Sons Company.

McGraw-Hill books are available at special quantity discounts to use as
premiums and sales promotions, or for use in corporate training programs. For
more information, please write to the Director of Special Sales, McGraw-Hill,
11 West 19th Street, New York, NY 10011. Or contact your local bookstore.

 This book is printed on recycled, acid-free paper containing a minimum of 50% recycled de-inked fiber.

Dedication

This book is dedicated to my wife, Deanna, and our children, Vernon and Andrew, who have given me both the love and encouragement that I needed to persevere for the twenty-three years that this book has been in process.

Contents

Foreword

Throughout a long and distinguished career as an educator, a significant piece of which was at Arizona State University in the College of Architecture and Environmental Design (of which I am currently the Dean), and then most recently at the University of Arizona (where he has only recently stepped down as Dean), Bob Hershberger has sustained in parallel an active architectural practice. This volume draws richly from this joint background. Donald Schoen has written vividly of the need for reflective practice. Perhaps no one should feel more powerfully that challenge than the educator/practitioner. In this book we all benefit from Dr. Hershberger's reflections on a career that has included the rigorous research required for his Ph.D., the careful structuring required to transform students into professionals, and his own work as a practicing architect.

I should declare immediately that I am the direct beneficiary of Bob Hershberger's efforts. For a brief period he was my Associate Dean before the University of Arizona called. The new addition to our College of Architecture and Environmental Design celebrates through the work of Alan Chimacoff of the Hillier Group an extraordinarily thoughtful program for which Bob Hershberger and Tim McGinty provided the major effort and guidance. And every day of my working life is spent in the context of Bob Hershberger's two efforts on Mill Avenue in Tempe, both of which are described in this book. I am referring to his influence that caused the city fathers to rethink their plan to bulldoze Mill Avenue, which was then replaced with a much more responsible plan to honor the historic heritage and create a richer and far more humane urban center. I also enjoy my daily salute to the Alleluia Lutheran Church on Mill Avenue where the existing modest house became the springboard for his design of the sanctuary.

This book is a contribution to the literature on programming and acknowledges its debt to its predecessors, most notably the work of William Peña whose series of volumes, all of which have the phrase "Problem Seeking" in their title, began in 1969. Other names familiar from the literature, such as Henry Sanoff, Wolfgang Preiser, and Mickey Palmer are invoked, as are institutions such as the AIA and GSA who have helped define the current practice.

This book differs, however, in several respects. First, it is clearly intended primarily as a text to be used in an educational setting. Second, it is much more discursive and inclusive, drawing heavily on the author's academic and professional experiences. Third, and most significantly, it emphasizes the qualitative, or value, issues as having priority while accepting as a competent professional that there remain quantitative, and particularly economic, realities that must be addressed.

As a text I suspect the book will be easy to use. The eight chapters relate nicely to a sixteen-week semester. The exercises at the end of each chapter are valuable pedagogical tools. And the instructor will be able to develop an interesting dialogue with the voice and ideas of the author. The voice, and those ideas, lend a personality to the text. The reader gets to know and admire the author as a reflective practitioner and a natural teacher, whose own values of respect and caring for his clients and his students are transparent.

Ever since Amos Rapoport wrote House Form and Culture, educators have been appropriately loath to refer to climate, site, technology, and use, as "determinants" of architectural form. Let me quote:

My basic hypothesis, then, is that house form is not simply the result of physical forces or any single causal factor, but is the consequence of a whole range of socio-cultural factors seen in their broadest terms. Form is in turn modified by climatic conditions (the physical environment which makes some things impossible and encourages others) and by methods of construction, materials available, and the technology (the tools for achieving the desired environment). I will call the socio-cultural factors primary, and the others secondary or modifying.

Given a certain climate, the availability of certain materials, and the constraints and capabilities of a given level of technology, what finally decides the form of a dwelling, and moulds the spaces and their relationships, is the vision that people have of the ideal life.

Amos Rapoport was writing primarily about buildings that were the product of what he calls the "preindustrial vernacular." That is to say, buildings that may have been built by craftsmen but were not the conceptual products of professional architects. I see this book as an effort to bring to the self-conscious work of the architect a similar priority of cultural value.

One of the questions that is always raised when programming is discussed is whether programming and design are necessarily separate and sequential activities, and the corollary question of whether the programmer and the designer can or should be the same individual. This book does not firmly answer those questions, while it does discuss the pros and cons behind them. As an architect who often has designed the buildings he has programmed, and who is intimately familiar with the dialogue that can be so fertile between program and design, Bob Hershberger clearly does not fit in the camp of those who would hold them firmly separate. Indeed, as a student, he studied under Louis Kahn, whose building designs are as much an interrogation of the program of an institution as they are a consequence of that program.

In closing, I have a suggestion as to how to read this book. I would start at the end, with the two sample programs. In particular I would start with the program for a Mikvah for an Orthodox Jewish Congregation. Dr. Hershberger is not an Orthodox Jew, indeed a significant part of his practice has been churches for the Christian faith that informs his life and values, but in this program there is evidence of the profound respect for the values of the institution which is being served. That is the very center of what this book is about. Having come to terms with it, one can turn with profit back to the beginning to follow the logic of the text in the comfortable company of its estimable author.

John Meunier
July 1997

Preface

This book is intended to be a teaching/learning tool-a text/ workbook that can be used in the college classroom to help students in architecture and other environmental design disciplines learn a sound basis for architectural programming. It will also be useful in the architectural office for practitioners who have not had sufficient educational background in architectural programming. Each reader can learn from the text about the theoretical and methodological aspects of programming and employ the suggested exercises to develop needed programming skills.

The intent of the book is to provide a strong philosophical basis and the appropriate methodology for programming that begins the process leading to architecture—buildings that accomplish the goals, meet the needs, and express the highest and most appropriate values of the clients, users, and architect to become works of art.

Because of its emphasis, the book should appeal to architects, architectural designers, architectural educators, and architectural students. Interior designers, landscape architects, and urban designers should also find this programming approach to be useful as they endeavor to create works of art in their own areas.

The book will also prove of interest and use to behavioral and social scientists engaged in architectural programming because the philosophical basis is not alien to their objectives, and the methodologies are decidedly biased toward those used by behavioral and social scientists. They will find themselves on familiar ground during discussions of literature search and review, observation, interviewing, questionnaire preparation, sampling, and the like. They will also find the emphasis on values to be of current interest in their own fields.

The point of view offered is that effective architectural programming can enhance the quality of design, and conversely that some programming approaches actually inhibit quality design. Those methods of programming that focus only on the collection of facts and figures about the presumed needs of the client or user group are likely to miss the most important information for design: values and goals. Without an initial understanding of these areas, there is a very high probability that many of the collected facts and figures will be irrelevant and misleading. The important values and goals must be identified for the programmer to know what facts and figures need to be articulated in the program. The designer, on the other hand, needs values and goals to know on which areas to focus the design effort. The designer can also use the expressed values and goals to evaluate the appropriateness of various design decisions. The behavioral scientist needs to understand the values and goals for meaningful post-occupancy evaluation.

The intent, therefore, is to provide the reader with a text/workbook that articulates a sound and general basis for architectural programming and sets forth the fundamental methods, techniques, and tools to be utilized. It differentiates itself from other texts and publications currently available in this area by:

1. Providing an extended theoretical discussion of the reasons for preparing an architectural program.

2. Stressing the importance of value identification prior to establishing specific program goals and requirements.

3. Covering in some depth the most essential and general procedures for developing programming information

4. Showing how work sessions can be used effectively at the conclusion of information gathering and the beginning of program preparation.

5. Showing what program documents should contain and how to assemble them.

6. Introducing specific exercises by which the reader can develop the skills necessary to do quality architectural programming.

7. Demonstrating how such an approach can help architects evaluate, and hence improve, their design solutions.

8. Providing two excellent examples of program documents in the appendix to show the reader how a final program document should be presented.

Finally, the organization of the text and abundance of illustrations should make reading both easy and enjoyable for those in or aspiring to be in a visually oriented design profession. They should find this book of use in their endeavor to create architecture.

Acknowledgments

As an architectural student I did not take a course in architectural programming. I was given the program, usually a brief one, by the studio instructor and was expected to begin to design. However, like other students in the typical five-year architectural program, I was required to do research and write a program for my bachelor's thesis. I selected a two-year medical school for my project, and in the process of literature review discovered Louis I. Kahn and his seminal work on the Richards Building at the University of Pennsylvania. I was amazed at the depth of his thinking about architecture, not just design but also questions about the nature of form and its relation to human institutions. I decided that I should study under this master architect and teacher. I must acknowledge the seed that he planted as he considered with his students the essential nature of various design projects—a house in Chestnut Hill, a consulate for Angola, a river boat on the River Thames and finally the Salk Center. It started me thinking about the nature of architecture. My sincere thanks to Louis I. Kahn.

In my first teaching job at Idaho State University, I regularly ate lunch in the Faculty Club where, to my constant amazement, I listened to other faculty talk about their research, statistics and the like. I found their conversations stimulating and baffling, because my education had practically nothing in these areas. The University of Pennsylvania had just begun a Ph.D. program in architecture, so I decided to go back and learn about research, especially as it might apply to architecture. This time I discovered Russell Ackoff, professor and head of Operations Research. He had graduated in architecture, but had found research more to his liking. He applied the problem solving mentality of the architect to this new field. His work and teaching were fascinating because, like Kahn, he looked beyond the obvious for the profound—for understanding, not just description. I gratefully acknowledge his influence on my way of thinking. Dean G. Holmes Perkins reinforced this type of thinking as he guided me through my dissertation study on Architecture and Meaning. His incisive directions and insistence that I manage the scope of the research also greatly contributed to how I think. I acknowledge and thank him. He is my model of a fine human being and an outstanding educator and administrator.

I presented my dissertation research at one of the first meetings of the Environmental Design Research Association (EDRA) in Blacksburg, Virginia. Here I met other architects and social scientists interested in research questions in architecture. A few, like Gerald Davis and Jay Farbstein, were practicing as architectural programmers. I have been greatly influenced by a number of these people including Walter Moleski, Robert Bechtel, John Zeisel, Kent Spreckelmeyer, and Wolf Preiser, to name a few. Returning to the annual EDRA conference every year for ten or more years influenced my thinking a great deal.

After receiving my Ph.D. at the University of Pennsylvania, I took a position as Associate Professor at Arizona State University where I began teaching research methods and architectural programming. I also began teaching design with Calvin C. Straub, who became a personal mentor. His devotion to site analysis and, especially, client/user analysis greatly influence how I think, how I teach design, and especially how I have come to think about and teach architectural programming. I especially acknowledge his contribution to this book.

And, of course, a professor's best teachers are students. I greatly appreciate the education that they have given to me. I especially acknowledge how their insights and concerns have gradually shaped the text on programming to its present state. I have been able to include some of their work in the text, but there has been so much more that could not be included. Thank you everyone. Your contributions are most appreciated. Similarly, the practicing professional's best teachers are clients! They often selected my firm because it offered programming services. I have had many outstanding clients and acknowledge their contribution, especially how they showed me that "values become issues," whether we want them to or not. They taught me how to program.

I began working on this book in the summer and fall of 1976. The book took second place to an active programming and design practice for about ten years, but was nearly complete when I left Arizona State University in 1988 to become Dean of the College of Architecture at The University of Arizona. I team-taught programming that spring with Susan Moody, who then taught the course for the next seven years using my nearly complete document. I very much appreciate the insights that she and her students gave me from that time period.

I thank Chuck Hutchinson for his encouragement and good advice over the years. I also thank Donna Duerk, Kent Spreckelmeyer, Wolf Preiser, and Walter Moleski for being thoughtful reviewers of the manuscript in its various stages. I deeply appreciate the thoughtful foreword by Dean John Meunier of Arizona State University. I thank Carl Okasaki for the many excellent sketch illustrations, Nancy Cole for her computer graphic images, and Claudette Barry for initial editing of the manuscript. I especially thank Audrey Brichetto Morris of the Herberger Center for Design Excellence at Arizona State University for her exceptionally thoughtful copyediting of the final manuscript. I stand in awe of her special abilities in this area. I am equally impressed with the expertise of Kelly Ricci, Lisa M. Mellott, Nadine McFarland, and Toya Warner of Barry E. Brown, Broker, in designing, formatting, layout, and graphic design of this book. Finally, I want to express appreciation to Mary Kihl, Director of the Herberger Center, and Wendy Lochner, Architectural Editor for McGraw-Hill, for their timely and incisive answers to my many questions about how to get the book published. Thank you all!

About the Author

Robert Hershberger is a professor and dean emeritus of the College of Architecture at the University of Arizona in Tucson and a practicing architect who has won numerous design awards. He is a fellow of the American Institute of Architects.

Architectural Programming

1.1 The Nature of Architectural Programming

Programming is the first, and perhaps the most important, stage in the architecture delivery process. Whether provided as an integral part of professional architectural services, as an additional service, or not consciously provided by anyone, programming takes place at one level or another in the interaction of the client, users, and the architect.

> *Programming is the definitional stage of design—the time to discover the nature of the design problem, rather than the nature of the design solution.*

The programming stage is a crucial time in which serious mistakes can happen or insightful, formative decisions can be made. The implications for the design solution are as enormous as the differences between the Taj Mahal (Fig. 1-1) and a car wash (Fig. 1-2). Both are appropriate architecture for very different problems.

Figure 1-1 Taj Mahal.
Photo Credit: Calvin C. Straub

Figure 1-2 Weiss Guys Car Wash.

It is the nature of the problem as expressed in the architectural program that has the most profound effect on the design solution in architecture. As one outstanding architect and educator, Calvin C. Straub, FAIA, stated (1980):

"The program is the design!"

He was not implying that the talents of the design architect are of little consequence, but that many of the most important "formative" decisions are made before the architect begins to design. For instance, the decision may have been reached to have only one building instead of two; or an auditorium within the fabric of a larger building rather than freestanding on its own site; or offices in a building separate from the classrooms, or vice versa. The budget could be set so low as to preclude any number of design opportunities, or the time span for completion of the design and construction could be so short that only the simplest of forms could be utilized in order to finish on schedule.

If the client and programmer are primarily interested in functional efficiency, organizational and activity decisions may be made that could significantly affect the form of the building. If the client and programmer are more concerned with the social and psychological needs of the users, prescriptions for form may be inherent in the listed spaces, sizes, characteristics, and relationships. If they are concerned with economics, it is possible that numerous material and system opportunities, as well as potentially unique spaces and places, will be eliminated from design consideration. Conversely, for any of the above illustrations, the lack of concern for and information on important design issues may restrict the designer's options. The point is that the values and concerns of the client and the programmer will have a significant impact on the form of the building, because they choose the information presented to the designer.

Some architects have expressed concern that poorly conceived programs limit their design decision-making freedom, and they have taken steps to be certain that architectural programs address their concerns as well as those of the client and programmer. William Peña of the architecture and engineering firm Caudill Rowlett Scott (CRS) developed and articulated a very systematic and successful approach to architectural programming, which attempts to define the "whole problem" by making certain that every program produced by the firm provides essential information in four distinct areas: function, form, economy, and time (Peña et al. 1969, 1977, 1987). It is apparent from the many design awards received by the firm that this approach to developing information about the whole problem has had a significant positive impact on the quality of the firm's design efforts.

Other architects, such as Louis I. Kahn, upset by the poor quality of architectural programs received from clients, insisted on going back to "original beginnings," rethinking with the client about the nature of the design problem (Kahn 1961). Numerous other practicing architects and programming specialists have dealt similarly with these issues and tried to bring understanding to this first stage of the architectural design process (Becker 1959; Demoll 1965; Horowitz 1966; Evans and Wheeler 1969; Davis 1969; White 1972; Farbstein 1976; Sanoff 1977, 1992; Preiser 1978, 1985, 1993; Davis and Szigeti 1979; Zeisel 1981; Palmer 1981; Marti 1981; Hershberger 1985; Spreckelmeyer 1986; Lang 1987; Duerk 1993; Kumlin 1995).

This book is deeply influenced by many of these efforts. It utilizes insights obtained from these sources and the author's experiences in practice and teaching to set forth a general programming approach applicable to a wide range of architectural design problems, and provides both theoretical and practical frameworks for learning how to do effective architectural programming.

1.2 Definitions of Architectural Programming

Definitions of programming in the design professions are as diverse as the people involved in its practice. These people have even had difficulty arriving at an appropriate modifier to distinguish the activity from the more pervasive "computer programming." Combinations such as building programming (Davis 1969), environmental programming (Farbstein 1976), facility programming (Preiser 1978), functional programming (Davis and Szigeti 1979), and design programming (GSA 1983) have been used to describe the activity.

The above-stated modifiers to programming and the resulting definitions do not set high enough standards. It is not enough to "facilitate" a client's operations. "Function," while important in most projects, is not the only reason for building. "Environment" simply implies that which surrounds, neither good nor bad. Even "design programming," with its process rather than product orientation, misses the essential reason why architects should be interested and involved in programming. For architects, the purpose of both programming and design should be to achieve architecture: buildings that respond effectively to the program, but in synthesis become works of art.

The objective, then, is to program for *architecture*, for environments that transcend the "problem" to create something of wonder that captures the essence of the institution; relates marvelously to the site, climate, and time; goes beyond immediate needs to enhance the potential of the users; expresses the highest aspirations of the client, architect, and society; and "moves" all users in some special way.

The terminology proposed here is the most generally used: "architectural programming." A carefully conceived program should promote architecture. It should not focus exclusively on "defining the problem." It should serve as a vehicle to "question the problem," to discover the nature of the "institution," to explore and discover the values of society, client, user, and architect; to uncover constraints and opportunities, so that in the pursuit of inspired design, the program becomes a guidepost for achieving architecture.

What then is an appropriate *description* for architectural programming?

Related: Programming is the first stage of the architectural design process in which the relevant values of the client, user, and society are identified; important project goals are articulated; facts about the project are discovered; and facility needs are made explicit.

The architectural program is the document in which the identified values, goals, facts, and needs are presented.

Programming is an essential part of the overall architecture delivery process, which can roughly be defined as having four stages: programming, design, construction, and occupancy. Between each stage is an appropriate time for evaluating the effectiveness of the previous stage (Fig. 1-3).

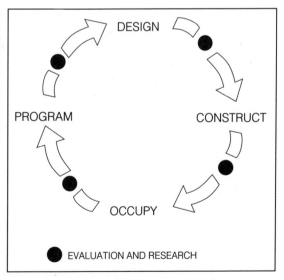

Figure 1-3 Architecture Delivery Process.
Credit: Nancy Cole

1.3 Approaches to Architectural Programming

Various programming methods have been developed and used over the years as clients, architects, and programmers have tried to arrive at appropriate definitions for particular architectural problems. These methods range from informal discussions between client and architect to carefully articulated research studies covering similar facilities and users leading to a comprehensive and detailed program. Most programming approaches fall between the two extremes.

Historically, programming appears to have fallen outside of normal architectural services. In fact, in the current AIA Standard Form of Agreement between Owner and Architect (AIA Document B141), programming is identified as an additional service. The expectation is that the owner will provide the architect with the needed program information. In England, this document is referred to as the "client's brief." Aptly named, these documents are typically very short lists of the required rooms and their square footages, with very little explanation of the values of client, users, or society; purposes to be served by the building; relationships between the spaces; requirements of the spaces; and so on. This type of program was adequate at a time when most institutions were relatively simple and slow to change, allowing architects to intuitively understand what was needed.

This client-based approach to architectural programming became less effective toward the middle of this century, as buildings became more complicated and difficult to understand. In these cases, when insufficient or inaccurate information was provided to the designer by the client, it proved costly during design, construction, and after occupancy because of the necessity for expensive changes to make the building work. As a result, architects such as Herbert Swinborne (1958), Nathanial Becker (1959), and Louis Demoll (1965) began to offer architectural programming services to their clients in order to achieve more reliable and valid programs.

In 1966, Harold Horowitz, an architect working at a federal research agency in the United States, wrote a seminal article on the nature of architectural programming and its relationship with research in the behavioral sciences: "The Architect's Programme and the Behavioral Sciences" (Horowitz 1966). In this article, Horowitz discussed 11 areas of information that should be included in an architectural program as well as how the work of behavioral scientists could contribute to the development of information in each area.

The article was of great interest to a number of architectural practitioners and social scientists. Indeed, it was highly influential and continues to define the essential elements of architectural programming today (Fig. 1-4).

1.4 Design-Based Architectural Programming

1. Objective of the master plan.
2. Special restrictions and limitations on design.
3. Characteristics of the site.
4. Site development requirements.
5. Functional requirements for the facility.
6. Characteristics of the occupants.
7. Specific facility requirements.
8. Relative location and inter-relationship of the spaces.
9. Budget.
10. Flexibility for future growth and changes in function.
11. Priority of need among the various requirements.

Figure 1-4 Horowitz Programming Areas.

Credit: (Horowitz 1966) 72–73. Permission: Architectural Science Review

Today's most frequently used programming method occurs simultaneously with the design process. In this method, a minimum amount of programmatic information is generated prior to initiation of the design process. Usually, the architect and client meet to discuss the client's design problem and the architect takes notes as the discussion proceeds. Sometimes the client has already prepared a short program statement or client's brief, which may list the spaces required, square footage for each, maximum construction budget, and occasionally some particular material or system requirements, or desired special effects.

In most cases, a minimum amount of time and effort are expended in generating the program, and the design proceeds forthwith—sometimes at the first meeting. This happens both when the client has already generated a plan for the architect "to draw up," and when the architect brings pencil and paper to the meeting and begins to sketch design ideas based on the client's brief and/or the discussion with the client. The programming process then continues over a number of meetings as the client reacts to the designs generated by the architect.

If something was left out of the brief and not covered in the discussion, it becomes evident in the drawings. The new information is then taken into account and a new drawing is produced. This process is repeated until the client and architect are satisfied that all problems have been uncovered and resolved in the design. This approach sometimes works, depending on:

1. The thoroughness and accuracy of the client's brief.

2. The effectiveness of the architect as an interviewer.

3. The scope of the project.

If the project is very simple, such as an artist's studio or a small house for an individual or couple, the hopes, dreams, and requirements of the client may be completely articulated in one or two meetings, and a satisfactory solution achieved with minimal formal programming or cost to the client or architect. However, if the client has prepared an inadequate brief and/or the architect is not an effective interviewer, problems may arise.

If the client has already prepared a plan, as is often the case for residences, the architect may try it and sketch some elevations to see how they look. What if they do not look good? This is quite likely, since the plan would have been prepared by a non-designer. What is the architect to do next? Tell the client that the plan is bad because the elevations do not look good? An adversarial relationship is likely to develop if this takes place. Or should the architect simply accept the plan even if the elevations do not look good? The architect, if interested at all in creating architecture, will probably be extremely uncomfortable doing this.

Conversely, if the client does not offer a plan, then the architect may come up with plan and elevation studies, and the process will be reversed. The client may find something missing from the plan that had not been previously discussed. Or, the elevations may not be considered satisfactory by the client, because the plan does not seem to work. A negative situation may develop in which the client always has the last word. The key problems here are that:

1. The process might become reactionary, rather than creative, in nature.

2. The interaction between client and architect may erode any initial confidence or rapport between them.

It may also shift the authority to make aesthetic decisions from the architect to the client. This is almost inevitably disastrous to the creation of architecture. The proverbial camel is created as the committee of client and architect react to each successive design.

Another problem with the design-based approach is that it can be expensive and time consuming. It is much simpler and less expensive to generate program requirements (words, numbers, diagrams) than to generate designs. An architect in a reactionary relationship with a client may be tempted to accept less than an excellent and artistic solution in order to cut financial losses. Or, an architect with artistic integrity may start a new design each time new information is generated, but it will be at considerable personal cost.

The author knows of one architect who prepared four complete schematic designs for a large house using design-based programming procedures. At that point, the client completely lost confidence in the architect's ability to solve the problem. The architect had spent nearly four times the normal budget for schematic design before the contract was terminated. What a terrible and foolish loss! All four of the designs had artistic merit, but none solved the client's inadequately defined problem. The client ended up thinking the architect was incompetent, and the architect ended up thinking even worse of the client (Fig. 1-5).

Figure 1-5 Are We Really Communicating?
Credit: Carl Okazaki

Louis I. Kahn is known to have completely redesigned buildings after he discovered something new about the essential character of the facility. He had the integrity to take substantial financial loss to produce a design of great significance. Perhaps, however, it would have been possible to understand the essential nature or "existence will" (as he might have called it) of the building before going through the great expense of preparing the designs he rejected. It would have saved a great deal of time and money for both the client and the architect. Fortunately, Kahn was interested in seeking out the very essence of a problem and the discoveries and insights were his own, not the result of client critiques of his designs. Clients were awed by how profound his discoveries were, rather than chagrined by the fact that something had been missed earlier. For lesser architects, however, such changes are often the result of inadequate programming—and the discovery by the client that needs are not being met. This circumstance can create serious problems for the architect.

Another exception to the often unsatisfactory approach of programming by design has been used and articulated by Joseph

Esherick, architect and professor of architecture at the University of California at Berkeley (Esherick 1987). Working primarily on single family residences, Esherick meets with the client several times- at their home, at the site, in the architect's office. At each meeting, he produces very simple analytic sketches and diagrams in response to the client's input. He leaves these sketches with the client and does very little, if any, work on the project until the next meeting, at which time the process repeats itself as the client provides new information and the architect generates new sketches. This goes on until the client is satisfied that the architect knows and appreciates the client's expectations for the house. Esherick then proceeds to develop the actual design for the house (Figs. 1-6 and 1-7).

Esherick avoids an adversary relationship because the conceptual diagrams and sketches are simply representations of what the client is discussing—manifestations of the client's own thoughts. The tendency of the client to become sole judge of design is avoided, because the sketches are not designs but reflections of the discussion. The high cost in terms of time, money, and especially lost rapport between client and architect is completely avoided, since the architect makes no investment in design between meetings (Fig. 1-8).

Figure 1-6 House: Sketch.

Credit and Permission: Esherick Homsey Dodge and Davis

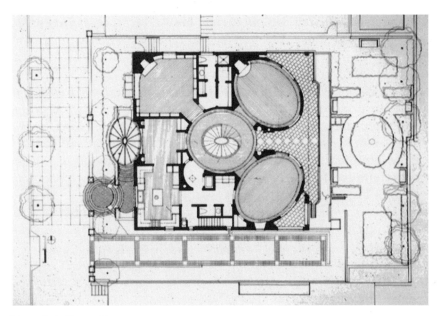

Figure 1-7 House: Plan.

Credit and Permission: Esherick Homsey Dodge and Davis

Figure 1-8 House: Interior.

Credit and Permission: Esherick Homsey Dodge and Davis

Similarly, an architect who sees his or her role as facilitator and resource to the client may be more comfortable with designs resulting from a highly interactive process in which the problem and its solution are not known until the design is complete (Sanoff 1977). Designers who delight in complex, contradictory, and even discordant final design statements may enjoy programming by design, because whatever turns up at the end of the process can be developed into an aesthetic statement satisfactory to the architect. The fact that the process is essentially reactionary and inefficient may be of little importance if the client and architect are happy with the results.

A fine example of this interactive process with outstanding results is the programming and design of St. Matthew's Episcopal Church (Fig. 1-9) in Pacific Palisades, California, by Moore Ruble Yudell Architects and members of the congregation, who worked together to assemble a three-dimensional model of the overall scheme (Knight 1984).

A cogent argument for "programming as design" has been advocated by Julia Robinson and J. Stephen Weeks of the University of Minnesota College of Architecture. Their premise is that "an architectural problem cannot be fully understood prior to design; thus any definition of the problem is premature until the design is

Figure 1-9 St. Matthew's Episcopal Church.

completed" (Robinson and Weeks 1984). The entire design process is seen as a process of problem definition. Robinson and Weeks further argue that the distinction is not between analysis and synthesis, nor rational and intuitive, but between verbal/numerical and formal/spatial exploration. Words and pictures are more powerful programming tools in concert than alone, and, thus, a program is not complete without them (Fig. 1-10).

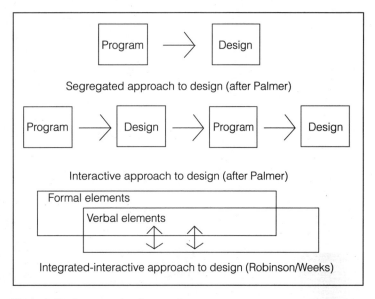

Figure 1-10 Programming Approaches.

Adapted from diagram by Julia Robinson in Robinson and Weeks, 1984, page 4, with permission from Julia Robinson.

The author agrees with some of the above assertions and feels that design exploration is appropriate during programming, especially in an academic setting where a real client, user, and/or site cannot be identified. However, in a professional setting, the earlier cautions about "programming by design" still apply. It is true that no problem definition is ever complete—even after design is complete! Our understanding of the problem becomes clearer as time progresses. Similarly, organizations, environments, and economic situations are constantly changing. They do not stop changing when the program is complete, the design is complete, the building is complete, or any time thereafter. This should not mean that an adequate problem definition cannot be generated from which to begin design.

Beginning design with a carefully developed program does not preclude some overlap of programming (verbal/numerical) and design (formal/spatial) activities late in programming and early in design, especially if the design architect is involved in programming, such as is the case with many fine architects. This overlap takes place in two ways: 1) when design ideas are articulated (verbally and visually) during the programming process by the client, users, and designer; and 2) as the programmer initiates design analysis by seeking clarification as to whether certain combinations of activities, spaces, and relationships will be viable. This

PROS

1. A minimum amount of time is spent on generating programmatic information.
2. Design can begin at the very first meeting of client and architect.
3. There is intensive and often positive interaction between client and architect.
4. The review of various design schemes may help the client recognize new ways to accomplish their objectives.
5. Both client and architect can claim the design solution as their own.

CONS

1. If the client's brief is flawed, it may be difficult to overcome with design.
2. If the client already has a plan, the architect may have difficulty adjusting to the limited aesthetic possibilities.
3. The client may assume authority to make all decisions, including aesthetic and technical ones.
4. The process may become reactionary and adversarial rather than creative.
5. In these cases, the process can be time consuming and costly for the architect.

Figure 1-11   Design-Based Programming.

kind of design exploration or analysis (rather than synthesis) is almost always helpful to both the architect and the client in understanding the architectural problem more completely. It may lead to changes to the previously accepted program. This is to be expected. If done systematically at the end of programming or at the beginning of design, such changes can be included in the final program statement or a suitable addendum.

In any case, the desirability of design exploration does not mitigate against developing the best possible architectural program as a beginning point for design. Also, there is no reason to confine programming activities to verbal/numeric data. There are good reasons to use visual information throughout the programming process to show site conditions, existing facilities both on and off the site, required furnishings or equipment, desired relationships, design ideas, and the like. Programming is not solely a verbal/numeric activity (Fig. 1-11).

1.5 Knowledge-Based Architectural Programming

In the late 1960s, a new group of people began to have an impact on architectural programming. These were social and behavioral scientists who began to direct some of their attention to the built environment. A new social science specialization alternatively referred to as environmental psychology, environmental sociology, or human ecology began to emerge (Conway 1973). Many of these social scientists became affiliated with the Environmental Design Research Association (EDRA), an organization in which architects, interior designers, and other design professionals began to interact with social scientists in the common concern that many buildings and other designed environments did not work particularly well for the people they were meant to serve. These interdisciplinary groups generally chose to utilize research methods, techniques, and tools developed by social and behavioral scientists to study human attitudes and behavior-literature search and review, systematic observation, controlled interviewing, questionnaires and surveys, sampling, and statistical analysis. This ushered in a time of extensive research oriented to developing knowledge about the environmental needs of various user groups.

Seminal studies of personal space and territoriality by Edward Hall (1966) and Robert Sommer (1969) were introduced to the architectural profession and influenced many architects, who gave consideration to their findings in both programming and design. Other behavioral scientists such as Irwin Altman (1975), Powell Lawton (1982), Bechtel et al. (1987), and Clare Cooper Marcus (1975) followed with more directed studies on privacy, special needs of the elderly, survey research, and special building types. A number of architects including Henry Sanoff (1977, 1992), Gary Moore (Moore and Gooledge 1976), Paul Windley (Lawton et al. 1982), Kent Spreckelmeyer (Marans and Spreckelmeyer 1981), and the author (Hershberger 1969) adopted some of the same methods, techniques, and tools to study problems of interest to them. Still other architects, such as Gerald Davis (1969), Jay Farbstein (1976), Wolfgang F. E. Preiser (1978, 1985, 1993), Walter Moleski (1974), and Michael Brill (1984) began to utilize research in actual programming practice. All have been successful in their own ways and have accounted for a large number of the programs produced for major clients in recent years (Fig. 1-12).

Typically, these programming efforts have been of great benefit when considering facility needs for large, complex building types such as prisons, hospitals, airports, research facilities, governmental office buildings, and the like, where the architect or even the key administrators may not have a very good conception of the

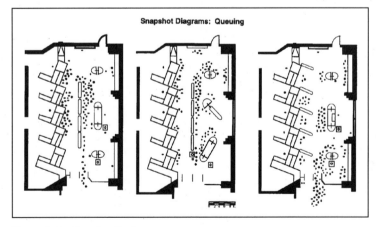

Figure 1-12 Queuing Study.

Credit: Jay Farbstein and Associates and Min Kantrowitz and Associates for Einhorn Yaffee Prescott, 1996. *Albuquerque Test Market Post Occupancy Evaluations: Summary.* United States Postal Service. Permission: Jay Farbstein and Associates

values, goals, and needs of persons in various divisions of the organization. In order to make these determinations, it is necessary to interview key personnel in the various divisions about their values and goals and to observe how people use their current environments. It may also be possible to review the research literature on special user needs, to visit other facilities to see how they respond to similar problems, and to devise questionnaires to sample typical users about their attitudes and ideas about specific facility, furnishing, and equipment requirements.

The information gained from the various research approaches is assembled, statistically analyzed, and summarized in a program document that attempts to cover all of the human requirements of the organization. Indeed, program sheets are developed for every space in the proposed facility. Such a systematic approach to programming provides highly reliable information that is of considerable value to the designer in preparing plans to meet the needs of the client and the various user groups of the building (Fig. 1-13).

Given the generally systematic approach to knowledge-based programming, there tend to be few problems with resulting programs. In some cases, the interest in being systematic in developing knowledge about users may tend to obscure issues of importance to the design architect. Similarly, the fact that oftentimes the design architect has yet to be hired prevents the designer's expertise and values from influencing the program. Utilization of high-powered research methods on comparatively easy problems can also require excessive amounts of time and money. Indeed, this is the primary problem with

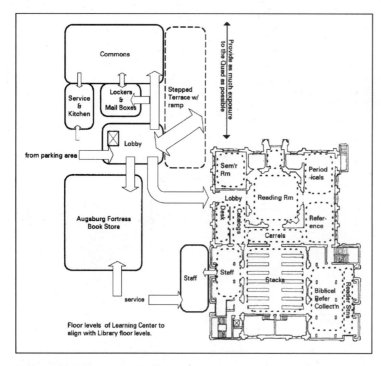

Figure 1-13 Lutheran Theological Seminary.

Credit: Walter Moleski, ERG/The Environmental Research Group, 1996. *Programming Study for Lutheran Theological Seminary*. Philadelphia, Pennsylvania. Permission: ERG/The Environmental Research Group

the knowledge-based approach to programming. Knowledge-based programming tends to consume great quantities of time in planning, making arrangements for the actual studies, doing the studies, and analyzing the large amounts of data generated. This is not a problem unless it leaves insufficient time or money to adequately consider the remaining environmental, technological, legal, temporal, economic, aesthetic, and safety issues in architecture. If something crucial to the eventual architectural solution is not studied sufficiently or covered adequately in the program, the resulting building could fail in one manner or another.

In a situation of unlimited time and resources, it would be ideal to devote an extensive systematic research effort to developing knowledge on every relevant design issue, so that no area of potential importance would be left unstudied. However, few programming projects are done in conditions where time and money are of little concern. Indeed, most programming endeavors are conducted under conditions where time and money are limited, and there is not enough of either to do the kind of job the programmer would prefer. If knowledge-based programming is to be utilized, it is important that the programming team isolate the crucial variables, in whatever issue areas they are found, and be sure to devote research efforts to these variables. The high costs of research, then, can be focused where the cost of error is high, and less expensive programming approaches can be used to obtain other kinds of information (Fig. 1-14).

1.6 Agreement-Based Architectural Programming

The agreement-based approach to programming has a number of advantages, especially when time and money are at a premium. This approach to programming relies on the knowledge of several key individuals in the client's organization to generate the required programming information. Often the key participants are officers of the organization and departmental heads who are appointed to a planning or

PROS
1. Brings to bear all currently available knowledge on the design problem.
2. Develops new knowledge using the systematic methods of the sciences.
3. Provides all of the information needed to design each space.
4. Especially useful on large, complex, or innovative projects, when no one has a clear grasp of the project requirements.

CONS
1. Can be time consuming and costly for typical building projects.
2. If a social scientist is the programmer, there may be a tendency to under emphasize non-behavioral science areas such as site/climate, economics, time, and technology.

Figure 1-14 Knowledge-Based Programming.

Figure 1-15 Work Session.
Photo Credit: Richard Brittain

building committee to generate the needed programmatic information, to hire the architect, and possibly to monitor construction.

The programmer works with this planning or building committee to arrive at a mutually acceptable set of design requirements. It is assumed that key individuals appointed to the committee will have sufficient knowledge of the organization to arrive at a satisfactory program, or they can access other information as needed (Fig. 1-15).

In this approach, the programmer serves as a knowledgeable catalyst to guide the committee in assembling the program. First, the programmer collects readily available information from the organization's records, local site and climate data, applicable governmental regulations, and the like, and sets forth areas where more information is needed from the client and users. In a working session with the programmer, the committee either responds directly with additional needed information, or the members return to their respective divisions to obtain needed information from others. The programmer points out potential areas of conflict or inconsistency in the information and leads the committee in working out differences to arrive at an agreeable program statement. The keys to the success of this approach are the understanding of the programmer relative to the information that will be needed by the designer, and the capability of the committee to provide reliable and accurate information in a timely way.

The most notable example of this approach to programming is the work of CRS of Houston, Texas (Peña et al. 1969, 1977, 1987). Their approach developed over a number of years under the able guidance of William Peña has been one of the hallmarks of the programming profession. In this approach, referred to by Peña as "problem seeking," the intent is to discover the nature of the whole design problem. In order to accomplish this, they proposed the completion of a predetermined information matrix, which the firm believed to be capable of providing a complete definition of the design problem. The completion of such a matrix and agreement on its content is the fundamental task in each programming situation.

The problem seeking matrix has four value, or issue, categories along one side: function, form, economy, and time. Peña argues that any relevant information in a design project can be placed in one of these categories. For example, site, context, climate, materials, technology, landscape, and aesthetics can be included under form. Similarly, building purpose, special users, way finding, task performance, safety, and security all fall under the function category.

Along the top of the matrix are five information areas: goals, facts, concepts, needs, and problem statement. If the resulting twenty cells of the program matrix, including the four problem statement cells, are filled with acceptable information about the project, then the problem is considered to be defined (Fig. 1-16).

	Goals	Facts	Concepts	Needs	Problem
Function					
Form					
Economy					
Time					

Figure 1-16 CRS Programming Matrix.

Adapted from Peña et al. (1969, 1977, 1987). Permission: American Institute of Architects and HOK

The approach to filling the twenty cells of the matrix is as follows: the programmers from the architecture firm independently search out readily available facts about any of the four information areas (function, form, economy, time). They then gather in "squatter" work sessions, usually at the client's existing facility, to interact with a representative group of the client/users, with an open invitation for anyone in the client's organization to participate. During these work sessions, specific project goals are identified, additional facts are generated, conceptual ways of dealing with the problem (programmatic concepts) are identified, and specific need statements are generated for each value category. A representative of the architect's design team joins the work session to fashion the problem statements in the fifth column of the matrix. This final column is included as a feedback mechanism to ensure the client and users that the designer really does understand the nature of the design problem.

The matrix is placed on a large plain wall in one of the client's meeting rooms—it often fills the entire wall. Cards indicating the value categories are placed along the left wall and cards indicating the other information areas are placed along the ceiling before the session begins. Strings are stretched between the category cards to indicate the twenty "cells" of the matrix. Five-by-eight-inch cards are prepared by the architect's programming team members and placed within the cells to visually and verbally display the information obtained (Fig. 1-17).

Cards are added throughout the programming work session, changed as necessary, and even moved from one cell to another until everyone agrees that the appropriate and complete problem definition is being presented on the wall (Fig. 1-18).

After the matrix is complete, the programming team continues to work with the client's programming group to develop specific lists of required spaces, square footages, and appropriate relationship diagrams. They do these on brown sheets of butcher paper (or on white grid paper), which, like the programming matrix, are attached to a wall in the work session room where they can easily be seen by all of the work session participants.

The brown sheets are developed using chalk on the butcher paper so they can be continuously modified until all work session participants agree that the information contained on them is correct. The participants also work together on these sheets to develop realistic budgets and schedules. They continue to work in

Figure 1-17 Completed Card Matrix.

Figure 1-18 Placing Cards on a Matrix.

Photo Credit: Richard Brittain

Figure 1-19 Completed Brown Sheet.

this manner until all elements of the program are agreed to by the members of the work session team, including the client, the programmers, and the designer (Fig. 1-19).

It should be noted that in the programming approach advocated by CRS, completing brown sheets containing information on space allocation, relationships, estimated costs, and schedule completes the active information gathering stage of programming. CRS consciously avoids the development of design development information, such as space program sheets, in order to maintain an exclusive focus on schematic design. Design development programming is conducted after the schematic design has commenced or even been completed. (See section 4.1 for full descriptions of schematic design and design development.)

There are several advantages to the above architectural programming process. First, it is a way to ensure that information is obtained for every area in which the architect has design concerns. Second, it is an economical method of generating the information needed to begin design. Very little effort is spent on time-consuming research on user needs. The firm relies, instead, on a representative group of users to communicate these needs during work sessions. Third, and perhaps most importantly, both client and architect agree on the nature and scope of the design problem before design commences. Fourth, time is conserved in the initial programming process by avoiding development of information not required to commence schematic design.

Because of the above listed advantages, this programming approach avoids both the misunderstandings and reactionary nature of the design-based programming process and the higher costs and time requirements of the knowledge-based process. And, the design results are generally very positive as evidenced by most projects by CRS including the Indiana Bell (Fig. 1-20) and Irwin Union Bank buildings (Fig. 1-21) in Columbus, Indiana.

There are, however, some disadvantages to the agreement-based programming approach as advocated by CRS. One disadvantage is the pre-fixing of the value categories. If the four categories chosen to define the whole problem appear to exclude certain value areas, there is a chance that the design problem will be inadequately defined. When trying to use the CRS system, this author always found it necessary to introduce a context category to accommodate issues such as site, climate, and urban setting, because it seemed unnatural to include them under the form category. Another firm that utilizes the problem seeking method, Anderson DeBartolo Pan (ADP), added an energy category, because

Figure 1-20 Indiana Bell.

Figure 1-21 Irwin Union Bank.

this issue was not easily absorbed within the four predetermined value categories (Pan 1985). I understand that CRS originally placed form first in the matrix until a number of clients indicated that function was their first concern. All of these changes indicate that limiting the matrix to four value categories may not be appropriate in every case. There will be other influences as well!

Another disadvantage of the CRS approach relates to how the information is obtained. If the client's selected programming group is not representative of the entire organization, or is unable to understand or communicate important user concerns and needs accurately during the on-site programming sessions, the resulting program data may be flawed. This would be most likely for unfamiliar building types.

Similarly, the information area identified as concepts in the CRS matrix appears to be appropriate only for certain types of projects, and perhaps only for firms that design numerous projects of the same building type. It has proven difficult for most student programmers and especially clients/users to separate "programmatic concepts" from "design concepts," hence there is a confusion of roles as clients and programmers begin to tie down "design" approaches, perhaps prematurely (Marans and Spreckelmeyer 1981). If the designer is on the programming team and primarily responsible for advancing the concepts, this may not be a problem, but if design concepts are advanced and accepted by others, they may be overly restrictive or inappropriate.

The purposeful separation of schematic design programming from design development programming in the CRS system eliminates detailed information that may be important to the design of individual spaces. Detailed information may be important to obtain and place in the program if a room must be of a particular shape to function appropriately, or if it must have access to natural daylight, or have a particular view or orientation. Even specific needed types or arrangements of furniture should be known by the designer so they can be accommodated appropriately.

Finally, it is not appropriate to fill in the problem statements for each value area if the designer is not a part of the programming team. This may not be possible if the programmer is hired before the architect (Fig. 1-22).

1.7 Value-Based Architectural Programming

Legend has it that Frank Lloyd Wright moved in with some of his clients for several days or weeks prior to designing them a new house. During this time he would have numerous conversations with the clients, see and experience how they lived, and have time to visit and analyze the site for the new house. By the end of this period, he had developed an excellent understanding of the family's values and goals for the new house. He also had developed an understanding of the constraints and opportunities of site, climate, budget, and the like.

PROS

1. Ensures that information is obtained for every area in which the architect has design concerns—the "whole problem."
2. Having a representative group develop the program information during work sessions is efficient and economical.
3. Visually displaying the programming information during the work sessions helps the participants to understand and influence the program.
4. The client, users, and architect agree on the nature and scope of the problem before design commences.
5. The costs of programming changes during design are generally avoided.
6. The design results are typically positive as evidenced in projects by users such as CRS and ADP.

CONS

1. The pre-fixed value categories in the CRS matrix may be too limiting for some projects.
2. Important information may be missed by using on-site work sessions as the primary information gathering method.
3. Limiting clients and users to programmatic concepts is frustrating when they have design ideas that they want to express and include in the program.
4. Not including detailed information on individual spaces may result in inappropriate schematic design decisions.
5. The problem statement requires the designer to be actively involved in the programming process.

Figure 1-22 Agreement-Based Programming.

The above legend also indicates that Wright returned to his office after the intensive time period with the client and site to "draw up" the design that he had already completely realized in his mind. There was no need to erase or redraw any element of the design. The truth of the story is not clear, but the result, inevitably, was architecture (Fig. 1-23).

Louis I. Kahn was similarly intense exploring the problem with his clients. In so doing, he came to an understanding of the most important issues to be confronted during the design process. For example, in programming for the Richards Building, a medical research facility on the campus of the University of Pennsylvania, Kahn discovered that the laboratory needs of the scientists were constantly changing and, thus, they required a large, high, open laboratory space to allow for different types of experiments. In order to make the laboratory spaces effective, Kahn also realized that there was a need for flexibility of service to and strict environmental control in these research laboratories. Indeed, he found that a very substantial portion of the construction budget would have to be expended on bringing mechanical, plumbing, and electrical service systems into and out of each laboratory. There

Figure 1-23   Kaufman Residence (Falling Water).

was a need for an effi-
cient and effective way
to bring in clean materi-
als and to dispose of
waste materials. His de-
sign for the Richards
Building (Fig. 1-24) took
into account this impor-
tant design issue, and in
so doing allowed him to
create an entirely new
form of academic re-
search building: a design
expressing the impor-
tance of the "served"
spaces for the scientists
(the offices and the laboratories) and of the "servant" spaces (the high
towers for the mechani-
cal, plumbing, and elec-
trical systems and for
egress in case of emer-
gency).

Calvin C. Straub,
FAIA, of the Southern
California architectural
firm of Buff, Straub and
Hensman, was similarly
intense in his architec-
tural programming activ-
ities. He was especially
sensitive to the lifestyle

Figure 1-24 Richards Building.

values and needs of the client/user in relationship to the opportunities offered by site and climate. The 1,400-square-foot
Thomson residence is a particularly good example of his work
(Figs. 1-25 to 1-27). In spite of its small size and modest budget, it is a spacious and beautifully articulated wood frame
house that fully meets the needs of the family and relates well
to the sloping wooded site and mild climate of Southern California.

Figure 1-25   Thomson Residence: Exterior.
Photo Credit: Julius Shulman

Figure 1-26   Thomson Residence: Interior.
Photo Credit: Julius Shulman

Will Bruder, architect, of New River, Arizona, is so thorough when interviewing his clients, so careful in discovering their values and goals and analyzing budget, site, climate, and other external influences, that he is able to develop initial designs that are usually accepted without change by the client. Bruder indicates that "by celebrating the client's poetic and pragmatic program aspirations as opportunities for unique solutions, the client takes ownership of the architecture from the beginning, as they see themselves reflected in the first drawings, models, and ideas" (Bruder 1997). The quality of Bruder's work, and his success in having original designs accepted and built, attests to his diligence and perception in the interviewing and analysis processes, as well as to his design ability (Figs. 1-28 and 1-29).

In their thoroughness of predesign analysis, Wright, Kahn, Straub, and Bruder avoid the pitfalls of design-based programming and accomplish something more akin to, but less formal than, the value-based approach to programming being advocated in this text.

Value-based programming tries to incorporate the best aspects and avoid the worst problems of all of the programming approaches discussed above.

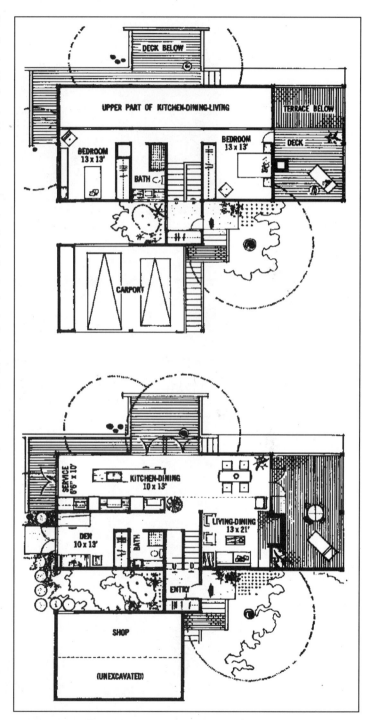

Figure 1-27 Thomson Residence: Plans.
Credit: Calvin C. Straub, FAIA

Figure 1-28 Platt Residence: Exterior Evening.
Photo Credit: Hans Lettner. Permission: William P. Bruder

Figure 1-29 Platt Residence: Entry Evening.
Photo Credit: Hans Lettner. Permission: William P. Bruder

First, value-based programming introduces an examination of the fundamental nature of the design problem into the earliest stages of architectural programming. Thus, it incorporates an intensive search for the essential purposes for which human institutions exist and are perpetuated. In order to do this, it relies heavily on the type of interviewing and discussion sessions between architect and client used by leading designers such as those discussed above to uncover the strongly held values and goals of the client. In addition, it employs this approach with other users and representatives of the community to discover their understanding of the nature of the organization. By conducting this search for values early in the programming process, rather than waiting until design, the value-based programming approach allows the entire balance of programming activities to be influenced by the important values uncovered. This is the crucial difference between this approach and other approaches to architectural programming. The reason for this difference is to make the program itself the first step in the quest for architecture, to program for architecture. An understanding of strongly held values is essential in this pursuit.

Value-based programming makes certain that the most important design issues are addressed in the programming document.

Second, the value-based programming process adopts the systematic procedures used in knowledge-based programming whenever they are needed to ensure that the information obtained during programming is reliable and valid. Literature search and review, interviewing, observation, questionnaire development and administration, and various sampling and statistical methods are used in the value-based programming process to establish values and goals; to collect, organize, and analyze facts; and to establish needs. Value-based programming, however, differs from a purely research-oriented approach in that it acknowledges the typically limited budgets and short time schedules allowed for programming activities. By determining the important values relating to the design problem early in the programming process, it becomes possible to identify those crucial areas in which more systematic research procedures should be used. This is done because of the potentially high cost of error if these areas are not carefully examined. In less crucial areas, the less structured information gathering systems employed in design- and agreement-based programming are utilized.

Value-based programming uses systematic information gathering procedures to ensure that important information is not overlooked in the programming process.

Third, the value-based approach to programming is heavily influenced in structure and approach by the agreement-based method of programming developed by CRS. It incorporates the objective of being comprehensive (of defining the complete architectural problem) and relies on a similar matrix format to ensure that all of the necessary information is collected, presented, and agreed to by the client's programming team. Important values are listed down the left side of the matrix, and categories for goals, facts, needs, and ideas are listed across the top of the matrix. Additional needs information is recorded on brown sheets or grid sheets. It utilizes the very efficient and effective work session method advocated by Peña to obtain much of the needed programming information and, especially, to obtain agreement.

Value-based programming recognizes the importance of obtaining agreement with the client, users, and community in open work session environments.

There are, however, four distinct differences from the agreement-based programming approach to obtaining agreement:

1. The CRS system maintains that the four value categories (Function, Form, Economy, Time) listed to the left of the matrix are complete, constant, and apply to all building types, user groups, and presumably architectural firms. The value-based approach, on the other hand, uses an eight-value starting point, but seeks to discover the unique set of values applicable to each design project. In value-based programming, the most important value areas are typically listed near the top of the matrix and decrease in importance as the list descends. In this way, a sense of priority is made known to the designer. Thus, the value-based programming approach avoids a commitment to a restricted list of values and asks: What about the reason for being of an organization, its institutional purpose? Does function alone define an organization? What about the natural environment and the urban context? What about history, tradition, and meaning? Some important value areas, at least for some architects, clients, and users, are hard to fit into the CRS programming matrix. The left column of the value-based programming ma-

trix, thus, might vary from project to project. In one case, it might include symbolic, institutional, functional, technical, environmental, temporal, and financial values. In another case, the list might include image, function, special users, safety, economics, and urban context as more appropriate values. The point is that it should be possible for the value areas to change for every project, client, and architect.

The intent in value-based programming is to let the most important values or issues set the tone of the programming effort, while making certain that recurring value areas are not inadvertently omitted.

2. The CRS system develops a listing of appropriate goals, facts, concepts, and needs for each value area, followed by a problem summary statement. The value-based programming approach is similar, but avoids the difficult task of developing programmatic concepts prior to finalizing the need statements. Rather, it allows for programmatic or design concepts to be introduced into the program simply as undifferentiated ideas to be considered by the designer. The kinds of ideas presented in the program are not really important, as long as the designer is not required to follow them. In value-based programming, they are presented simply as ideas which the programming group hopes will be explored by the designer. Some will be programmatic ideas. Others will be design ideas. Many will prove to be preconceptions that will be considered, but then will be discarded by the designer because, during careful design analysis, they prove to be inappropriate.

Value-based programming encourages the clients and users to set forth both their programmatic and design ideas for the project so that the designer will have benefit of their unique perspectives.

3. The CRS system assumes that the designer is part of the programming team, hence, is available to provide a summary problem statement as part of the program. The value-based system attempts to state the design problem in such a way as to allow the designer to develop an understanding of the important design issues whether or not the designer is part of the programming team. Thus, it does not advocate including a cursory problem statement by the designer in the matrix. The ordering of the values in the matrix helps the designer to recognize what the client, user, and programmer consider to be the most important values and goals. The rest

of the matrix, along with the accompanying brown or grid sheets, display the agreed upon nature of the design problem. The programmer is expected to summarize the nature of the problem in the executive summary of the program document and the designer is expected to confirm the program with the client before commencing schematic design.

The value-based architectural program is prepared in such a way as to completely define the architectural problem whether or not the designer is a participant in the programming process.

4. The value-based programming approach does not seek to differentiate between schematic design and design development programming. In interviews and work sessions as well as in the literature search and observational studies, considerable information is forthcoming that relates more to design development than to schematic design. There is no reason to avoid collecting this information during the programming process—if it is known, why not collect it? This information typically relates to specific requirements for individual spaces, areas, or systems in the new facility. As such, it can be developed and presented on space program sheets in the overall architectural program. These sheets are like mini-programs for each of the rooms, public spaces, service spaces, and exterior spaces of the new facilities. Rather than get in the way of effective schematic design, these space program sheets provide the designers with detailed knowledge about each space so they can place them appropriately in the new facility. Some rooms may need to be on outside walls for fenestration, others on the interior to avoid outside light or temperature fluctuations, others isolated from public spaces to minimize noise disturbances, etc. This information is also helpful to the designer to decide on room configuration. Should a room be long and narrow, or nearly square, or odd shaped for one reason or another? Without space program sheets or a lot of prior knowledge about a particular room type, the designer has little basis to decide such questions. Having this information will allow the designer to make appropriate schematic design decisions.

Complete value-based programs include design development information presented on space program sheets in order to help the designer make informed schematic design decisions.

1.8 Exercises

1. Write down a definition of architectural programming without looking back over the chapter.

   Compare your definition with the one in Section 1.2. What are the differences? Are they important? Would programming based on your definition be different from or similar to the definitions described in Sections 1.4 through 1.7?

2. Discuss the advantages and disadvantages of design-, knowledge-, agreement-, and value-based programming with some of your colleagues.
   a. Is value-based programming an improvement over the other programming approaches?
   b. Is flexibility in establishing value areas an improvement over the CRS fixed matrix?
   c. Would one fixed value list be better for you? Would it be the CRS list, another list, or one of your own? Would it be appropriate for every commission? Is there a better way than any discussed so far?

3. Set aside a couple of hours to begin the design of a house for a friend. Select a site (or make one up), bring drawing paper and a soft pencil, and sit down with your friend. Begin to design as you discuss your friend's desires and needs for the house. Be sure to get beyond the plan view to at least one elevation and a perspective sketch in the two-hour period.

   Consider what you accomplished and the nature of the interactive process. Was it positive? Fun? Were there any problems? Do you personally like the result? Does your friend?

4. Pick another friend for whom to design a house on the same site. Spend approximately an hour discussing this friend's aspirations and needs and write them down on a sheet of paper. Have the friend review the information you have recorded and confirm that it is correct. Spend another hour by yourself coming up with a preliminary design including a plan and at least one elevation and a sketch perspective.

   Consider what you accomplished and the nature of the interactive process. Was it positive? Fun? Were there any problems? Do you personally like the result? Does your friend?

5. Compare the two processes. What were the advantages and disadvantages of each? Which process produced the best results? Which process worked best from your friends' point of view?

Were there differences in the types of information discussed? Were there differences in the nature of the designs related more to the processes used than to the differences in the friends' ideas? Keep these differences in mind as you proceed through the text and the exercises at the end of each chapter.

Remember to have fun as you read the text, consider what it says, and do the exercises at the end of each chapter. Programming and design are interactive processes which can be accomplished in a number of ways. You should try to discover the approach or approaches that work best for you.

1.9 References

Alexander, Christopher. 1965. "The Theory and Invention of Form. *Architectural Record*. 137(4): 177-186.

Altman, Irwin. 1975. *The Environment and Social Behavior: Privacy, Personal Space, Territory, Crowding*. Monterey, Calif.: Brooks/Cole Publishing Company.

Bechtel, Robert, Robert Marans, and William Michelson, eds. 1987. *Methods in Environmental and Behavioral Research*. New York: Van Nostrand Reinhold.

Becker, Nathaniel. 1959. Space Analysis in Architecture. *American Institute of Architects Journal*. 31(4): 40-47.

Brill, Michael, Stephen T. Margulis, Ellen Konar, and BOSTI. 1984. *Using Office Design to Increase Productivity*. Buffalo, N.Y.: Workplace Design and Productivity, Inc.

Bruder, William. 1997. Letter to the author. 10 August.

Conway, Donald, ed. 1973. *Social Science and Design: A Process Model for Architect and Social Scientist Collaboration and Report of a Conference*, October 1973, Coolfont Conference Center, Berkeley Springs, W. Va. Washington D.C.: American Institute of Architects.

Davis, Gerald. 1969. The Independent Building Program Consultant. Building Research. 18(2) 16-21.

Davis, Gerald, and Francoise Szigeti. 1979. "Functional and Technical Programming: When the Owner/Sponsor is a Large or Complex Organization." Paper presented at the Fourth International Architectural Psychology Conference, 10-14 July 1979 at Louvain-la-Neuve.

Demoll, Louis. 1965. Operations Programming and Planning. In *Comprehensive Architectural Services: General Principles and Practice*, edited by William D. Hunt Jr. New York: McGraw-Hill.

Duerk, Donna P. 1993. *Architectural Programming: Information Management for Design*. New York: Van Nostrand Reinhold.

Esherick, Joseph. 1987. Lecture on the work of Esherick Homsey Dodge and Davis, Arizona State University, Tempe, Ariz.

Evans, Benjamin H., and C. Herbert Wheeler, Jr. 1969. *Architectural Programming: Emerging Techniques of Architectural Practice—A Continuing Study by the Committee on Research of Architects*. Washington, D.C.: American Institute of Architects.

Farbstein, Jay D. 1976. Assumptions in Environmental Programming. In *The Behavioral Basis of Design: Proceedings of the Seventh International Conference of the Environmental Design Research Association*, Vancouver, British Columbia, Canada, edited by P. Suedfeld and J. Russell. Vol. 1. Stroudsburg, Pa.: Dowden, Hutchinson and Ross.

GSA. 1983. *Design Programming*. PBS 3430.2. Washington, D.C.: General Services Administration.

Hall, Edward T. 1966. *The Hidden Dimension*. Garden City, N.Y.: Doubleday.

Haviland, David, ed. 1994. *The Architect's Handbook of Professional Practice*. Washington, D.C.: American Institute of Architects Press.

Hershberger, Robert. 1969. A Study of Meaning and Architecture. Ph.D. diss., The University of Pennsylvania.

_____. 1985. Values: A Theoretical Foundation for Architectural Programming. In *Programming the Built Environment*, edited by Wolfgang F. E. Preiser. New York: Van Nostrand Reinhold.

Horowitz, Harold. 1966. The Architect's Programme and the Behavioural Sciences. *Architectural Science Review*. 9(3): 71-79.

Kahn, Louis I. 1961. Design studio discussion at the University of Pennsylvania, Philadelphia, Pa.

Knight, Carleton. 1984. Built on Religious, Regional Traditions: St. Matthew's Episcopal Church, Pacific Palisades, Calif. *Architecture*. 73(5): 178-185.

Kumlin, Robert R. 1995. *Architectural Programming: Creative Techniques for Design Professionals*. New York: McGraw-Hill.

Lang, Jon. 1987. *Creating Architectural Theory: The Role of the Behavioral Sciences in Environmental Design*. New York: Van Nostrand Reinhold.

Lang, Jon, Charles Burnette, Walter Moleski, and Steven Vachon, eds. 1974. *Designing for Human Behavior: Architecture and the Behavioral Sciences*. Stroudsburg, Pa.: Dowden, Hutchinson and Ross.

Lawton, Powell, Paul Windley, and Thomas Byerts, eds. 1982. *Aging and the Environment: Theoretical Approaches*. New York: Springer.

Marans, Robert, and Kent Spreckelmeyer. 1981. *Evaluating Built Environments: A Behavioral Approach*. Ann Arbor, Mich.: Survey Research Center, University of Michigan.

Marcus, Clare Cooper. 1975. *Easter Hill Village: Some Social Indications of Design*. New York: The Free Press.

Marti, Manuel. 1981. Space Operational Analysis: A Systematic Approach to Spatial Analysis and Programming. West Lafayette, Ind.: PDA Publications Corp.

Michelson, William, ed. 1975. *Behavioral Research Methods in Environmental Design*. Stroudsburg, Pa.: Dowden, Hutchinson & Ross.

Moleski, Walter. 1974. "Behavioral Analysis in Environmental Programming for Offices." In *Designing for Human Behavior: Architecture and the Behavioral Sciences*, edited by Jon Lang, Charles Burnette, Walter Moleski, and Steven Vachon. Stroudsburg, Pa.: Dowden, Hutchinson & Ross.

Moore, Gary, and Reginald Golledge, eds. 1976. *Environmental Knowing: Theories, Research and Methods*. Stroudsburg, Pa.: Dowden, Hutchinson & Ross.

Palmer, Mickey, ed. 1981. *The Architect's Guide to Facility Programming*. New York: Architectural Record Books.

Pan, Solomon. 1985. Programming Seminar at ADP offices in Tucson, Arizona.

Peña, William, and John W. Focke. 1969. *Problem Seeking: New Directions in Architectural Programming*. Houston, Tex.: Caudill Rowlett Scott.

Peña, William, William Caudill, and John Focke. 1977. *Problem Seeking: An Architectural Programming Primer*. Boston, Mass.: Cahners Books International.

Peña, William, Steven Parshall, and Kevin Kelly. 1987. *Problem Seeking: An Architectural Programming Primer*. 3rd ed. Washington, D.C.: AIA Press.

Preiser, Wolfgang F. E., ed. 1978. *Facility Programming: Methods and Applications*. Stroudsburg, Pa.: Dowden, Hutchinson & Ross.

_____. 1985. *Programming the Built Environment*. New York: Van Nostrand Reinhold.

_____. 1993. *Professional Practice in Facility Programming*. New York: Van Nostrand Reinhold.

Robinson, Julia, and J. Stephen Weeks. 1984. *Programming as Design*. Minneapolis, Minn.: Department of Architecture, University of Minnesota.

Sanoff, Henry. 1977. *Methods of Architectural Programming*. Stroudsburg, Pa.: Dowden, Hutchinson & Ross.

_____. 1992. *Integrating Programming, Evaluation and Participation in Design: A Theory Z Approach*. Brookfield, Vt.: Avebury.

Sommer, Robert. 1969. *Personal Space: The Behavioral Basis of Design*. Englewood Cliffs, N.J.: Prentice-Hall.

Spreckelmeyer, Kent. 1986. Environmental Programming. Chapter 8 in *Methods in Environmental and Behavioral Research*, edited by Robert Bechtel, Robert Marans, and William Michelson. New York: Van Nostrand Reinhold.

Straub, Calvin C. 1980. Lecture on architectural programming at Arizona State University, Tempe, Arizona.

Studer, Raymond. 1966. On Environmental Programming. *Arena*. 81(902): 290-296.

Swinborne, Herbert. 1967. Change is the Challenge. *American Institute of Architects Journal*. 47(5): 83-90.

White, Edward T. III. 1972. *Introduction to Architectural Programming*. Tucson, Ariz.: Architectural Media.

Zeisel, John. 1981. *Inquiry by Design: Tools for Environment-Behavior Research*. Monterey, Calif.: Brooks/Cole Publishing Co.

Values and Architecture

2.1 Importance of Values

The first responsibility in architectural programming is to articulate the values to which the architect should respond in design. Values in this context mean those beliefs, philosophies, ideologies, understandings, purposes, or other deeply held ideas or feelings that are the reason for building and should influence how the building is designed. It is these underlying values and purposes that serve as the framework for an architectural program. The identification of these values in the program is crucial if the program is to help the designer achieve architecture.

Every program will involve somewhat different values, depending on the nature of the client, users, site, climate, and even the programmer and designer. The client's reasons for building vary widely. User groups have different views of the world and especially of the types of environments suitable for their diverse activities. Site and climate change from project to project. Programmers and designers vary considerably in the values they bring to

41

Figure 2-1 Hershberger Residence.

Photo Credit: Andrew Hershberger

the programming process. It should be expected that the values identified for each project will be different. The following discussion covers a number of values that often have a significant impact on architectural form.

The values discussed are not a definitive set applicable to all architectural problems. The author contends that there is no such definitive set, only sets that apply to certain architectural problems. For example, the Tucson, Arizona, house that the author designed for his family in 1988 is a reflection of the client/user, site, climate, designer, and other values identified during the programming stage of design. For example, the exterior of the house with its second- and third-story roof decks reflect the value of views—the family's desire to see the surrounding mountains and sky even from a flat, mid-town location (Fig. 2-1).

2.2 Enduring Values of Architecture

- Survival (to protect)
- Good Life (to nurture)
- Art (to transform)

The enduring values of architecture were first discussed by the Roman Vitruvius in the first century BC as *firmitas*, *utilitas*, and *venustas* (Vitruvius 1960). These values were modified somewhat by Sir Henry Wotton in the seventeenth century as "firmness, commodity, and delight" (Wotton 1970), and reassessed by several authors in the twentieth century including Talbot Hamlin (1952) and Christian Norberg-Schulz

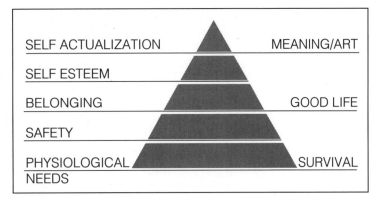

Figure 2-2 Maslow's Pyramid & Enduring Values.
Adapted by Nancy Cole from Maslow 1973

(1963). These values are now sometimes addressed in terms of their effect on people, rather than as qualities of a building, and as such can be seen to parallel the categories of the value pyramid (Fig. 2-2) originated by the psychologist Abraham Maslow (1973). In this same sense, and enlarging the meaning of each category to encompass contemporary architectural issues, these values cover Survival (to protect), Good Life (to nurture), Art (to transform) (Fig. 2-2).

Survival (To Protect)

Certainly the primordial value of architecture was to promote human survival by protecting its occupants. Shelter from the elements allowed the occupants an opportunity to take care of human needs such as sleep, food preparation, socialization, procreation, and child rearing. It is important that a building be programmed, designed, and constructed so that it will not collapse and harm the occupants (Fig. 2-3).

Figure 2-3 Leaning Tower of Pisa.
Credit: Carl Okazaki

The structure of the building must be firm. This can be ensured only if the architect and engineer are apprised of the kinds and locations of loads that are likely to be imposed. The program must specify unusual loads so that the designers can make certain that the loads will not result in building failure.

The same is true for mechanical and electrical loads. If unusual requirements are not specified in the program, then the building is likely to fail in some respect, possibly resulting in a threat to human survival, such as fire or inadequate ventilation. Thus, human survival and protection are much broader categories than structural strength alone as implied by the term *firmitas*, or firmness.

The program must also set forth guidelines for human safety and security as available in the work on "defensible space" by Oscar Newman (1972), on crowd behavior in fires and other emergency situations (Stahl 1976; Canter 1980), on crucial requirements of special user groups such as the handicapped and the frail elderly (Steinfeld 1979; Lawton et al. 1982). There is a growing body of knowledge about how buildings can be designed to limit threats to occupants from other human beings as well as from physical hazards that are often built into the environment (Greenberg 1982). The architectural program must provide information to help the designer avoid problems in these areas. And these are not trivial or unusual problems. They are survival problems!

If a person cannot get out of a building during a fire, this is serious business. If a handicapped person must use stairs or an excessively steep ramp, an accident might result in their injury even death. Similarly, many of our nation's streets, parks, and housing areas have become such a threat to those who use them that specific strategies of accessibility, visibility, lighting, landscaping, and the like have been developed to overcome the severe consequences of inadequate design. For example, locating balconies and windows overlooking exterior pedestrian areas helps to make them safe to use.

An excellent example of this can be found in the Martin Luther King Square public housing project by Kaplan McLaughlin in San Francisco (Fig. 2-4). It provides for surveillance of and ready access to children's courtyard play areas near walk-up apartments with views from balconies and kitchen windows.

The increase in terrorist attacks directed at American citizens and officials in foreign countries and, more recently, within the

Figure 2-4 Martin Luther King Square.

United States has created a keen interest in the survival value. These attacks are frequently directed at government, military, or diplomatic compounds in which the buildings and surrounding landscaping serve as the first line of defense. In these cases, safety and security become dominating concerns in the design of such buildings and their grounds (Fig. 2-5). Unfortunately, it requiring architects to surround these buildings with fences, walls, bollards, and the like to prevent vehicles loaded with explosives from coming near them.

Programmers are in a unique position, as they spend time with clients and users, to discover still other survival issues that could affect the user's health or safety. They may be

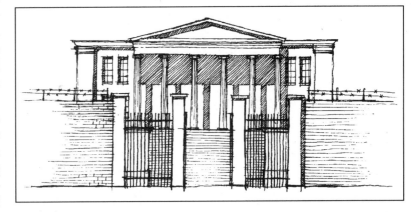

Figure 2-5 Fortified Government Building.

Credit: Carl Okazaki

Figure 2-6 Hill Hall Women's Dormitory.

able to discover waste products that could be hazardous—if not directly to the user, then to society at large. If so, the program should specify that care must be taken in the disposal and treatment of the hazardous material. The concern need not be just for the immediate survival of the client/user, but for the long-term survival of the community or society. Ian McHarg has written very convincingly in this regard in his book *Design with Nature* (McHarg 1969). A whole body of literature on ideas of sustainability has developed in recent years (Crosbie 1994).

If some of these survival issues are seen as more than just routine by the designer, they may become the stimulus for a unique and perhaps wonderfully creative design idea—an opportunity for architecture. Eero Saarinen's castle-like women's dormitory at the University of Pennsylvania, complete with what appears to be a drawbridge and other features typical of a fortification, is a wonderful and even humorous example of how a security problem identified in the program can lead to a particular aesthetic expression in the architecture (Fig. 2-6).

Good Life (To Nurture)

A concern for the good life should also be present in design. Architecture should not merely promote survival, it should make survival good. Buildings should enable users to accomplish their purposes and tasks without great effort, and they should promote the comfort of the users in all of their sensory modalities: visual, aural, olfactory, tactile, and kinesthetic. Architecture has the obligation and opportunity to nurture its occupants and the programmer must discover how this can be ensured.

The underlying value or purpose of the early modern movement in architecture was to bring the "good life" to all people. The architects of this movement were not content with providing the good life only to the wealthy elite. They wanted to make the benefits of well-designed buildings available to the people as a whole: housing, schools, hospitals, and other institutions. The Tuberculosis Sanitarium by Alvar Aalto exemplifies this approach to architecture (Fig. 2-7).

Some early modern architects developed elaborate theories as to how architecture could promote the good life. Large buildings set in green parks with plenty of light, air, and special playground facilities for children were advocated for housing (Le Corbusier 1946). Standards for minimum room sizes, lighting, and ventilation were developed. New materials, systems, equipment and furnishings promoted the efficiency and comfort of occupants of buildings. The whole mood was to go well beyond survival issues to those that would make life more enjoyable for everyone. This concern for quality of life has not been lost on most

Figure 2-7 Tuberculosis Sanitarium.
Credit: Carl Okazaki

Figure 2-8 Demolition of Pruitt Igoe.

Credit: Carl Okazaki

contemporary architects and continues to be a major concern in programming.

Interestingly, some ideas advanced to create the good life led to problems of survival. The Pruitt Igoe public housing development in Saint Louis, which purported to follow some of these ideas, was completely demolished after several years of occupancy due to the health and safety problems created by its design (Fig. 2-8).

Fortunately for programmers, designers, and especially the users of the buildings and cities they create, the failures of early modern architecture led social and behavioral scientists to explore how architecture creates problems of survival and difficulties in achieving the good life. The involvement of a large number of these scientists in research and programming in the past 15 to 20 years has ensured that the survival and good life values will continue to be considered in architectural programming. Functional, personal, social, and security values are generally well articulated in programs influenced by social and behavioral scientists.

Art (To Transform)

Finally, as an art, architecture has the opportunity to transform users, to help them see beyond their immediate needs for protection and nurturing. The architect has the responsibility to please the users in some manner or another: to excite and stimulate or to calm and assure. Architecture should enrich the meaning of the users' lives and move them in some special way. The program should identify the aesthetic values of society, client, and user to encourage the designer to express them in the architecture.

This urge to create objects of beauty and meaning has been present since humans first began to build. Cave dwellers placed figures on cave walls, perhaps for magical purposes. Even so, they were often proportioned and stylized to become beautiful and meaningful objects. Early builders similarly developed architec-

tural details where walls met the
ground, roof, and sky that went beyond mere building or functional accommodation. By the time of
classical Greece and Rome, this urge
to art had developed to the point
where every part of a building had
specific requirements for both form
and meaning.

Similarly, a concern of the Gothic
and Renaissance periods was to create works of art that would transform the viewer by their formal
power and beauty. Gothic buildings,
such as Chartre Cathedral (Fig. 2-9)
in France, with their elaborately dec-
orated openings, windows, and towers, went far beyond shelter and
accommodation in trying to express
the highest religious aspirations of
the people of their time.

The architecture of the Renaissance, Revival, and Eclectic periods
that followed became increasingly
concerned with the importance of
art in architecture. Many history
books have been written about the
architecture of these and other periods of architectural history. Such
books should be studied by students
interested in architectural program-

Figure 2-9 Chartre Cathedral.

ming, for much of what they discuss has to do with the aesthetic
qualities of the buildings of those times (Hamlin 1952; Roth
1979; Trachtenberg and Hyman 1986). Some more recent books
on architectural history are more likely to address social and cultural concerns of the architecture of these periods and should also
be studied (Kostof and Castillo 1995).

The early modern architects reacted strongly against the extreme emphasis on aesthetics of the Revival and Eclectic architecture. Some even objected to the words meaning and art in
reference to architecture. Hannes Meyer advocated that primary

Figure 2-10   German Trade Union Federation School.

Credit: Carl Okazaki

attention be directed toward functional and constructional issues (Schnaidt 1965). His German Trade Union Federation Building (Fig. 2-10) is an example of this approach to architecture.

Most modern architects consider meaning and art to be essential to architecture and develop their designs accordingly. Many reject specific references to previous styles of architecture in trying to fashion an architecture uniquely appropriate to their own time. In so doing, they show a preference for abstract or presentational form, as opposed to referential meaning in architecture (Langer 1942). The IIT Architecture Building (Fig. 2-11) in Chicago by Ludwig Mies Van der Rohe is

Figure 2-11   IIT Architecture Building.

representative of this approach to art and meaning in modern architecture.

A number of contemporary architects and their clients have reacted against what they perceive to be the limitations of modern architecture relative to meaning and art and have adopted a post-modern attitude about architecture. Some of these architects are once again looking at historical architecture for suitable expressive forms and relationships. Others are rejecting previously accepted tenets such as simplicity and clarity for complexity and contradiction in architecture (Venturi 1977). This later tendency is certainly the case in Robert Venturi's design for his mother's house in Chestnut Hill, Pennsylvania (Figs. 2-12 through 2-14). The house is small, but appears large in scale. Its apparent simplicity in the frontal view is belied by views from the side and rear. The inside has numerous similar contradictions.

Whatever approach architects take, they are generally concerned with aesthetic issues: with meaning and art, with transformation. Here again, as with survival and good life issues, the programmer is in a unique position to uncover what is particularly meaningful to clients and users, to discover what architectural objects are most likely to move these people. What do they appreciate? What are their traditions? What art do they value? This

Figure 2-12 Vanna Venturi House: Front.

Figure 2-13 Vanna Venturi House: Side/Rear.
Photo Credit: George Pohl. Permission: Venturi, Scott Brown and Associates

Figure 2-14 Vanna Venturi House: Interior.
Photo Credit: Rollin La France. Permission: Venturi, Scott Brown and Associates

information can be uncovered and articulated in the architectural program for the designer's benefit in their endeavor to create architecture. For example, the design by the author for the Alleluia Lutheran Church (Fig. 2-15) in Tempe, Arizona, incorporated a handsome old house that the client wanted to see preserved and restored as part of the project. He used the old house as the basis for the aesthetic expression of the much larger addition.

Figure 2-15 Alleluia Lutheran Church.

Finally, as programmers seek out the important values of the client, user, and community relative to an architectural project, they must continue to remember that the enduring values of architecture remain as a primary basis for design.

2.3 Contemporary Values of Architecture

The three enduring values elaborated above are certainly important in architecture. However, it is difficult to use them to describe the whole range of values that are important in contemporary architecture. For example, Wotton's conversion of the original terms used by Vitruvius, substituting "commodity" for utilitas, de-emphasized Vitruvius' concern for the functional and economic values of architecture and increased the importance of comfort. But all are contemporary concerns! Similarly, it is hard to see how other important issues for contemporary architects, such as responsiveness to site and climate, energy costs, urban context, building costs, growth, and change, can be adequately covered by the three traditional categories. Hence, it is important to rethink and enlarge the value categories during programming so all potential architectural values can be anticipated.

Various programmers have attempted to develop comprehensive lists of values and issues. As noted in Chapter 1, CRS uses

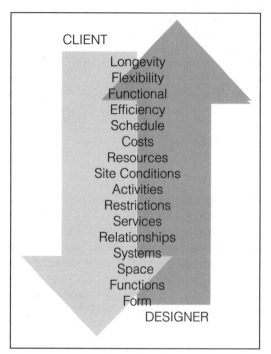

Figure 2-16 Client versus Designer Interests.

Adapted by Nancy Cole from: Palmer 1981, 17. Permission:
McGraw-Hill

function, form, economy, and time in their programming process. Mickey Palmer, in *The Architect's Guide to Facility Programming* (1981), advocates coverage of Human Factors, Physical Factors, and External Factors with numerous subcategories covering practically every imaginable value area. He also uses an expanded list of issues, which provide an interesting view of how designers and clients differ in what they value in architecture (Figs. 2-16).

Barton Myers, a well known and respected contemporary architect, has articulated what he considers to be important values for his work (Fig. 2-17):

1. Context
2. Space/environment
3. Climate
4. Technology
5. Social implication
6. Tradition

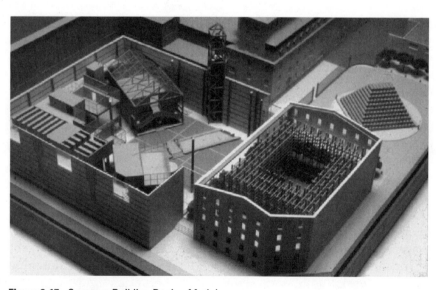

Figure 2-17 Seagram Building Design Model.

Photo Credit: Ian Samson. Permission: Barton Myers

George Hoover (1996) of Hoover Berg Desmond Architects of Denver, Colorado, indicated in a recent lecture at The University of Arizona that his firm looks metaphorically at issues of transformation ("the curving path"), permanence and change ("rocks and clouds"), embedding ("Russian dolls"), and coupling of the human with the environment ("I and Thou") in their mostly institutional commissions. These issues are evident in the design of the new Aerospace and Mechanical Engineering Building at The University of Arizona (Fig. 2-18). The building's material relationship to the rest of the campus suggests embedding. Its response to the local climate, with a central courtyard and shaded windows, couples the human and natural environment. Its permanent horizontal and vertical circulation suggests growth to the east and the open, flexible research and teaching spaces speak to permanence and change. Transformation of ordinary to extraordinary can be seen throughout the building complex.

Other architects and programmers have similar lists of values or concerns that they think are important. These can be considered the philosophic base or set from which these professionals approach both architectural programming and design.

Figure 2-18 Aerospace and Mechanical Engineering.

2.4 HECTTEAS (TEST EACH)

The following eight value areas, with subsets of issues to be discussed later in the text, cover the values advanced by most programmers and architects as well as the enduring values discussed in the previous section. This comprehensive easy-to-remember list, with the acronym "HECTTEAS," or "TEST EACH," will be used in this text to represent important contemporary values in architecture. It should be understood, however, that there are as many ways to classify value areas as there are persons to do the classification, and that for a particular architectural program the important values may or may not conform to the HECTTEAS categories either in name or number.

- *Human:* Functional, social, physical, physiological, and psychological.
- *Environmental:* Site, climate, context, resources, and waste.
- *Cultural:* Historical, institutional, political, and legal.
- *Technological:* Materials, systems, and processes.
- *Temporal:* Growth, change, and permanence.
- *Economic:* Finance, construction, operations, maintenance, and energy.
- *Aesthetic:* Form, space, color, and meaning.
- *Safety:* Structural, fire, chemical, personal, and criminal.

Exploration of the HECTTEAS list should allow the programmer to develop a comprehensive understanding of the important design issues for any building project. What are the basic purposes of the institution? What activities must be accommodated? Are there special users with unique physical or emotional needs? Is the site of great importance? Are there views that the client particularly treasures? Is the climate so severe that special considerations of form are warranted? Are there special processes or procedures that must be precisely followed to prevent the organization's failure? Is safety an important issue? Are only certain materials and systems available? Acceptable? Will future growth be a major factor? Is there a limit on building cost? Is tradition valued over novelty, or vice versa? These are typical issues that architects must deal with as they program and design buildings.

These values should be identified and prioritized with respect to their importance for each project. It then becomes relatively easy for the programmer to establish the scope of the project, appropriate goals and objectives, specific space/place needs, and mandatory spatial relationships. The potential impact on design decision making of the identified value areas is so great that they can be considered as the primary design issues in architecture (Duerk 1993).

2.5 Case Study: Alleluia Lutheran Church

A recent award-winning programming and design commission by the author for a campus-related church facility demonstrates how a variety of values and issues come into play during programming and design. Cultural, aesthetic, environmental, human, economic, and technological values combined as major issues in the design of the facility.

The existing building on the site was highly valued by the clients because it had once been a home. They felt that this home-like character had a positive impact on the use and enjoyment by students because it provided them with a place that had the feeling of a home away from home. Therefore, the clients wanted to keep and use the house as an integral part of the total church facilities. However, they also wanted to expand the facilities to create new worship, fellowship, and education spaces so that the center could become a full-service church. These were the important cultural, institutional, and human issues for design that were stated in the program and responded to in the design.

The architect also valued the home because of its aesthetic and historic qualities. It was a fine old bungalow-type house with red brick walls, hip roofs, porches, eaves, white wood trim, high ceilings, and abundant window areas, all of which provided a sense of quality and history (Fig. 2-19).

Figure 2-19 Alleluia: Axial View.

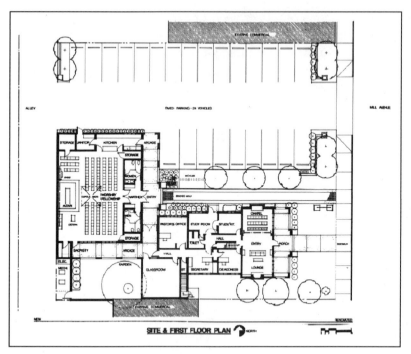

SITE & FIRST FLOOR PLAN

Figure 2-20   Alleluia: Site/Floor Plan.

The building committee and the architect decided that the new development should reflect the character of the old house. As a result, the historic, aesthetic, and technological qualities of the house became important design issues for the entire complex (Fig. 2-20).

The location of the existing house and a beautiful large Aleppo pine tree on the small site also had an important impact on design. The site planning was essentially determined by the location of the existing house at the street frontage and the tree near the side and rear property lines. The additions had to be placed to the rear of the site, behind but slightly offset from the house in order to save the tree. The parking was located on the other side of the site, extending from street to alley to obtain the required spaces and needed access. The offset of the new building from the old house allowed the architect to create a quiet courtyard at the base of the tree as well as an entrance walkway along the side of the old house on axis with the centerline of the new building. The walkway was realized by filling the center of an old strip concrete driveway with new brick paving. A line of fruit trees along the walkway creates a ceremonial approach to the entrance of the church.

Human and economic issues also came into play. As mentioned above, the client desired new worship, fellowship, and educational spaces in addition to the office, library, study, and lounge spaces that could be accommodated in the existing house. The budget, however, was limited by a fixed maximum construction cost. This required careful consideration of what spaces and sizes were absolutely required, as well as of the associated construction costs for new facilities versus renovation of the existing house. In fact, in order to stay within the limited budget, the clients had to accept a smaller facility than desired that combined the worship and fellowship spaces and provided a single rather than double classroom. So, while still very important, the functional requirements gave way to budgetary limitations and desired quality of materials and systems in order to obtain a satisfactory overall development (Fig. 2-21).

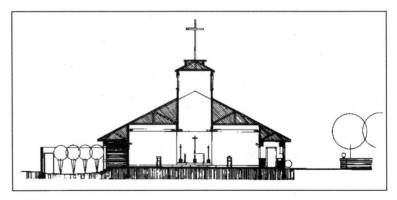

Figure 2-21 Alleluia: Section through Sanctuary.

There were other lesser influences on the design, such as the city's requirements for storm water retention, automobile and bicycle parking spaces, handicap accessibility, and landscaping. All of the existing windows leaked air badly, so they were tightly sealed, while new windows were double glazed to help reduce energy costs. Provisions were also made to accommodate sound partitions within the worship/fellowship space to allow for future subdivision into two additional classrooms and a high central chapel (Figs. 2-22 and 2-23).

Survival concerns were dealt with in several ways, including provision of fire separations between the new and old facilities, the addition of a required fire exit from the second floor of the house, complete rewiring of the house, and meeting code requirements for all systems. Improved air conditioning and lighting as well as complete renovation of the interior surfaces of the existing house helped to provide for the comforts of the good life and returned the interior

Figure 2-22 Alleluia: Interior of Church.

Figure 2-23 Alleluia: View of Cupola.

to the high quality of the original house. All of these issues were accounted for in the program and in the design, but had a lesser impact on the architectural character of the complex than the first-mentioned issues. Thus, they were not major architectural issues.

2.6 Case Study: Hershberger Residence

Programming for the house that the author designed for his family in Tucson, Arizona, has both parallels to and differences from the process used for the Alleluia Church. For Alleluia, the programming process was condensed into a two-week period, owing to time deadlines. For the house, the author and his wife had years of living together with their children in other Arizona houses to consider when they decided what would be appropriate in a house that they programmed and designed for themselves. In both cases, the expectations of the client/users were deeply felt and demanding of the talents of the designer.

Location

The house had to be within ten minutes of the university to the east of campus. The clients do not enjoy long commutes to work or the pollution caused by driving long distances to work. They wanted to show that a very satisfactory and less costly and polluting lifestyle could be maintained in town close to campus. They also felt that the very bright morning and afternoon sun was dangerous to face while driving. Location became an important consideration.

Views

The mountain and sky views in Tucson are truly spectacular. Although location dictated an in-town residence, the clients were unwilling to sacrifice views. The site had to have good ground level views to the mountains and the design would have to recognize the views to the often brilliant sunset and starlit skies. Views were an extremely important issue.

Resources

The house had to respond appropriately to the hot, arid climate, with energy and water conservation being major values strongly held by husband and wife. Water needed to be conserved and harvested for use only on plants that bore fruit or beautiful flowers. The house had to turn away the hot summer sun and capture the needed winter sun, and to use daylight throughout to conserve energy. Conservation and appropriate use of freely provided resources to help create a sustainable environment were strongly held values.

Lifestyle

The house would have to be a wonderful, peaceful yet stimulating place in which to live and entertain visiting family and guests. It would have to serve as an effective retreat for wife and husband, a place for them to live and work and garden, a place to gather the family members on holidays, and a place to entertain guests on the many social occasions required of a dean and a development officer.

Art

The house had to be a work of art that masterfully accomplished all of the goals and expressed the primary values of the clients. It had to use forms, textures, colors, and light to create a place of peace and happiness. Aesthetic quality was the bottom line.

Time

The house had to be constructed within a six month time period to allow the client/users' oldest son to serve as the construction superintendent while taking off a semester from his construction management program in college.

Budget

The house also had to be designed within a budget that would result in affordable mortgage payments.

The first job was to find a suitable site. The first selected site, in very close proximity to the university and with excellent views to the mountains over an adjoining city park, turned out not to be purchasable within time constraints because of liens on the property. The second site, which was purchased, met the ten minute

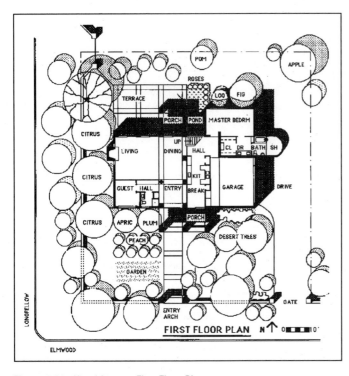

Figure 2-24 Hershberger: First Floor Plan.

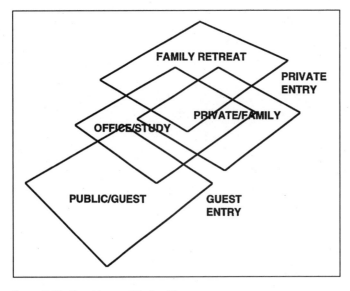

Figure 2-25 Hershberger: Zoning Diagram.

travel criterion by automobile and had an equally nice view to the mountains. It was preferred by the wife, because of concerns for safety at a site fronting on a public park.

The selected site was in an existing residential area on a vacant quarter of a large property surrounded by a low stuccoed adobe wall. The owner agreed to sell this unused portion of the property with the understanding that no walls would be put up to separate the houses within the walled precinct, so that all properties would seem more spacious. It also meant that the owner would be maintaining the backyard view from the new house, an added benefit in purchasing this property, but without the safety issues of a public park. The owner also agreed to a "first right of refusal" clause in the purchase agreement to allow the author and his wife to acquire the adjoining vacant property should the owner decide to sell it at some future time. This allowed the new house to sit on the cor-ner of the property with a large expanse of open space on either of its street sides.

The desire for safe ingress and egress dictated that entry be off the quiet street to the south. This allowed for a unique, sun-filled front yard to show off the existing native vegetation and to grow vegetables and fruit trees (Figs. 2-24 and 2-25).

The plan of the house responds to the various value areas, particularly to lifestyle. There are two primary areas on the first floor: the entertainment/guest area to the west with entry, living, dining, guest bedroom, and guest bathroom; and the private area to the east with kitchen, breakfast room, garage, and master bedroom, bath, dressing, and shower. The living and dining rooms face north toward the mountains and the landscaped west yard of the neighbor's house. The guest bedroom and bath face south with views under the deciduous fruit trees placed in front of the windows. The entry is protected by a large covered porch for protection from the weather. The kitchen is located next to the dining room and a small breakfast room facing a covered patio to the south. The master bedroom faces north and is situated for optimum control of exterior light and sound for sleeping. The dressing room and walk-in closet are skylighted and adjoin the bathroom that faces east into a completely private outside shower area. The garage faces east, avoiding a direct view from the street (Figs. 2-26 and 2-27).

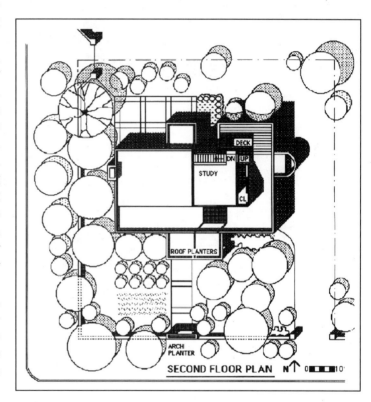

Figure 2-26 Hershberger: Second Floor Plan.

The study is located on the second floor with a spectacular view of the Catalina Mountains to the north and to a trellised rooftop planting area to the south. It is reached by a straight-run stair up from the living area, which allows for a

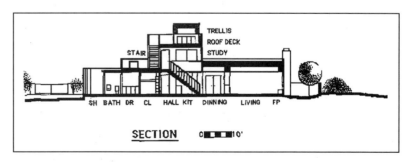

Figure 2-27 Hershberger: Section through House.

Figure 2-28 View to Catalina Mountains.

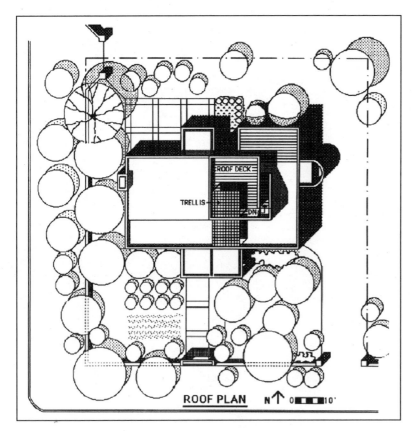

Figure 2-29 Hershberger: Roof Plan.

future wheelchair lift to access the second floor, should it be needed. The room has access to a rooftop patio and to a third-story outdoor family room, with magnificent views of the sky and mountains to the north and east (Figs. 2-28 and 2-29).

The house responds to the clients' wishes to capture the magical views. It also relates to the desire to promote a sustainable lifestyle by carefully protecting south-facing windows from the hot summer sun, minimizing windows to the west, and protecting windows facing east with adjustable shading screens. It uses a separate high-efficiency heat pump for each of the three zones to reduce non-renewable energy consumption. It captures roof and patio water and channels it to fruit-bearing landscaping surrounding the house. The landscaping features low water use native vegetation outside the wall and drip-irrigated vegetables and fruit trees within (Fig. 2-30).

Figure 2-30 Hershberger: from Northwest.
Photo Credit: Andrew Hershberger

Aesthetically, the house is conceived of as a "desert mountain" or "sky island," offering views to the luminous sky and surrounding desert areas. It is also considered to be representative of the Sonoran Desert as a whole. The south is Mexico, with the "ripple gates" in the masonry archway reminiscent of the Gulf of California and the Mexican tradition of walled and gated properties. The property then echoes the desert and agricultural areas of Arizona ending at the house as "mountain." The hanging gardens over the masonry lintels and columns provide a sense of permanence. The two-by-eight-foot spacing of columns and expression of the masonry bond beams create a rhythm and tectonic theme appropriate to the nature of concrete block (Fig. 2-31).

The porch provides a shaded summer place to eat with a view of the surrounding landscape and garden areas. The low winter sun warms the same porch, allowing year-round enjoyment of these beautiful site amenities (Fig. 2-32).

The interior of the house also represents the Sonoran Desert with the traditional red concrete floor symbolic of the hot desert floor, the varied texture of the masonry and green gallery walls, the

Figure 2-31 Hershberger: Gate, Porches, Trellises.
Photo Credit: Andrew Hershberger

Figure 2-32 Hershberger: Covered Entrance/Patio.

Photo Credit: Andrew Hershberger

interior plantscape, and the blue ceiling reminding us of the changing flora ascending up the desert mountains to the cool blue sky above (Figs. 2-33 through 2-36).

The trellised roof deck provides a wonderful outdoor living place and transition zone from the land to the sky (Fig. 2-37). It captures the panoramic and sky views as well as the cooling breezes that often cannot be felt on the desert floor below.

The final value area was only partially resolved to the satisfaction of the client. The short time frame for construction was realized through the diligent efforts of the construction foreman. The costs of the project, however, stretched beyond the budget, rising from an estimated $85 per square foot to $95 per square foot for the building. Landscaping and irrigation took the cost up to over $100 per square foot, much more than the client wanted to spend.

Figure 2-33   Hershberger: Living Room.

Photo Credit: Andrew Hershberger

Figure 2-34   Hershberger: Dining/Living Room.

Photo Credit: Andrew Hershberger

Figure 2-35 Hershberger: Dining Room/Gallery.

Photo Credit: Andrew Hershberger

Figure 2-36 Hershberger: Stairs to Upper Levels.

Photo Credit: Andrew Hershberger

Figure 2-37 Roof Deck and View to Mountains.
Photo Credit: Andrew Hershberger

2.7 Exercises

1. Ask another person to join you and take 15 to 20 minutes to each write down the important issues and requirements for a personal space: a study space at home, a studio space at school, or some similar space.

2. Trade your issues and requirements and spend 20 to 30 minutes making a preliminary design for their space.

3. After the design session, trade again and evaluate the design prepared for your space.

4. Discuss which issues and requirements were most clearly stated and how the designs either fulfilled or missed the intent of the user.

This exercise should help you understand the importance of the architectural program. The discussion should reveal what kind of information allows flexibility in design and what kind of information restricts design.

If an entire class is involved with the exercise, each member should state what information seemed to have the greatest implications for design. This information can be listed for all to see. A discussion should follow about the issues that seem to be crucial to successful design. The discussion might also highlight the need for clear and complete communication.

2.8 References

Canter, David, ed. 1980. *Fires and Human Behaviour.* Chichester, England: John Wiley & Sons.

Crosbie, Mike. 1994. *Green Architecture: A Guide to Sustainable Design.* Rockport, Mass.: Rockport Publishers.

Duerk, Donna P. 1993. *Architectural Programming: Information Management for Design.* New York: Van Nostrand Reinhold.

Greenberg, Stephanie W., William M. Rohe, and Jay R. Williams. 1982. *Safe and Secure Neighborhoods.* Washington, D.C.: National Institute of Justice.

Hamlin, Talbot. 1952. *Forms and Functions of Twentieth-Century Architecture.* New York: Columbia University Press.

Hoover, George. 1996. Personal correspondence, April 3.

Kostof, Spiro, and Greg Castillo. 1995. *A History of Architecture: Settings and Rituals.* 2nd ed. New York: Oxford University Press.

Langer, Susanne. 1942. *Philosophy in a New Key: Study in the Symbolism of Reason, Rite and Art.* Cambridge, Mass: Harvard University Press.

Lawton, Powell, Paul Windley, and Thomas Byerts, eds. 1982. *Aging and the Environment: Theoretical Approaches.* New York: Springer.

Le Corbusier. 1946. *Towards a New Architecture.* London: Architectural Press.

Maslow, Abraham. 1973. Dominance, Self-Esteem, Self-Actualization: Germinal Papers of A. H. Maslow. Monterey, Calif.: Brooks/Cole Publishing Company.

McHarg, Ian. 1969. *Design with Nature.* Garden City, N.Y.: Natural History Press.

Myers, Barton. 1991. Personal correspondence, October 10.

Newman, Oscar. 1972. *Defensible Space: Crime Prevention through Urban Design.* New York: The MacMillan Co.

Norberg-Schulz, Christian. 1963. *Intentions in Architecture.* London: Allen and Unwin.

Palmer, Mickey A., ed. 1981 *The Architect's Guide to Facility Programming*. New York: Architectural Record Books.

Peña, William, William Caudill, and John Focke. 1977. *Problem Seeking: An Architectural Programming Primer*. Boston, Mass.: Cahners Books International.

Roth, Leland M. 1979. *A Concise History of American Architecture*. New York: Harper & Row.

Schnaidt, Claude. 1965. *Hannes Meyer: Buildings, Projects and Writings*. Teufen, AR/Schweiz: Negli Ltd.

Stahl, Fred. 1976. Some Prospects for Simulating Human Behavior in Fires. In *The Behavioral Basis of Design: Proceedings of the Seventh International Conference of the Environmental Design Research Association, edited by P. Suedfeld and James A. Russell*. Vol. 1. Stroudsburg, Pa.: Dowden, Hutchinson & Ross.

Steinfeld, Edward. 1979. *Access to the Built Environment: A Review of Literature*. Washington, D.C.: Department of Housing and Urban Development.

Trachtenberg, Marvin, and Isabelle Hyman. 1986. *Architecture, from Prehistory to Post-Modernism: The Western Tradition*. Englewood Cliffs, N.J.: Prentice-Hall.

Venturi, Robert. 1977. *Complexity and Contradiction in Architecture*. New York: Museum of Modern Art.

Vitruvius Pollio. 1960. *Vitruvius: The Ten Books on Architecture*. Translated by Morris Morgan. New York: Dover Publications.

Wotton, Sir Henry. 1970. *The Elements of Architecture*. New York: Da Capo Press.

CHAPTER
3

Values Become Issues

In Chapter 2, the argument was made that architecture most often results when the architect responds to and expresses important human values. Three enduring values of architecture—Survival, Good Life, and Art—were discussed, and while obviously important, were found not adequate to describe all of the important issues that contemporary architects must address. An expanded list of eight important value areas—Human, Environmental, Cultural, Technological, Temporal, Economic, Aesthetic, and Safety (HECT-TEAS or TEST EACH)—were shown to encompass the three traditional and other important values that might have a significant impact on architectural decisions. It was noted that design decisions for all buildings are influenced to some degree by each of the values, but that really good buildings respond to and express the most important values in such a way as to produce true works of art: architecture.

Who, then, decides what values are important enough to become design issues, and what values are important enough to express for any particular architectural commission? Initially, it is the architectural programmer who must identify what is highly valued by the client, users, and designer, and make certain that specific project goals, facts, and needs relating to these values are developed and set forth in the architectural program. The designer for the project then selects the values upon which to focus. Finally, the client's values come into play when approving or rejecting the designer's decisions. Values become issues when one of the participants in the design process decides that they are important.

In this chapter, the value sets covered under the HECTTEAS headings will be considered as the focusing issues of architecture that should influence the form, character, and/or quality of buildings (Feerer 1977; Duerk 1993). These issues cover various aspects of the human enterprises to be accommodated; the available technology; the physical, cultural, and economic environments; the philosophies and preferences of those who build; and concerns for the public health, safety, and welfare.

All of these issues are not of equal importance for every project. It is essential that the programmer uncover, and the designer carefully consider and decide, which values should be the focusing issues for each project or part of a project. Ultimately, the values to which the designer responds are what make some buildings very good (architecture) and other buildings either mediocre or possibly very bad, failures in some manner or another.

The Phoenix Central Library (Fig. 3-1) by Bruder DWL Architects, also shown on the cover, is an outstanding contemporary building that responds to important issues to create a marvelous work of architecture. The south and north

Figure 3-1 Phoenix Central Library.

elevations are particularly responsive to site and climate while providing excellent daylighting into the interior.

Each of the sections of this chapter will concentrate on one focusing issue of architecture to show its importance. Be aware that other issues came into play during the design of each of these buildings.

3.1 Human Issues

- Functional

- Social

- Physical

- Physiological

- Psychological

Architecture is a social art. There would be no reason to build, no reason to seek out and analyze a site, to consider any other issue, were it not for some human activity or enterprise needing to be housed in some manner or another. Architects respond to most human needs, including accommodation, social contact, and comfort. They do not simply paint or sculpt something. Architects are commissioned to design something that someone needs. Human purposes and activities are the basis, the raw material for their art.

The human issues of architecture include:

1. The functional activities to be housed.

2. The social relationships to be maintained

3. The physical characteristics and needs of the users.

4. The physiological characteristics and needs of the users.

5. The psychological characteristics and needs of the users.

All are important and should be carefully considered and articulated in the architectural program.

Functional

If a building is to be successful, it must allow for the intended activities to be accommodated. Sometimes the activities are very simple. For example, the Lincoln Memorial (Fig. 3-2) by Henry

Figure 3-2 Lincoln Memorial.

Photo Credit: Howard Olson

Bacon, as far as the public is concerned, needs only to allow the public to enter and view the statue of the seated image of President Lincoln, to circulate freely in order to read several important speeches recorded on the stone walls, and then to leave. Accommodation of these activities, while simple, is very important.

Note that function was not the most important issue addressed by the architecture of this public monument. Issues of time, meaning, and aesthetics were far more important. It was essential that the memorial be built to last virtually forever. It was essential that it express the achievements and importance of this president of the United States. It was essential that the monument be of the highest possible aesthetic quality.

An industrial plant, on the other hand, may have such a specific production sequence or such unique functional requirements that they seem literally to "determine" the form of the resulting building (Fig. 3-3). All other potential issues pale in comparison to function. However, even here, the author would argue that the architect has the obligation and, generally, the discretion to propose a variety of formal solutions to the problem.

Figure 3-3 Hop Factory in Northern California.

Most buildings are somewhere between the extremes. Houses, schools, churches, office buildings, and museums all have major functional requirements that must be satisfied to allow the occupants to accomplish their tasks. Function may be a focusing issue for the design of such buildings; but there are other considerations as well. All of these buildings must relate to their natural and/or urban contexts, conform to cultural norms or legal requirements, be built within the client's budget, and so on. These considerations may also be important enough to influence the form of the building design. No single issue determines building form.

Alvar Aalto's Baker House dormitory at the Massachusetts Institute of Technology is a wonderful example of function playing a primary role, influencing all aspects of the building form. Aalto considered the lives of the students carefully as well as their relationships to each other, to the campus, and to the community. This resulted in a building with unique form, but suitable only to its site along the Charles River and beside a major campus open space (Figs. 3-4 and 3-5).

In order to provide unique rooms and views for the students, Aalto placed all of the student rooms along an undulating facade with views over a park to the Charles River and to the City of Boston beyond. He thoroughly understood the need for personal expression of the students and the value of such a magnificent view.

On the campus side of the dormitory, Aalto placed all of

Figure 3-4 Baker House: River Side.
Credit: Carl Okazaki

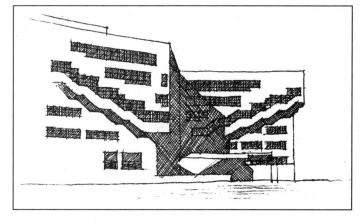

Figure 3-5 Baker House: Campus Side.
Credit: Carl Okazaki

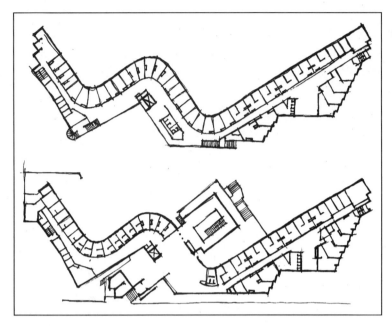

Figure 3-6 Baker House: Typical Floor Plans.
Credit: Carl Okazaki

Figure 3-7 People in a Typical Airport.

the common and service rooms, along with a set of stairs that collected students from every floor (Fig. 3-6). This resulted in the dominant angular exterior form on the campus side of the building. The stairs deliver the students to a handsome skylighted commons/dining room on the second floor, also with a view over the Charles River. From here, the students can descend just one floor to the main entrance of the dormitory, located on the campus side of the structure. The exterior form of the building related to its function, but also to its site.

A similar example is the Dulles Airport by Eero Saarinen. In this case, a very thorough review of major airport design during programming revealed that the long walks between boarding areas result in considerable human discomfort and angst, as people scurry to their next flight with hands full of luggage and children (Fig. 3-7).

As an alternative to this hassle, Saarinen proposed a completely new system, one where the planes remained out on the runway areas and giant lounge cars gathered up the people in a very compact area of the terminal, so that no one would have to carry luggage or children very far (Figs. 3-8 to 3-10).

Even kitchen and bathroom facilities require thoughtful design taking into account functional needs. For example, male architects may lack an understanding of the basic

Figure 3-8 Dulles Airport: Exterior.
Photo Credit: Howard Olson

Figure 3-9 Dulles Airport: Exterior Loading.
Photo Credit: Howard Olson

Figure 3-10 Dulles Airport: Interior.
Photo Credit: Howard Olson

Figure 3-11 Women's Powder Room.

Credit: Carl Okazaki

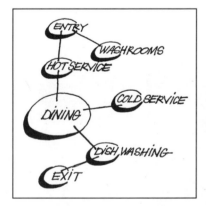

Figure 3-12 Functional Relationship Diagram.

Credit: Fourth Year Design Studio, Professor Poster, 1990. Salvation Army Homeless Facility: Program and Site Analysis. College of Architecture, The University of Arizona

functional requirements for women's toilet facilities (Fig. 3-11), and provide far less counter and hanging space than is typically required (Brown 1967).

While function is only one of the issues that must be acknowledged in design, it typically is very important and is given special consideration by both the programmer and the designer. This often means more than simply articulating the minimum or even optimum spatial layout to accommodate some activity. It also includes providing information on the hierarchy or relative importance of various activities, essential relationships, adjacencies or proximities of activities, specific space sizes and equipment needs, furnishings, and other materials necessary to support the functional activity. This is an area where a lot of information must be collected and analyzed. A number of the specific information gathering and presentation techniques described in Chapters 5, 6, and 7 are directed toward improving programming skills in this area (Fig. 3-12).

Social

Very few functional activities in a building are accomplished by only one individual. In most cases a group or interacting groups of people combine efforts to accomplish a task. In consequence, the programmer must learn how such groups work together. If they work in teams, are they horizontally or vertically structured? Is one person the leader, with a couple of captains, and the remainder workers of one type or another? Or are all of the participants of similar stature, cooperating to accomplish some purpose? How the group is structured has important implications for design, so this information must be articulated carefully.

The designer also needs to know the preferred way that people in a group communicate. Do they need to communicate face-to-face? Or can they be remote from one another and use the telephone, interoffice memos, or e-mail? What do various people need in the way of personal space, territory, and privacy in order to accomplish their tasks (Sommer 1969)? Who needs private offices, semiprivate offices, conference rooms? For example, the executive officer, with little paperwork, typically has the largest desk on the top floor and the clerical staff, with much paperwork, have the smallest desks on the lowest floor (Fig. 3-13).

Who can accomplish their tasks in an open office environment or even in a completely open workroom? If people are crowded tightly together, can they still accomplish their goals effectively? Should the teacher stand behind a lectern in front of the class, or should the class be organized in a circle with the teacher as just one participant on the perimeter (Sommer 1969)? The designer needs to know the social relationships that will help the participants accomplish their objectives most effectively. If this can be established during the programming process, it will greatly aid the designer in developing creative design solutions (Deasy 1974).

The social aspects of design can lead to primary expression in form. This is particularly true

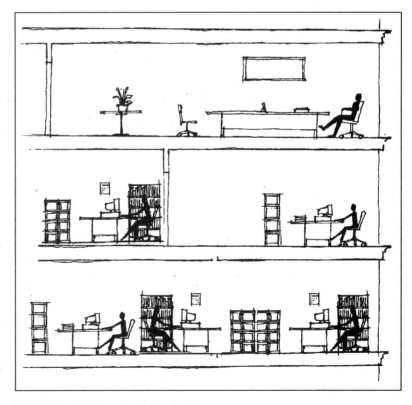

Figure 3-13 The Executive Office Syndrome.
Credit: Carl Okazaki

Figure 3-14   Kresge College: Courtyard.

at the Kresge Residential College at the University of California at Santa Cruz, designed by Moore, Lyndon, Turnbull and Whitiker (MLTW), for which they anticipated social events in the interior courtyard and surrounding balconies (Fig. 3-14).

Another example of response to social issues is the Lake Anne Village Center in the new town of Reston, Virginia, which was designed by William Conklin to ensure ample exterior recreation, socialization, meeting, and pedestrian circulation areas that are completely separated from the automobile circulation of the community (Fig. 3-15 and 3-16).

Figure 3-15   Reston, Virginia: Public Area.

Figure 3-16   Reston, Virginia: Separated Walk.

Physical

The physical characteristics of the occupants can have a profound influence on the form of a building. Special user needs of all kinds are encountered in architectural problems. Facilities for children, such as in preschools and day care centers, need to acknowledge the size of the principal occupants in terms of the heights and dimensions of windows, counters, and various furnishings. The size of rooms needs to acknowledge the child's natural tendency to learn through movement and various space-consuming activities (Figs. 3-17 through 3-19).

Buildings that accommodate the elderly and physically handicapped must provide suitable door openings, room

Figure 3-17   Baby by Stairs.
Credit: Carl Okazaki

Figure 3-18 Baby by Toilet.

Credit: Carl Okazaki

Figure 3-19 Young Child by Door.

Credit: Carl Okazaki

sizes, furnishings, equipment, surfaces, lighting, and mechanical systems. Requirements for accommodating persons with various disabilities, especially those confined to wheelchairs, are very specific and are outlined in mandatory standards and codes (ANSI 1996). They set forth the minimum width of halls; the size, location, and swing of doors; the height and location of various bathroom fixtures; and numerous other requirements depending on the needs of the people to be accommodated. The designer working without this information, or with inaccurate or inappropriate information, is likely to design non-accessible facilities—requiring redesign upon rejection by local building officials. This can be especially embarrassing and costly when the errors are found during or after construction of the facility.

The designer must understand how people with various disabilities actually use toilet facilities in order to design them appropriately. For instance, the frail elderly require stalls that are just three feet wide, with a higher than normal toilet seat, and with grab bars on both sides to help them get up from the toilet. Wheelchair confined persons, on the other hand, must have ample room in the toilet stall to allow them to make a lateral mount and dismount as shown below (Fig. 3-20).

These are not trivial problems. They can pose difficulties for the disabled that can prevent them from leading normal lives and, in some cases, can cause serious injury or even be life threatening (Fig. 3-21).

Even information on typical users can be important when it comes to such things as accessible heights for shelves, work surfaces, turning radii for various vehicles, and sizes of various appliances. Much of this information is available in such documents as *Architectural Graphic Standards* (1994), *Humanscale* (1974), and other standard references that cover both ergonomics and anthropometrics. However, many facilities have special appliance and/or equipment needs that are not contained in these standards and must be discovered during programming. This is extremely important in helping the designer avoid making assumptions which may result in costly errors.

Physiological

Information about human physiology may seem a very unlikely concern for programming or architectural design, but in some cases it is not. The elderly, for example, may have very special needs resulting from sensory losses. Letters on signs may need to be bolder and larger. Glare can be a major problem, making it very uncomfortable for the elderly to find their way. Acoustics may need to be carefully studied to be certain that messages can be heard by the hard-of-hearing. Oftentimes, the elderly experience a decrease in blood supply to their extremities, causing them to be more sensitive to

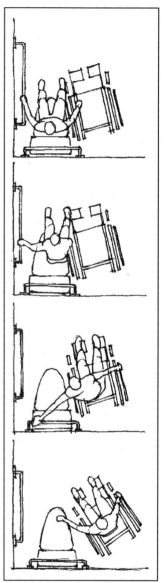

Figure 3-20 Handicapped Toilet Usage.

Credit: Carl Okazaki

Figure 3-21 Wheelchair by a Curb.

Credit: Carl Okazaki

Figure 3-22 Church of the Palms: Interior.

cold drafts on their feet or on the back of their necks than persons from other age groups. The designer of facilities for the elderly must be aware of these physiological changes, so that appropriate design decisions can be made. For example, in the Church of the Palms (Fig. 3-22) in Sun City, Arizona, Robert Hershberger and Ernest Nickels of Par 3 Studio designed the air conditioning system to bring in low-velocity air through long linear diffusers located high in the ceiling (dark strips on the photo) and to return it high at the rear of the sanctuary (behind a spaced wood screen), to ensure that there would be no drafts at the floor level or on the backs of the elderly members of the congregation and, also importantly, to provide an attractive ceiling and back wall.

Similar considerations were made on the exterior of the church, where a wide, covered arcade extends to a drop-off and pick-up area near the parking area. This walkway is flanked by a fountain courtyard surrounded by ample seating, covered walks, and landscaping to provide protected, shaded, and sunlit areas for the users. This is extremely important for the elderly, who often cannot tolerate the extreme heat from direct sun in the summer, or standing while waiting to be picked up. It also creates a quiet and pleasant environment in which anyone can choose to sit and meditate (Fig. 3-23).

Figure 3-23 Church of the Palms: Courtyard.
Photo Credit: Koppes Photography

Young children of pre-school or elementary school age are quite the opposite of the elderly relative to circulation to the extremities. They are little heat machines who can be comfortable in a considerably cooler room with plentiful ventilation. This can be a problem when a middle-aged teacher turns up the thermostat to keep his or her feet warm. The children are likely to become too warm, disruptive, or sleepy, and make the teacher wonder why they are not paying more attention to the lesson! Sensitivity to this kind of information by the programmer can be a great help to the designer (Fig. 3-24).

Figure 3-24 Teacher's Ideas versus Child's Ideas.
Credit: Thomas Dieterle, 1993. Computer Graphics Assignment. College of Architecture, The University of Arizona.

Psychological

There is an increasing body of information on the psychological needs of people in buildings and urban areas. In the past 25 years, environmental psychologists and sociologists have been actively studying just how people perceive, behave in, and feel about their physical environments. Some of this information has become well known and might be considered as knowledge that all designers should incorporate into their designs (EDRA 1969-96).

If there is psychological information peculiar to a particular type of project or user group, include it in the architectural program. This could include needs for apparent stability or security in environments for the elderly, for reducing environmental stimulation for people with certain mental disabilities, or for privacy or territoriality for hospitalized or institutionalized individuals. Books such as *The Hidden Dimension* by Edward Hall (1966), *Personal Space* by Robert Sommer (1969), and *A Graphic Survey of Perception and Behavior for the Design Professions* by Forrest Wilson (1984), provide good generalized coverage of many of these psychological interactions with architecture.

There are also quite a number of articles and books on various facility types or user groups that would be extremely valuable for particular projects. Current research is reported in journals such as *Environment and Behavior* and *The Journal of Architecture and Planning Research*. Powell Lawton's book *Planning and Managing Housing for the Elderly* (Lawton 1975) contains many important insights on the psychological needs of the institutionalized elderly; Oscar Newman's book *Defensible Space* (1972) includes information on the safety and security needs of both low-income families and the elderly; and Jean Wineman's book *Behavioral Issues in Office Design* (1986) takes an in-depth look at psychological needs of persons in office settings such as the one the following page (Fig. 3-25).

It is the architectural programmer's responsibility to conduct a suitable survey of the literature so as to be able to advise the client and the designer of important psychological issues for design. The degree to which the client and users value this type of information will help determine to what degree specific project goals and facility needs relating to human psychology are included in the program and subsequently in the design. A discussion of appropriate approaches to literature search and review is contained in Chapter 5.

Figure 3-25 Open Office Setting.

3.2 Environmental Issues

- Site (including views)
- Climate
- Context
- Resources
- Waste

The environmental concerns that may become focusing issues in architecture include site, climate, urban and regional context, available resources, and waste products. These are often very important issues in architecture because their influence is very direct and crucial, impacting the survival of the building or its occupants. If the designer ignores these issues and designs an inappropriate building for the particular site, climate, or other environmental concern, the building or occupants will suffer some loss over time, if not immediately. The building may neglect some wonderful view or be oriented to receive sun penetration in hot summer months or cold breezes during the coldest part of the winter. It may deteriorate as harsh weather takes a toll on inappropriate materials. It may sit in a floodplain or drainage area, such that it will be destroyed or washed away in a major storm. Its waste products may pollute a nearby stream or lake. If the programmer fails to inform the designer of such important design issues, how can the designer make the appropriate response? Complete environmental information is essential for a successful design solution.

Site (Including Views)

Frank Lloyd Wright repeatedly said, "The character of the site is the beginning of the building that aspires to architecture" (*House Beautiful* 1955). A colleague once said, "The site is the most important design consideration. It comes first. It was there before the architect and client and will be there long after they are gone" (Straub 1970). Both obviously valued the site very much, but does every client, user, and architect? If so, how much? Is it the first consideration, or is it only something to be dealt with after more important matters are considered? For some architectural problems, the site is a very important issue that can not be ignored during design.

The author, residing in the largest desert environment in the United States, advised a client (during the master planning stage of architectural services) not to build a retreat center on a cherished desert site near Sedona, Arizona, because most of the site was within a one-hundred year floodplain. In that particular case, there was a hundred-year flood just two years after the client decided not to build. The site was devastated. In two other instances, because of site locations that would be backwater areas in a flood, it was possible for the author to propose the use of earth fill to raise the sites above the floodplain. The clients proceeded with the design and construction of the projects. The floods have come, but the buildings have escaped any damage. These are clearly cases where the issue of site could not be ignored, because it related to the survival of the buildings (Figs. 3-26 and 3-27).

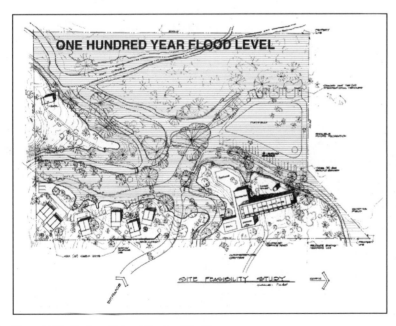

Figure 3-26   Sedona Retreat Center: Site Plan.

Figure 3-27 Building in Floodplain.
Photo Credit: The Arizona Daily Star

Topography is often a major consideration in the location of buildings. Les Wallach, principal of Line and Space, an architect/ builder in Tucson, Arizona, is very sensitive to site analysis and design, often saving significant landscape elements to incorporate their beauty as he designs and builds his projects. His own home, the Arroyo House, is an excellent example (Figs. 3-28 through 3-30). He saved most of the vegetation, including several ancient saguaro cacti, and safely bridged an

Figure 3-28 Arroyo House: Exterior.
Photo Credit: Henry Tom. Permission: Line and Space

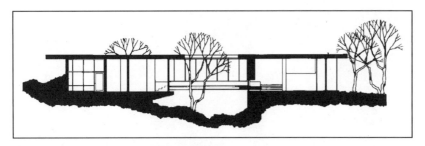

Figure 3-29 Arroyo House: Section at Wash.

Drawing Credit: Henry Tom. Permission: Line and Space

Figure 3-30 Arroyo House: Saguaro Cactus.

Photo Credit: Henry Tom. Permission: Line and Space

arroyo that runs full during heavy rainstorms.

In designing the Ventana Canyon Resort (Fig. 3-31) in Tucson, the firm of Frizzell, Hill and Moorehouse was very sensitive in site analysis and design, preserving the pristine desert area and selecting materials and colors that blend with the existing landforms and landscape.

The analysis for the Lawrence Hall of Science (Fig. 3-32) in Berkeley included a visibility analysis relating to major highways and important views in the Bay Area (Spencer 1962). The site selected for the building is the most visible of all sites considered, as well it should be for such an important public building.

In many cases, a careful site analysis during programming will reveal both significant external and internal site views. It might also indicate negative views or uncover current or potential developments that would destroy an apparently good view. In Beirut, Lebanon one family is reported to have built a "spite house" on their property to destroy a coveted view from an adjacent family (Hall 1966). Similar things happen all too frequently in subdivisions around our country, where designers design for views, only to have later buildings interfere (Fig. 3-33).

Figure 3-31 Ventana Canyon Resort.

Figure 3-32 Lawrence Hall of Science: Visibility.

Permission: William Busse of Spencer, Lee, Busse Architects

Figure 3-33 House in View of Another House.
Credit: Carl Okazaki

The author has designed a number of houses in the Sonoran Desert of Arizona in which views have been a very important issue. In one house, Thirsty Earth (Figs. 3-34 and 3-35), the client wanted to take advantage of spectacular views of the Superstition Mountains, including a pinnacle called Weaver's Needle, to the east and the McDowell Mountains and city lights to the west. A careful site analysis located each far and near view precisely, so that the design could respond to each. The final orientation provides for an axial view of Weaver's Needle as one enters the living room of the house. The other views are similarly captured from various rooms.

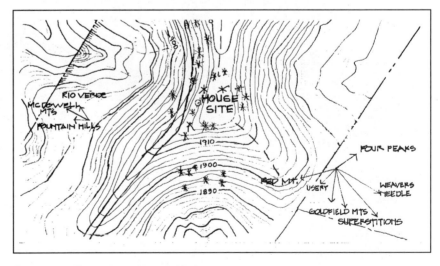

Figure 3-34 Thirsty Earth: View Analysis.

Figure 3-35 Thirsty Earth: House and View.

Geology and hydrology are also major site considerations. Will the building sit on bedrock, sand, an historic site of archaeological significance, or perhaps on a large abandoned sanitary fill or dump site? This information has a tremendous impact on the type and form of a building that might be constructed, or it may show that it would be unwise to build at all. This is especially true for sanitary landfills, where subsiding and outgassing would be crucial problems for human safety.

A building constructed on sand or in a marshy area likely will have a significantly different form than one solidly anchored on bedrock. It is also important to know if a building is to be located in an active seismic zone, as anyone in California or Mexico will testify. Buildings designed without sufficient care in such areas will fail in a major earthquake (Fig. 3-36).

A number of building programs have been delayed significantly

Figure 3-36 Failed Building after an Earthquake.

Credit: James Strata, Ted Canon, C. Martin Duke and Lawrence Selna (1976) Harvardian College East End, Fig. 30. Permission: Earthquake Engineering Research Institute

in recent years because they were found to be located over important archaeological sites that had to be explored and recorded before building could proceed. Similarly, in crowded urban areas with very high land costs, abandoned dumps and landfills are being reclaimed for higher uses, which include major building projects. In these cases, a great deal of time and money can be expended before building on the site can even be considered. The impact on the resulting architecture can also be substantial. It is vitally important that the client and architect be informed of such conditions prior to beginning design. A programming study by the author on such a site in the Phoenix area resulted in the conclusion that the site could not be used for the intended purpose because of excessive foundation costs and potential outgassing.

Climate

Climate considerations are of great importance when programming for architecture. A very severe climate will have profound effects on what should be built. The igloo is a clear response to the cold environment of the arctic, both in its use of available material and in its hemispherical form, which maximizes internal space and minimizes surface area to avoid heat loss and reflects interior-generated heat and light back into the interior. Here the architectural form is very much in response to climate. Environment and human survival are clearly values of great importance in this case (Fig. 3-37).

Similarly, a house on stilts with a thatch roof and open lattice floors and walls is an appropriate response to a warm, humid climate where shade and ample ventilation are the principal requirements for comfort (Fig. 3-38).

Figure 3-37   Igloo and Boy in Parka.
Credit: Carl Okazaki

Adobe construction in warm desert areas is also a primary response to climate, with its usually tiny windows and thick walls, which keep the heat out in the daytime but allow it to be transferred in through the walls to warm the interior during the course of the cool or even cold night hours (Fig. 3-39).

An example where climate was a major programmatic and design issue is at Sea Ranch (Figs. 3-40 and 3-41) in northern California, where Lawrence Halprin, Charles Moore (MLTW), and other architects responded to the prevailing cold breezes off the Pacific Ocean with shed roof forms to deflect the wind over the buildings. This creates quiet eddies on the east sides of the buildings where people can gather in comfort even on cold and windy days.

The wide-brimmed sombrero and the shade structures of the southwestern U.S. deserts are also examples of appropriate responses to hot and dry climates . . . shade! Judith Chafee's Solomon House, with its prevalent shade structure, is a bold use of this response (Fig. 3-42).

Similar illustrations can be made for environments with plentiful rain or snow. Even very temperate climates, such as those found in Southern California and the San Francisco Bay Area, impact architecture by allowing the indoor/outdoor living relationships that are characteristic of buildings in this part of the world. The Thomson House and other houses by Calvin C. Straub in Southern California are excellent examples of the development of these relationships (Fig. 3-43).

Figure 3-38 Stilt House and Boy with Hat.
Credit: Carl Okazaki

Figure 3-39 Adobe House and Boy with Sombrero.
Credit: Carl Okazaki

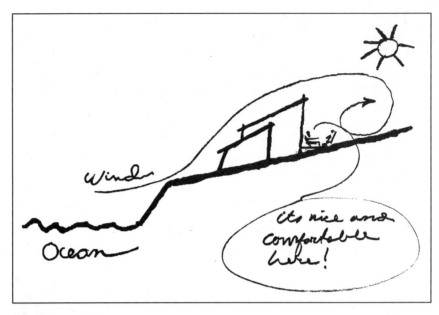

Figure 3-40 Sea Ranch: Wind Diagram.

Figure 3-41 Sea Ranch Lodge.

Figure 3-42 Solomon House.

Figure 3-43 Thomson Residence.
Credit: Julius Shulman

Context

One of the most important, but often overlooked, focusing issues of architecture is environmental context. This includes all of the natural landforms and built features beyond the immediate site. Views are often to off-site objects. Natural features or adjacent buildings may cast shadows over the site daily or only at certain times of the year, influencing where a new building should be located. Flight patterns from a nearby airport may have a noise or safety impact on a site. In an urban situation the height, shape, and other physical characteristics of surrounding buildings might influence what the designer chooses to place between them. A formal pattern may have been established, which would be very insensitive to ignore. Traffic on adjacent streets might similarly affect a site. For example, high levels of traffic on adjacent streets are essential to the economic survival of many projects. Gas stations, shopping centers, and many other commercial facilities are typically located at intersections of major traffic arteries to ensure their economic survival.

The operations research group of the Wharton School at the University of Pennsylvania study on why some gas stations succeed and others fail illustrates the extreme importance of context in programming and design (Ackoff 1966). A major petroleum company was baffled as to why some of their gas stations were successful while others failed. It seemed as if there was no plausible explanation for the problem, because each station was located at the intersection of heavily traveled arterial streets in accordance with established company policy. But even when the amount of traffic passing the sites was essentially identical, one station would be very successful while another would not.

The cause of failure apparently had nothing to do with the physical design of the station, because the company had several standard designs for its stations and there was no correlation between successful stations and the particular design utilized. Careful research also indicated that the friendliness of the operator or employees, the speed or quality of service, the cleanliness of the rest rooms, differential advertising, or even the comparative cost of gas had little impact on success or failure.

There being no readily apparent reason for success or failure, the research group decided to focus all of its attention on the vehicular traffic passing the station, because traffic is obviously of major importance. No station could succeed without automobile traffic. Was it the quantity of the traffic? Was it a characteristic of the traffic? The study revealed that characteristics of the traffic were the primary reason for success and failure of the stations, and were even more important than the amount of traffic passing the station (Fig. 3-44).

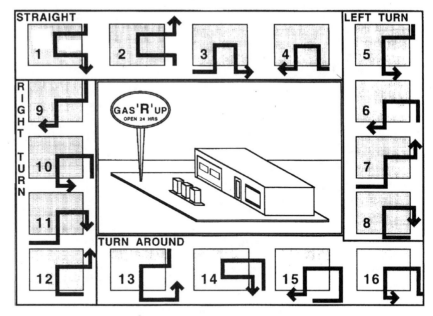

Figure 3-44 Traffic Options through an Intersection.

Credit: Chris Barta

At first glance, it appeared that there were two major streams of traffic, one along each artery. More careful analysis revealed that there were two lines of traffic on each artery and that there were turning movements from one artery to the other, some right turns, some left turns, even the possibility of U-turns. In all, there were sixteen different ways that traffic could pass through an intersection. The research group decided to focus on these sixteen alternatives in terms of the number of vehicles entering stations for service. It was discovered that about 90 percent of a station's customers came from three of the 16 alternatives. Vehicles turning right around the station accounted for as much as 70 percent of the use. Vehicles continuing in the same direction accounted for an additional 15 percent. Vehicles turning left around the station accounted for another five percent. The remaining 13 ways of passing through the intersection each accounted for less than one percent of the use of the station.

The researchers discovered that it was most important for the station to be located at an intersection where there was a high count of traffic turning right around the station. This characteristic alone could account for the success or failure of a station. A station with a large number of vehicles turning right around the station would succeed. A station without a large number of vehicles turning right

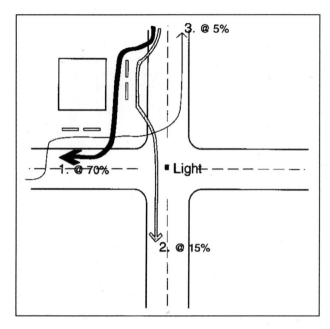

Figure 3-45   Routes to Avoid Traffic Light.

Credit: Nancy Cole

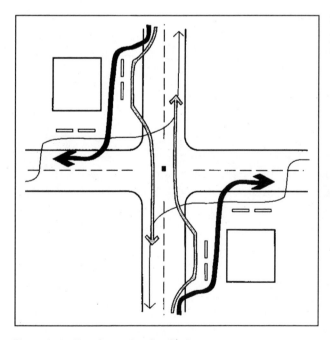

Figure 3-46   Non-Competing Gas Stations.

Credit: Nancy Cole

around the station would fail. The benefit from the right turns, the continuing straight movements, and the left turns were found to be tied closely to the stop-and-go lights at the intersection. People drove their vehicles into the station when it appeared that they could avoid waiting for the light by entering the station to get gas. They could get gas, then continue to the right, or straight ahead, or left to avoid the light (Figs. 3-45 and 3-46).

The persons turning right and left could avoid the light entirely by driving through the station. It is not as dangerous as it might first appear to make the two left-turn movements because the red light was, in fact, stopping oncoming traffic. In the case of the persons continuing straight ahead, the effect was similar, but the person had the choice after being serviced of entering the arterials either by a right or a left turn, whichever would help the driver avoid waiting for the light. Indeed, the study team discovered that drivers select service stations to save time!

What can a designer do to take advantage of this information? If the site is located on a corner, the designer can plan the station to allow the above movements to be accomplished with ease. Perhaps the designer can make it evident to motorists that these movements are easy to accomplish. However, if the station is located on a corner with very little traffic making right turns, there would be practically nothing the designer could do to make the station successful.

Clearly, anyone desiring to locate a gas station must place great value on the characteristics of traffic passing the station. The impact of other values of the client or designer would be minimal relative to the ultimate financial success or failure of the station. Traffic in this case is the most important issue—all others pale in comparison.

Resources

Environmental resources—water, air, fuel, building materials—can have a profound influence on built form. Whole civilizations have vanished when water became unavailable. In climates where a continuous supply of water is uncertain, buildings are sometimes designed as collectors of water, with cisterns beneath them to store precipitation for use during periods of drought. The impact on architectural form can be significant. In western Pakistan, the prevailing breezes are collected and channeled down through chimney-like stacks to ventilate interior rooms (Fig. 3-47).

Middle-Eastern and Mediterranean cities have also developed with a consciousness to the benefits of sun and shade to create natural ventilation. The courtyard house and narrow streets of towns in Morocco are particularly effective in this regard (Fig. 3-48).

Before air-conditioning was invented, buildings in every region of the United States were designed appropriately for the local climate. In southern Arizona there were two proto-types—the thick-walled and flat-roofed adobe courtyard houses similar to those found in the Mediterranean area, and high-ceiling

Figure 3-47 Wind Collectors on Buildings.
Credit: Carl Okazaki

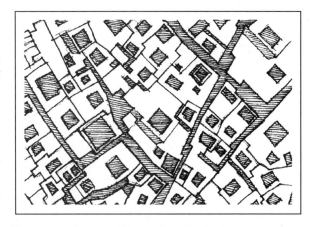

Figure 3-48 Courtyard Houses Creating Shade.
Credit: Carl Okazaki

Figure 3-49 Old Main: Exterior.

Figure 3-50 Old Main: Surrounding Porch.

sloped-roof buildings with broad shaded porches on all sides, adapted from European traditions. James Creighton's Old Main, the first building on The University of Arizona campus, is a very effective example of the latter tradition (Figs. 3-49 and 3-50). Its large surrounding porches shade the walls and windows to keep out the heat of the sun. Its high ceilings and vented attic remove the heat from the areas in which people work. Its sunken lower porches take advantage of both the shade and the cooling effect of the surrounding earth, which serves as a heat sink to draw heat away from the area. Even before air-conditioning made it possible to maintain a constant indoor temperature, it was a very comfortable building in which to work.

The energy crisis of the 1970s alerted the world, and especially the architectural profession, to the prospect of a time when conventional petroleum-based heating and cooling technologies might not be available. Suddenly a completely new value, energy, began to have a significant impact on the practice of architecture. Previously, architects could build buildings without much concern for orientation, solar penetration, and the like, and rely on air conditioning run on cheap petroleum-based energy to overcome the resulting high heating and cooling loads.

It became mandatory to conserve energy as costs skyrocketed and the possible unavailability of petroleum products for energy use loomed as a distinct possibility. Indeed, the energy crisis resulted in a completely new aesthetic expression in architecture, where large areas of south-facing glass, attached greenhouses, dark-colored Trombe walls, and roof-mounted solar collectors became expressed parts of the architecture. This is a contemporary case in which a newly held value became an architectural issue, just as it had been for nearly all primitive buildings where energy issues could not be ignored. Cases in point are the cool towers and insulating shade structures of the Environmental Research Laboratory (ERL) of The University of Arizona (Fig. 3-51).

Figure 3-51 ERL Cool Tower and Shade Structures.

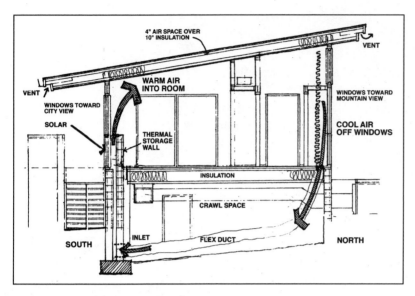

Figure 3-52 Trombe Wall and Vented Roof.

Credit: Robert Hershberger and Nader Chalfoun

The under-window Trombe wall and vented roof structure of the Mittal Residence in Tucson, Arizona, also exemplify this contemporary concern (Fig. 3-52).

The availability of building materials also may have a significant effect on built form. Since time began, builders (and later architects) have used the most readily available building materials: timber and stone in forested mountain areas; adobe and brick in desert environments; reeds, mud, and thatch in tropical regions; ice and animal hides in arctic areas. Only with modern technology and the resulting transportation capabilities have many materials become nearly universally available. Nevertheless, materials still have an impact on design, depending on their economic availability and appropriateness relative to conditions of climate, available labor, and other local conditions.

Waste

Waste products from buildings and their ultimate disposition is a design problem that rarely receives attention during the programming process, but can be an important issue in architecture. In site planning, for example, the type and location of dumpsters to receive trash can have a major impact on parking and circulation layout. Every municipality has its own system for waste pickup and screening which must be discovered and accommodated. The designer needs to know the particular requirements for locating dumpsters so that their placement will not interfere with other more important design considerations. A particularly onerous example of the misplacement of trash containers is at golf resort restaurant (Fig. 3-53). While partially screened behind wooden

Figure 3-53 Entry and Trash Conflict.

gates, the trash area is immediately adjacent to the covered main entrance to the restaurant. This exposes customers to the obnoxious odors of the decaying food products and to the flies that make trash areas their home. It also results in occasional noise and traffic obstruction by vehicles collecting the trash. This is a terrible way to handle restaurant waste. The program must make such things clear to the designer.

Where to dispose of the collected trash is also a major problem. In many cities in the southwestern United States, the urban washes have been the location of choice for wildcat dumps and even municipal landfills. These seemed like logical places because occasional flooding made them poor choices for building sites. So, there they were, open and available to receive trash. This has created problems with water pollution as the occasional storms and flooding disrupt the landfill areas and leach contaminants such as TCP into the aquifers. This is not an easy problem to solve. Waste recycling programs are one of the obvious ways to reduce the problem. Employing only recyclable materials in both building and manufacturing processes can also help tremendously.

Similar problems are occurring in rapidly developing suburban and rural areas with wildcat dumping, septic systems, and even agricultural pesticides and fertilizers that overcome the capability of the surface materials to absorb them so that clear water streams are being contaminated by waste products. Here again, recycling combined with carefully planned landfills away from watercourses and self-contained or development-sized sewer treatment systems can greatly reduce the amount of pollutants reaching the aquifer. Use of biodegradable nutrients and biological methods of pest control can also help to reduce pollution. In some rapidly growing urban areas, the existing communities do not have a sufficient tax base to provide sewage disposal systems. Developers must provide their own systems as part of the overall project. The location of these facilities and their costs have a serious impact on project design.

Similarly, airborne waste, once unregulated, has become a serious concern in most states and municipalities, such that special systems in buildings and automobiles are often necessary to reduce waste products (pollutants) to an acceptable level. Reduction of auto emissions is beginning to have an effect on how we plan and design our cities and buildings. Provisions for shorter trips, carpooling, public transportation, and charging electric vehicles may become the norm.

While waste management is rarely a primary issue in the design of buildings, managing waste is nevertheless an important issue and should be valued by anyone not wishing to be unpleasantly surprised by its impact on architecture or the surrounding community. The programmer is responsible for advising clients and designers about special facility needs in this area.

3.3 Cultural Issues

- Historical
- Institutional
- Political
- Legal

Cultural issues are sometimes difficult to distinguish from human issues. However, the reader can make the distinction by thinking of human issues as those that are immediately involved with the client and users of the building, while cultural issues are the expectations of society—the community at large. These issues vary widely from project to project, but no project is totally immune to or divorced from cultural influences.

How people perceive and use space, the meanings they attribute to various forms, and what they expect in terms of art all relate to culture. Virtually every human institution is in some sense a product of the values of the culture in which it is located. In this section, we look at several aspects of culture that often have an impact on what is designed.

Historical

In every place in the world, there is a history of development that relates to the particular region and its human, environmental, cultural, technical, temporal, economic, aesthetic, and safety traditions. All new developments must fit within this cultural context. If the place is characterized by a free market economy, the way that buildings are planned, designed, and built will be different from similar facilities in a centrally controlled economy. If there is a strong central government, concerns for safety and security from unfriendly neighbors may be dealt with by an armed police force. If there is not a strong central government, it might be necessary to deal with protection in a more immediate way, such as the castles used in feudal times (Fig. 3-54).

If a country has an official religion, virtually all of the institutions may revolve around the precepts of

Figure 3-54 Manzanares Real Castle, Spain.

that faith. If a country and its people are relatively rich, how something is made will be very different from one in which great numbers of the people are very poor. This historical background will establish the cultural context into which any new development will be placed. It will have a strong impact on what is programmed and designed, even if some of the issues are not clearly articulated by anyone (Hall 1966).

There will also be a tradition of language and art that conditions how people actually think, use space, and interpret architectural forms. In the words of the noted anthropologist Edward Hall, there will be both a "silent language" and a "hidden dimension" to deal with as the programmer and designer work to achieve architecture (Hall 1959, 1966). This is typically no great problem for architects working in the region in which they live. These traditions will likely be an inherent part of the architect's way of dealing with architecture. The same is true for regional building traditions based on available materials and labor. There will be materials that are much less expensive to use than others, and craftsmen available to work on one kind of system, but not on another. The Arizona Inn by Merrit H. Starkweather in Tucson, Arizona, with its adobe walls, skylights, trellises, and oasis—like courtyards, is a particularly sensitive example of design for the Sonoran Desert region (Fig. 3-55).

Figure 3-55 Arizona Inn.

It is a much more difficult problem when architects do work in another country, region, or culture. Without careful environmental research and sensitivity, there is a good chance that such architects will create something appropriate for their own place, but not for the place in which the building is to be constructed. There may be times of the year when everyone will be on vacation, so no work can be accomplished, or rainy seasons or other conditions that might interfere with construction schedules. Introduction of some equipment or systems might guarantee that with the first breakdown, the entire operation would come to a standstill because people from the architect's place of residence would have to be brought in to make repairs. This is particularly true in some of the Central and South American countries. There may also be traditions of community life that should be known to the designer, so that if a departure from the norm is selected, it will be with an understanding of its likely effect. For example, what would be the reaction to a supermarket in a community accustomed to using an open market or small neighborhood stores? (Fig. 3-56)

It is important that the architectural program clearly set forth the conditions that establish the context for a project to be situated outside of the architectural designer's immediate region. Otherwise, the designer will need to do research on the culture or

Figure 3-56 Market Place in Curitiba, Brazil.

to rely on intuition appropriate in one place, but possibly not in another. This can lead to problems in getting a design approved, built, and then properly used and maintained.

A particularly interesting commission relating to historical traditions in our own country dealt with downtown Tempe, Arizona, referred to as "Old Town Mill Avenue." This part of the city was destined, by vote of the city council, for complete demolition and rebuilding at the time when the author had arrived in town as a new assistant professor, fresh from graduate school in Philadelphia. He felt that much of what was to be torn down was quite handsome and capable of restoration, particularly since it had been built some 200 years after many of the still functioning buildings in Philadelphia. Fortunately, another young architect, Ernest Nickels, felt similarly and was writing letters to the editor of the local paper criticizing the shortsightedness of the decision.

The author met with Nickels and together they developed a strategy to preserve the area. They helped organize the older residents and current business owners to resist the urban renewal approach in favor of an old town revitalization program, to bring back the lost qualities and to reinvigorate the business climate of the district. This group of people ultimately prevailed, and the council reversed their earlier decision and appointed a project area committee to see how this revitalization could be achieved.

A year later, the city hired the two young architects, who had subsequently organized a firm together, to make a thorough study of the area and to draft a specific revitalization plan. This was accomplished after a very careful analysis of the district, including the condition of the old structures, and extensive interaction with the project area committee members and other residents and users of the area.

The proposed plan included reducing traffic on Mill Avenue, increasing the sidewalk back to its original generous width, planting street trees, and adding street furniture and other amenities. It also included adding considerable off-street parking and bringing in new city buildings, a hotel, and some other major business anchors. The plan included preserving many of the old structures through careful augmentation of seismic capabilities and refurbishing exterior materials and finishes, including the additions of canopies and awnings. It also specified signage appropriate to the time that the buildings were constructed. The intent was to make this an active, pedestrian-oriented shopping district filled with small stores, galleries, eateries, and entertainment to bring students from the neighboring university and residents of the community back downtown, especially at night.

The strategy and specific plan were adopted by the city council. Improvements by the private sector, led by architects as developers, began almost immediately and have continued ever since. The district has quadrupled in size and is the strongest and most attractive entertainment district in the metropolitan area. Interestingly, it has converted a town relying on regional shopping centers into one that now loves its "open market" in the old downtown (Figs. 3-57 and 3-58).

Institutional

If the client is involved with an activity that has a continuity or history of development in society, the architect will be designing for a human institution. This is the area of value identification to which the architect Louis I. Kahn made such a great contribution (Kahn 1961). What is the nature of the institution? What is its reason for being? What is the purpose for building? These were

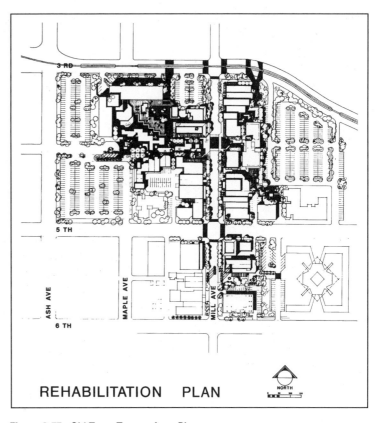

Figure 3-57 Old Town Tempe: Area Plan.
Credit: Robert Hershberger and Ernest Nickels, Par 3 Studio

Figure 3-58 Old Town Tempe: Street Fair.

Figure 3-59 Salk Center: Courtyard.

Figure 3-60 Salk Center: Exterior.

important questions that Professor Kahn asked for all of his commissions, from bathhouses to churches to great research institutions. For these great research institutions, he realized the importance of differentiating between served and servant spaces, and he made an architecture that recognized both types of spaces. This is clearly the case in the Salk Center in La Jolla, California, where he designed mechanical/electrical floors above and below laboratory spaces to allow supply and removal of air, gas, water, electricity, exhaust, and sewage at any location in the laboratories (Figs. 3-59 through 3-61).

If the institution is a hospital, what important human values are being served? Is it a place where doctors operate? A place where nurses care? Where patients heal? Where patients die? Where investors make a good return on investment? Or some or all of the above? The institution's essential place in society should be considered and articulated so that the designer can express this value in the form, space, and meaning of the design. Imagine the different hospital designs that would result if only one of the above institutional values was considered primary for each design. For example, Stanford Hospital was conceived by Edward D. Stone as a place for patients to heal (Fig. 3-62). This attitude resulted in a hospital only a few stories high, with patient access to patios on the ground floor and views of trees from upper levels. Its long halls made access to patient rooms inconvenient for the doctors, who generally prefer high-rise buildings, with elevators for quick access to patient areas.

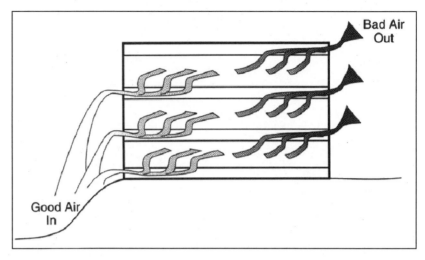

Figure 3-61 Salk Center: Systems Diagram.
Credit: Nancy Cole

An even more interesting case is that of the prison or penitentiary. Are they institutions whose primary purpose is *custody*—to keep the prisoner away from society? Or are they for *therapy*—to prepare the prisoner to return to society as

Figure 3-62 Stanford Hospital: Model.
Photo Credit: Office of Communications, Stanford University Medical Center. Permission: From the collection of Lane Medical Library, Stanford University Medical Center

a better person? Or are they for *punishment*—to make the prisoner pay a high price for their crime? The prison official's perception of the role and function of a prison can greatly affect prison design. Robert Sommer (1974) has serious concerns that society in general, and prison institutions in particular, do not have clearly defined values relative to housing social misfits; hence, they cannot decide upon appropriate goals for accommodating these people (Fig. 3-63).

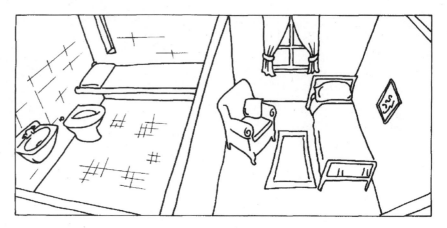

Figure 3-63 Hard and Soft Prison Spaces.

Credit: Goldman and Peatross (1993), 376. Permission: Wolfgang F. E. Preiser

A mental hospital is a similar case relative to the values it should serve in society. If the purpose of the mental hospital is to prepare people to better cope in society, it seems inherently wrong to remove the patients from society and confine them with other persons with similar or worse problems! Our society needs to define more clearly the purposes of such institutions, or to change them or the types of patients they house. These are cases where established institutions of society may be products of conflicting or outmoded values.

A case for carefully articulated institutional values could be made for practically any human institution: educational, religious, commercial, or residential. What is the true value or purpose of the airport, the school, the retirement community? What are the implications of these values relative to specific goals, objectives, needs? It is important that the designer know the building's reason for being. Will it be a very important facility for the neighborhood, the entire community, the state, or even the nation? Or is it only intended to serve the purposes of some individual or private organization? What, then, is its appropriate image in the community? Should it be a foreground or background building? Or somewhere in between? What should it communicate to those who pass by, to those who enter, to those who occupy and use the building? The programmer has an obligation to make these things clear. The values that an institution embraces should have a strong influence on its form. If made clear in the program, the designer should be able to express these values in the resulting architecture.

If the building is to be a city hall, it will have considerable importance within the community, both functionally and symbolically. What is the nature of a city hall in our culture? Is there a fundamental difference between a city hall in our country and one in Mexico, Poland, or Turkey? Is it a place of great power and central authority or an easily accessible place to service the people of the community? This needs to be determined so that the architect can find an appropriate solution.

In a master planning study for the Miami/Dade County Center, Robert Geddes, Architect, proposed a long, low building rather than the typical high-rise, feeling that a government center in our country should be close to the people. He believed that citizens should be able to get to the public service areas without having to enter an elevator. Is this a correct understanding of this institution? Apparently, few big-city governments have come to this realization. Indeed, the programmer for the government center in Miami assumed it would be a high-rise, and developed all of the floor-by-floor spatial relationships typical of high-rises found in Manhattan, where the programming firm was located. And years later when Miami/Dade County actually built the center, it was comprised of several high-rise buildings, each one for a different governmental unit. So, how should a governmental center be organized?

The Boston City Hall by Kallman, McKinnell and Knowles was a very bold scheme set in a great urban square (Fig. 3-64). The smaller Tempe City Hall by Michael and Kemper Goodwin was equally strong conceptually (Fig. 3-65). Are they appropriate designs?

A very interesting architectural problem that the author dealt with, as both the programmer and designer, was a training and workshop facility for handicapped adults. The organization had always

Figure 3-64 Boston City Hall.

Figure 3-65 Tempe City Hall.

been housed in leased space in existing industrial or warehouse facilities. These facilities lacked appropriate spaces for training activities and flexibility for rapidly changing needs. They were unsatisfactory in terms of convenience and safety for the handicapped workers and projected an inappropriate image. Fortunately, the staff and directors of the facility were able to articulate the true nature of the institution.

The center was not merely a place where handicapped adults could learn to be gainfully employed. The fundamental reason for the facility was the belief that "the handicapped are individuals with the potential for growth and development" and that "handicapped individuals have the right to self respect and deserve the opportunity to be contributing members of society." This undergirding value system required that the facility be much more than a workshop in a leased industrial space. It had to be a place where the handicapped could reach their full potential as contributing members of society. It had to communicate to the occupants and to the public at large that individuals with disabilities can be contributing and valued members of the community. And, it had to do this within very severe economic constraints. This was a considerably different design problem than would have been the case had the architect only received information on specific functional requirements for the facility.

The extremely limited financial resources of the organization had to be directed to expressing the high quality of the operation, not just to providing space to meet functional requirements. The design solution was a simple rectangular building with flexible and expandable interior spaces, but constructed of high-quality exterior materials, including an exterior shade canopy for breaks and lunches, that would convey to the public the high standards and expectations of the organization (Fig. 3-66).

Figure 3-66 Tempe Center for the Handicapped.
Credit: Robert Hershberger and Kyun Kim, Hershberger-Kim Architects

The new building's impact on the community was enormous. Tempe Center for the Handicapped became a symbol of a progressive city, recognized for its quality design and used as a prime example in the city's successful application for All-American City status. More importantly, it was recognized as an institution capable of delivering quality services, and its annual contract work and community financial support increased threefold. Applications for placement of the handicapped and additional services also increased substantially, such that in just three years the client returned to the architect for a major renovation and expansion with cash in hand to pay for it. Virtually every function had outgrown its original space allocation. Was this a problem with the original program or design? Of course not! In the ten years of existence prior to the building program, the center had a very slight upward growth curve. Its rapid growth after occupying the new building was the result of excellent programming and design.

Although *institutional* is properly located in the cultural section of the HECTTEAS list, the author believes that it is the most important value area in architectural programming. Indeed, the identification of institutional purpose at the beginning of the architectural programming activity and within the program document is important to establish the direction of the rest of the programming and design activities. If a clear understanding of the nature and purpose of an organization can be established early in programming, it is an important step on the way to producing architecture. To help ensure its place when programming, the author thinks of the overall list as "I HECTTEAS" or "I TEST EACH" with the letter "I" standing for institutional.

Political

Most communities determine the kind of place they want to be through political processes. Some seek to be full-service cities, others seek to be limited service places, perhaps bedroom communities. Most eventually evolve general plans that include the infrastructure of the community: streets, utilities, storm drains, water, sewage treatment, and the like. Location, disposition, and costs to tie in to these services often have a strong impact on private building development. Zoning regulations spell out the kinds of buildings that can be located in parts of the community, at what density, to what height, etc. In short, the general plans and zoning regulations adopted by communities have a significant impact on what can be designed.

Most communities also have citizen boards to interpret the general plans and ordinances and hear citizen and/or developer appeals for deviations. The architectural program must identify the various community ordinances and procedures that will affect the design of a facility. Unusual requirements such as extra large lots or setbacks, height restrictions, or complete storm water retention must be included. If the community has particular requirements for signs or landscaping, these too should be made known. Communities, through their elected officials, decide what they want their city to look like, and each building within the community must contribute to that image, or the architect must convince the leaders that a deviation is appropriate (Fig. 3-67).

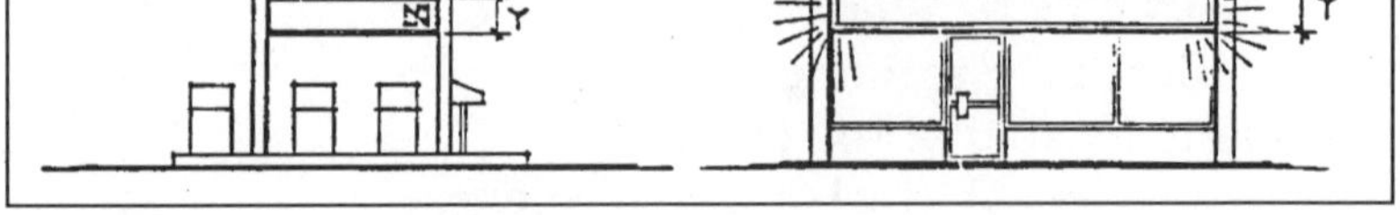

Figure 3-67 City of Tempe: Sign Requirement.
Credit: City of Tempe, 1996. *Sign Regulations.* City Ordinance No. 808, Section 7, page 89.

Legal

Most political decisions of a community, county, or state become a matter of law. Most states now require that architects have an accredited professional degree and practical experience, and that they pass a lengthy exam to demonstrate their ability to design buildings that will protect the public health, safety, and welfare. This, of course, has had an effect on both who can practice architecture and the overall quality of the built environment (Figs. 3-68 and 3-69).

National standards and codes are also adopted by communities as a further means of protecting the public health, safety, and welfare. Building, plumbing, electrical, and mechanical codes are usually adopted by cities and other governing authorities. Life safety and handicapped standards are also frequently adopted that specify how buildings can be

ORDINANCE 808
ZONING REQUIREMENTS
YARD, HEIGHT, AREA AND DENSITY

ZONING DISTRICT SYMBOL	DISTRICT NAME	MAXIMUM			MINIMUM						
		DENSITY d.u./acre	BUILDING HEIGHT in feet	LOT COVERAGE %	NET SITE AREA	LOT WIDTH in feet	LOT DEPTH in feet	SETBACKS in feet			
								FRONT	SIDE	REAR	STREET SIDE
AG	AGRICULTURAL	1	30	20	1 acre	115	150	40	20	35	25[A]
R1-15	ONE FAMILY RESIDENTIAL	2.40	30	40	15,000 sq. ft.	115	120	35	15	30	20[A]
R1-10	ONE FAMILY RESIDENTIAL	2.80	30	40	10,000 sq. ft.	90	100[B]	30	10	25	15[A]
R1-8	ONE FAMILY RESIDENTIAL	3.35	30	40	8,000 sq. ft.	80	100[B]	25	7	20	10[A]
R1-7	ONE FAMILY RESIDENTIAL	3.75	30	40	7,000 sq. ft.	70	100[B]	25	7	15	10[A]
R1-6	ONE FAMILY RESIDENTIAL	4.00	30	40	6,000 sq. ft.	60	100[B]	25	7	15	10[A]
R1-5	ONE FAMILY RESIDENTIAL	6	30	NS	5,000 sq. ft.	NS	NS	20	5	15	10[A]
R1-4	ONE FAMILY RESIDENTIAL	8	30	NS	4,000 sq. ft.	NS	NS	20	O[D]	15	10[A]
R1-PAD	ONE FAMILY RESIDENTIAL (J)	NS	NS	NS	1/2 acre	NS	NS	NS	NS	NS	NS[A]
R-2	MULTI-FAMILY RESIDENTIAL	10	30[C]	40	7,200 sq. ft.	60	100	25	10	15	25
R-3R	MULTI-FAMILY RESIDENTIAL RESTRICTED	15	15[C]	40	6,000 sq. ft.	60	100	25	10	15	25
R-3	MULTI-FAMILY RESIDENTIAL LIMITED	20	30[C]	40	6,000 sq. ft.	60	100	25	10	15	25
R-4	MULTI-FAMILY RESIDENTIAL GENERAL	24	35[C]	40	6,000 sq. ft.	60	100	25	10	15	25

Figure 3-68 City of Tempe: Zoning Requirement.

Credit: City of Tempe, 1996. City Ordinance No. 808, Section 7, Zoning Requirements

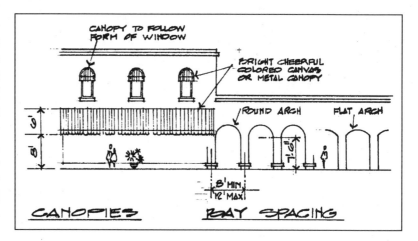

Figure 3-69 Old Town Tempe: Design Standards.

Credit: Robert Hershberger and Ernest Nickels, Par 3 Studio, 1973. *Old Town Tempe-Mill Avenue Rehabilitation Feasibility Study*, Tempe Arizona

designed and constructed. The architectural programmer must diligently seek out and identify those that apply to the particular project under consideration. Here again, if some code requirements are unusual, or a city interprets them differently, or has modified them for its own purposes, these irregularities should be pointed out in the program.

Some architects complain bitterly that codes and ordinances design their buildings. We are convinced that the architects who complain loudest are the ones who did not take time to learn about the codes and ordinances during the programming phase and, hence, were rudely introduced to them after design decisions had already been made. They were then forced to go back and redesign to accommodate the law. This hurts! If the designer is fully aware of the rules and regulations before commencing design, the legal requirements become just another design issue. Generally, regulations to protect the public health and safety are neither arbitrary nor capricious. Nor are they there to give architects a hard time. Indeed, as one of my colleagues, a structural engineer, has told his students, "They are there because somebody got killed!" (Sheydayi 1985). They provide important programmatic information that can have a profound impact on design (Fig. 3-70).

GROUP AND DIVISION	SECTION	DESCRIPTION OF OCCUPANCY
A-1		A building or portion of a building having an assembly room with an occupant load of 1,000 or more and a legitimate stage.
A-2		A building or portion of a building having an assembly room with an occupant load of less than 1,000 and a legitimate stage.
A-2.1	303.1.1	A building or portion of a building having an assembly room with an occupant load of 300 or more without a legitimate stage, including such buildings used for educational purposes and not classed as a Group E or Group B Occupancy.
A-3		Any building or portion of a building having an assembly room with an occupant load of less than 300 without a legitimate stage, including such buildings used for educational purposes and not classed as a Group E or Group B Occupancy.
A-4		Stadiums, reviewing stands and amusement park structures not included within other Group A Occupancies.
B	304.1	A building or structure, or a portion thereof, for office, professional or service-type transactions, including storage of records and accounts; eating and drinking establishments with an occupant load of less than 50.
E-1		Any building used for educational purposes through the 12th grade by 50 or more persons for more than 12 hours per week or four hours in any one day.
E-2	305.1	Any building used for educational purposes through the 12th grade by less than 50 persons for more than 12 hours per week or four hours in any one day.
E-3		Any building or portion thereof used for day-care purposes for more than six persons.
F-1		Moderate-hazard factory and industrial occupancies include factory and industrial uses not classified as Group F, Division 2 Occupancies.
F-2	306.1	Low-hazard factory and industrial occupancies include facilities producing noncombustible or nonexplosive materials which during finishing, packing or processing do not involve a significant fire hazard.
H-1		Occupancies with a quantity of material in the building in excess of those listed in Table 3-D which present a high explosion hazard as listed in Section 307.1.1.
H-2		Occupancies with a quantity of material in the building in excess of those listed in Table 3-D which present a moderate explosion hazard or a hazard from accelerated burning as listed in Section 307.1.1.
H-3	307.1	Occupancies with a quantity of material in the building in excess of those listed in Table 3-D which present a high fire or physical hazard as listed in Section 307.1.1.
H-4		Repair garages not classified as Group S, Division 3 Occupancies.
H-5		Aircraft repair hangars not classified as Group S, Division 5 Occupancies and heliports.
H-6	307.1 and 307.11	Semiconductor fabrication facilities and comparable research and development areas when the facilities in which hazardous production materials are used, and the aggregate quantity of material is in excess of those listed in Table 3-D or 3-E.
H-7	307.1	Occupancies having quantities of materials in excess of those listed in Table 3-E that are health hazards as listed in Section 307.1.1.

Figure 3-70 Uniform Building Code.

3.4 Technological Issues

- Materials
- Systems
- Processes

Available technology, at least historically, has been one of the major influences on architecture. If a masonry unit was the only material available for construction, the arch was the only way to span openings. If wood was readily available, timbers and trusses were used to span major spaces. The form of the building directly reflected the possibilities of the available materials.

Today, what the architect selects from the tremendous variety of available building materials, systems, and processes is often a matter of personal preference, based on availability, cost, and aesthetic potential. Whether any of the technological selections become an important part of the architectural expression is usually at the designer's discretion.

Materials

Occasionally, a client will have a very strong preference for one material or another and may insist that the preferred material be used in a project. This is often the case in housing, where some people have a strong preference for masonry and others for wood construction. It also occurs in other building types, depending on material and installation costs and the client's previous experience with particular materials. There are also preferences that relate to the historic availability of materials and skilled craftsmen in the region where a building is to be constructed. The programmer, while not dictating the choice of materials for the building, should include client preferences or requirements in the program so the designer will be able to give these materials special consideration when developing the form of the building. This includes structural materials such as wood, masonry, steel, and concrete, as well as finish materials such as plaster, wall board, marble, brick, tile, glass, and aluminum.

For example, the author programmed and designed a medium-sized landscape nursery for a client who had purchased hundreds of used 12" × 12" Douglas fir timbers from a Central Arizona Project

Figure 3-71 Greenworld Nursery: Structure.

Figure 3-72 Greenworld Nursery: Entry.

trestle bridge. The client wanted to use them in the nursery facility. What an opportunity! The limited project budget would not have allowed the purchase of new timbers of this size (Figs. 3-71 and 3-72).

Systems

Preferences and decisions about systems should be handled in a manner similar to that used for construction materials. Structural systems vary depending on the nature of the materials used. For the American Pavilion (Fig. 3-73) at the Montreal World's Fair, R. Buckminster Fuller and Shoji Sodao chose to use lightweight steel members to construct their noted geodesic dome. The Cambridge Seven used a contrasting structure of concrete to differentiate the internal exhibit from the enclosing structure.

Norman Foster used exposed structural members to construct the exquisitely detailed Hong Kong and Shanghai Bank (Fig. 3-74).

If a particular system is required by the client, it must be noted in the program. Generally, however, structural systems tend to be selected by the designer to meet other goals and requirements of the program.

Mechanical and electrical systems can also be identified during programming. One client may have a strong preference for fluorescent over incandescent lighting because of the economics of operation. Another client may prefer incandescent over fluorescent lighting because of the quality of the light. One client may prefer to heat and cook with gas, while another may prefer electricity. Some clients may insist on dropped, easily maintained ceiling surfaces for quick cleaning and easy access to mechanical and electrical systems and equipment, while others may wish to have a more formal plastered or paneled ceiling, and still others may be willing to expose all systems and have no ceiling at all.

In the Richards Building (Fig. 3-75) and the Salk Center, Louis I. Kahn determined that there needed to be entire structures devoted to handling the various mechanical, plumbing, and electrical systems. In the Richards Building, the systems were housed in separated towers and delivered to the spaces through exposed verandale trusses supporting each floor. The fresh air intakes were at the lower level of the towers located on the south side and the exhaust was at the top of dissimilar towers located on the other sides of the building. This solved the problem of possible contamination of the air supply and expressed the differences with the bold forms used in the design.

Aldo Giurgola of Mitchell/Giurgola Architects saw a similar potential for the mechanical systems in high-rise buildings, which are often hidden in penthouses at the tops of these buildings or in basement service areas. For

Figure 3-73 American Pavilion: Interior.

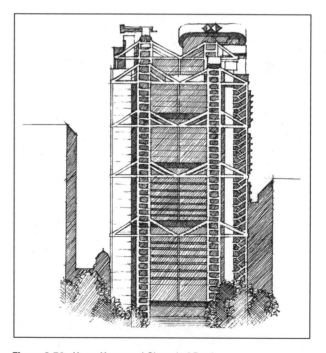

Figure 3-74 Hong Kong and Shanghai Bank.
Credit: Carl Okazaki

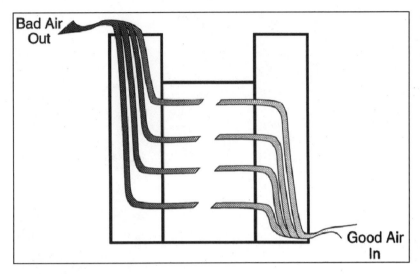

Figure 3-75   Richards Building: Systems.

Figure 3-76   Two INA Plaza.

the Two INA Plaza building in Philadelphia, Giurgola chose to locate these systems near the center point of the building and used the location as a primary aesthetic expression of the building (Fig. 3-76).

Other architects, such as Hardy, Holzman and Pfeiffer, expose brightly colored mechanical systems as significant elements of architectural expression, even in major public buildings where all systems have traditionally been kept hidden. The Discovery Park Multi-Tenant Facility by Russell Vandiver Architects Partnership in Vancouver, British Columbia, is a good example of mechanical ducts being used as elements of architectural expression (Fig. 3-77).

If the architect is not sensitive to the aesthetic potential of systems, they can destroy the building's appearance. Probably the most usual situation is one in which interior equipment requires large and possibly unsightly elements on the roof. The programmer should make the designer aware of this fact. Otherwise, the result could be disastrous from an aesthetic standpoint. A glaring and ironic example of unsightly unscreened mechanical equipment is on the roof of the Arizona State University Art Annex (Fig. 3-78).

Figure 3-77 Multi-Tenant Facility.

Photo Credit: Simon Scott. Permission: Che-Cheung Poon

Figure 3-78 Unsightly Rooftop Equipment.

The program needs to state if the client, users, or community prefer or require a particular material or system. The designer, having been apprised of these preferences or requirements, can evaluate their appropriateness and incorporate them into the design or try to convince the client, user, or community why the preferred material or system would not be appropriate. While some may argue that no one but the architect should have any say as to materials and systems selection, the reality of who is approving the design, paying the bills for construction, and ultimately maintaining the building, dictates that it is appropriate to let the designer know the preferences of these people.

Processes

The effect of process on architecture is very significant but is rarely consciously planned. The architect who proceeds without a program will program the building through design. This is an inefficient process that generally results in a substantially different building than one based on a written program. Similarly, the methods, techniques, and tools employed in the design process have a profound influence on the resulting architecture. A designer who really understands the client's and user's values, and who has discovered the fundamental nature of the institution, is likely to produce a very different building than an architect who is concerned only with providing the required spaces, in proper relationships, within the client's budget. Similarly, if a designer uses a parallel bar and a 30-60 degree triangle as the principal tools for design, he/she is likely to end up with a building characterized by right and possibly 30-60 degree angles in its form. Frank Lloyd Wright was known for designing with a T-square and a 30-60-90 degree triangle. The Unitarian Church in Madison, Wisconsin, is one example of his using this combination during design (Figs. 3-79 and 3-80).

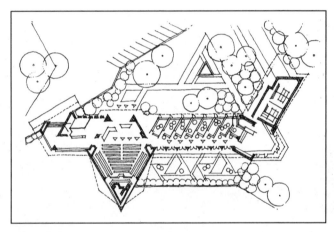

Figure 3-79   Unitarian Church: Exterior.
Credit: Carl Okazaki

Figure 3-80   Unitarian Church: Plan.
Credit: Carl Okazaki

If an architect uses freehand sketches during the design process, his/her buildings are likely to be less rectilinear than buildings by architects who rely on a straightedge while designing. Erich Mendelsohn often used freehand charcoal or soft pencil sketches during design, which allowed him to develop very fluid, dynamic, and organic-appearing buildings. This was certainly true of the Einstein Tower (Figs. 3-81 and 3-82) designed by Mendelsohn in Potsdam (Hart 1995).

The author, using freehand pencil sketches in the early stages of design, often develops irregular forms, as can be seen in the sketch plan and elevation for the Thirsty Earth Museum project (Figs. 3-83 and 3-84).

Designers who use chipboard or clay models are likely to generate forms that are in some way a reflection of these media. Similarly, the ease of drawing and building radially defined curves with computer-aided design (CAD) systems is reflected in the designs by firms using these systems.

The firm of Eric Owen Moss Architects combines freehand sketching and computer imaging in their design process. The Exhibition Hall for Imagina published in Architectural Record (Novitski 1996) involved videoconferencing to communicate the design to a collaborating architect and client based in Monaco. These methods help the firm imagine and develop the

Figure 3-81 Einstein Tower: Architect's Sketch.

Permission: Staaliche Museen PreuBischer Kulturbezitz, Kunstbibliothek, Berlin

Figure 3-82 Einstein Tower: Exterior.

Photo Credit: Vaughn Hart

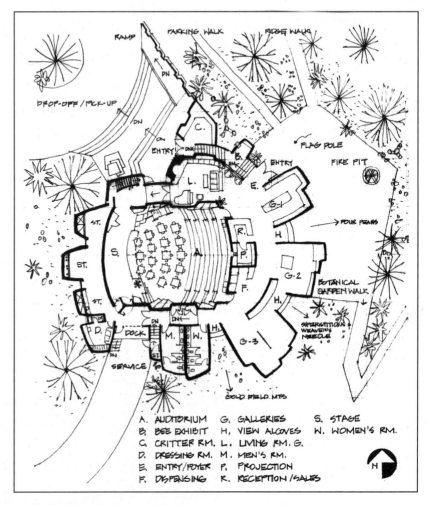

A. AUDITORIUM   G. GALLERIES   S. STAGE
B. BEE EXHIBIT   H. VIEW ALCOVES   W. WOMEN'S RM.
C. CRITTER RM.   L. LIVING RM. G.
D. DRESSING RM. M. MEN'S RM.
E. ENTRY/FOYER   P. PROJECTION
F. DISPENSING   R. RECEPTION/SALES

Figure 3-83   Thirsty Earth Museum: Plan.

Figure 3-84   Thirsty Earth Museum: Sketch

highly innovative designs that characterize their work (Figs. 3-85 and 3-86).

Construction processes also can have an impact on the form of a building. A case in point is the Hilton Palacio Del Rio Hotel by Cerna and Garza, Architects, built along the Riverwalk in San Antonio prior to the 1968 world's fair. It was not possible to have the building ready for the fair using conventional design and building processes. The architect developed a design that allowed room units to be completed and furnished in advance of completion of the building structure, so that when the structure was in place these room systems, including furnishings, could be inserted within the structural framework, and the hotel could be ready for immediate occupancy. This fast-tracking of construction became a dominant theme in the design of the building (Fig. 3-87).

A similar need for fast-tracking resulting in a very different modular solution can be found in the Habitat Housing project by Moshe Safde for the Montreal World's Fair in 1967 (Fig. 3-88).

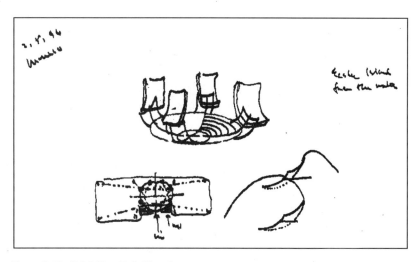

Figure 3-85 Exhibition Hall: Sketches.
Credit and Permission: Eric Owen Moss Architects

Figure 3-86 Exhibition Hall: Computer Image.
Architect: Eric Owen Moss. Design Team: Paul Groh, Scott Nakao and Gevik Hovsepian. Computer Image and Photo Credit: Paul Groh. Permission: Eric Owen Moss Architects.

Figure 3-87 Hilton Hotel Under Construction.

Credit: Carl Okazaki

Figure 3-88 Habitat Housing.

3.5 Temporal Issues

- Growth

- Change

- Permanence

Time has an impact on architecture in a variety of ways (Duffy 1990; Brand 1994). It can impact the design and construction processes, as discussed under process issues. It can also have a very strong influence on the design of institutions that are characterized by growth and change, as well as for buildings that are intended to last a very long time—where permanence is highly valued.

Growth

Most design commissions are for buildings that will be expanded in the future to reflect natural growth in the organization. In fact, most successful enterprises will expand numerous times during their existence. Sometimes this can be done on the original site. Often, an organization will have to move to a new location because their existing site is not large enough to accommodate additional building expansion.

Churches can be striking examples of this kind of growth. They often begin with a small group of people in a home, grow into a rented facility, and then into a first small building of their own. If they have the financial resources or denominational support, they generally purchase a parcel of land of sufficient size to accommodate the projected future growth, but begin with only one or two buildings of sufficient size to accommodate their present congregation plus space for modest growth. Once the first phase is complete and the size of the congregation is near capacity, the church typically begins a second phase of design and construction, and so on, until the capacity of the site is reached. At such time, the church faces the prospect of limiting growth; finding a new, larger site and beginning the process of growth again; or possibly spinning off smaller mission churches to absorb additional growth. In many cases, initial worship facilities are enlarged to achieve greater capacity. In other cases, old worship facilities are converted to new uses, such as education or fellowship, which often require less space, and a new worship facility is built. It is important that the growth potential in churches be recognized as an issue in the initial planning and programming, so that adequate provision can be made for future additions and new facilities. If this is not done, it is likely that future work will be hampered by facilities located in inappropriate places.

Figure 3-89 Covenant Baptist Church: Model.

The master plan for Covenant Baptist Church by Hershberger Kim Architects includes a future sanctuary, classrooms, and expanded parking (Figs. 3-89 and 3-90).

The architectural programmer must discover if the facility being programmed has a potential for growth, determine in what particular areas and what manner the growth

Figure 3-90 Covenant Baptist Church: Exterior.

is most likely to occur, and include strategies acceptable to the client for accommodating the growth. This is probably one of the most glaring omissions in many traditional programs. It results in added future costs to clients when they discover that growth is difficult or even impossible to accommodate, given the locations of existing facilities on the site.

Change

Well-designed buildings are able to accommodate changes in occupants or occupant needs. A characteristic of university buildings is the likelihood of internal change. It is a rare academic building that serves the same purpose for long periods of time. A

building may begin as a multipurpose liberal arts college for a number of departments, be taken over by one department as others move out to new facilities, then be given over to still another department as the first outgrows the facility and moves into another larger facility. Between actual moves, there may be constant internal change as the departmental focus moves from teaching to research or service, as equipment and furnishings are modernized, as new faculty are fitted into already crowded offices, and so on. The programmer must discover if the need for change is characteristic of the building being programmed.

High-rise buildings have similar needs to accommodate change. The Citicorp Center in Manhattan, New York, designed by The Stubbins Associates Inc. (TSA), has, like most high-rise office buildings, an unobstructed span from the central core to the exterior wall to allow the flexible partition system to accommodate changing tenants and uses over time (Figs. 3-91 and 3-92).

Figure 3-91   Citicorp Center: Exterior.

Photo Credit: Edward Jacoby. Permission: The Stubbins Associates

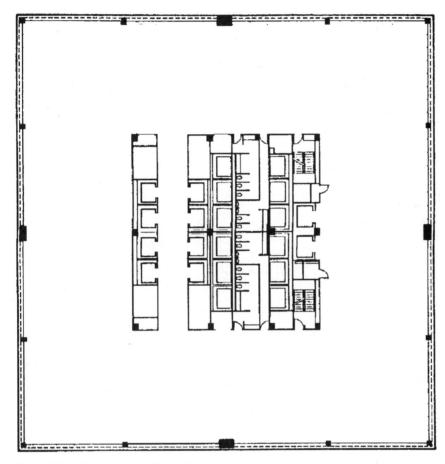

Figure 3-92 Citicorp Center: Plan of Tower.

Adapted from the preliminary design drawings of HSA. Permission: The Stubbins Associates

Robert Hershberger and Ernest Nickels of Par 3 Studio designed a relocatable church in which change was a crucial issue. The denomination's board for new church development wanted a church building that could be placed on the permanent site at the time that a minister was assigned. The client believed that quality facilities for exclusive use of the new congregation would enhance church growth and commitment. The intent was to have this relocatable church on the site no longer than five years, when it would be moved to another site in the region to begin another new church. This would give the founding congregation three years to establish itself, to hire an architect to design permanent

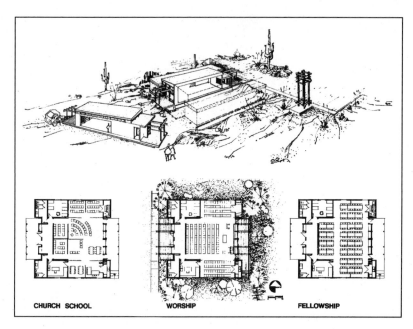

CHURCH SCHOOL   WORSHIP   FELLOWSHIP

Figure 3-93 Relocatable Church: Concept.

facilities, and to have them built and ready to occupy before the relocatable facility would be moved (Fig. 3-93).

In order to accommodate this program for change, the author's firm proposed using four completely finished and transportable units built off-site, which could be moved down the highway on "low-boy" trailer units and assembled on-site to form a 50-foot-square facility.

The assembled unit further responded to change to meet the programmatic requirement that the church accommodate all typical activities of a congregation of 100 persons. In order to accomplish this within a very restricted budget, it was necessary to have a facility that could quickly change to first accommodate church school, then worship, and then fellowship—all in the same morning. The design included moveable sound partitions and furnishings that are easily stacked, moved, reassembled, or stored to meet this requirement.

All of this accommodation for change was done in the context of other important issues such as the functional requirements for education and fellowship being met in a facility that is aesthetically satisfactory for worship. The relocatable building also needed to be attractive enough to be welcome in newly developing upscale neighborhoods.

Jon Jerde's design for Horton Plaza (Fig. 3-94), a major shopping center in downtown San Diego, also responded to requirements for change, but in a slightly different way. Jerde speaks about "scripting" places in the city for a variety of uses at different times of the day, week, and year, so that changing activities can be accommodated seamlessly (Jerde 1992). He has been par-

Figure 3-94 Horton Plaza: Mall.

ticularly successful at designing for these changes, because he recognized change as a crucial urban design issue.

Most building types are affected by the need to change internally as technologies become obsolcte and new equipment and systems are introduced. It is often hard to predict the nature of this kind of change. In addition, the demands of new technology are often so specific that modifications of facilities are difficult to make, sometimes resulting in extremely high remodeling and renovation costs. Making spaces more general, with free spans from exterior wall to exterior wall will help to accommodate change. Oversizing of ducts, chases, and other service systems is another strategy that helps to mitigate such problems. Providing for ease of expansion can also be helpful.

Some buildings change even more dramatically. World fair exhibition buildings are often designed to be dismantled at the end of the fair, so other uses can be made of the fairground site. Other structures, like those for circuses, are designed to be erected and dismantled repeatedly in different locations. The tent structure designed by Richard Larry Medlin for a ten-day concert series in Big Sky, Montana, was intended to be this kind of temporary structure (Fig. 3-95).

The character of this kind of temporary structure varies considerably from buildings intended to remain in one location. They must be easily assembled and dismantled, lightweight, and made of relatively short members so that they can be shipped from one site to another.

Figure 3-95 Tent Structure.
Credit: Richard Larry Medlin Architect, Inc.

Permanence

The flip side of growth and change is the issue of permanence. Most buildings are intended to have a long life, even though there may be repeated remodelings or additions to accommodate needed change.

Even buildings constructed for world's fairs are often intended to remain long after the event is over as functional or symbolic parts of the city in which the fair was held. This was certainly the case for the Seattle World's Fair— city officials and planners decided that the fair was a great opportunity to develop needed permanent buildings for the community. So, they planned quite a number of structures, including the Space Needle and Monorail (Fig. 3-96), for use after the fair was over. The same has occurred for buildings planned for most of the fairs and Olympic celebrations that have been held throughout the world.

There is also a need for certain buildings that will last a long time and the client or society at large will value for their permanence. Key governmental buildings or monuments

Figure 3-96 Space Needle and Monorail.

to great leaders, such as those found in the capitols of countries around the world, are excellent examples. The people of each country want these buildings to be permanent symbols of their national culture. Therefore, such buildings need to be constructed of materials and systems of the highest quality and permanence, so they will last as long as the country itself. Clearly, the United States Capitol (Fig. 3-97) is intended to last this long.

What about other buildings? Which buildings in society should be the most permanent? For which should the image of permanence

Figure 3-97 United States Capitol.
Photo Credit: Howard Olson

be an important characteristic of the architecture? Which buildings should be readily capable of change of one type or another? Which buildings will continue to grow over long periods of time? Programmers should give some attention to these questions for each new design problem.

3.6 Economic Issues

- Finance
- Construction
- Operations
- Maintenance
- Energy

Concern for cost may be of little interest to the student, novice programmer, or designer. But anyone who has been professionally involved for some time in either programming or design will agree that the most frequent misunderstandings between clients and architects will be over money—something costing more than the client expected. The bottom line, as far as most clients are concerned, is what the project is going to cost.

Often, clients seem to be most concerned with the initial construction cost, or even the amount of the architect's fees. They want to keep both as low as possible. However, in the 1980s the very high interest rates for construction and permanent financing, steadily increasing energy costs, and realization that costs for operations and maintenance go on for the life of the building made it apparent to many clients that life cycle costs are really much more important (Crosbie 1994). Financing costs go on for up to thirty years, usually at a constant level. The costs of operations, maintenance, and energy continue and usually increase over the life of a building. Thus, a building constructed of cheap materials and systems may soon lose the benefit of low initial cost because of substantial operations, maintenance, and energy costs.

An unrealistically low architect's fee is likely to result in increases in all of these costs because of the resulting lack of careful planning and design. It takes time to solve the functional and technical problems of building. It takes even more time to compare the life cycle costs of various materials and systems. The most effective money that the client can spend to solve these problems will be for architectural services, including architectural programming.

It is also a truism that clients very soon forget their willingness to accept lower quality to obtain a building within a fixed budget. Once built and occupied, clients always expect the building to perform as if only the highest quality materials and systems were installed. It is mandatory, therefore, to precisely spell out in the program what the owner is willing to accept initially, so that subsequent misunderstandings can be resolved without added cost to the programmer or to the architect.

Finance

Project financial feasibility analysis is an important pre-design service for most commercial, industrial, and housing facilities. It involves both market assessment and financial planning for the project. If there is no market for a particular facility, it matters little how well it is designed—it is likely to fail. This is not simply a matter of whether a facility can be located in a particular area. Market analysis must establish the appropriate size of the facility, the acceptable level of quality, and even the types of amenities that can be absorbed within the current market. The financial analysis must then establish an acceptable project cost, given current costs of construction, the cost of financing, comparable property costs/rental rates, expected profitability, and the like. Such studies are not always a direct part of programming, and if not, usually precede programming to determine if the project is feasible and, if so, to help establish the size and quality of the project.

For example, a financial feasibility study for a speculative office building would identify the current market conditions; the likely types and numbers of tenants; the lease rates that can be expected; availability of financing, including points and interest rates; the square footage costs allowable for construction; typical square footage requirements for prospective tenants; reasonable bay sizes to accommodate typical tenants; and various amenity requirements such as exterior windows and landscaping.

It is advisable for the novice programmer to retain professionals capable of conducting market studies and developing financing packages in order to be certain that various assumptions made in the programming studies are credible.

Construction

A building whose cost exceeds budget can be devastating to both the client and the architect. If discovered during programming, excessive building costs can be eliminated by reducing either the size of the project or the quality of materials and systems. On the other hand, this can involve the architect in a substantial amount of redesign if not discovered early in the design process. If excess costs are discovered during bidding, after many months have been spent in developing detailed construction documents, it can cost the client considerably in terms of lost time, temporary facilities costs, land holding costs, financing costs, or inflation of construction costs. It can cost the architect, too, if the agreement stipulates that redesign will be at the architect's expense. If discovered during the course of construction because of inadequate programming or construction documents, increased costs can be disastrous, sometimes resulting in bankruptcy for the client and lawsuits against the programmer and the architect.

Careful delineation of the building budget and accurate assessment of probable construction costs in the architectural program are the most beneficial and least costly ways to ensure that a project can proceed within the client's budgetary limitations. If, at this point, it is clear that the desired facility cannot be built within the budget, then the client can either raise the budget to obtain what is needed, reduce space requirements, quality of materials or systems, or use other strategies to allow the project to proceed. The costs of making adjustments are less during programming stage than in any other stage of the design/construction process. A simple and direct statement of maximum construction cost such as the one below can do much to keep both the client and the designer from attempting to obtain more than the budget will allow (Fig. 3-98).

Figure 3-98 Construction Cost Card.

Operations

Costs of operating a facility are not independent of either programming or design. In programming, it is necessary to understand and set forth information that directly relates to operating costs. If a client intends to retain one doorman to monitor all ingress and egress from the building and parking, this must be clearly stated. A design requiring several doormen or sophisticated electronic equipment to monitor a facility could seriously jeopardize the financial feasibility of a project. Inefficient planning of office or industrial space, requiring additional personnel or causing extra time to be consumed in developing a product, could also seriously impact operating costs. Ineffective programming relating to the client's plan for operating a facility can have a serious negative financial impact. This is important information that must be included in the program!

Maintenance

Maintenance, like operations, is often overlooked in programming because of the client's desire to obtain a building at the least initial cost. However, with many materials and nearly all systems, initial costs are inversely related to maintenance costs. If inexpensive, low-quality materials or systems are used in design, they typically require greater maintenance and earlier replacement than higher quality products. Roofing systems, for instance, vary greatly in initial cost and in durability over time, but almost invariably those which cost the least require the greatest maintenance and earliest replacement. On the other hand, elaborate landscaping or luxurious interior materials and treatments may require care beyond the owner's maintenance budget.

If a client absolutely must obtain a facility of a certain size for a very limited construction cost, it may be necessary for the designer to utilize some high maintenance systems to stay within the construction budget. In this case, the responsibility in programming is to clearly set forth that the value of the size of the facility exceeds the value of potential maintenance costs, and that the client is willing to assume the liability for the increased maintenance costs. Or, perhaps in so stating in the first draft of a program, the client(s) will realize that they are unwilling to carry such high maintenance costs, and they will either reduce the amount of space required or increase the budget to a level where the needed space can be obtained at an acceptable level of maintenance cost.

Energy

In Section 3.2 we discussed energy as an environmental issue. In the context of this section, however, energy costs are considered as a subset of operating costs. A recent project in which the author served as both programmer and designer brought home the seriousness of energy costs. In an effort to reduce initial construction cost, client, architect, and engineer decided to use package air conditioning equipment with electrical heat strips instead of heat pumps or gas-fired heating. While the initial building costs were somewhat lower, the heating bills were so high that the owner decided to retrofit the original units with gas to reduce the operating costs to an affordable level. Here, the operating costs were shown to be much more important than the initial project costs. The client should be made aware that lower operating costs are sometimes purchased with higher initial costs!

Langdon Wilson Architecture Planning Interiors, designers of the new Phoenix City Hall, were concerned with the operating costs of this high-rise building (Fig. 3-99). In order to control

Figure 3-99 Phoenix City Hall.

Photo Credit: Timothy Hursley, The Arkansas Studio. Permission: Langdon Wilson Architecture Planning Interiors

the heat gain on the east-, south-, and west-facing walls, they designed a number of sun control devices that also provide the primary aesthetic expression for the building. The energy savings resulting from this design feature resulted in the elimination of a 1,000-ton chiller and all of the accompanying annual energy costs (Larson 1997).

The cost of construction is a one-time event or, more typically, is spread over a number of years with a constant monthly mortgage payment. The costs of operations, maintenance, and energy, on the other hand, continue for the life of the building and, in an inflationary economy, can increase to become major costs. It is important that both client and designer know the relative importance and magnitude of each of these costs, so that no misunderstanding will be manifested in the design. The best time to make these determinations is during the programming process. It can be very costly to make them later.

3.7 Aesthetic Issues

- Form

- Space

- Meaning

Although most clients consider economics to be the bottom line, many architects see aesthetics as the bottom line. This concern for aesthetics separates architects from most engineers and other participants in the building industry. The "art" of architecture is what motivates most designers. This comes from the architect's view of self as artist and relates to the architect's developed preferences for form, space, and meaning when responding to the other issues affecting design. However, most architects also want to understand and express the aesthetic preferences of clients, users, and society in the design. And, nearly all clients and users have legitimate goals and needs relative to the physical appearance of the buildings they occupy. They may wish to express the nature of their enterprise to the rest of the community; prefer certain materials, shapes, and colors; have strong preferences as to how the building should relate to its context; and so on.

This does not mean that the architect must utilize all of the client's aesthetic preferences in the design. It means only that the architect should know about these preferences and make an effort to understand them, so they can be taken into account during design. The responsibility of the programmer relative to aesthetic concerns of the client, user, and community is to communicate the preferences to the architect.

Form

Many communities have ordinances that are quite specific in terms of the acceptable form of buildings, signs, parking, and landscape areas. They define maximum heights, setbacks, land coverage, and the like, all of which have important effects on building form. Some municipalities even specify acceptable openings on facades relative to neighboring land or buildings. Signs are often limited in terms of their size, shape, color, and location. Parking is similarly restricted in terms of location and requirements for lighting and screening. Landscape areas are sometimes specified in terms of size, location, and acceptable planting materials. Some planned communities go still further, in specifying acceptable materials and colors for buildings.

At least one planned community in Arizona permits only earth tone colors for building materials, prohibits roof-mounted air conditioning equipment including evaporative coolers, specifies how solar collectors must be placed and screened, and dictates location, height, and style of fences and freestanding walls within setback areas. These restrictions on form are quite common and need to be described in the program.

Building owners and clients also have preferences for form. If there are existing buildings to which the new building will relate, many owners will insist that the new building conform in terms of color, materials, or configuration. This is often the case for university campuses. The administration or regents determine if a consistent design image for buildings is desirable. Indeed, clients responsible for a large number of buildings in one geographic area will often have a design review policy, which typically requires that individual buildings conform in some respect to a larger design idea.

Seaside, a new community in Florida planned by Andres Duany and Elizabeth Plater-Zyberk, is a case in point (Figs. 3-100 and 3-101). They developed not only the planning and urban design scheme, but also a set of design guidelines that they refer to as an "Urban Code"—relating to yard setbacks, height requirements,

Figure 3-100 Seaside: Street View.

Photo Credit: Xavier Iglesias. Permission: Duany/Plater-Zyberk & Company

Figure 3-101 Seaside: Yard View.

Photo Credit: Duany/Plater-Zyberk & Company

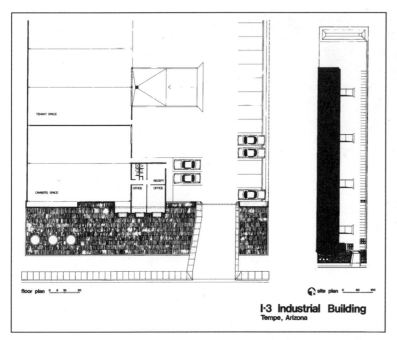

floor plan 0 5 10   20

site plan 0   50   100

I·3 Industrial Building
Tempe, Arizona

Figure 3-102   Rollo Industrial Building: Plans.

Figure 3-103   Rollo Industrial Building: Exterior.

parking, and even specific elements such as porches, balconies, and roof slopes, in order to ensure that the community's desired character would be achieved and maintained.

The clients may also have preferences for specific forms. Some will insist on pitched roofs because of an earlier bad experience with leaks from flat roofs. Some will insist upon certain materials and appearances because they want to appeal to a certain market. Occasionally, a client will insist on a specific product because they make it, own it, or have special reason to use it. Each desired product will, of course, have important formal implications for design. The program must clearly articulate all formal preferences so that the architect can consider them in design.

The design for the I-3 Industrial Building by Hershberger Kim Architects utilized giant concrete pipes for the window openings at the request of the owner, an underground contractor (Figs. 3-102 through 3-105). The designers considered this an opportunity to do

Figure 3-104   Rollo Industrial Building: Pipes.

Figure 3-105   Rollo Industrial Building: Court.

something more figural than normal in a speculative industrial building. The large pipes became part of a facade stretching the entire width of the property in order to provide more presence to the building, following some of the thinking of Robert Venturi (1977). The balance of the building is less than half of the site's width, as can be seen on the site plan diagram (right side) and court view.

Frank Gehry has proven to be a contemporary master of form, with many of his innovative structures using materials, systems, and form in new and unusual ways. The Norton Residence at the beach walk in Venice, California, is one of many of his very fresh and exciting designs (Fig. 3-106).

Figure 3-106 Norton Residence.

Space

Space preferences can be very important to some clients. That space is the essence of architecture is argued effectively by Bruno Zevi (1957) and shown dramatically by some of the masters of modern architecture. Frank Lloyd Wright is considered the master of masters in this regard. His Guggenheim Museum (Figs. 3-107 and 3-108) is the extreme case—the spatial experience on the inte-

Figure 3-107 Guggenheim Museum: Exterior.

rior as moving as the art being exhibited. The exterior form as a reflection of the interior spatial organization gives a preview of the form to be found in the interior.

Le Corbusier showed his mastery of both space and form in a beautiful chapel at the small nunnery in Ronchamp, France. The dramatic form of the building's exterior, said to resemble a nun's cap, created an implied exterior space at the crown of the hill for outside services. Inside is one of the most potent, moving, spiritual spaces the author has ever experienced, with its floating roof form and the mysterious play of light created by the splayed openings at the windows (Figs. 3-109 through 3-111).

Architects like Mies van der Rohe treated space in a very different way, creating *universal spaces* (Hoag 1977) that can be used in a variety of ways and, with interior furnishings, adapted to the particular needs of the occupants. This is

Figure 3-108 Guggenheim Museum: Interior.

Figure 3-109   Ronchamp: Exterior.

Figure 3-110   Ronchamp: Interior.

a very sensible approach in many office and institutional settings, where the only constant is change. In these cases, a very specialized space will soon be outmoded and likely will be expensive to alter to meet the changing needs of the organization.

CRS, through their programming activities, took a leadership position in the design of open classroom schools which allow teachers to adapt their spaces to frequently changing educational approaches. CRS's Fodera School in Columbus, Indiana, is an excellent example of the freedom and architectural interest of open space planning (Fig. 3-112).

In both offices and residences, some clients prefer an open plan, while others are more comfortable in clearly defined rooms. Some people enjoy high, lofty spaces while others prefer lower, more intimate spaces for essentially identical activities. It is appropriate to advise the designer as to the type of person(s) who will be occupying the building. There is perhaps nothing more troubling to a designer than to return to a building where the aesthetic qualities have been destroyed by users who violate the spatial order of the original design.

One of the author's professors in graduate school, a highly respected designer, told the story of a house for which the client had given him a free hand in design, but who in occupying the house had subdivided the major rooms with partitions and painted the previously white sculptured walls chartreuse and pink. He lamented that he could have designed a very nice building with smaller spaces and even

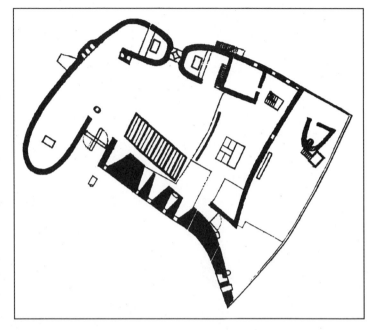

Figure 3-111 Ronchamp: Plan.
Credit: Carl Okazaki

Figure 3-112 Fodera School.

using those colors, if the client had let him know what she preferred. Once constructed and occupied, the architect has little or no control over changes to the design. The designer's best defense is to know and respond to what the client values in such a way that the client will not want to alter the aesthetic statement.

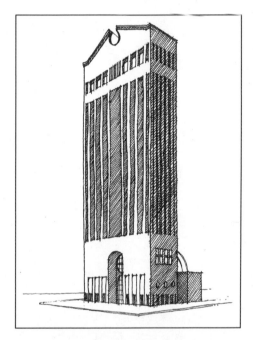

Figure 3-113 AT&T Headquarters.
Credit: Carl Okazaki

Meaning

Some clients have a desire to communicate a specific image to the community and perhaps to the building's users. Sometimes the image involves a level of quality or concern that needs to be conveyed to the users. At other times, the image relates to specific referential meanings. Occasionally, the desired meaning is more emotional or affective (Hershberger 1969).

Many clients simply want a building that appears to have been designed and constructed with care. This sort of meaning is easy to achieve and gives the architect great freedom in determining which other values to express. Other clients want to make a unique statement that conveys the special qualities of their organization or product. The Lever House by Skidmore, Owings and Merrill; the Seagram Building by Mies van der Rohe; and the General Motors Technical Center by Eero Saarinen were all such buildings and have brought great public recognition to their companies. More recently, the American Telephone and Telegraph Headquarters building by Johnson and Burgee, with its "Chippendale" top, has served the same purpose (Fig. 3-113).

The broken facades of the Best Company buildings by SITE Architects, even with great individual variety, have also served to produce a national image for this company (Fig. 3-114).

Figure 3-114 Best Company Building: Entry.
Credit: Carl Okazaki

Some companies have an image that they try to maintain wherever they locate new buildings. This is particularly true of some hotel, motel, and restaurant chains. An architect agreeing to design one of these buildings must accept and express these required symbols in the design of the new building. Still other building types are characterized by more or less traditional typologies which come to have a particular meaning. This is true for certain religious denominations, and was once the case for banks, theaters, and many other institutions. If there is some desired referential meaning, then the designer needs to be informed in the program. It is still within the architect's power to decide how this meaning will be interpreted in the design.

Figure 3-115 Plazzetto Zuccari: Entry.
Credit: Belinda Watt

The meaning of the entry at the Plazzetto Zuccari is one of the most direct and potent referential uses of the human figure to convey an idea about what it would be like to enter a building (Fig. 3-115).

Eero Saarinen's TWA Terminal at LaGuardia Air-

Figure 3-116 TWA Terminal: Exterior.

port in New York City has been characterized as an eagle about to take off, as is evident in the exterior view. Its curving sinuous lines and ample skylighting convey the image of loftiness and even flight on the interior (Fig. 3-116 and 3-117).

Figure 3-117 TWA Terminal: Interior.

Figure 3-118 Vietnam War Memorial.

Photo Credit and Permission: Howard Olson

Affective meaning is also highly prized by some clients. Certain church clients want worship spaces that will move people toward a more spiritual feeling. Some governmental monuments commemorating heroes of one kind or another should instill some sense of reverence or awe in observers. The Vietnam War Memorial by Maya Ying Lin is a special example of such a monument (Fig. 3-118).

The Franklin Court Bicentennial Exhibit by Venturi, Scott Brown and Associates is a case where the design project has been reduced to a silhouette of the original Franklin House. This proved to be an effective and memorable way to convey the shape and scale of the original house while, at the same time, allowing thousands of viewers to pass through the courtyard each day to see the archeological and other exhibits situated around the courtyard area (Fig. 3-119).

Unlike Mies van der Rohe, with his philosophy that "less is more," Robert Venturi prefers "complexity and contradiction" in architecture and believes that "less is a bore" (Ven-

Figure 3-119 Franklin Court.

turi 1977). This is evident in the complex and contradictory exterior of Fire Station 4 in Columbus, Indiana, by Venturi, Scott Brown and Associates (Fig. 3-120).

A more subtle use of meaning in architecture was intended by Robert Hershberger and Ernest Nickels of Par 3 Studio in the design of the chancel area of the Church of the Palms in Sun City, Arizona. In this case, the firm designed a high window with a cross in it to the east of the chancel in order to obtain a shadow of the cross on the center of the chancel wall during Easter morning services. The shadow works its way across the wall during the Lenten Season (Figs. 3-121 and 3-122).

Figure 3-120 Fire Station 4.

Figure 3-121 Church of the Palms: Section.
Credit: Robert Hershberger and Ernest Nickels, Par 3 Studio

Figure 3-122 Church of the Palms: Chancel.
Credit: Robert Hershberger and Ernest Nickels, Par 3 Studio

Figure 3-123 Church of the Palms: Interior.
Credit: Robert Hershberger and Ernest Nickels, Par 3 Studio

In addition, the window's brilliant white light on the chancel contrasts with the very soft light of twelve candles mounted on the chancel wall, to symbolize for the congregation the great light of God and the halting and sometimes failing light of believers.

The architect also provided a subtle distinction in meaning for those parishioners who wanted to gather around the communion table setting as shown on the previous illustration, and those who wanted to sit in traditional straight-on style as shown below. They all sit under the soft, warm light of a stained glass clerestory, in contrast to the white light on the chancel (Fig. 3-123).

Sometimes the designer will be more interested in the meaning of pure form or geometry. For example, in the design for an artist's studio, Hershberger and Nickels sought to express the client's desire for natural light, complexity, and inexpensive construction in abstract form (Figs. 3-124 through 3-126).

The designer must know in which area(s) of meaning the client/

Figure 3-124 Waddell Studio: East Elevation.
Credit: Robert Hershberger and Ernest Nickels, Par 3 Studio

Figure 3-125   Waddell Studio: Exterior.

Figure 3-126   Waddell Studio: Interior.

user is most interested, so that appropriate attention can be given to communicating these meanings effectively. It is important to remember that it is the purview of the architect as designer to determine how such preferences will be incorporated into the design, because the architect will be held accountable if the building is unattractive or lacks appeal in some way. As William Peña noted when lecturing about programming, "The person to be held responsible for a decision must have authority to make it" (Peña 1980).

3.8 Safety Issues

- Structural
- Fire
- Chemical
- Personal
- Criminal

If the bottom line for clients is economics and for architects, aesthetics, the bottom line for the government is the protection of the "public health, safety, and welfare." This is why architects are licensed professionals. We must be qualified practitioners so that we will not design buildings that threaten the health, safety, or welfare of the public. Therefore, architects must be carefully educated and pass extensive licensing examinations to protect occupants from harm, illness, injury, even death!

Structural

The first consideration is, of course, the strength of the structure. It must not fall down under its own weight or the weights that might be imposed upon it. These loads include the dead load (the load of the building itself including all fixed materials, systems, equipment, and other permanent parts of the building) and the live loads (the estimated weight of unfixed materials, equipment, furnishings, wind, snow, and seismic, as well as the weight of the expected human occupants). The programmer is not responsible for identifying typical dead and live loads. These are a matter of code with which the architect must be familiar.

The programmer's responsibility is to identify any unusual loads. These might include loads imposed by special equipment or furnishings, unusually high occupant loads, or external loads associated with wind, earthquake, snow, or other similar conditions. This must be done so that the architect will not underdesign the structure and, thus, introduce the possibility of failure and consequent injury or death.

Bridge structures are designed almost totally in response to the structural and traffic loads which they must carry with primary attention to safety. Even so, they can be great works of art as is evident in this concrete bridge in Switzerland designed by Robert Maillart.

Note: Structural issues for more complex buildings were covered in Section 3.4 Technological Issues.

Fire

Buildings must also be safe in case of fire. The programmer should discover and let the designer know if there are any especially hazardous situations in the building(s) to be designed. The designer should be aware of normal exiting requirements, but the programmer must reveal any unusual situation. For example, how can suitable exits be provided in high-rise buildings for persons incapable of safely descending many flights of stairs? This is not easy to accomplish. However, one method that is required in some codes is the design of safe zones, or places of refuge, on each floor of a building. These allow the elderly, infirm, or handicapped (and all others) to go from one section of a floor to another through a specified fire separation. Those unable to do so need not go down a flight of stairs or seek the help of someone else—they can move horizontally to reach a safe place.

In places of public assembly such as major auditoriums and stadiums, the need for safe egress in unusual situations must be thoroughly explored, requirements documented, and potential solutions outlined, so that the designer is made thoroughly aware of the nature of the fire safety problem. It may even become an opportunity for architectural expression. Frank Lloyd Wright used exit ramps to parking areas as an opportunity for formal expression in Grady Gammage Memorial Auditorium at Arizona State University in Tempe, Arizona (Fig. 3-127).

A similar use of required fire exiting as part of the aesthetic expression of a building can be found at the John C. Ross-William C. Blakley Law Library

Figure 3-127 Memorial Auditorium Ramp.

building on the same campus, by Scogin, Elam and Bray with Leo E. Daly (Fig. 3-128).

Once again, I would caution the reader that while an issue like safety may have a significant impact on the design of a facility, other issues will also come into play. For the law library, as an example, the architects were interested in creating a sensitive relationship with nearby buildings. They also responded to the campus context in the use of materials, to the climate of Arizona with sun controlling features, and, of course, to their own aesthetic preferences (Figs. 3-129 and 3-130).

The architects also showed a keen regard for and understanding of the inner workings of a law library in the formal and spatial development, as well as in the daylighting of the interior spaces (Fig. 3-131).

Chemical

Other threats to the health of building occupants can be important for a programmer to recognize. Is the site downwind from a major industrial polluter?

Figure 3-128 Law Library: North Side Fire Exit.

Figure 3-129 Law Library: South and East Sides.

Figure 3-130 Law Library: West and South Sides.

Figure 3-131   Law Library: Interior.

Dairies have been relocated because of possible contamination of milk by chemical pollutants. Some forms of air or water pollution could, of course, directly threaten the health of occupants, when long-term exposure might result in diseases such as cancer and emphysema.

The building being programmed could, itself, be a producer or user of products that might damage the health of the occupants or even of persons off-site. The now familiar problem of carcinogenic building products containing asbestos is such an instance. What if an existing facility with such products must undergo a major renovation? The programmer should point out such products, so that the architect can deal with the problem appropriately in designing the new facilities.

If by-products of activities within the facility are hazardous, this should be documented so that suitable means can be designed for their containment, destruction, or removal and appropriate disposal. Here, a concern should be manifest not only for the building occupants, but also for people off-site. If pollutants are to be disposed of into the atmosphere, waterways, or aquifers, they must be within acceptable limits, generally as specified by governmental authorities. The designer(s) needs to be advised of these limits.

Similarly, many commonly used building products and equipment give off chemical or biological contaminants to such an extent that they become a threat to the occupants of buildings in which they are used. This phenomenon has been referred to as the "closed building syndrome." The aforementioned and now carefully regulated asbestos products are good examples. However, other products still in use can pose problems in tightly sealed spaces or in cases of fire where contaminants are created as a by-product of burning. If it is known that such products must be used in a project, then the programmer should point out the potential hazards so that the designer can make proper allowances in design to mitigate against the potential hazard.

Personal

Other threats to the safety of occupants are dangerous equipment and situations within the building and on the site. If a building is expected to house equipment with moving parts in which a person could be caught and injured, the program should make a note about each such piece of equipment, along with acceptable safety precautions and required spatial separations. Similarly, if conditions of the site or surroundings could be a threat to user safety, these should be pointed out in the site analysis. Abandoned mine shafts, wells, and cisterns can collapse under the weight of vehicles or other heavy objects, and people can fall into unprotected openings. If adjacent streets are heavily used or have blind spots due to configuration or topography, these conditions should be noted so the designer can avoid introducing traffic at unsafe locations.

If a site is directly in the path of low-flying aircraft, this must be mentioned because of the dangers of aircraft crashing into the site and any tall structures on it. Indeed, in more than one major city, proposals for very tall buildings have been rejected by aviation authorities because of alignment with existing flight paths. Another consideration is the danger of damage to hearing and nerves associated with low over-flights of jet aircraft. There are, in fact, numerous federal and municipal regulations about development in high noise zones with which the programmer should become familiar, if a site is located in such a zone. For instance, housing developments may be prohibited in some higher noise zones. If not prohibited, it may prove difficult to obtain financing.

Criminal

Even the characteristics of the building occupants or of people in the immediate vicinity may create design problems. In a prison, both guards and inmates must be protected from injury by inmates. A more typical situation, however, is in ordinary living environments where criminals prey on residents. Oscar Newman (1972) and a number of other architects and social scientists have studied ways that architecture can help make living and working environments safe for users.

Lighting of public walkways and courtyards, surveillance of such places from surrounding windows, and direct access from housing units to pedestrian walkways increase the safety of public areas—in effect making these places semipublic in nature by allowing residents to monitor the activities occurring within them. Physical and psychological barriers such as fences, grade changes, surface texture changes, and the like can also be used to help residents develop feelings of ownership and undertake territorial behavior in the surveillance, maintenance, and defense of spaces.

The architect must know if there are likely to be problems that threaten the physical safety of users so that strategies can be employed to mitigate these problems. The *Richard Allan Homes Site Safety and Security Analysis* by Walter Moleski of ERG/Environmental Research Group with Roberts, Wallace and Todd (architects) is a particularly good example of how research can be used to develop recommendations for improving planning and design decisions (Moleski 1990) (Figs. 3-132 and 3-133).

Each of the above issues is important to consider for inclusion in an architectural program. Several of the architects of the buildings shown in this section considered safety issues to be important enough

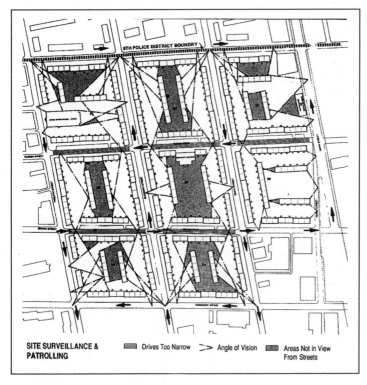

Figure 3-132 Richard Allen Homes: Analysis.

Credit: Walter Moleski with Wallace Roberts and Todd, 1990. *Richard Allen Homes Analysis and Objectives.* Philadelphia, Pennsylvania. Permission: ERG/Environmental Research Group.

to influence the aesthetic character. Similarly, it should also be understood that while specific buildings were used throughout the chapter to show how one issue or another can be expressed in design, the architect(s) consider several issues at various stages of the design process. It is important for the programmer to identify what issues the client, users, and community believe should influence design. It is important for the architect to deal with these issues responsibly and creatively when designing the building.

3.9 Exercises

1. Examine your favorite building to see if you can determine the values that became design issues and, therefore, dominated the design decision making.

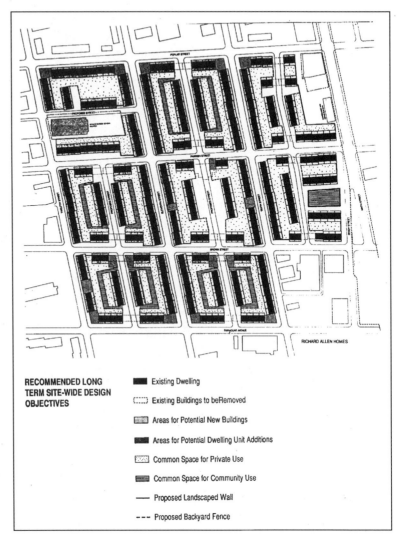

RECOMMENDED LONG TERM SITE-WIDE DESIGN OBJECTIVES

- ▬ Existing Dwelling
- ▭ Existing Buildings to beRemoved
- ▦ Areas for Potential New Buildings
- ▬ Areas for Potential Dwelling Unit Additions
- ▨ Common Space for Private Use
- ▤ Common Space for Community Use
- — Proposed Landscaped Wall
- --- Proposed Backyard Fence

Figure 3-133 Richard Allen Homes: Objectives.

Credit: Walter Moleski with Wallace Roberts and Todd, 1990. *Richard Allen Homes Analysis and Objectives*. Philadelphia, Pennsylvania. Permission: ERG/Environmental Research Group.

2. Read about the theories and methods of your favorite designers to see if you can discover the dominant values that become issues and influence their designs.

3. Examine the building you are in at the moment to see what values are expressed in its design. Compare the outside

with the inside. What values would you like to see more vividly expressed? Which ones should have lower priority? Which values should become design issues?

4. List what values should become design issues for the following:
   A. an artist's studio
   B. a small doctor's clinic
   C. a branch bank
   D. a major hotel
   E. an industrial building

5. Would a set of value areas different than HECTTEAS work better for you? Are any important values missing in the HECTTEAS set? If so, prepare an alternative list of value areas for you to use when beginning to program. Would this list be modified for some projects?

6. Try to think of buildings in which the design expression has been dominated by just one issue. Can you think of any such building(s)? If you can, ask a colleague if they agree with you. Will they be able to identify other issues that they feel had an impact on the design of the building?

3.10 References

Ackoff, Russell. 1966. Classroom lecture and discussion in Operations Research at The University of Pennsylvania, Philadelphia, Pa.

ANSI. 1996. New York: The American National Standards Institute.

Brand, Stewart. 1994. *How Buildings Learn: What Happens After They're Built*. New York: Viking.

Brown, Denise Scott. 1967. "Planning the Powder Room." *AIA Journal*. 47(4): 81-83.

Crosbie, Michael J. 1994. *Green Architecture: A Guide to Sustainable Design*. Rockport, Mass.: Rockport Publishers.

Deasy, C. M. 1974. *Design for Human Affairs*. Cambridge, Mass.: Schenkman Publishing Company.

Diffrient, Niels, Alvin R. Tilley, and Joan C. Bardagjy. 1974. *Humanscale 1/2/3: A Portfolio of Information*. Cambridge, Mass.: MIT Press.

Duerk, Donna P. 1993. *Architectural Programming: Information Management for Design*. New York: Van Nostrand Reinhold.

Duffy, Francis. 1990. "Measuring Building Performance." *Facilities*. May: 17.

EDRA. 1969-96. Proceedings of the Annual Conference. Publisher varies.

Feerer, Michael. 1977. *Family Services Ward: Environmental/ Architectural Programming*. Program for Atascadero State Mental Hospital, Atascadero, Calif.

Goldman, Mark, and Frieda D. Peatross. 1993. *Planning for a Captive Audience. In Professional Practice in Facility Programming*, edited by Wolfgang F. E. Preiser. New York: Van Nostrand Reinhold.

Hall, Edward T. 1959. *The Silent Language*. Garden City, N. Y.: Doubleday.

_____. 1966. *The Hidden Dimension*. Garden City, N. Y.: Doubleday.

Hart, Vaughan. 1995. "Erich Mendelsohn and the Fourth Dimension." *ARQ Architectural Research Quarterly*. 1(2): 50-59.

Hershberger, Robert. 1969. "A Study of Meaning and Architecture." Ph.D. diss., The University of Pennsylvania, Philadelphia.

Hoag, Edwin, and Joy Hoag. 1977. Masters of Modern Architecture: Frank Lloyd Wright, Le Corbusier, Mies van der Rohe, and Walter Gropius. Indianapolis: Bobbs-Merrill.

House Beautiful. 1955. The Character of the House is the Beginning of Architecture. November: 248, 292.

International Conference of Building Officials. 1994. *Uniform Building Code: Administrative, Fire- and Life-Safety, and Field Inspection Provisions*. Volume 1 of Uniform Building Code. Whittier, Calif.: ICBO.

Jerde, Jon. 1992. Public lecture in the College of Architecture at The University of Arizona.

Kahn, Louis I. 1961. Masters design studio discussions at the University of Pennsylvania.

Lawton, M. Powell. 1975. *Planning and Managing Housing for the Elderly*. New York: Wiley.

Marans, Robert, and Kent Spreckelmeyer. 1981. *Evaluating Built Environments: A Behavioral Approach*. Ann Arbor: Survey Research Center, University of Michigan.

Moleski, Walter, with Roberts, Wallace and Todd. 1990. *Richard Allen Homes Site Safety and Security Analysis*. Philadelphia, Pa.

Newman, Oscar. 1972. *Defensible Space: Crime Prevention through Urban Design*. New York: Macmillan.

Novitski, B. J. 1996. "Telecommuting Design: Merging Technologies Change the Rules of Collaboration." *Architectural Record*. 184(10): 46-51.

Pastalan, Leon A., and Daniel H. Carson, eds. 1970. *Spatial Behavior of Older People*. Ann Arbor, Mich.: Institute of Gerontology, University of Michigan; and Wayne State University.

Peña, William. 1980. Lecture at continuing education seminar at the University of Wisconsin, Madison.

Ramsey, Charles George. 1994. *Ramsey/Sleeper: Architectural Graphic Standards*. New York: J. Wiley.

Sheydayi, Yury. 1985. Lecture by faculty colleague at Arizona State University, Tempe.

Sommer, Robert. 1969. *Personal Space: The Behavioral Basis of Design*. Englewood Cliffs, N.J.: Prentice-Hall.

_____. 1974. *Tight Spaces: Hard Architecture and How to Humanize It*. Englewood Cliffs, N.J.: Prentice-Hall.

Spencer, Eldridge. 1962. *Site Location Analysis for Lawrence Hall of Science*. Spencer and Lee, Architects, San Francisco, Calif.

Straub, Calvin C. 1970. Design studio discussion at Arizona State University, Tempe.

Stratta, James L., Ted J. Canon, C. Martin Duke, and Lawrence G. Selna. 1976. *Reconnissance Report Mindanao, Philippines Earthquake, August 17, 1976*. Oakland, Calif.: Earthquake Engineering Research Institute.

Venturi, Robert. 1977. *Complexity and Contradiction in Architecture*. New York: Museum of Modern Art.

Wilson, Forrest. 1984. *A Graphic Survey of Perception and Behavior for the Design Professions*. New York: Van Nostrand Reinhold.

Wineman, Jean D., ed. 1986. *Behavioral Issues in Office Design*. New York: Van Nostrand Reinhold.

Zevi, Bruno. 1957. *Architecture as Space: How to Look at Architecture*. New York: Horizon Press.

Preparing to Program

P re-design services occur at a number of times and places, beginning with the client's first thoughts about a project. Commercial projects often begin with a financial feasibility study. Some projects also require a site suitability study to determine if an owned or desired site will accommodate the contemplated project. Wise clients will then want a master planning study to determine how best to utilize the selected site. The next pre-design service, referred to as architectural programming, typically consists of developing information necessary to complete schematic design and to begin design development for a project.

4.1 Pre-Design Services

- Planning

- Programming

Several services are conducted prior to design studies in architecture. Generally, these pre-design services are accomplished by different people at different times. Occasionally, they are done by one programming team at the beginning of a project.

Planning

- Financial Feasibility
- Site Suitability
- Master Planning

Three different types of planning studies may be required before commencing architectural programming. All such studies require development of at least some programmatic information. However, the architectural programmer is frequently only a minor participant or possibly not even involved in the first type of planning study.

FINANCIAL FEASIBILITY

A financial feasibility study may be conducted even before a site has been selected. This involves predicting if the market conditions, available financing, site situation, and building costs will combine in such a way as to lead to a successful project, one that will provide a favorable return on investment. This is an important pre-design activity when developing plans for speculative developments. It makes little sense to do architectural programming for a facility until it is certain that what is being proposed is economically viable.

Financial feasibility studies involve collecting demographic information about the market situation in the targeted area. Is there a need for a new hotel, shopping center, or other venture? Do too many exist in near proximity? Is another in the planning stage? Will another similar facility have a definite market advantage because of a more favorable location? Is there, or will there soon be, enough traffic past the site to ensure that customers will be available to purchase the product, whatever it may be? Will the traffic be passing the site at such a time and in such a manner that it will be easy, even desirable, to stop and take advantage of the services available? As was shown earlier, it is even important to know on which corner of an intersection a gas station should be located. The same is true for shopping centers and grocery stores. If a street-oriented business is located on the morning rush hour side of the street, it may not get as much business as one located on the return trip side, when the people passing by are running errands on their way home.

It is also necessary to determine the availability and cost of money. Will local financial institutions provide the necessary financing? They may not be willing to support what seems to be a risky financial venture. Will the required interest rate and points keep project costs low enough to offer competitive rental rates to tenants? The same question is relevant for costs of land and construction. If your client is planning to purchase an overpriced site, that alone may compromise the potential success of the project. The financial feasibility study should show this to be the case, and it might be possible to use the study to convince the seller that the site is overpriced. Similarly, the probable cost of construction must be determined. If market conditions are leading to very high construction costs, it might be wise to delay the project until construction costs come back into line so that a feasible project can be developed. The following four-way financial feasibility analysis was done as part of a larger study by the author for a site that he planned to develop. It showed that the project would not be feasible given the asking price for the land, current interest rates, construction costs, and rental rates (Fig. 4-1).

All of this information is oriented toward the prediction of future events. Developing some of this information may not be what a person with an architectural background is best prepared to do. Architects are typically well prepared to discover information on the site and surrounding physical features, as well as on site and building costs. Fortunately, there are other people available with marketing, real estate, and financial skills to aid in the development of the financial feasibility study. Their services should be sought and utilized by a programmer involved in such a study. There are also several books, articles, and sophisticated computer programs that address financial feasibility analysis (Rushman 1986; Barrett and Blair 1988). A team of

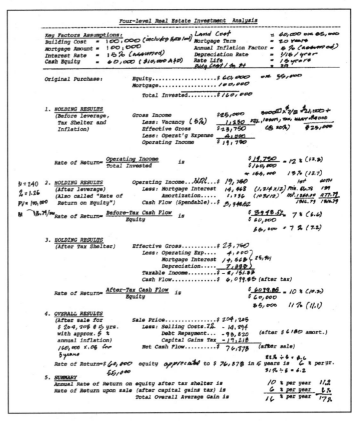

Figure 4-1 Four-Way Financial Feasibility Analysis.

knowledgeable persons with varying interests, skills, and resources will be required to do an effective financial feasibility study.

SITE SUITABILITY

Once a project has been determined to be feasible, it is important to discover if the intended use can be accommodated on the prospective site. This can be accomplished with a site suitability study. If the owner does not currently own the site, it is wise to do this study before the site is purchased. Unlike the financial feasibility study, a person with a design education is generally well prepared to undertake site suitability studies.

The information required for a site suitability study tends to be more limited and general than that required for a master plan or schematic design study, because the end product is simply one or more two-dimensional diagrams, rather than a plan with strong three-dimensional implications or an actual design for a building. The site suitability study needs only to demonstrate that a site is large enough and configured properly to allow a number of suitable plans to be developed. The study need not articulate a particular plan that will satisfy all of the requirements of the client or architect. It does need to verify that the necessary infrastructure of streets and utilities are available to support the proposed development. It also needs to verify that city codes, ordinances, and services will allow the development to take place (Lynch 1971).

The following study by the author for a small religious building to be located near an existing courtyard explores the pros and cons of three alternative locations. For major projects, like a new hotel, three or more completely different sites with much more complex conditions may need to be analyzed (Fig. 4-2).

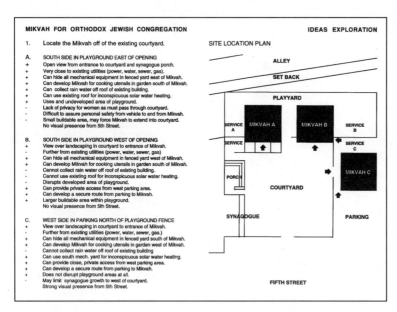

Figure 4-2 Site Suitability Study.

MASTER PLANNING

The program for a master plan is only one step removed from that of the site suitability study. Once the site has been selected and purchased, it is common practice to prepare a master plan for the development of the site. Such a plan ordinarily shows the various stages of the proposed development so that an orderly and economical growth pattern can be maintained throughout the life of the enterprise. To do this requires information on the immediate and long-range needs of the organization, so that the designer can explore how the site can be arranged to accommodate the planned phases of development (Rubenstein 1987; Dober 1963). The primary programmatic data required for master planning relates to major development, growth, and change over time. It is still a planning activity, where prediction of what might or should occur in the future is important.

In order to prepare a master plan, the designer needs information about the client's values, goals, and expectations relative to site development, the type and overall size of facilities to be provided, the probable order in which they will be built, and an approximation of their size, both initial and ultimate. It is not necessary to develop detailed information about each building facility, internal space needs and relationships, or specific building technologies. It is necessary to include basic information about the nature of the site—its drainage patterns, soil conditions, and existing structures—as well as the characteristics of traffic on adjacent streets, including where automobiles, service vehicles, and pedestrians can enter and leave the site; the general character of the surrounding area; major neighboring structures; site orientation; views; prevailing breezes; average and extreme temperatures; and so on. Other considerations include zoning ordinance requirements such as types and sizes of buildings allowed, set-backs and height restrictions, on-site storm water retention, fire access to all buildings, and parking and landscaping requirements. The overall human, cultural, and environmental issues must also be considered.

The program should articulate desired images or meanings for the development so the architect can consider appropriate three-dimensional design in the layout of buildings, parking, etc. Aesthetic issues can and should have an impact on a master plan. The only issues of little importance for master plan programming are those that relate to specific human and technological requirements for the buildings.

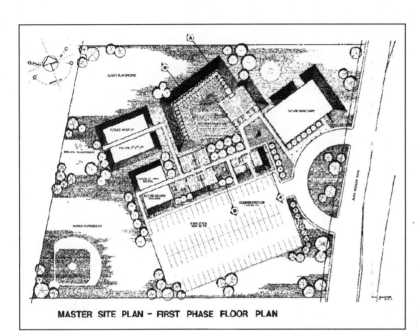

MASTER SITE PLAN - FIRST PHASE FLOOR PLAN

Figure 4-3 Covenant Baptist: Master Plan.

Credit: Hershberger - Kim Architects.

A transition can be seen from the almost pure planning information needed for a financial feasibility study to the combination of both planning and design information needed for the site suitability and master planning studies. This is to be expected. It is a rare occasion when any architectural programming activity has an exclusive need for just the planning, design, or selection levels of information. For example, the master planning study for the Covenant Baptist Church by Hershberger Kim Architects shows the physical configuration of the first phase of development, but also shows how subsequent phases of development might occur to fully utilize the site (Fig. 4-3).

Programming

- Schematic Design
- Design Development
- Construction Documents

Programming for schematic design begins where master planning leaves off. It requires much of the same information needed for master planning, but considerably more information on the specific facilities to be designed. Design programming tends to be more extensive and complex than master planning, because information must be provided that will influence the specific three-dimensional development and character of each building, and especially the size and relationships of the spaces within them. It may or may not involve considerations for growth or change over time. It is programming for "design" rather than for "planning";

for a developmental problem in which new, three-dimensional form will be the result. There are three types of programming that relate to the corresponding phases of design services.

SCHEMATIC DESIGN

Programming for schematic design must provide the information the designer needs in order to decide on the basic formal and spatial organization and aesthetic character of the proposed building(s). It must provide information on the human and cultural issues essential to making appropriate design decisions about building organization and relationships. It must set forth the client's expectations relative to building image and any other aesthetic requirements. It should also include information on environmental issues, urban or rural context, growth and change, special material or system needs, and economic opportunities or constraints. The purposes of schematic design programming are very much like those of master planning, but schematic design programming requires additional information relating to the specific performance and design requirements for architectural development.

Schematic design programming need not focus on particular products, systems, or equipment that can be accommodated within a range of potential architectural concepts or solutions. The schematic design program should provide information on the performance requirements of materials, products, equipment, furnishings, and systems that would meet the needs of the client user group. The type of information needed is that which could affect the basic spatial and formal decisions made during schematic design.

If needed equipment will require an elaborate chimney or exhaust system that might be seen above the roof, this information should be evident in the schematic design program so the designer can deal with it. If a certain space will require extensive windows, this must be stated, because such spaces cannot be buried in the interior of the building. If a particular type of material or system will provide the required level of comfort, but others will not, this should also be made known. It is also necessary to know the specific activities and furnishings that must be accommodated, as well as their configuration and size, in order to make an accurate estimate of the size and character of each space. The key question in schematic design programming is:

Can the information make a design difference?

Figure 4-4 Thirsty Earth House: Design Drawing.

If the answer is yes, the information belongs in the schematic design program.

A good example of schematic design programming was for the author's Thirsty Earth house. The clients indicated a strong desire during programming to have their house placed into the land. As the husband said, "Critters in the desert keep cool by burrowing into the ground." This information went into the architectural program and the resulting schematic design concept was for a house dug into a ridge and completely covered by earth and desert plants. This allowed for spectacular views from either side of the house, but with a building form that appeared to be part of the earth itself (Fig. 4-4).

DESIGN DEVELOPMENT

It is essential for design development programming that the designer be aware of requirements for material finishes, illumination levels, lighting control, electrical outlets, conditioned air distribution and control, plumbing fixtures, built-in cabinets or shelves, and fixed and moveable furnishings and equipment for each required space. There may also be specific requirements for other systems needed to satisfy the client, users, or community. A design development program typically includes all such requirements that differ from or exceed accepted standards. If this information is gathered after the schematic design has been approved, it typically will be collected by members of the design team in a secondary programming effort (Peña et al. 1977). In this case, only the persons involved with particular aspects of the proposed facility will be consulted for the supplementary information.

If design development information is collected as part of the initial programming effort, much of it can be included on space program sheets in the program document and the balance can appear in an appendix.

Space program sheets typically include the special values, goals, facts, needs, and ideas, as well as the spatial relationships for each identified space in the schematic program. In a sense, each space program sheet is a microprogram for a particular space (Fig. 4-5).

CONSTRUCTION DOCUMENTS

The detailed programming required for construction documents is most often accomplished informally by the person(s) charged with producing the construction documents. This aspect of programming involves obtaining the information necessary to select particular building materials, equipment, furnishings, and systems needed to complete construction documents. The selections are often made in direct consultation with the client's staff or with professional engineers and other specialist consultants who have developed expertise in the building type being designed. The information can also be obtained directly from manufacturers' product catalogs and in such sources as the *Sweet's Catalog Files* (1997).

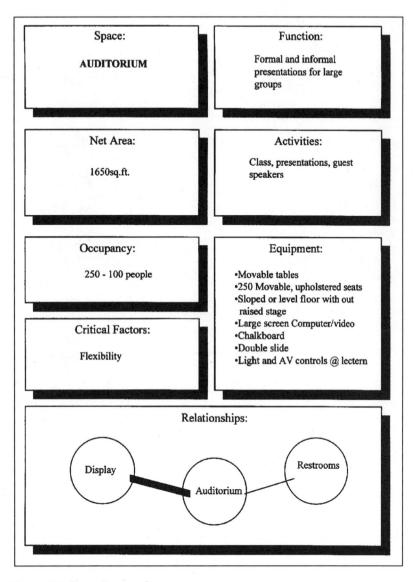

Figure 4-5 Space Program Sheet.

Credit: Kelly Angell, 1997. *Architecture Expansion Program*. College of Architecture, The University of Arizona.

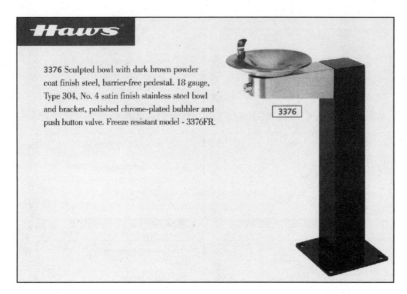

Figure 4-6 Product Manufacturer Literature.

Credit: Catalog #197 in 1997 Sweet's General Building & Renovation Catalog File, The McGraw-Hill Companies. Permission: McGraw-Hill

This information might make a design difference in the details of a building, but generally not in its overall formal or spatial organization. It is, of course, important to most architects that the detailed development of the project be in accordance with the major conceptual thrust of the architecture, so that the project as a whole will be consistent in projecting the desired image to the community (Fig. 4-6).

Why is this information not collected during design development programming? Actually, some of it is. However, the great amount of detailed information necessary to make final material and equipment selections when preparing working drawings and specifications is not gathered during design development programming. It is left out to avoid encumbering the designer with information that is not required to make schematic design and design development decisions. Furthermore, there generally are many ways to solve a design problem and each way will require different equipment, furnishings, and systems. There is little point in collecting detailed information during design programming that will not be needed as the design is developed. It is better to leave this information out of the program, so that the designer can obtain a clearer picture of the major design issues which need to be resolved. Detailed information collected during design programming need not, of course, be discarded. It should be documented and placed in an appendix or filed for possible use in preparing the construction documents

4.2 Architectural Programming

Architectural programming typically involves the collection of information relating to the schematic design and design development phases of architectural services. Whether the programmer will collect information for financial feasibility, site suitability, or master planning depends on how the problem has developed up to the time the architectural programmer is hired by the client. Some of these studies may have been accomplished before architectural programming is initiated. If not, the architectural programming process can be expanded to include them. On the other hand, it is rarely necessary or desirable in architectural programming to collect all of the detailed information necessary to make final selections of products, equipment, and furnishings for construction documents. This information will be more appropriately generated after schematic design and design development decisions have been made.

4.3 Discovering Crucial Issues

At each level of architectural programming, the objective is to isolate the crucial issues, the areas of knowledge that are most likely to make a design difference. In other words, the objective is to develop a better understanding of those areas where the costs of designer error could be great. If it is too expensive to relocate buildings to a new site in order to expand, the initial building(s) must be located in such a way as to allow future expansion on the present site. If it is crucial that a certain image be maintained to ensure continuing patronage for a commercial enterprise, then it is important to communicate this image with clarity. If it is important that operational costs not rise substantially over the life of a building, materials and systems selected must be either very durable or inexpensive to replace.

Interestingly, the cost of error is rarely the same in both directions. If a room is too small, it may not accommodate the intended equipment and personnel. The cost of error of a room being too small can be substantial—a new room or addition might be required to rectify the problem created. On the other hand, if a room is designed to be somewhat larger than required, the cost for this additional space might be comparatively small, consisting only of the extra cost of the additional floor area and surrounding surfaces, and perhaps a very small increase in utility costs. The additional space would definitely be advantageous as the enterprise expands or requires new equipment, storage, or personnel. In short, it is often less costly in the long run to err in the direction of over-sizing a space. Similarly, a modest increase in the initial cost of roofing materials may save a great amount of subsequent cost in roof repairs as well as costs of possible damage to interior systems and furnishings. The programmer should consider the potential cost of error, and tailor the program information to minimize the cost of error (Ackoff 1968; Brill et al. 1984).

The same is true in matters of public health and safety. Engineers typically allow for a margin of error in the systems they design, over-designing them by a factor of two or three to allow for occasional imperfections in materials and equipment, or poor workmanship in the field. The cost for the margin is quite low in comparison with the costs of a building system failure. Architects, on the other hand, often provide no more than the minimum number of exits required by code, even though the added initial cost of providing more exits would be low in comparison to the cost in human lives that could result in case of fire or panic. Architects need to change their mind-set in this regard. Wherever cost of error is likely to be very high, the architect, both as programmer and designer, must learn to pay attention and to err in the direction where added costs will be small. If moral compunction is not an adequate argument, perhaps major liability problems will be convincing.

4.4 Program Planning

- Schedule

- Costs

In order to plan a programming activity, it is necessary to have a preliminary understanding of the scope and complexity of the design problem. If the project is to be a small house or studio, a few visits with the client and to the site may be enough to understand and describe the design problem, particularly if the programmer will also be the designer. If the project is significantly larger, it will be necessary to develop a complete programming plan, such as the one below, detailing all of the activities that must take place to produce the program document. The following diagram by Walter Moleski for The Philadelphia Orchestra Hall Project is a verbal and graphic illustration of typical information gathering activities used to arrive at an architectural program for a complex building project (Fig. 4-7).

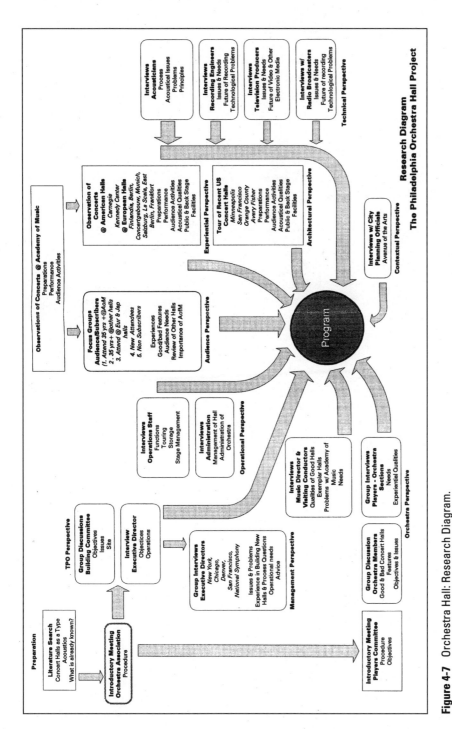

Figure 4-7 Orchestra Hall: Research Diagram.

Credit: Walter Moleski, 1995. *The Philadelphia Orchestra Hall Project.* Permission: ERG/Environmental Research Group

Schedule

Program scheduling is a process requiring the programmer to estimate the time needed to do a responsible program, before the nature of the problem is known. Sometimes the programmer has the benefit of a financial feasibility study and/or a completed master plan which sets forth the scope of the project. Often, the budget restricts the size of the project. Sometimes the continuing nature of the institution makes clear the level of complexity to be expected. Occasionally clients will have prepared a brief or a call for proposals which spells out their thinking about the nature and scope of the programming project. The programmer must develop the schedule based on this information.

Scheduling first involves preparation of a list of all of the activities necessary to develop the program, such as shown in Figure 4-7. For complex projects, this list might include interviews with the client(s) and other knowledgeable persons, review of relevant literature, observation of existing and similar facilities, site and climate analysis, preparation and administration of questionnaires, sampling and data analysis, client/user work sessions, and preparation of the program document.

The following illustration from "Programming the Third Dimension" (Goldman and Peatross 1993) indicates the percentage of time spent on information gathering tasks for correctional facility programming. Be aware that much of this work is done by a few firms that specialize in these facilities, so that previous research is often applicable to new commissions, and thus does not need to be repeated (Fig. 4-8).

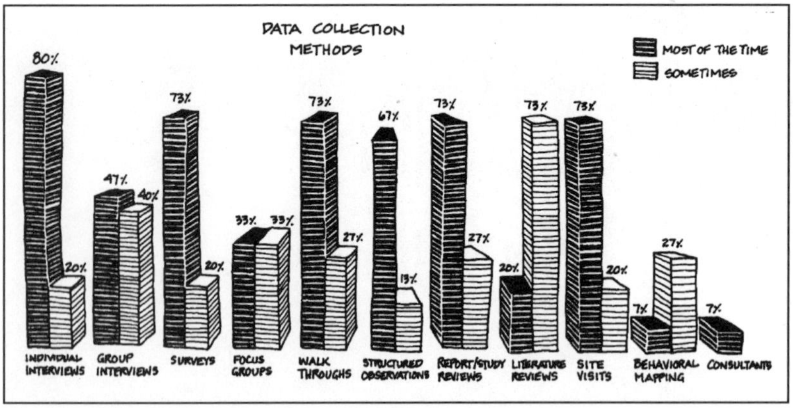

After deciding on the programming activities, a time allocation schedule is formulated. This schedule typically itemizes every activity, sets up a bar chart in-

Figure 4-8 Data Collection Methods.

Credit: See Tustler et al 1993. Permission: Wolfgang F. E. Preiser

dicating when each activity will be conducted, and indicates the number and type of personnel to be involved for each task. This process is helpful in determining how long the programming will take and what it will cost (Figs. 4-9 and 4-10).

Costs

Like most other architectural services, the costs of programming will vary depending on the type, size, and complexity of the project, and with the scope of services. A normative figure for an architectural programming budget for most projects is between one-quarter and three-quarters of one percent of the construction cost, or between $2,500 and $7,500 for a million dollar construction project (Peña et al. 1987; Preiser 1993a; Moleski 1997; Farbstein 1997; Pan 1997). Programming for a ten-million-dollar project might run between $25,000 and $75,000. The exact amount will, of course, vary depending on the building type and size.

The costs of programming for a residence would likely be absorbed within the normal fee of the architect and might actually involve no more than three or four extended meetings with the client family—one or two at their existing home, one on the prospective site, and perhaps

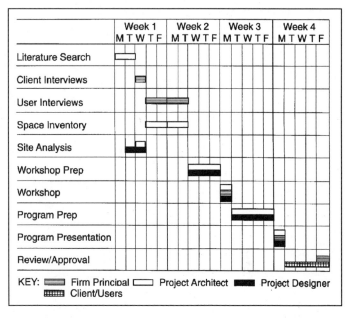

Figure 4-9 Simple Programming Schedule.
Credit: Nancy Cole

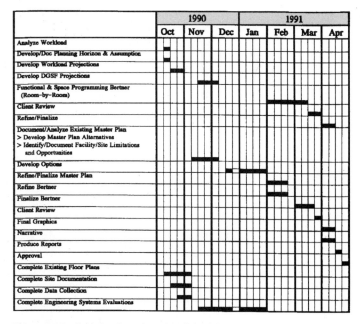

Figure 4-10 Complex Programming Schedule.
Credit: See Tustler et al.1993. Permission: Wolfgang F. E. Preiser

one in the architect's office. The results might then be prepared as a short program document (or brief) for confirmation by the client that they agree with what the architect has stated. The costs of such a program, usually prepared by the design principal of a small firm, if billed at an hourly rate of between $75 and $100 per hour, would run between $1,200 and $2,000 for 16 to 20 hours of work. If projected as a percentage of construction cost, this would imply a construction cost between $160,000 and $800,000 if the normative figures of one-quarter to three-quarters of one percent were to be used. In actuality, the programming costs for a small custom house are very similar to those for a larger custom house. Therefore, the percentage rate should be greater for the smaller house—one-half to three-quarters of one percent for the $160,000 house ($800 to $1,200 fee) and one-quarter to one-half of one percent for the $800,000 house ($2,000 to $4,000 fee). In other words, to make $75 per hour on the least expensive house, the programmer would have to charge three-quarters of one percent and complete the programming in 16 hours. To make $100 per hour on the most expensive house, the programmer could charge one-quarter of one percent and complete the programming in 20 hours. Obviously, the larger the fee, the more time that can be spent on programming and still make the desired hourly rate. In other words, the potential for profits increases with the size of the project, given a standardized percentage-based fee structure.

The same situation holds true for other building types—the smaller the project, the larger the percentage for the architectural programming fee. This is because there is a minimum level of service required, regardless of the size or expense of a project. In the case of the house, there is the need to meet with the family at their home and at the site, at least one more meeting to discuss what was programmed, analysis of the particular site, search of local codes and ordinances, and time to document the results so that no misunderstandings will occur later. Sometimes a smaller project, particularly those operating under tight budgetary constraints, will cost more to program because a lot of time will be necessary to sort out aspects of the project which the client desires, but cannot afford.

Costs for programming also range considerably for projects of different levels of complexity. Programming costs for a hospital will likely be very high in comparison to programming costs for an equally expensive high-rise office building. In the case of the hospital, there are many unique spaces with particular requirements, and a relatively high cost of error if each space is not satisfactory in most respects. For the high-rise office building, there may be only a few space types that must be programmed, and they will tend to be general in nature. This is particularly true for speculative office buildings, where unknown tenants will come in later and program and design their own spaces within the framework provided. The programming cost for such a development may be very small, since most developers use a number of space standards repeatedly. The program may need only to relate to specific conditions of site and climate, city codes and ordinances, and the particular market image desired. Financial feasibility studies may already have determined the appropriate size and particular nature and characteristics of the project. In any case, the programmer must become familiar with programming costs associated with the various types, sizes, and complexities of a project in order to make an appropriate estimate for the cost of programming services.

Similarly, a program intended only for master planning purposes will cost much less than one intended for the schematic design of a building. A program that includes some detailed information needed for design development will cost more than one intended only for schematic design. How to determine the exact cost of programming is not easy for the novice programmer. Most programmers use a standard percentage fee to begin with, then develop a history of actual costs from which to make more precise programming cost estimates.

It should also be possible for the programmer to develop a breakdown of costs based on the expected programming procedures to be used, including costs for gathering information on values and goals, discovering factual information, negotiating and coming to agreement with all programming participants relative to specific facility needs, and preparing and publishing the programming document. The comparative costs for preparing relationship matrices and diagrams, determining and illustrating space sizes, and setting forth specific requirements for each space in a programming document can also be established. Developing costs for each service will, of course, relate to the amount of time and effort required by personnel at each pay scale.

Wolfgang F. E. Preiser (1993), in a survey of architectural firms found that the vast majority did not bill programming separately from their overall fee, with only 11 percent of the firms

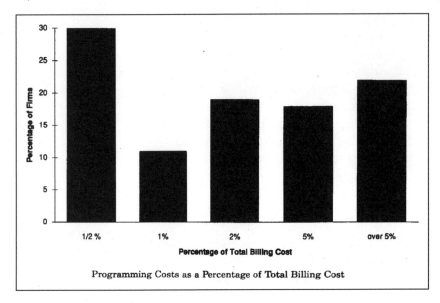

Figure 4-11 Comparative Programming Costs.

Credit: See Preiser 1993, 17–20. Permission: Wolfgang F. E. Preiser

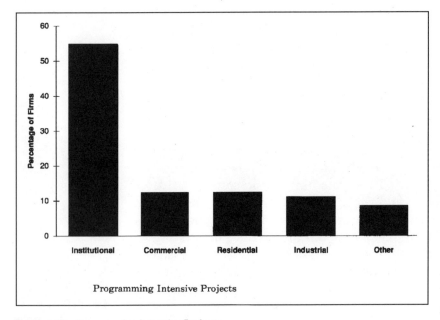

Figure 4-12 Programming Intensive Projects.

Credit: See Preiser 1993, 17–20. Permission: Wolfgang F. E. Preiser

billing programming as a separate service. These firms reported that one-half to over five percent of billable time is devoted to programming (Fig. 4-11).

In this same report Preiser found, as would be expected, that programming was much more intensive for institutional projects (Fig. 4-12).

He also found that less than ten percent of the architectural firms responding to the survey conduct any information gathering activity beyond interviewing (Fig. 4-13).

Is it any wonder that many architects have such a poor reputation relative to programming?

The fact is, the education of many of today's architectural firm leaders predates the teaching of programming in architectural schools, so these firms tend to rely on the client to

produce the program-
ming documents. Or
they produce the best
program that they can
within their standard
fee, simply by sitting
down with the client
and trying to resolve
what is needed
through the interview-
ing process. Is this an
adequate way to pro-
gram? Sometimes it
appears to be—or at
least the architects
and clients seem satis-
fied with the results.
Often, however, it is
not. In these cases,
the client gets much

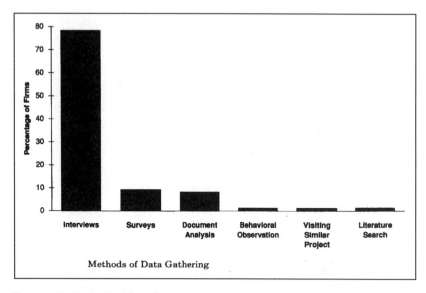

Figure 4-13 Methods of Data Gathering.
Credit: See Preiser 1993, 17–20. Permission: Wolfgang F. E. Preiser

less than hoped for or even major problems requiring complete redesign and alteration of recently completed facilities. This is unfortunate and costly in many ways. These problems can be avoided
by first completing a competent architectural program.

What would the added costs be to have architects or professional
programmers prepare
better programs? They
are relatively small
compared to design,
construction, and pro-
ject costs. They are
extremely small when
compared to life cycle
costs. This is shown
clearly on the follow-
ing diagram from a
study relating to cor-
rectional facilities (Fig.
4-14).

The savings to the
client for competent

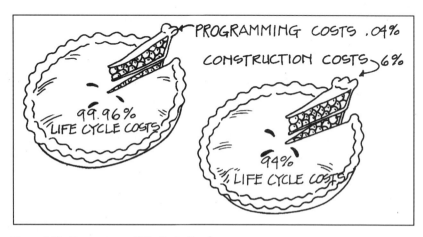

Figure 4-14 Percentage of Life Cycle Costs.
Credit: See Preiser 1993, 380. Permission: Wolfgang F. E. Preiser

architectural programming can be substantial because programming mistakes have major impacts at every subsequent phase of the project, often involving considerably greater costs to overcome the mistakes than the total cost of preparing the architectural program. Architects should make this case clearly when considered for architectural commissions. It will add a small amount to the architect's fee, but will save everyone a great deal of time, money, and good will in the long run.

4.5 Exercises

1. Visit an older existing church or synagogue site near where you are located. Is there adequate automobile access and parking? Are the various units of the facility appropriately related to each other? Is pedestrian circulation clear and unimpeded by driveways or excessive stairways? Are there provisions for handicapped individuals in the parking areas and throughout the buildings?

   Prepare a sketch drawing of the site including all buildings, parking, and landscape areas. Pace off the perimeter of the site and of the various buildings to make the drawing roughly to scale.

   Imagine that the owners now need to add a new "Family Life Center" and related parking to provide for daily activities, particularly for the old and young of the congregation. Where would this facility best be located on the existing or on an adjoining site? Assume that they could purchase an adjoining site if no room is currently available on the owned property.

   If you were to start over, where would you have located the existing facilities and the family life center? Would they be in different locations from the present locations? Why?

2. Develop a short list of crucial issues and related goals for master planning the above site again, assuming that there was no existing development.

   After having done this, reassess where you would locate the various facilities, including the family life center. Would they be in different locations than your original placement? If so, why? Did the crucial issues and related goals make a difference?

3. Without reference to either of the above master planning ideas, develop a short list of crucial issues for schematic design of the new family life center. Would responding to these issues cause you to re-assess the location of this center?

4. Given the characteristics of the existing development, of the neighborhood, and the local climate and conditions, what would be the appropriate systems and materials to use for the new family center? Would they relate to existing materials and details? Would they be different?

5. Assume that you have been asked to master plan the site and prepare an architectural program for the family life center.

   Develop a list of all of the information gathering techniques that you would need to use to become knowledgeable enough to prepare a competent program for a completely new facility for the church or synagogue.

   Develop a bar chart schedule showing when all of these activities would be accomplished and who would be doing them.

   What would you charge the church for your programming efforts? How would you determine your costs? How long would it take you to do the programming? Is this a good way to estimate your costs? Are there better ways?

   What would be your personal hourly take home pay based on the fee and time needed to do the study? Would it be adequate to make a good living? What do you think is a good living?

4.6 References

Ackoff, Russell L. 1968. *Scientific Method: Optimizing Applied Research Decisions*. 1st corrected edition. New York: Wiley.

Barrett, G. Vincent, and John P. Blair. 1988. *How to Conduct and Analyze Real Estate and Market Feasibility Studies*. New York: Van Nostrand Reinhold.

Brill, Michael, Stephen T. Margulis, Ellen Konar, and BOSTI. 1984. *Using Office Design to Increase Productivity*. Buffalo, N.Y.: Workplace Design and Productivity.

Dober, Richard P. 1963. *Campus Planning*. New York: Reinhold Publishing Corp.

Farbstein, Jay. 1997. Discussion by telephone.

Goldman, Mark, and Frieda D. Peatross. 1993. *Planning for a Captive Audience. In Professional Practice in Facility Programming*, edited by Wolfgang F. E. Preiser. New York: Van Nostrand Reinhold.

Lynch, Kevin. 1971. *Site Planning*. Cambridge, Mass.: M.I.T. Press.

McGraw-Hill Construction Information Group. 1997. *Sweet's General Building & Renovation Catalog File*. New York: McGraw Hill.

Moleski, Walter. 1997. Discussion by telephone.

Pan, Solomon. 1997. Discussion by telephone.

Peña, William, William Caudill, and John Focke. 1977. *Problem Seeking: An Architectural Programming Primer*. Boston, Mass.: Cahners Books International.

Peña, William, Steven Parshall, and Kevin Kelly. 1987. *Problem Seeking: An Architectural Programming Primer*. 3rd ed. Washington, D.C.: AIA Press.

Preiser, Wolfgang F. E. 1993a. *Recent Developments in Facility Programming. In Professional Practice in Facility Programming*, edited by Wolfgang F. E. Preiser. New York: Van Nostrand Reinhold.

Preiser, Wolfgang F. E., ed. 1993b. *Professional Practice in Facility Programming*. New York: Van Nostrand Reinhold.

Rubenstein, Harvey M. 1987. *A Guide to Site and Environmental Planning*. 3rd ed. New York: Wiley.

Rushman, Stephen. 1986. *How to Perform an Economic Feasibility Study of a Proposed Hotel/Motel*. Chicago: American Society of Real Estate Counselors.

Tustler, Wilbur H., Frank Zilm, James T. Hannon, and Mary Ann Newman. 1993. *Programming: The Third Dimension. In Professional Practice in Facility Programming*, edited by Wolfgang F. E. Preiser. New York: Van Nostrand Reinhold.

Information Gathering

No matter which method or approach to architectural programming is used, it will feature techniques and tools for
gathering information about the client, users, site, and other factors in order to define the nature of the architectural problem. If
the data gathered is extensive, then various techniques and tools
of analysis will be necessary to distill the raw data into useful information. This chapter covers the most basic and frequently
used information gathering and data analysis techniques and
tools. It does not cover every approach currently used by professional programmers. However, careful reading and application of
the materials presented should allow the programmer to develop
the information needed for most commissions. It will also advance the beginning programmer to the point where other techniques and tools can be evaluated and used as appropriate for a
particular programming problem.

A person can learn a great deal about architecture by reading
and going to lectures, as well as from conversations, movies, and
television. Much can also be learned by general observation of

people interacting with their physical and social environments. The more diverse and varied an architect's experience with the environment, the more knowledge that person can draw upon in any architectural programming or design situation. But what one has experienced and learned may not apply to a particular problem. What we think is true may not be true. What we think is false may be true. It is important to study the particular situation for which a new building is being considered before deciding what the new building should be. Information should be gathered on client and user values, goals, and needs as well as on facts about the site, climate, context, and existing facilities in order to understand what is required.

The most obvious, but often overlooked, approach to obtaining information about a particular architectural problem is to see what others have written about it. Literature search and review techniques can be employed to uncover a great deal of useful information about a project. The problem is doing this in an efficient and reliable fashion. Several successful techniques of literature search are covered in this chapter.

There are also likely to be a number of people available who have not written about or published their experiences, but nevertheless have a wealth of knowledge concerning the problem at hand. Certainly the client will have much to share. So will the users of the existing facilities, if there are any. Others who would have knowledge to share include persons responsible for similar enterprises and the users of similar facilities. There are also experts in particular building types, and other design and engineering professionals, social scientists, and public officials who should be consulted. These people can be interviewed or asked to respond to questionnaires to obtain the knowledge they can contribute. It is also possible to observe persons in existing facilities or environments similar to the proposed project to discover more about actual behavior patterns. Several strategies for gathering firsthand information through interviews, questionnaires, and observation techniques are also covered in this chapter.

If large numbers of personnel or settings are involved and time or budget is limited, as is almost always the case, then it will be necessary to select exactly who and what should be studied. A sampling plan will be needed to select representative persons from whom to gather the information. It will also be necessary to develop procedures to reduce the gathered information to manageable amounts for the designer to assimilate. These are significant problems that will be discussed.

The procedures covered in this chapter should prove sufficient for most small- to medium-scale programming problems. Persons wishing to expand their understanding of programming to include more advanced or specialized information gathering or data analysis techniques and tools should review books such as *Facility Programming* (1978) and *Programming the Built Environment* (1985) edited by Wolfgang F. E. Preiser, *The Architect's Guide to Facility Programming* (1981) by Mickey A. Palmer, *Methods of Architectural Programming* (1977) by Henry Sanoff, *Problem Seeking* (1987) by William Peña et al., and *Architectural Programming: Creative Techniques for Design Professionals* (1995) by Robert Kumlin. These books contain case studies and detailed examples of programming procedures used by professional programmers, and include references to a number of other texts and articles that contain even more detail on specific procedures. *Methods in Environmental and Behavioral Research* (1987) edited by Robert Bechtel, Robert Marans, and William Michelson; *Inquiry by Design* (1981) by John Zeisel; and *Creative Design Decisions* (1988) by Stephen J. Kirk and Kent F. Spreckelmeyer are examples of literature that concentrates on some of the more useful advanced information gathering procedures.

5.1 Literature Search and Review

- Information Needs
- Literature Sources
- Library Search Procedures
- Non-Library Search Procedures
- Literature Review Procedures
- Matrix Summary
- Sampling Plan

Nearly all architectural students that the author has encountered feel that they have learned quite enough about literature search and review in their freshman English courses. But few of these students have been effective in finding information appropriate for programming a particular architectural project. This is not because the information is unavailable in print, but because it is typically not found in the same libraries and reference sources appropriate for English or history research papers. Indeed, in many cases the information needs, sources, and requirements are so different in architectural programming that the strategies for search and review must be revised significantly to be effective.

Information Needs

- Precommission

- Programming

- Design

The above list indicates three distinct time periods or phases when literature resources can be of great value to the architect. Each phase requires different types of information and involves somewhat different search strategies in order to be successful.

PRECOMMISSION

For the architectural firm seeking a commission for a project type that team members have not previously programmed or designed, it is vitally important to know as much as possible about the potential client and the client's facility needs prior to the first meeting or interview. Literature on or by the particular organization is very useful: its own publicity, news releases, newsletters, etc. The information contained in these documents can be most helpful in obtaining a feeling for the organization, its manner of operating, financial resources, and potential as a client. It can provide a preliminary understanding of the purposes and goals of the organization as well as the potential for growth and facility development. It can also be helpful in securing the programming commission.

Clients, like most people, typically are flattered and impressed when others show a sincere interest in their particular concerns. Familiarity with the client's organization is a concrete demonstration of this interest and can make the difference in being hired or not hired—it can be an effective marketing tool for architectural firms that specialize in or offer programming as a primary service.

After all, not much of what follows is very important if you do not get the commission!

Where do you obtain this information? Visit their offices. Request copies of their printed materials. Show your interest in them and the proposed project before the formal interview. This will help to ensure that your firm will stand out from others being interviewed.

Likewise, it is important to familiarize yourself with the general space vocabulary and facility requirements of the organization. Nearly every business or institution has a particular jargon with which the architect should be familiar during the interview. If you are trying to get a commission to do a church for an unfamiliar denomination, will the members of the building committee refer to the primary meeting space as the "church," "sanctuary," "worship center," or will they use another term? Similarly, there may be a particular arrangement of spaces about which you should be aware. Lack of familiarity with their organization may result in losing the commission.

Most institutions belong to larger groups, such as church denominations, that publish guidelines for appropriate physical development. Sometimes these can be found in the local offices. If not, correspond directly with the organization headquarters to obtain the appropriate literature. This literature will typically provide both the typical vocabulary and space standards. *Strategic Planning and Building Planning for New Congregations* (1990) of the Board of Church Extension of Disciples of Christ is an excellent example (Fig. 5-1).

Figure 5-1 Planning and Design Guide: Cover.
Permission: Board of Church Extension of Disciples of Christ

An excellent job interview strategy is to bring up the special vocabulary, typical space standards, or unique relationships which the organization prefers to demonstrate your interest in discovering the special character of their institution. *Time-Saver Standards for Architectural Design Data* (Callender 1982) and other similar standards can also serve as helpful beginning points to obtain basic information on the building types that reoccur in our society. Monographs on particular building types are available in many libraries and can serve to familiarize the architect with special requirements of the building type and provide an understanding of precedent. Are there particular formal arrangements that occur repeatedly in different times and places, even at very different sites? It is important to understand the reasons behind such formal arrangements, to determine if some strong institutional value is being expressed, and to show your awareness of these values, should the potential client show an interest.

PROGRAMMING

Once the commission is obtained, programming can begin in earnest. The same information obtained earlier can be reviewed for applicability to the problem at hand. Further vocabulary building and understanding of the organization can go on as well. An examination of the records and archives of the organization can also be very fruitful. Is there a program for the existing facilities? What were the goals and objectives then? What projections were made for growth and change? Was there a master plan showing where future facilities were anticipated? What about the actual construction documents? Were specific provisions made to accommodate growth and/or change in the organization or facilities? Were some walls designed as knock-out panels to allow additions? Were certain utilities extended in anticipation of future expansion? Is there an organizational chart showing how various departments and people relate to each other? Are there annual reports or files which reveal special developments? This can be useful information at the beginning of the programming stage and should be sought out in cooperation with the organization's staff.

If the organization has a library, it might include trade journals containing special information about this and similar organizations. If it is a subsidiary of a larger entity, the headquarters may have a more comprehensive library that can be accessed for additional information. What concerns do the people in the organization find to be of enough importance to publish? It may be possible to identify the principal purposes or "institutional values" of the organization, as well as primary goals and directions for advancement and/or change. Guidelines for space size may be provided in some degree of detail as shown in Fig. 5-2.

Information on the site and its surroundings, as well as on the urban infrastructure, can be obtained from various governmental agencies. Cities typically have extensive files containing plans and other documents relating to specific sites that are available to the developers of new projects. They also have planning and development documents such as general plans, zoning ordinances, design review policies, building permit guidelines, and the like. The key provisions of these should be documented in the program. Cities also develop or adopt building codes (building, mechanical, plumbing, fire safety, etc.) which contain information that is important to include in the architectural program. Current versions of all of these documents are likely to be available at city offices. They may also be available in the government documents section of the local public or university library. Those that contain useful information should be obtained for reference during both programming and design. The *Tucson Historic Districts: Criteria for Preservation and Development* (City of Tucson 1972) is typical of this kind of document (Fig. 5-3).

As pointed out in earlier sections of the text, information about the needs of special user groups applying to a particular problem can be obtained in the literature. There is also an abundance of environmental design research available covering the territorial, privacy, community, safety, and

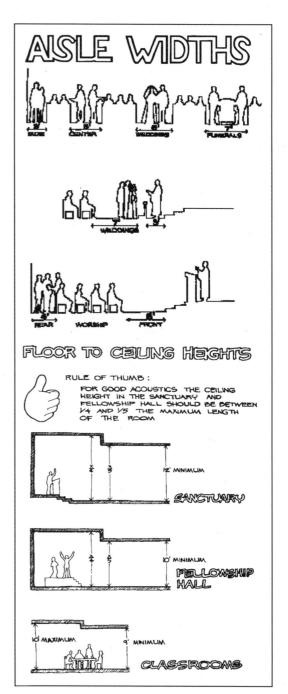

Figure 5-2 Organization Design Standards.

Credit: Board of Church Extension of Disciples of Christ, 1990. *Strategic Planning & Building Planning for New Congregations.* Permission: Board of Church Extension of Disciples of Christ.

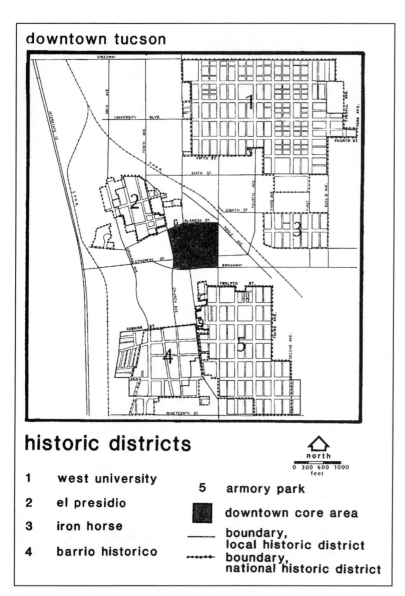

downtown tucson

historic districts

1   west university
2   el presidio
3   iron horse
4   barrio historico

5   armory park

▨   downtown core area

──   boundary,
     local historic district
╍╍╍   boundary,
     national historic district

△
north
0 300 600 1000
     feet

Figure 5-3 Planning and Development Guide.

Credit: Tucson Historic Districts: Criteria for Preservation and Development, 1972. City of Tucson, Department of Community Development/Planning Division, Tucson, Arizona.City of Tucson, Department of Community Development/Planning Division

other social and psychological needs of various user groups: the elderly, young, handicapped, incarcerated, and so on. This type of literature typically is available in major public and university libraries.

DESIGN

Prior to or during design, an entirely different body of printed information becomes important to the architect. The journals of the architectural profession, such as *Architecture* and *Architectural Record*, as well as related publications dealing with values and design methodologies such as *Oppositions* and the *DMG Newsletter*, are of continuing interest to the designer. Issues devoted to particular building types may be of considerable interest in terms of the spatial and formal organization of the facility. Books and other publications on the history of a building type or the architecture of particular places, such as *Precedents in Architecture* (Clark and Pause 1996), might also be of interest, as they can aid in the analysis and evaluation of potential solutions to the architectural problem.

During the design development phase of architectural services, there is a whole body of information that can be obtained from reference books such as *Architectural Graphic Standards* (American Institute of Architects 1994) and monographs on particular building materials and systems such as the excellent one on *Metal Design and Fabrication* by architects David Frisch and Susan Frisch (1998). Manufacturer's literature on building products and equipment are also available. This literature typically is not available within a university or public library system, but is readily available to architectural or programming firms upon request. There are also general catalog files that include the products of many suppliers, such as *Sweet's Catalog File* (McGraw-Hill Construction Information Group 1997), which are updated yearly and may not be available in public libraries. They will be found in most architectural libraries and in the offices of most practicing architects (Fig. 5-4).

Figure 5-4   Sweet's Catalog File in Library.

Literature Sources

- Building and Planning Standards
- Historical Documents/Archival Materials
- Trade Publications
- Research Literature
- Professional Publications
- Codes and Ordinances
- Government Documents
- Manufacturers' Publications
- Popular Literature
- World Wide Web

As is evident from the above discussion, the types of literature and printed material available and useful to the architectural programmer are diverse both in nature and location. Each of the ten categories of printed materials may contain useful information. A brief description of each of these information sources is included in the following paragraphs, along with their most likely location and the areas of programming in which they would be of benefit. Representative titles are also noted.

BUILDING AND PLANNING STANDARDS

Time-Saver Standards for Architectural Design Data (Callender 1982), *Architectural Graphic Standards* (American Institute of Architects 1994), and *Interior Graphic and Design Standards* (Reznikoff 1986) are examples of printed documents that contain standards for site development, building types, space types, and systems within buildings. These and other similar documents can be found in most architectural libraries and should be part of an architect's reference library. They can be useful in developing a general understanding of a building type or system in the early stages of programming or even prior to obtaining the commission, and the more specific systems-oriented standards can be useful for design development and construction documents (Fig. 5-5).

HISTORICAL DOCUMENTS/ ARCHIVAL MATERIALS

These are the community's or client's own records. They include newspaper

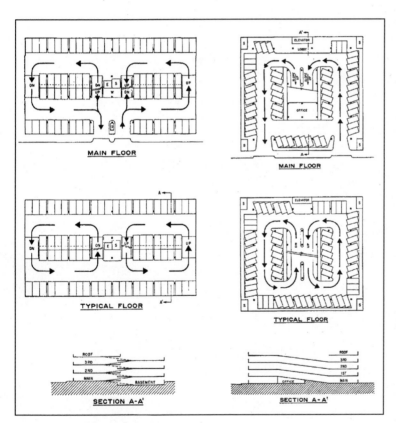

Figure 5-5 Planning Standards.

Credit: De Chiara & Callender, 1973. *Time Saver Standards for Building Types.* McGraw-Hill Book Co., NY, NY, p. 677 . Permission: McGraw-Hill

coverage of events relating to the proposed development; legal descriptions and restrictions; records of street and utility alignments and easements; zoning and design review decisions; and the client's records of building programs, plans, and specifications, and plans for development.

Newspaper archives may be in a public library or the publisher's office. Most legal descriptions of property can be located in a county recorder's office. City documents are usually available through the public works, engineering, and/or planning offices. The client's records are sometimes carefully stored in files, but quite often are within the client's dead storage areas or lost forever because no one thought they were worth saving. Occasionally, formal archives are established to preserve the records of an establishment or an area of knowledge. Information located in all of the above areas can be valuable during programming and design. The adjoining plate is from the architect's drawings for the Pima County Court House that are being preserved in the Arizona Architectural Archives of the College of Architecture, The University of Arizona (Fig. 5-6).

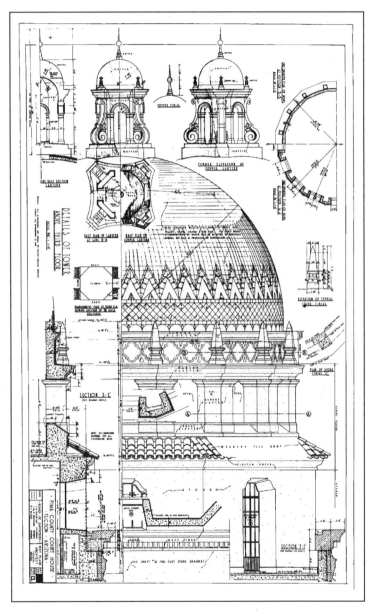

Figure 5-6 Pima County Court House.

Credit: Roy Place Architect, Pima County Court House, Tower Details. Permission: From the Arizona Architectural Archives, College of Architecture, The University of Arizona

TRADE PUBLICATIONS

Trade publications include magazines, newsletters, journals, conference proceedings, and monographs relating to a specific organization or institution. Newsletters may be generated by a local organization or by a state, regional, national, or international association. Journals and conference proceedings are usually benefits of membership in the association. These publications are often maintained at the association headquarters, in major research collections at university libraries, and if the magazine, journal, or monograph is of community interest, within public library systems. Such publications are useful in vocabulary building prior to obtaining a commission and in the early stages of programming when establishing the important values and issues to be considered in the design. They are also important sources for obtaining an understanding of an organization's current concerns, occasionally including very helpful critiques of how previously designed buildings have worked.

RESEARCH LITERATURE

Literature on human behavior in buildings can be found in the conference proceedings of the Environmental Design Research Association (EDRA 1969-); journals such as *Environment and Behavior*, *The Journal of Environmental Psychology*, *The Journal of Architectural and Planning Research*; and in a variety of monographs such as *Planning and Designing the Office Environment* by David A. Harris (1981), *Tight Spaces* by Robert Sommer (1974), *A Graphic Survey of Perception and Behavior for the Design Professions* by Forrest Wilson (1984), and many others.

These publications are typically available in major public libraries and university architectural libraries. Architectural firms should have the more generally applicable books and journals in their own libraries, and those wishing to be involved in particular building types should acquire monographs and journals on that building type in order to have the material at hand during programming and design. Information in these journals and monographs should become a part of the architect's understanding of the field. Information on particular user groups and facility types would be appropriate before obtaining a commission and especially during schematic and design development (Fig. 5-7).

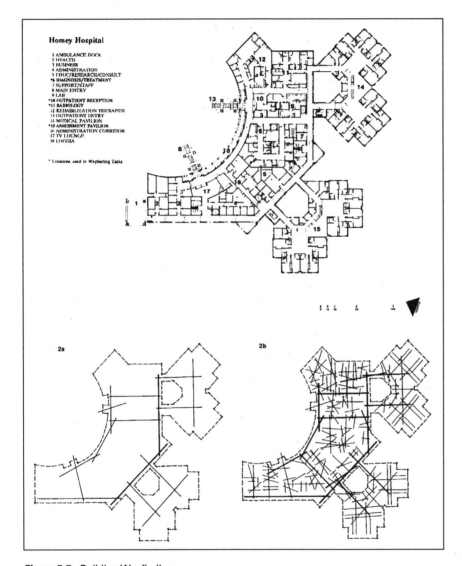

Homey Hospital

1 AMBULANCE DOCK
2 HEALTH
3 BUSINESS
4 ADMINISTRATION
5 EDUC/RESEARCH/CONSULT
*6 DIAGNOSIS/TREATMENT
7 SUPPORT/STAFF
8 MAIN ENTRY
9 LAB
*10 OUTPATIENT RECEPTION
*11 RADIOLOGY
12 REHABILITATION THERAPIES
13 OUTPATIENT ENTRY
14 MEDICAL PAVILION
*15 ASSESSMENT PAVILION
16 ADMINISTRATION CORRIDOR
17 TV LOUNGE
18 LOGGIA

* Locations used in Wayfinding Tasks

Figure 5-7 Building Wayfinding.

Credit:(Peponis et al 1990), 555–590. Reprinted by permission of Sage Publications, Inc.

PROFESSIONAL PUBLICATIONS

These include professional journals such as *Architecture*, *Architectural Record*, and *Architectural Review* as well as numerous monographs, architectural history books, and related books and journals in urban planning, landscape architecture, and interior design.

Figure 5-8 Professional Journal cover.

Photo Credit: Paul Warchol. Makuhari Housing Complex, China, Japan. Steven Holl Architects. Permission: Architectural Record

These are, of course, the publications most likely to be available in the architectural libraries of both the professional schools of architecture and architectural offices. They contain information appropriate at all levels of architectural programming and design. Issues of professional journals and conference proceedings contain articles relating to almost every building type, occasionally with in-depth analysis and evaluation of specific examples, making them highly useful in the programming process (Fig. 5-8).

Monographs by firms specializing in particular building types such as hospitals, schools, and commercial office buildings can also be extremely useful since the firm's experience is available to the reader. History and theory books may assist the architect in the development of appropriate design concepts, as well as in the development of details for a particular situation.

CODES AND ORDINANCES

These include federal, state, county, and municipal standards, codes, and ordinances typically geared to protecting the public health, safety, and welfare. They are often legal documents that must be complied with, so are of paramount importance in programming and design. Standards are often promulgated at the federal level and include requirements for the workplace such as those included in the Occupational Safety and Health Act (Blosser 1992); for the handicapped as covered in publications of the American National Standards Institute (ANSI); and for asbestos and other materials as published by the American Society for Testing and Materials (ASTM). States often have codes covering portable or relocatable structures since they can be moved across city and county boundaries. Counties usually adopt building codes for unincorporated areas. Cities either develop their own building codes or adopt in whole or part uniform codes such as the *Uniform Building Code* (International Conference of Building Officials 1994) or *National Building Code* (BOCA 1990) as well as related documents for mechanical, plumbing, and electrical requirements. They also develop general plans and zoning ordinances that restrict the type, size, and nature of facilities that can be built in various parts of the community.

Sometimes these ordinances are quite specific in terms of building size, setbacks, heights, sign location and size, and even of building and landscape materials and treatments. These documents are typically available at the county or local planning and building departments at cost. They are sometimes available in public and university libraries in the government documents section. Check if they are kept current by the library because of constant updates and modifications. Because these documents contain legal requirements for building, it is mandatory that they be referenced and that key provisions likely to impact design be articulated in the program (Fig. 5-9).

EXCERPTS FROM CHAPTER 16   1994 UNIFORM BUILDING CODE

FOOTNOTES TO TABLE 16-B—(Continued)

[9]Intermediate rails, panel fillers and their connections shall be capable of withstanding a load of 25 pounds per square foot (1.2 kN/m²) applied horizontally at right angles over the entire tributary area, including openings and spaces between rails. Reactions due to this loading need not be combined with those of Footnote 8.

[10]A horizontal load applied at right angles to the vehicle barrier at a height of 18 inches (457 mm) above the parking surface. The force may be distributed over a 1-foot-square (304.8-millimeter-square) area.

[11]The mounting of handrails shall be such that the completed handrail and supporting structure are capable of withstanding a load of at least 200 pounds (890 kN) applied in any direction at any point on the rail. These loads shall not be assumed to act cumulatively with Item 9.

[12]Vertical members of storage racks shall be protected from impact forces of operating equipment, or racks shall be designed so that failure of one vertical member will not cause collapse of more than the bay or bays directly supported by that member.

[13]The 250-pound (1.11 kN) load is to be applied to any single fire sprinkler support point but not simultaneously to all support joints.

TABLE 16-C—MINIMUM ROOF LIVE LOADS[1]

	METHOD 1				METHOD 2		
	Tributary Loaded Area in Square Feet for Any Structural Member			Uniform Load[2] (pounds per square foot)	Rate of Reduction r (percentage)	Maximum Reduction R (percentage)	
	× 0.0929 for m²						
	0 to 200	201 to 600	Over 600				
	Uniform Load (pounds per square foot)						
ROOF SLOPE	× 0.0479 for kN/m²						
1. Flat[3] or rise less than 4 units vertical in 12 units horizontal (33.3% slope). Arch or dome with rise less than one eighth of span	20	16	12	20	.08	40	
2. Rise 4 units vertical to less than 12 units vertical in 12 units horizontal (33% to less than 100% slope). Arch or dome with rise one eighth of span to less than three eighths of span	16	14	12	16	.06	25	
3. Rise 12 units vertical in 12 units horizontal (100% slope) and greater. Arch or dome with rise three eighths of span or greater	12	12	12	12			
4. Awnings except cloth covered[4]	5	5	5	5	No reductions permitted		
5. Greenhouses, lath houses and agricultural buildings[5]	10	10	10	10			

[1]Where snow loads occur, the roof structure shall be designed for such loads as determined by the building official. See Section 1605.4. For special-purpose roofs, see Section 1605.5.

[2]See Section 1606 for live load reductions. The rate of reduction r in Section 1606 Formula (6-1) shall be as indicated in the table. The maximum reduction R shall not exceed the value indicated in the table.

[3]A flat roof is any roof with a slope of less than $^1/_4$ unit vertical in 12 units horizontal (2% slope). The live load for flat roofs is in addition to the ponding load required by Section 1605.6.

[4]As defined in Section 3206.

[5]See Section 1605.5 for concentrated load requirements for greenhouse roof members.

1–246

Figure 5-9 Uniform Building Code.

Reproduced from the Uniform Building Code™, copyright © 1994, with the permission of the publisher, the International Conference of Building Officials

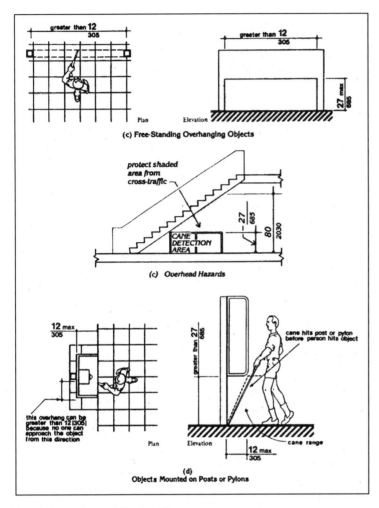

Figure 5-10 Accessibility Guidelines.
Federal Register, Vol. 56, No. 14, Jan. 22, 1991, p. 20

GOVERNMENT DOCUMENTS

In addition to codes and ordinances, both federal and state governments generate a tremendous amount of printed material. This includes information on particular organizations and building types, special manufacturing or other processes, special systems and materials, and a host of other topics. These publications are generally found in the government documents section of public and university libraries. Government documents have their own catalog and methods of access. Request help from the government documents librarian about how to proceed. Be sure to look at these documents because they may contain programmatic information on the exact type of facility for which you are preparing a program. For example, the Small Business Administration (SBA) publishes information on how to set up many small businesses. The *Federal Register* publicizes rules for various laws such as from the Proposed Rules for the Americans with Disabilities Act (ADA) (Fig. 5-10).

MANUFACTURERS' PUBLICATIONS

Manufacturers' catalogs and other similar publications almost always relate to the specific materials or systems that they produce. As previously noted, *Sweet's Catalog File* (McGraw-Hill Construction Information Group 1997) is the most generally available form of product literature in the United States. Many manufacturers include small brochures of their product line in these catalogs, which cover every aspect of building construction. These manufacturers, and many others not included in Sweet's, also have their own more extensive catalogs, which include standard details, cut sheets, samples, and the like. They generally will make these available to architectural firms at no cost in the hope of having their products specified in a building, so almost any architectural firm will have copies of the Sweet's file and many other product catalogs in their firm library. Again, these materials are rarely available in public libraries, but should be available and up-to-date in architectural libraries and offices.

Figure 5-11 Sweet's Catalog File: Contents.

Credit: Contents, 1999 Sweet's Contract Interiors Catalog File, the McGraw-Hill Companies. Permission: McGraw-Hill

This type of information is primarily used during the design development and construction document phases of architectural services when particular materials and systems are being selected. This information may also be of help to the programmer in establishing the physical dimensions of required equipment and systems (Fig. 5-11).

POPULAR LITERATURE

Occasionally it is possible to find useful information in the popular literature, such as *Time*, *Life*, *The New Yorker*, and *Better Homes and Gardens* nationally, as well as in *Sunset*, *Arizona Living*, and other regional publications. These may have feature stories on the client's organization or articles and commentary on architects or architecture of interest to the readership. This type

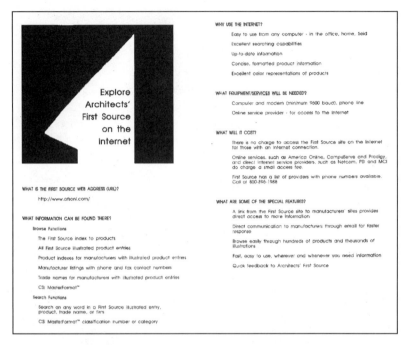

Explore
Architects'
First Source
on the
Internet

WHY USE THE INTERNET?

Easy to use from any computer - in the office, home, field

Excellent searching capabilities

Up-to-date information

Concise, formatted product information

Excellent color representations of products

WHAT EQUIPMENT/SERVICES WILL BE NEEDED?

Computer and modem (minimum 9600 baud), phone line

Online service provider - for access to the Internet

WHAT WILL IT COST?

There is no charge to access the First Source site on the Internet for those with an Internet connection.

Online services, such as America Online, CompuServe and Prodigy, and direct Internet service providers, such as Netcom, PSI and MCI do charge a small access fee.

First Source has a list of providers with phone numbers available. Call at 800-896-1988

WHAT IS THE FIRST SOURCE WEB ADDRESS (URL)?

http://www.afsonl.com/

WHAT INFORMATION CAN BE FOUND THERE?

Browse Functions

The First Source index to products

All First Source illustrated product entries

Product indexes for manufacturers with illustrated product entries

Manufacturer listings with phone and fax contact numbers

Trade names for manufacturers with illustrated product entries

CSI MasterFormat™

Search Functions

Search on any word in a First Source illustrated entry, product, trade name, or firm

CSI MasterFormat™ classification number or category

WHAT ARE SOME OF THE SPECIAL FEATURES?

A link from the First Source site to manufacturers' sites provides direct access to more information

Direct communication to manufacturers through email for faster response

Browse easily through hundreds of products and thousands of illustrations

Fast, easy to use, wherever and whenever you need information

Quick feedback to Architects' First Source

Figure 5-12 *Architects' First Source.*

Permission: Architects' First Source, Inc.

of information is likely to be most useful when familiarizing oneself with a particular client, rather than for obtaining information relevant to a particular commission.

WORLD WIDE WEB

Students have recently been successful in finding current information on the World Wide Web. This information is variable in nature and spotty in building-related areas at this time, but is likely to increase dramatically in quantity and quality over time. It is also only as reliable as the source, so programmers would be wise to confirm information found on the Web with other sources. *Architects' First Source* (Diercks 1996) is helpful in finding product manufacturers (Fig. 5-12).

Library Search Procedures

- Decide generally what information would be helpful to discover
- Consult with the librarian on special sources
- Follow up on the special sources
- Check the appropriate subject headings in the catalog system
- Consult the appropriate indexes to periodical literature
- Investigate the government documents index
- Conduct a computer literature search
- Obtain and review the most promising sources of information

Library search procedures will vary from library to library, but all have many of the same general characteristics. The above listed literature search steps are generally appropriate (Yao 1987). Systematically following such a procedure will almost always result in a more efficient, hence less time consuming and costly, search than if more casual procedures are utilized. Browsing through the shelves of the stacks of a library and thumbing through the current periodicals are not efficient nor cost-effective methods of retrieving information.

DECIDE GENERALLY WHAT INFORMATION WOULD BE HELPFUL TO DISCOVER

A few minutes thinking about what you hope to accomplish with the literature search is always time well spent. If you have already done programs or designs for a number of similar projects, you may not need to conduct a literature search at all. If the project appears to have only one or two significant differences from earlier projects, you might concentrate only on these areas. But if the commission is for a project type with which you are essentially unfamiliar, you should conduct a thorough review—it could help you get the commission. In all but the first case, identification of what you need to know will help streamline the steps that follow.

CONSULT WITH THE LIBRARIAN ON SPECIAL SOURCES

Introduce yourself and the task at hand to the architectural librarian, if there is one at the library where you are doing your research. Otherwise, ask for a librarian generally familiar with the areas in which you will be seeking information. Librarians are experts in literature searches and know a great deal about the resources in their library, and will almost invariably save you time. Ask if there are any authoritative reference sources in your area of concern. There may be sources which can provide you with all of the information needed—the search is over! Often, there will be several sources known to the librarian that contain limited, but nevertheless useful, information (Fig. 5-13).

Figure 5-13 Librarian Helping with a Search.

The published standards mentioned in the previous section may be available. There may also be monographs directed more specifically to the subject at hand. The librarian may also know about a specially prepared bibliography on the specific subject. These lists of references may be annotated as a result of a previously organized research effort on the subject by a knowledgeable person, perhaps another architectural programmer. For instance, *Vance Bibliographies* includes a large number of special topic bibliographies on architectural subject material. Here again, if the bibliography is current, several of the other steps in the literature search may be unnecessary as you proceed directly to find and review the most promising sources listed in the bibliography.

FOLLOW UP ON THE SPECIAL SOURCES

Obtain and review all of the special sources to which you are directed by the librarian. At the very least, this will give you enough information to identify what you are seeking. Often, however, these sources will provide all that is needed for pre-programming activities and may be sufficient even for programming if an abundance of information is found in the subject area. If the information is not sufficient, it is well to peruse the references and bibliographies contained in the various publications for other leads, and especially to continue to develop the appropriate terminology and subject headings needed to continue with the search.

CHECK THE APPROPRIATE SUBJECT HEADINGS
IN THE CATALOG SYSTEM

If no special bibliography is available or if additional resources are needed, it is advisable to conduct your own search for books in the library's catalog. Use appropriate subject headings for your topic, as listed in the *Library of Congress Subject Headings* or in accordance with the library's catalog system. Using this terminology, you can proceed to find additional sources on the subject. When relevant books are located, write down the complete bibliographic information for each: author, title, place of publication, publisher, year of publication, and call number. This consumes some initial time, but saves effort in the long run. Also note the subject heading(s) under which the book was found so that it will be easy to return to the same heading if additional information is desired at a later date. The catalog entry for a book will also note if it contains illustrations, drawings, plans, and a bibliography. Such information may help you decide if the particular document is worth pursuing.

CONSULT THE APPROPRIATE INDEXES TO PERIODICAL LITERATURE

The librarian may also be able to refer you to the appropriate indexes to periodical literature. Some of the appropriate indexes for architectural periodicals include the *Avery Index to Architectural Periodicals*, *Art Index*, and *Architectural Index*. The *Avery Index* can be accessed in some libraries with a computer search. A valuable resource for finding appropriate indexes is *Information Sources in Architecture*, edited by Valerie J. Bradfield (1983). The librarian may also be able to refer you to appropriate indexes, bibliographies, or abstracts in other fields. As in the references for books, write down the complete citation for each article: author, title of article, title of journal, volume and issue number, full date of issue, and inclusive page numbers, as well as the index and subject headings consulted. If the particular periodicals in which you are interested are not covered in a standard index, a time-consuming review of the tables of contents of each publication may be necessary to find articles or chapters applicable to the problem at hand. In this case, always try to find relevant information in the most current documents. They may make reference to earlier publications, so you can avoid a seemingly endless search through the contents of numerous periodicals. This is an especially good strategy in using unindexed trade journals and newsletters (Fig. 5-14).

Figure 5-14 Indexes in Architecture Library.

INVESTIGATE THE GOVERNMENT DOCUMENTS INDEX

Government documents are generally located in a special section of major libraries. You must work with the section librarian to locate the desired materials, because they are not referenced in either the library's main catalog system or indexes. The librarian will likely refer you to specific materials as well as acquaint you with the use of the *Monthly Catalog of United States Government Publications* and other special reference tools. As mentioned earlier, some government documents can be invaluable in a programming effort. For instance, many government documents sections maintain complete up-to-date codes and ordinances applicable within a specific area of the country.

CONDUCT A COMPUTER LITERATURE SEARCH

In many libraries, it is also possible to conduct a literature search on CD-ROM or over the Internet. It is also possible to request a special computer literature search. Features of such searches are speed of retrieval, access points beyond the standard author-title-subject approach of a printed index, and other specialized search capabilities. Some data bases currently available include *Art Literature International (RILA)*, *Avery Index to Architectural Periodicals On-line*, and the *Architectural Database of the Royal Institute of British Architects*. Similar data bases exist for other fields which may be of interest for a particular project. One example is Medline for medical facility design issues. Such searches are worth pursuing if speed is an object. A charge may be involved for the search.

OBTAIN AND REVIEW THE MOST PROMISING
SOURCES OF INFORMATION

With all of the bibliographic information in hand, it is now time to find the most promising sources. The books contained in the catalog should be available in the library. If checked out, request a recall. If available, they can either be accessed directly on the shelves or brought to you from closed stacks. Most libraries will also have public serials lists, which indicate if a periodical is available in the library and if it is in paper copy or some microformat. It is likely that some sources will not be available in the library. In this case, it may be necessary to utilize the services of interlibrary loan to obtain the materials. Be prepared, however, to wait several days to obtain the materials and to pay a small charge for the service.

Non-Library Search Procedures

Traditional literature search procedures such as those described above are appropriate for only some of the printed documents needed for architectural programming and design. Many documents will not be in a library or indexed, so the search can be time consuming and even fruitless if not approached systematically. This is especially true for organization archives. First the archives must be found, then the filing system determined, and finally the search for specific useful information undertaken. An excellent approach to retrieval of useful archival information is provided in the book *Inquiry by Design* by John Zeisel (1981). This book should be available in any architectural library.

Often, copies of the needed information can be obtained from appropriate agencies, such as the city planning, building, and engineering departments. Documents relating specifically to the site for a building project are typically stored in the files of local, county, and state offices and can be accessed through their catalogs or filing systems.

Manufacturers' catalogs are available in the architect's library and accessed in accordance with a uniform specification numbering system. If information on a particular product is not available in the architect's library, calls to the Sweet's BuyLine (1-800-892-1165) or to local building product distributors will usually result in a response from a product representative who will bring the needed materials to the office.

Some trade publications may be found lying around the client's facilities. If their content appears to be promising, it may require correspondence or calls to parent organizations to locate original publications. This may involve exasperating delays in obtaining ordered materials. Depending on the nature of the problem, it may be very important to obtain this missing information. An historic preservation or restoration project, for instance, may take a great deal of research in a variety of places to establish the original design characteristics of a building. Should one proceed without it? Probably not. The same is true for many other problems.

Literature Review Procedures

There is probably much to be said for the systematic note taking advocated in most bibliographic research procedures. The author, on the other hand, has found for a programming search that photocopying of title pages and appropriate content pages onto 8½" × 11" sheets is more efficient and effective, and in the long run produces more readily retrievable information than notes on cards.

If the information source is available on an on-line data management system, it can be called up using a personal computer and the desired pages printed. Original copies can then be filed for future use and, when appropriate, the pages can be incorporated into an appendix to the program. Key statements can be highlighted or marked in the margin for easy retrieval. If an entire book or journal contains appropriate material, then it should be checked out for the duration of the programming process, or purchased for the programmer's permanent collection.

The actual relevance of material will, of course, be determined by the person doing the literature review. Here, as in all areas of information gathering, the best tests of relevance are whether the information is likely to make a design difference and whether there will be a substantial cost of error if the design is not done properly. Some care must also be taken relative to reliability and validity. Just because something has been published does not make it true. A notation system relating to the reliability of the information may be appropriate for any materials excerpted from a questionable source.

Matrix Summary

In the first stages of literature review, it is best to summarize the information within the eight value categories covered in Chapters 1 through 3 or a similar comprehensive set of categories with which the programmer is comfortable, as well as to designate whether the material appears to relate to project goals, facts, and needs for the new facility. Using such a system of classification and summary can help in the development of the ultimate programming matrix (Fig. 5-15). It can serve as the original basis for determining the direction of the firsthand information gathering techniques: interviewing, observing, and questioning.

Areas of the programming matrix in which there is limited or no information may indicate the need for more directed literature search or firsthand information gathering techniques. Areas where much has been discovered in the literature will be of great help in defining the problem, but the information will need to be

Values	Goals	Facts	Needs	Ideas
Human				
Environmental				
Cultural				
Technological				
Temporal				
Economic				
Aesthetic				
Safety				

Figure 5-15 Value-Based Programming Matrix.

confirmed for the specific project using firsthand information gathering techniques.

Sampling Plan

As with any information gathering procedure, only the amount of information that can be reasonably processed and summarized within the constraints of time and budget should be collected. A plan should be developed before beginning the search. The plan must address one fundamental issue—what does the designer need to know? In other words, what can be found that will make a design difference? The plan must also be made with respect to the available time and money for conducting the literature search, review, and summary. And there must be time and money left after this activity to obtain and summarize firsthand information and to meet and work directly with the client/user group to develop and publish the program document. So, the literature search and review process must fit within a general research and programming plan. Once this is determined, the programmer should develop a particular search strategy. Which of the sources are likely to contain the most useful information? Go to these first! Which of the sources are likely to contain valuable information not available using other information gathering techniques? Check out these sources also! In other words, try to decide where the highest return on invested time is likely to occur. After searching the areas of high return, summarize what you have found using the matrix as a guide. If something is missing, go directly to the most likely source of information. Do not wander aimlessly through the library or interesting periodicals hoping that something will turn up—it usually does not.

When the search time budget is nearly used up, summarize what you have found for each category of the matrix and use this as the basis for planning the next stages of information gathering. What has been found that is sufficient? What needs to be confirmed by firsthand observation or interviewing? What has to be completely developed from original sources? Is there still something that must be obtained in the literature? If so, what can be shortened in the balance of the programming process in order to obtain the necessary information by further literature search?

Ask yourself, what is the likely cost of error if the missing information is not obtained? If the cost is likely to be great, then the information must be obtained. If the cost is likely to be very small, then it may not be worth the time and money needed to go after it. The specific design solution may accommodate the expected problem satisfactorily and no one will know the difference. But, if the information could make a great difference, like the existence of an unbuildable easement through the property, it must be found. Otherwise, design decisions may be made or the building may be constructed in such a manner that it must be removed from the easement at great cost to everyone involved. The programmer must always be alert to the crucial variables and make certain that they are adequately covered. If we do not discover and note such important information in the program, the architect could even design a building on someone else's property—a very costly error (Fig. 5-16).

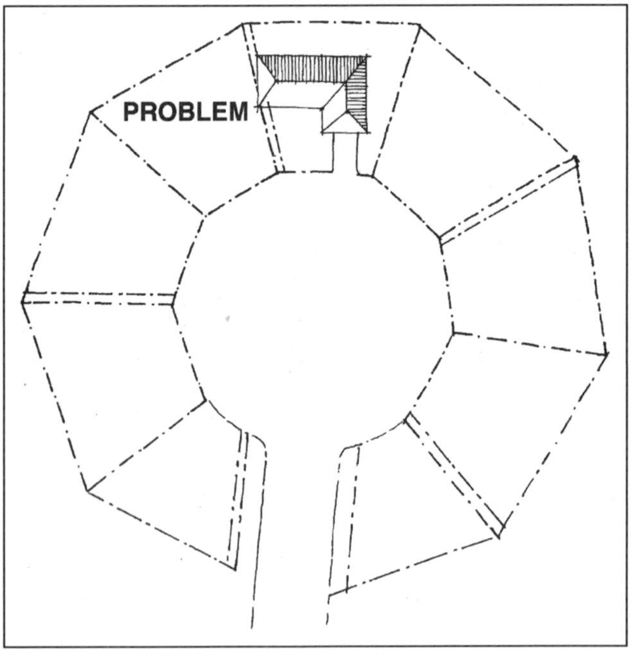

Figure 5-16 Building Over Property Line.

Credit: Carl Okazaki

5.2 Diagnostic Interviewing

- Value and Goal Seeking
- Planning the Interviews
- Interviewing Process
- Interviewing Skills

Interviewing is the most frequently used method for gathering information in architectural programming. The very first contact with the client, even before obtaining the commission, tends to be an interviewing situation in which the client attempts to determine if the architect or programmer is qualified to do the work, and the architect or programmer tries to obtain an initial understanding of the nature of the proposed project. They interview each other.

After obtaining the commission, the programmer begins in earnest to interview the client, and then various users, expert consultants, and others who may have special knowledge. The goal is to discover the primary reasons that a new facility may be needed: the particular values and goals of the client; requirements for the master plan; requirements for the first phase of development; expected growth and/or change; any special conditions or restrictions relative to site, materials, and systems; the construction budget; and possibly the client's expectations regarding the image or aesthetics of the project. The programmer, thus, tries to obtain a complete understanding of the design problem to be undertaken. If the project is quite large or complex, with a sizable staff having important information to share, or with special users whose needs might be rather unusual, an extensive series of interviews may be needed to help discover the special nature of the proposed project. The activity is very much like that of a doctor trying to make a medical diagnosis, but the architect is looking for information that will help to define the architectural problem rather than the medical problem. We, therefore, refer to the process as "diagnostic interviewing."

Note that this type of interviewing is sometimes referred to as "unstructured interviewing." However, this is inappropriate terminology, because there is a great deal of structure required in carrying out such an interview successfully. The required methodology and the associated techniques and tools of diagnostic interviewing are covered in the following sections.

Value and Goal Seeking

The main purpose of diagnostic interviewing is to discover the primary architectural values and project goals of the clients, staff, and users of an architectural facility. This helps the programmer obtain an early understanding of the important values and goals of clients and users in order to develop a framework in which to consider facts, needs, and ideas relating to the project. This may not be easy to do. Some clients already will have decided what they need, and will have difficulty trying to discover the values and goals that led to their decisions about needs. Nevertheless, it is important to get them to back up a bit to determine if their needs relate to the essential values and purposes of the organization, or if they are not needs at all, but wishes—something that is desirable, but by no means essential (Marans and Spreckelmeyer 1981).

It is necessary to identify the various values and goals in order to help the designer gain an understanding of the important design issues and, thus, to give the designer a basis on which to evaluate design decisions. Continuing with the medical analogy, it is important to make the appropriate diagnosis before deciding upon the treatment. Understanding the values and goals of an organization changes architectural design from a problem solving activity into an activity in which important goals can be achieved and important values can be expressed.

Planning the Interviews

- Defining the "Whole Problem"
- Natural Categories
- Sampling Plan
- Logistics
- Priming
- Documentation
- Analysis

As with any information gathering activity, planning can save one a great deal of time and effort both in collecting the needed information and analyzing it later. Planning typically involves some type of preliminary resolution of how the whole problem can be defined; what data can make a design difference; which persons can provide the most useful information; which persons have authority to make tradeoffs and establish priorities; what timeframe and budget are available; how interviewing fits into the several methods that will be used to gather the needed information.

DEFINING THE "WHOLE PROBLEM"

If a programmer can establish the goals, facts, and needs relating to the eight value areas outlined in Chapter 2, there is a good chance of developing a comprehensive definition of the architectural problem. As discussed earlier, a programmer can begin with an entirely different set of value categories, such as Peña and Focke's (1969): function, form, economy, and time; or Palmer's (1981): human factors, physical factors, and external factors.

Planning for an interview requires that the interviewer remember the various value areas that may significantly influence the design of the facility, so as to be able to use them as a kind of checklist during the interview. As noted previously, the author uses the acronyms "HECTTEAS" or "TEST EACH" to remember the eight value areas. Any number of similar associations can be used to recall each of these or similar issue areas.

The interviewer will receive essentially five types of programmatic information from interviewee: values, goals, facts, needs, and ideas. Each area should be included in a *mental matrix* so that significant information can be sought, particularly with respect to important values and goals:

Values	Goals	Facts	Needs	Ideas
Human				
Environmental				
Cultural				
Technological				
Temporal				
Economic				
Aesthetic				
Safety				
Other?				

NATURAL CATEGORIES

In a series of interviews, some of the above listed value categories may not be considered to be important by the person(s) being interviewed. This is okay! Only the programmer need be concerned about defining the whole problem. The programming approach should be flexible enough to admit new categories of information if they arise and especially to allow "natural" categories to surface and be substituted for the value categories listed above. *Image* may be very important to the client, and if so, *image* could be used in place of *aesthetics*. Similarly, a client may be interested in *building systems* and, if so, *building systems* could be substituted for *technological*. If *economics* was found to be of very little concern, as is possible in academic problems but rarely in real world problems, this category could be left out all together. *Economics* would not be necessary to the definition of the "whole" problem.

The point is that the final programming matrix should include the value areas that the client, programmer, and designer agree cover the important issues for a particular design problem. They may or may not be the eight HECTTEAS areas used as the beginning point in structuring the interviews.

SAMPLING PLAN (PERSONS, PLACES, TIMES)

If the project is a very simple one such as a home, it may be readily apparent who should be interviewed: the wife, husband, children, grandparents . . . anyone who would ultimately live in the house. If the project is for a large institution, it may not be so apparent who should be interviewed. The programmer should request an organizational chart and review it with the client to identify the key officers, department heads, and other persons who are likely to be knowledgeable about or have the authority to make decisions regarding facility needs. The client should also be asked about other persons in the organization who might have some special knowledge. The client should identify users and visitors who are not part of the organization, but who nevertheless must use the facility. These could be patrons, suppliers, service persons, city fire department personnel, and many others. For some projects this would include customers—the most important users of the facility (Figs. 5-17 and 5-18).

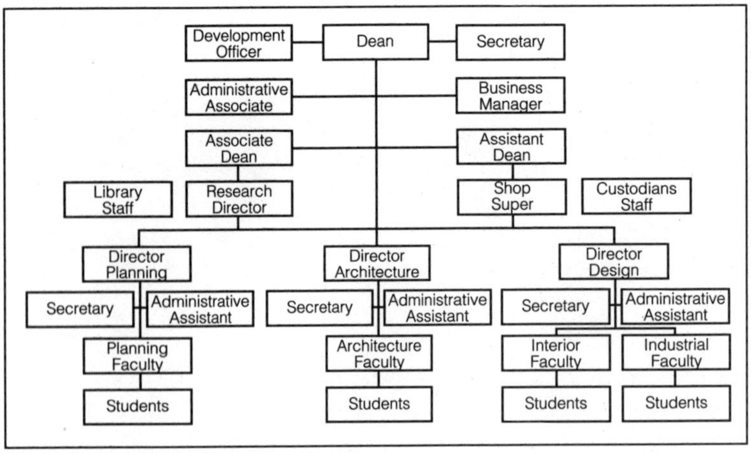

Figure 5-17 Organizational Chart.
Credit: Nancy Cole

Dean	Director of Architecture	Director of Design
Associate Dean	Administrative Assistant	Administrative Assistant
Assistant Dean	Secretary	Secretary
Administrative Associate		
Business Manager	Architecture Faculty	Interior Design Faculty
Administrative Assistant	First year students	First year students
Development Officer	Second year students	Second year students
Receptionist	Third year students	Third year students
Shop Superintendent	Fourth year students	Fourth year students
Librarian	Graduate students	Graduate students
Archivist	Graduate Assistants	Graduate Assistants
Head Custodian		
	Director of Planning	Industrial Design Faculty
University President	Administrative Assistant	First year students
University Provost	Secretary	Second year students
Advisory Council Pres.	Planning Faculty	Third year students
AIA President(s)	First year students	Fourth year students
Campus Planning Dir.	Second year students	Graduate students
Facilities Director	Third year students	Graduate Assistants
Facilities Management	Fourth year students	
	Graduate students	
	Graduate Assistants	

Figure 5-18 Architecture Interviewees.

It is not always advisable or even possible to interview only individuals. Group interviews have the advantage of time efficiency, because they cover the interests of a number of persons with presumed similar concerns at one time. If they are "primed," the persons involved can meet and discuss their concerns prior to the interview and possibly arrive at a consensus on some issues. The danger is that some persons' viewpoints may be suppressed because others might dominate the exchange, or there may be fear of some type of reprisal. The gain in efficiency in obtaining the views of larger numbers of people must be weighed against the possible cost of error of obtaining biased information. There is no way to anticipate the size of this error, but if it seems like the cost might be great, precautions must be taken. The groups might be reformed. Or any individual wishing a personal interview should be granted one.

In any case, a listing of persons to be interviewed should be prepared for each new programming commission. If the list involves a great number of individuals, it may be necessary to develop a sampling plan whereby only a representative sample of each category of user is interviewed. The objective is not to see how many people can be interviewed, but rather how few can be interviewed to obtain complete and reliable information (Figs. 5-19 and 5-20).

Figure 5-19 Individual Interview.

Figure 5-20 Small Group Interview.

When possible, interviews should take place in the client's or user's existing environment. This is especially true if the interviewee will be relocated to the new facility. This tends to make the person more comfortable in answering questions, but also makes it easier for the person to focus on his/her own architectural environment. If something is difficult to explain, the interviewee can point out characteristics of the existing facilities that are satisfactory or unsatisfactory. The one exception to this is if the interviewee's environment is simply too uncomfortable: too noisy, too cluttered, lacking in privacy, or some other circumstance that would make conducting an interview very difficult. In this case, it would be important to identify a nearby conference room or other suitable space where more favorable interviewing conditions could be found, but close enough to his/her own place for the interviewee to recall issues of importance and even to take the interviewer to the appropriate location to point out key problems or solutions.

The time of the interview is also important. Select a time when the interviewee is not being expected to produce work. Ideally, the client or someone on staff should arrange an interview schedule in which everyone to be interviewed would be prepared to undertake the interview at an appointed time. If this cannot be arranged, then the interviewer will simply have to be somewhat flexible and prepared to adjust the interview schedule as circumstances require.

LOGISTICS

The first interview should not take more than an hour. If more than one hour is required, another interview should be scheduled. There are several reasons for this. First, the primary purpose of the first diagnostic interview is to get at the key issues that are of concern to the interviewee. It should not take longer than an hour to get at a person's primary values and goals, a number of important facts and needs, and some key ideas for reorganization or design. Second, it is generally more productive to obtain a clear picture of the values and goals of the different participants before attempting to obtain all of the factual information and specific needs that might best serve the organization. Third, interviewing fatigue is a reality that should not be ignored. If too much time is spent in the interview, most people will lose interest and want to return to activities of more concern to them. In other words, it is best to use

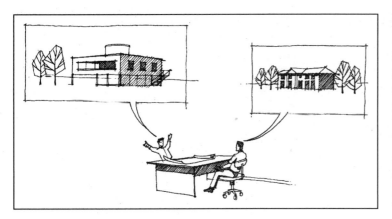

Figure 5-21 Interviewer versus Interviewee Ideas.
Credit: Carl Okazaki

the first interview to establish a framework for later, more directed research. This research may involve focused interviews to obtain more factual information, but because of time and budget considerations, may also involve a structured questioning and/or an observation period followed by group work sessions to cut down on both the time and expense of further information gathering.

Interviewing is a very effective but inefficient way of obtaining information. It is undoubtedly the most effective way to get at the owner's, client's, user's, and customer's values and goals. It generally is not an efficient way to obtain facts or to establish needs for the facility. Facts can be obtained more efficiently through literature search and review, observation, measurement, and by structured questioning procedures. Needs, on the other hand, can be established most efficiently during client/user work sessions, where several people can review the values, goals, and facts before arriving at a conclusion regarding needs. What interviewees express as needs may be personal ideals, wants, or wishes that are not necessary to satisfy the purposes of the organization. More importantly, however, the interviewer must not project what he or she thinks are the purposes of the organization onto the interviewee. The interviewer must learn to listen (Fig. 5-21).

PRIMING

It is a good idea to give each person to be interviewed some advance notice of what is to be accomplished in the interview, so he or she can think about key programming issues and requirements. This should not be a list of specific questions. Rather, it should include broader categories of information such as:

- The purposes of the organization
- How a department or position supports those purposes

- Key values or design issues

- Specific goals that could be better met with improved facilities

- Constraints that must be considered

- Important performance or design requirements.

For interviews with staff, the priming issues should include value areas identified earlier by the leadership of the organization as important areas of concern for the persons being interviewed. However, it should be made clear that the categories listed are only a stimulus to get the interviewee(s) thinking about the nature of the architectural problem and that they should feel free to bring up other areas of concern during the interview. It is also important to tell them how their response will be useful to the designer (Fig. 5-22).

To: Interviewee's Name
Fr: Programmer's Name
Re: Interview date, time, and place
Please consider the following as you prepare for the interview:

1. The purposes of [name of organization]

2. The role of your department in serving these purposes

3. Specific goals that should be accomplished by improving the facilities

4. Important conditions or constraints that must be considered

5. Specific requirements for your department

We will try to remain focused on these topics throughout the interview, because our time will be limited to one hour.

We appreciate very much your thoughtful consideration of these issues and look forward to talking with you on [date, time, place].

Figure 5-22 Priming for an Interview.

DOCUMENTATION

The purpose of the interview is, of course, to obtain information that can be kept and analyzed with other information gathered in the programming process. It is necessary, therefore, to have a systematic way of recording the information obtained for later retrieval and analysis. It is best to plan ahead for both the documentation and the analysis to be certain they can be done efficiently and in a manner that does not bias the results. This is not easy to do. Regardless of how an interview is documented, the information obtained tends to have less structure than other more quantitative information. If one is not careful in documenting the interviews, the amount of information gathered can be so vast as to be unfit for analysis within time or budgetary restrictions.

There are some general techniques for ensuring that some of the worst problems do not occur. First, it is important to develop a recording instrument that will allow easy identification of the project, interviewee, his/her position or title, interviewer, and the time and location of the interview. This information should be at the top of each sheet or card on which the data will be recorded. Second, all of the issues that the programmer wishes to cover during the interview should be listed just below in a compact, readable form so as to allow maximum room for recording the information obtained (Figs. 5-23 and 5-24).

Contrary to the normal practice for "structured" interviews, it is important not to provide a number of specific questions on each page with a limited amount of space to record each answer. This does not allow the interviewee the flexibility to approach the subject from her/his point of view, but rather forces her/him into the interviewer's framework. This can have disastrous results in terms of omitting important ideas and information that may have come out had the interviewee(s) been allowed to discuss the topic more

SMALL COMMERCIAL BUILDING INTERVIEWING SCHEDULE

Commercial Building Name and Address TROPHY DEN 707 S. MYRTLE TEMPE
Interviewee Title OWNER Interviewer Name SCOTT WALKER Date 3-31-87

Values, goals, facts, needs and ideas for a new building to house the commercial enterprise with which the person being interviewed is associated. Consider such areas as the Human, Environmental, Cultural, Technological, Temporal, Economic, and Aesthetic issues which might be important design determinants in the minds of those being interviewed.

1. NEED LARGE WORK + STORAGE ROOM SO THAT A LARGER ASSEMBLED INVENTORY COULD BE KEPT ON HAND. CURRENTLY EVERYTHING MUST BE ORDERED BY THE CUSTOMER BEFORE HAND. (NEED)
2. LOOK FOR A MORE PROMINENT LOCATION, OR AT LEAST A MORE WELL KNOWN STREET NAME. CURRENT STREET (MYRTLE) IS UNFAMILIAR TO MANY. (GOAL)
3. ALTHOUGH MOST BUISNESS IS REFERRAL AND NOT WALK-IN, WANTS MORE WINDOWS ON THE STREET FOR PEOPLE TO SEE IN. (NEED)
4. WANTS SOMETHING ABOUT THE STORE FRONT TO CATCH PEOPLES ATTENTION. (CURRENTLY THE BUILDING IS BRIGHT RED, AND HE SAID THAT WORKS GREAT. PREVIOUSLY THERE WAS A LARGE TROPHY PAINTED ON THE OUTSIDE WALL.) (GOAL)
5. HAS SPECIAL COMPUTERIZED ENGRAVERS (3) THAT NEED AREAS TO SET ON. ROUGHLY 2' SQUARE (EACH). (NEED)
6. EXPRESSED AN INTEREST IN CONSERVING ENERGY BY LIMITING WINDOWS IN SUNLIGHT ETC. (CURRENT BUILDING HAS ONE MAIN FRONT WINDOW.) (NEED)
7. SHOWROOM SPACE NEED BE NO LARGER THAN CURRENT SET-UP. (FACT)
8. SATISFIED WITH A FEW WALLS TO SHOW TROPHY'S + PLAQUES AND MAYBE A FEW STAND OR DISPLAY TABLES. (FACT)

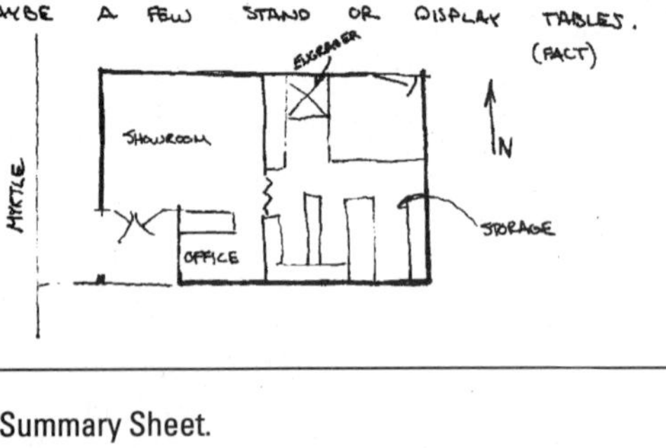

Figure 5-23 Interview Summary Sheet.

Credit: Scott Walker, 1987. *Program for Trophy Den.* Permission: School of Architecture, Arizona State University

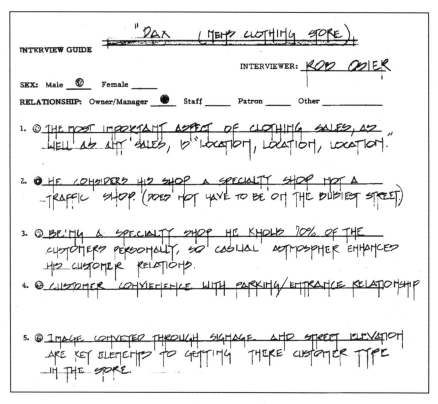

Figure 5-24 Interview Summary Sheet.

Credit: Rob Osier, 1987. *Program for DAX.* Permission: School of Architecture, Arizona State University

freely. Conversely, if the interviewer has a restrictive recording format but allows the interviewee(s) to move about freely, the interviewer is constantly required to search through the recording sheets to find the category into which the information should go. This may make it very difficult for the interviewer to concentrate on the interview, and it is distracting to the interviewee. Finally, not everything discussed needs to be recorded, only the conclusions. If care is taken in this regard, the recorded information can be both understandable and manageable to analyze.

ANALYSIS

The analysis of the results of the interviews is difficult because each respondent is likely to have brought up different values and issues. Even when considering the same value area, the interviewees may have expressed different goals, as well as facts and needs. Here, again, it is helpful to use a matrix format to organize the information obtained. The analysis could use a numerical designation for each person interviewed, beginning with the highest ranking person as number one. A check could then be placed under the number of each respondent that mentioned the particular value, goal, fact, need, or idea. These could then be tabulated to determine the relative importance of each item (Fig. 5-25).

Category	\			Respondents						
	1	2	3	4	5	6	7	8	9	TOTAL
VALUE										
1. [name]	/	/	/	0	/	/	0	0	0	5
2. [name]	/	/	0	/	/	0	0	/	/	6
3. [name]	0	/	0	/	0	0	/	0	0	3
GOAL										
1. [name]	/	/	0	/	/	0	0	0	0	4
2. [name]	/	/	/	/	/	/	0	0	/	7
3. [name]	0	/	/	/	/	0	0	0	0	4
FACT										
1. [name]	/	0	0	/	0	0	0	/	0	3
2. [name]	0	/	/	0	0	/	0	/	/	5
3. [name]	0	/	/	/	/	0	/	0	0	5
NEED										
1. [name]	/	/	0	/	/	/	0	0	0	5
2. [name]	0	/	/	/	0	0	0	0	/	4
3. [name]	0	0	/	/	0	0	0	/	0	3
IDEA										
1. [name]	0	/	0	0	/	/	0	0	0	3
2. [name]	0	/	/	0	/	0	/	0	0	4
3. [name]	0	/	0	0	0	0	0	/	0	2

Figure 5-25 Interview Coding Sheet (1).

An alternative would be to designate if the value, goal, fact, need, or idea was considered to be extremely important (3), very important (2), important (1), or not mentioned (O). The numbers could be added to get a more sophisticated idea of the relative importance of each entry (Fig. 5-26).

Note that even here the tabulation does not reflect the whole picture. In a number of cases the highest ranking person (person

Category				Respondents						
	1	2	3	4	5	6	7	8	9	TOTAL
VALUE										
1. [name]	3	3	3	1	2	3	2	1	1	19
2. [name]	2	2	1	3	3	2	1	3	3	20
3. [name]	1	2	0	2	0	1	3	2	1	12
GOAL										
1. [name]	3	2	0	3	2	1	0	0	0	11
2. [name]	2	3	3	3	3	3	2	2	3	24
3. [name]	1	2	3	2	2	0	0	2	0	12
FACT										
1. [name]	3	1	0	3	1	1	0	3	0	12
2. [name]	2	3	3	0	0	3	2	3	3	19
3. [name]	1	3	3	2	3	0	3	2	0	17
NEED										
1. [name]	3	2	0	3	2	1	0	0	0	11
2. [name]	2	3	3	3	2	2	2	2	3	22
3. [name]	0	0	3	2	2	0	0	2	0	09
IDEA										
1. [name]	0	2	0	0	2	1	0	0	0	05
2. [name]	0	3	3	0	3	0	2	0	0	11
3. [name]	0	2	0	0	0	0	0	2	0	04

Figure 5-26 Interview Coding Sheet (2).

1) has been out-voted in terms of which values, goals, facts, needs, and ideas are most to least important. Should the majority rule? Should the person(s) who will be held responsible for the success or failure of the project have more say? This must be determined in order to have a meaningful analysis of the data.

There will also likely be more value, goal, fact, need, and idea statements expressed for each category [value, goal, fact, need, idea] than the three shown on the preceding matrix. It is therefore best to use a separate coding sheet for each category and to increase the statements in each category as they occur.

It should be expected that persons with different responsibilities in an organization will have different values and goals, be aware of different facts, have different needs, and desire different resolutions to the perceived design problem. The interview coding sheets will allow the programmer to see the areas of consensus as well as

Key Values and Goals

1.	Location	Having lots of pedestrian traffic in the area is essential.
2.	Visibility	The store must be seen by passing pedestrians and vehicles.
3.	Image	It must convey its purpose with signs, displays, materials, and colors.
4.	Inviting	The entry must be convenient, ample, and protected.
5.	Display	The merchandise must be displayed under the most favorable conditions

Figure 5-27 Interviews Analysis Summary Statement.

of division. The results can be summarized on a series of lists, such as the adjoining one, or placed in a programming matrix, with controversial areas flagged so they can be considered later during client/user work sessions (Fig. 5-27).

Because the purpose of diagnostic interviewing is to obtain a feeling for the important design issues, this works quite well. But it must be understood that this is only the beginning of the information gathering. Controversial areas that might be settled through input from a larger sample of people can be followed up with additional focused interviews or a questionnaire-based survey. Questions of fact can be checked using observation techniques and by returning to the appropriate literature. Ultimately, in value-based programming, the areas of importance and difference are sorted out in a group session typically involving most of the interviewees. The results are placed before the group in an initial matrix and discussed until a decision is reached about the inclusion and importance of each item. This procedure will be discussed thoroughly in Chapter 6.

Interviewing Process

- Introduction
- Appraisal
- Diagnosis
- Recording
- Review
- Open Ending

The introduction, review, and open ending each occur just once during each interview. Appraisal, diagnosis, and recording, on the other hand, occur numerous times as the interview shifts from one topic to another.

INTRODUCTION

The introduction involves a few very important activities. First, it is important to recognize the different roles of the interviewer and interviewee(s). The interviewer should state briefly his/her name, position, what should be accomplished, and how long the interview should take. The fact that the interviewer is part of the design team is generally enough to make interviewees both cooperative and interested. Long introductions or rapport building are neither necessary nor desirable. Second, confirm that the interviewee(s) are correctly identified by name and title and record the time and location of the interview. Third, outline the categories of information that will be covered during the interview.

If the interviewee(s) have already been primed for the interview, it does no harm to reiterate the issues of concern. This will help keep the interviewee on track. The interviewer should take charge and make clear that the interview is a time for architectural business, not casual conversation or complaining about personal problems with staff or superiors:

1. Introduce the interviewer: name and position.

2. Indicate what is to be accomplished.

3. State the length of interview.

4. Confirm the interviewee's name and position.

5. Record the time and location of the interview.

6. Outline the categories of information to be covered: values, goals, facts, needs, and ideas.

The final part of the introduction is to mention the first issue, such as:

Let's begin by discussing the central purpose(s) of your organization.

In what ways will the new building help your organization meet its objectives?

APPRAISAL

This step should consume 90 to 95 percent of the time of the interview (Ripley 1980-85). It is the time spent actively listening as the interviewee(s) discuss what they know or think they know about the proposed project. It involves only minimal question asking by the interviewer. In fact, many times it is better not to ask a question at all, but rather to begin with a statement about an area on which the interviewer would like to obtain information—something like the following:

Tell me your feelings about the overall purposes of the organization and how they should influence the design of the new facility.

This is generally enough to get a response from the interviewee. The purpose of appraisal is to keep the interviewee talking about architectural issues until something is learned that could make a design difference. To do this involves a whole series of listening skills, supporting gestures, comments, and probes to keep the interviewee talking until an accurate diagnosis can be made for some aspect of the building problem. The key is to listen for what the interviewee(s) think are the important values, goals, facts, needs, and ideas to be addressed in the program while providing the necessary cues to support and encourage them to continue at this level of discourse. There are five essential skills used in the appraisal stage of an interview: acceptance, reflection, clarification, amplification, and redirection. These techniques will be discussed in detail under Interviewing Skills.

DIAGNOSIS

This is the crucial stage when the interviewer attempts to interpret and summarize the concerns of the interviewee(s). The important kernels of information about values, goals, facts, and needs, as well as ideas, that shed light on the nature of the architectural problem are distilled from what the interviewee has said. This generally involves interpretation of what has been said, stepping a little beyond the information presented, and restating it in terms that will fit into the programming matrix. This demonstrates to the interviewee(s) that the interviewer has heard them and understands and appreciates their concerns. It also allows the interviewer to bring a certain topic to closure so as to be able to go on to the next. There are two important diagnostic skills that the interviewer needs to learn: interpretation and summary. These will also be covered in detail in the Interviewing Skills section.

RECORDING

Whenever a diagnostic summary statement has been made by the interviewer and affirmed by the interviewee, it is time to record the diagnosis. This is all that is recorded! The interviewer does not try to take down everything that the interviewee says. This would be much too laborious, would interfere with the ongoing interview, and would provide a mountain of data that would be very time consuming and costly to analyze. The intent is to record only those items of information that have been identified as important by the interviewee(s).

The first attempt at a diagnostic statement may not be agreeable to the interviewee(s). If so, the interviewer must try again, and perhaps again, until the interpretation is agreed to by the interviewee(s). When several interpretations have been agreed to, such that an area of discussion is complete, then the diagnosis is summarized and recorded while the interviewee(s) watch—knowing that their concerns are having an influence on the programming process. In this way a major part of information analysis is accomplished in the field. This is an extremely important point—only the verified conclusions are recorded and carried forward into the programming process. This has the psychological advantage of showing that the interviewee's concerns have been articulated while avoiding the recording and analysis of everything that has been discussed.

The interviewee(s) will feel comfortable and can relax while the interviewer records the important information that has just been summarized, confident that their concerns have been heard. This also provides a time break when the interviewee(s) can be thinking of other areas of concern. It may be appropriate for the interviewer to indicate what the next area of discussion will be, or conversely simply to suggest that the interviewee(s) be thinking of something else to discuss.

Please be thinking about _____ while I write this down.

This type of recording works well for interviews with up to three interviewees. When the interview is with a larger group, it generally works better to record the same information, but on newsprint or graph paper set before the group on an easel, or perhaps on 5" × 7" cards taped to a wall surface, so that the entire group can confirm that what is recorded is correct. This technique, which typically involves more than one interviewer, will be outlined in Section 6.1.

Note that the use of a tape or video recorder is rarely desirable during diagnostic interviewing. Not only is this intimidating to most people, especially those who are lower in a hierarchy, but it also leaves all of the raw data to re-analyze after the interview, when the person(s) who can correct or clarify are no longer present. This can be a tremendous waste of time and result in serious misinterpretations of the interviewee's comments.

REVIEW

Review takes place toward the end of the interview. It is a verbal summary by the interviewer of everything that has been recorded.

The review of the summary verifies that the interviewee's concerns have been recorded and will be carried forward in the programming process. It often stimulates the interviewee to add other important thoughts to be recorded.

The review also serves as a time for the interviewer to determine if all of the programming categories have been discussed. If not, this can be pointed out, and the interviewing process repeated for the category(s) remaining to be covered (Fig. 5-28).

OPEN ENDING

This is the time to acknowledge the value of the information that has

---

Interviewer: Jennifer Keaton   **Position:** 2nd Year Student

Interview Time: 10:10 AM , 3/26/97   **Location:** Room 308

Intended Accomplishment: to gain insight on what you think are the central purposes of the architecture college and how the new addition of planning and landscape can help the college meet its objectives

Interviewee: Anne Nequette   **Position:**

Values/Issues: To show ourselves to the community. Reflected in building. Integrate. Express the place we inhabit. Building should respond to culture & climate, time & technology. Have balance between two groups. Take full advantage of technology.

Goals: Getting everyone under same roof. (3 colleges) Bring us together. Presence in community.

Facts: Tough for visitors to get to building. Shortage of small classrooms. Need small, quiet rooms for discussion groups. We use CCP lecture hall, but maintenance is not kept up. Architecture building behind in technology. Graduate studio blocks traffic from one side of building to another.

Needs: To be open to community. Have a presence on Speedway. Be a welcoming place in community. Need more small classrooms!

Ideas: Have identity on Speedway. Make small classrooms more functional. Open bridge (graduate studio area). Have more windows. Nice to have our own lecture hall, but not necessary.

Figure 5-28   Interview Summary.

Credit: Jennifer Keaton, 1997. *Architecture Expansion Program.* Permission: College of Architecture, The University of Arizona.

been provided and to briefly point out what will be done with it, what the balance of the programming effort will involve, when the interviewee(s) might be involved again, and to offer thanks for their help. If it appears that additional interviewing time would be productive, as with the principal officers of a corporation or other persons with a wealth of information, then it is also an appropriate time to make an appointment for another interviewing session, work session, or whatever else would be useful.

If it becomes clear early or at some point in an interview that a person has little to offer, is extremely preoccupied with a deadline, has an important phone call, has become bored with the discussion, or is otherwise unable to concentrate, the interviewer should be sensitive to this and terminate the interview. If appropriate, another interview time can be scheduled or an early open ending can occur, with the person advised when it will be possible to review the results of the interviewing session.

Interviewing Skills

- Acceptance
- Reflection
- Clarification
- Amplification
- Redirection
- Interpretation
- Summary

The successful diagnostic interview requires the development of a number of interviewing skills to be used during the appraisal and diagnosis stages of the interviewing process (Ripley 1980-85; Rae 1988; France and Kish 1995). These are crucial to the success of the interview. The first three skills (acceptance, reflection, clarification) relate to the appraisal portion of the interview and are known as "active listening" skills. The next two skills (amplification, redirection), known as "management" skills, also are part of the appraisal process and involve short verbal probes to manage the interview. The final two skills (interpretation, summary) relate to the diagnostic portion of the interview and bring closure to a portion of the interview.

ACCEPTANCE

Acceptance is both an attitude and a technique. As an attitude, it conveys respect for the worth of the interviewee. It implies that that interviewee has inherent value as a person and has important things to contribute. As a technique, it involves both verbal and non-verbal responses. The verbal responses are very simple, such as "uh-huh," "interesting," and "yes, go on." Any simple phrase implying that the interviewer is listening and what the interviewee is saying is okay will do. The technique is employed throughout the appraisal portion of the interview and is especially useful in keeping the interviewee talking.

There are also several non-verbal aspects of acceptance that are at least as important as the verbal acceptance skills, and together they are very powerful tools:

- *The facial expression and nodding of the interviewer:* The facial expression of the interviewer, including eye contact, must convey genuine interest in what is being said. A smile and vertical nod of the head when the interviewee has said something of interest encourage the person to continue speaking. If an interviewee is rather hesitant in speaking, these gestures should be both frequent and exaggerated (like an actor) to be most effective. The nodding can be of the entire upper body. While this may seem silly and contrived at first, it is very effective.

- *The tone of voice and inflection of the interviewer:* The small comments are essentially meaningless, except in the sense that they communicate that the interviewer is there and is interested. The tone and inflection of voice are important in expressing interest in what is being said.

- *The distance and posture of the interviewer:* If the interviewer sits at a comfortable distance and leans slightly forward, the interviewee will infer a friendly interest on the part of the interviewer. It will help them to feel secure in responding to the interviewer's questions. On the other hand, if the interviewer sits fairly far away, then leans back, crosses her/his legs, or looks away, disinterest will be communicated. This combination usually will prevent any interviewee from continuing with their responses.

In fact, many people are very sensitive to the semiverbal and nonverbal cues, and react to them more than to anything the interviewer has to say. The slightest negative gesture of the interviewer may be interpreted as rejection or disinterest. Yawning, crossing the legs or arms, stepping back, and looking away are all negative cues that may be interpreted as disinterest and may stop the interview cold. The down-beat "umm-hum" of the bored compared to the up beat "uh-huh" of the interested can make a world of difference in whether an interviewee decides to continue with what she/he is saying.

Indeed, the interviewer needs to learn when to use both positive and negative techniques! If the interviewee is talking too quickly or heading in the wrong direction with irrelevant banter, the interviewer should use no active listening techniques at all. This will usually slow the person down. If not, stepping or leaning back or some similar negative gesture can often stop an irrelevant line of discussion. Then a forward, open motion and simple probe can be used to get an interviewee back on track without telling them they are wandering. But if the interview is to be successful, the upbeat tone and gesture must be used frequently and the downbeat tone and gesture used only very rarely. Otherwise, the interviewer will be seen as manipulative and the interviewee may become uncooperative or guarded in what he/she says.

REFLECTION

Reflection is the restatement or paraphrasing of the interviewee's comments. It involves both content and affect. Reflecting content involves feedback of what has been said, often in a more concise manner. The following are examples of reflection of content:

Interviewee: I am really most concerned about the safety of the clients. (nod) *They simply do not look after their own best interests and often walk into equipment or throw open doors without any concern as to who might be beyond them.* (I see) *They . . . etc.*

Interviewer: Your primary concern is the safety of the clients.

or:

Interviewee: If I had my way around here, we would have a copy machine in every department, rather than one central one which always takes me away from my desk, and has people waiting when I need something done right away. (uh-huh, nod) *Besides, the machine is broken down half the time, so we must send our materials out for reproduction, which is even more inconvenient.* (I see, nod) *A copy machine in the department, even a small one, would make my job much easier and more productive.*

Interviewer: The centralized reproduction department doesn't meet your needs as well as would a departmentalized system.

Interviewee: That's right. As often as I use the copy machine, I probably need one right by my desk! (smile)

or

Interviewee: We need to communicate to those passing on the street that they are welcome to come in and shop.

Interviewer: A welcoming appearance at the street is important.

Note that the interviewer is adding nothing new to what has been said, but is distilling the essence of a more lengthy discourse.

The exact statement is not repeated. A parrot-like response should be avoided, because it can be irritating, especially if repeated several times during an interview. Crystallizing the interviewee's comments in new words shows that the interviewer is really listening to what is being said. This is generally taken to be a compliment and reacted to favorably by interviewees. It must not be done too often, however, or it will soon become stilted and old. It needs to happen only when the interviewer feels something has been said that could be important for the program.

A reflection can also be of the expressed attitude. An interview for Frank Lloyd Wright's Kaufman House (Falling Water) might go something like the following (Fig. 5-29):

Interviewee: When I visited the Kaufman house, I was really awed by the incredible site. (yes!) *Then as I approached the house I became aware that the environment was closing in on me.* (nod, uh-huh) *When I reached the entry, I was completely enclosed and in a tight space. But when the door opened, it was as if the world had opened up to me. The space was huge and I could see out over the wonderful forest beyond. I was really dumbstruck!*

Interviewer: This was an incredibly moving experience for you!

Figure 5-29 Kaufman House (Falling Water).

The reflection should be the essence of the experience. The interviewee will feel both understood and affirmed. The key is to make a fresh, new statement with the same meaning as the words of the interviewee. Do not worry about getting it just right. The client will let you know when your reflection is wrong. The fact that you are actively listening will help him/her feel comfortable about telling you more.

CLARIFICATION

If the interviewee is vague in the discussion, or talking about things with which the interviewer is unfamiliar, it may be necessary to seek some additional information to clear up the interviewer's understanding. In these cases, it is necessary for the interviewer to insert some gentle probes into the discussion.

An excellent example of clarification in an interview could be taken from an interview that the author had with a member of First Presbyterian Church, Sun City, Arizona (Fig. 5-30).

Interviewee: The problem with the south aisle is the blasted "head knockers."

Interviewer: I don't understand what you mean.

Interviewee: Oh, the "head knockers" are those confounded structural members that come down at an angle over the side aisle of the church.

Interviewer: Go on, I am still confused about the problem.

Interviewee: Well, the people going down the south aisle, if they are not really careful, may wander to the left a little and bang their heads against the wood members. (oh!) *It really hurts!* (ouch!) *Some people have even been knocked down or cut their heads!*

An alternative way of seeking clarification is simply to use the confusing term again as a question. The

Figure 5-30 Head Knockers.

interviewer might have followed up the first interviewee statement somewhat as follows:

Interviewer: Head knockers? (silence)

Interviewee: Oh yes, you wouldn't know. (nod, for sure!) *Those are those structural members that come down at an angle over the south aisle and hit people on the head when they are not watching.*

Interviewer: Hit people?

Interviewee: Well, if people don't watch where they're going, they may get too close to the member and bump their heads. It really hurts, you know! (I would think so!)

AMPLIFICATION

If you are not getting enough information on the topic using the three active listening techniques, it might be necessary to introduce some additional verbal probes to obtain the needed information. These could involve simple questions or statements such as the following for almost any issue being discussed:

Could you tell me more about that?

What else?

That's useful information. Tell me more!

An amazing tool for amplification is silence. If the interviewee needs encouragement to talk, one of the best techniques is for the interviewer to remain quiet and let the interviewee fill the silence. There are very few people who can stand to look at an interviewer for long without saying something. Once they begin to talk, the other skills can take over. The interviewer should consciously develop his/her own tolerance for silence, so as to "outlast" the interviewee and cause him/her to continue the conversation.

REDIRECTION

If an interviewee is extremely talkative, it may be necessary to remind him/her gently that time is going quickly and that unless attention is paid to the architectural issues, there will not be time enough to cover all areas that might be of concern. This might involve such statements as:

Let's get back to _____ issue.

That is really interesting, but we need to focus on _____.

It may be necessary to redirect after each recording session. This generally involves two techniques. Early in the interview when the interviewer is clearly trying to discover what is on the interviewee's agenda, these probes (not specific questions) are generally as follows:

That was excellent. Now what else is of concern to you?

Okay. Is there something else I should know?

If the interviewee is persistently too focused, particularly the client or another leader of the organization, it might be necessary to be more specific:

Now that we've covered some key problem areas of the current facilities, let's redirect our attention to plans for the future. What are some key issues there?

Later in the interview, as the interviewer considers what is needed to complete the mental matrix, the questions may be even more focused, but still not specific. These may follow an intermediate review of what has already been recorded.

Now, let's go to the second area. Where does your department fit within the overall organization? How should this affect design of the new facilities?

or

We have now covered _____, _____, _____, and _____. What about safety or budget? Are these issues of concern to you?

The amplification and redirection probes are ways to keep people talking about the areas in which the interviewer is interested. Notice that the interviewer asks very few direct questions, especially ones that can be answered yes or no. This is very important—when the interviewer asks a direct question, he/she may get only a direct answer, often a very simple one, then silence returns as the interviewee waits for the interviewer's next question. The interviewer may feel he/she must go on to the next question to fill the silence. This should be avoided by using the techniques described here. For instance, if the last question about concerns for safety or budget had been answered, "Yes," the interviewer should follow up with something like:

Uh-huh (nod and smile)

Go on! (silence)

If this is not enough, add a redirect such as:

Tell me more about safety concerns! (questioning look with brows raised, then silence)

Notice that neither of the follow-up techniques involves a question. The interviewee is first directed to a new subject area, then essentially forced to elaborate on the brief answer. After the second probe, the interviewer should remain silent until the interviewee responds.

It would, of course, be better if the final redirection did not involve a question at all.

We have covered _____, _____, _____, and _____. Now, let's talk about safety or budget.

This redirect can not be answered with a yes or no. It requires some discussion of the two issues.

INTERPRETATION

Once the interview reaches the stage where the interviewer feels that an important point has been made (i.e., a point with design implications), then it is time to offer an interpretation in terms of values, goals, facts, needs, or ideas. This usually involves going beyond what has actually been said to make an initial diagnosis of some kind. For example, in the illustration on the "head knockers," the interviewer might offer the following conclusion:

Interviewer: You're saying that you do not want any "head knockers" in the addition to the building.

Interviewee: That's true. But we also want to get rid of the head knockers in the existing building!

Note how the interviewee will clarify any incorrectness in the interpretation. This paves the way for a summary statement.

SUMMARY

After one of the issues or focus areas has been completely discussed and several diagnostic interpretations made, it is well to recapitulate, to condense, and to crystallize the essence of what the interviewee has said. This will help to close out a phase of the interview or possibly to stimulate the interviewee to bring up additional thoughts. When the topic has been covered sufficiently the interviewer says something like the following:

Interviewer: Okay, relative to the head knocker issue, we are agreed that all circulation areas in the new addition must be clear of obstructions and that the existing "head knockers" will have to be removed, even though they are important structural elements in the existing building. Is this correct?

Interviewee: Yes. Enough people have been hurt by those darn things!

The above is a summary statement for project needs. There could also be a more general summary statement after several such items had been discussed:

Interviewer: A most important value for this project is safety for the users of the building. A specific goal would be to eliminate all building hazards that threaten the health or safety of the building occupants.

The summary should be used to close out an area of discussion, but not restate every point made (Fig. 5-31).

Once stated the interviewer should say something like:

This is really important. I would like to record it while you begin to think about _____.

As you can see, diagnostic interviewing is a very powerful and effective way to get at the issues of greatest concern to the interviewee(s). Is it very difficult to master the techniques? Not for some individuals. They have learned to be active listeners on their own, usually because they are people who have a sincere interest in what other people have to say. They have already learned many of the techniques during informal conversation. They need only to develop a few of the specialized skills.

Figure 5-31 Solution to Head Knockers.

For those of us who would rather hear ourselves talk, it takes a concerted effort to learn all of the techniques and to use them. Good luck!

5.3 Diagnostic Observation

- Different than the Diagnostic Interview
- Understanding
- Types of Observation
- Observation Formats
- Photographic Methods

Although most architectural programming commissions begin with an individual or group interview session, it is not possible for most programmers or designers to understand and define the architectural problem fully or to offer appropriate design suggestions until they have personally experienced the project site and existing and/or other similar facilities. It is like a physician asking the patient about symptoms to discover important clues as to the nature of an illness, but observing the patient to find further, often more reliable, clues. Such observation includes visual inspection, listening to the heartbeat, and taking the patient's temperature, blood pressure, and so on to check for abnormalities or other problems. This analogy is appropriate for architectural programming and design. It is important to observe all areas of environment and human interaction to discover what seems to be working satisfactorily and where there are significant problems that could be eliminated by appropriate design.

This section will include discussions on the kinds of observation that are most useful, alternative levels of focus, the importance of scale and time, examples of various observation formats, and comparative levels of obtrusiveness.

Different than the Diagnostic Interview

Observation and interviewing are at opposite ends of the spectrum in the way that information is obtained. With interviewing, the client or user is treated as a subject. Each person is considered as a potential source of information, knowing something that can be communicated to the interviewer. The interest is in the interviewee's values, feelings, beliefs, and attitudes as well as their perception of the goals, facts, needs, and ideas related to the project being programmed.

When observing, on the other hand, the client or user is treated as an object. The interest is in what they do, their actual behavior. By careful observation the programmer can develop an understanding of how the activities of the client, user, or other building occupants are supported or inhibited by the architectural environment. Quite often the observer finds that what people say they do is not really true. Conversely, what one observes may not predict very well what the observed person is really thinking or feeling.

Interviewing and observation are complimentary. They serve to verify each other, to be reliability checks. Taken together they help the programmer diagnose the nature of a design problem and consequently help the designer understand what needs to be accomplished. The interviewer is more effective in obtaining an understanding of a person's strongly held beliefs, values, attitudes, ideas, and the like. Observation is more effective in obtaining an understanding of the relationships of buildings to users, of buildings to their surroundings, and of patterns within the building itself. The point of both is diagnosis, to understand the nature of the architectural design problem (Deasy and Lasswell 1985).

Understanding

Observation can be used to gain understanding of nearly all of the design issues discussed in the earlier chapters. Observation of the relationships of form and content can shed light on human, temporal, safety, and aesthetic issues. Observation of the relationships of form to context can lead to understanding of the physical, temporal, and cultural environments. Similarly, observation of the relation of the building to its own parts and the principles of its organization, like syntax in language, should clarify both technological and aesthetic values.

Sometimes it is possible to detect causal relationships, when one factor changes in response to changes in another factor. In contrast to Louis Sullivan's (1949) statement that "form follows function," Winston Churchill said, "We shape our buildings: thereafter they shape us!" (Bardens 1969). Churchill's argument was that the parliamentary system of the United Kingdom, with

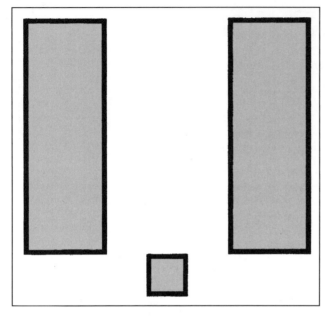

Figure 5-32 House of Commons: Plan Diagram.

Credit: Nancy Cole

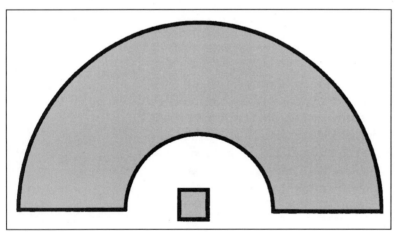

Figure 5-33 French Assembly: Plan Diagram.

Credit: Nancy Cole

the parties of the "government" and of the "loyal opposition," was at least partially the result of the equally divided sides of the halls of parliament, in essence forcing a two-party system of government. On the other hand, the aisle-less hemicycle of the French assembly allowed for many political parties and fractions of parties moving from the left to the right. It was easy for a member to make a slight move to the left or right and, thus, to change political affiliation. In the United Kingdom, on the other hand, it was very difficult politically to move across the center aisle to change dramatically from one party to the other. Churchill believed that this helped to create the stability of the British government and the instability of the French government. This was understanding resulting from a lengthy period of observation by Churchill (Figs. 5-32 and 5-33).

Similarly, the object of both interviewing and observation is to increase the programmer's understanding of the nature of the design problem. As Russell Ackoff and others have said, "An ounce of explanation is worth a ton of description" (Ackoff 1967). It is possible to gather extensive amounts of description from either interviewing or observation, but to obtain understanding takes diagnostic skills. The objective should not be to gather as much information as possible, but to observe those things that have the potential to make important design differences, to gather only as much information as is necessary to understand the problem—that is, to obtain the "ounce of explanation." A carefully planned and executed interview and observation program can do much to ensure that useful information is collected and useless information is not.

Types of Observation

- General Observation
- Walk-Through
- Space Inventory
- Trace Observation
- Behavioral Mapping
- Systematic Observation

There are several distinctly different types of observation, each of which can be included in the information gathering activities of architectural programming. The extent of use of each will vary for any particular commission.

GENERAL OBSERVATION

As human beings, and especially as architectural programmers and designers, we are constantly involved in general observation of the world around us. This observation typically is simple and unstructured. We watch the world to understand it. The more we concentrate on the relationships of various things to the architectural environment, the more we build our intuition as to how architecture can best relate to and support the human activities to be accommodated. We also gain understanding of organizational and aesthetic principles, and which materials, systems, and forms respond best to external influences. We gradually build our understanding to the point where we can easily and quickly decide how something should be designed.

But this sometimes leads us to err! The problem with general or undirected observation is bias. We look for things that interest us and ignore things that do not. We may even color our perception of how well something works by whether we think it is attractive, or perhaps come to consider something attractive if it works very well. Even so, constant alertness to the physical and aesthetic attributes of buildings and their relationships to content and context is very important for programmers and designers. We

Figure 5-34 Dislocated Parking Bumpers.

should begin observing for programming when we first step onto the client's property, and continue during interviews, when visiting similar projects, and on the first visit to the new site. This provides a sensitivity to environmental issues and a head start in knowing where to look as we begin more directed types of observation.

For example, casual observation at the University of Texas at Austin revealed that bicycles were parked almost anywhere on campus where there was a means to lock them to something, but not in university-provided racks that required locking through the wheel spokes where the spokes could easily be damaged. Could this influence how to design bicycle parking? Similarly, at The University of Arizona, it is easy to observe that the surface-mounted automobile bumpers are soon dislocated and present a very unsatisfactory appearance (Fig. 5-34).

WALK-THROUGH

A combination of observation and interviewing takes place simultaneously in the building walk-through, an information gathering technique used frequently in architectural programming. If a client has come to the point of being unable to conduct operations satisfactorily in an existing facility, they often seek out an architect to design an addition or new facility. The architect first discusses the problem with the client in a diagnostic interviewing session, often in the client's office or conference room. But as various problems are discussed, the client invariably suggests that they get up and go look at some of the problem areas. A walking observation and interviewing situation has begun. They get up together and go from place to place to observe and discuss the key issues and problems as the client sees them.

This approach to information gathering is very beneficial to the architect in that it couples the objectivity of direct observation with the subjective viewpoint of the client as to the nature of each problem. It is an excellent way to begin preparation for more systematic observation. If planned in advance, the walk-through can be very effective in generating hypotheses about the nature of the problem; for instance, if combined observation/interview forms are used. This is especially effective if arrangements can be made for each department or section leader to meet the client and programmer as they enter their area, because experiences of these persons can be shared as the walk-through proceeds. This can enhance the information obtained by involving those with more direct experience in that particular environment.

It is also important to walk through similar facilities to those for which you are programming. Arrange to visit other projects of the same or similar types and sizes to listen and observe how they work, perhaps in contrast to your client's facilities.

Recording observations and comments during a walk-through is not easy, because the walk-through usually proceeds rapidly and covers many important issues. A clipboard with a number of sheets of paper folded vertically down the center, with observations down the left side and commentary down the right side, works well, if the programmer can remember to record the room name and location prior to each observation and the commentator's name prior to each comment (Zeisel 1981).

The recorded notes should be brief, but detailed enough to remind the programmer of the entire observation and associated commentary. This is important, because the programmer may want to return to an apparent problem area later on to observe it more carefully. The walk-through notes can also serve effectively in generating a more thorough and systematic observation effort (Figs. 5-35 and 5-36).

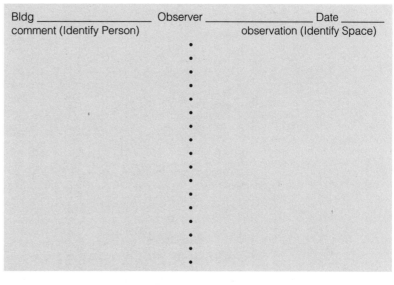

Bldg _____ Observer _____ Date _____
comment (Identify Person)   observation (Identify Space)

Figure 5-35 Walk-Through Observation Sheet.

SMALL COMMERCIAL BUILDING WALK THROUGH OBSERVATION

FACILITY PET SHOP OBSERVER PERRY VETTRAINO DATE 4/13/87

Observation (Identify space)	Comments (identify commentator)
CASHIERS DESK IS LARGE AND SEEMS FUNCTIONAL	IT IS GOOD EXCEPT WHEN FEEDING BIRDS. MESSY (MANAGER)
DISPLAYS FOR PUPPY'S ARE SMALL AND THERE DOSNT SEEM TO BE VERY MANY BREEDS	MORE KENNEL SPACE WOULD BE DESIRABLE BUT WE DONT HAVE THE ROOM.
LARGE BIRDS HAVE A LARGE NATURAL INCLOSED SETTING SEEMS TO BE THE FOCAL OF STORE. 23'X12'	LARGE BIRDS ARE VERY GOOD SELLERS THE LARGE SPACE IS GOOD THE CAN FLY INSIDE.
RABBIT KENNELS TAKE UP CONSIDERABLE SPACE ON NORTH WALL SEEM TO BE MESSY.	THE RABBITS ARE ONLY TEMPORARY. STAY UNTILL EASTER. THEY ARE VERY MESSY.
SMALL ANIMAL ROOM IS CRAMPED 6'X8' I DONT WANT TO GO IN ROOM TO SMALL	PEOPLE ARE AFRAID TO ENTER ROOM THEY JUST LOOK AT ANIMALS THROUGH GLASS.
FISH ROOM IS ADEQUATE DARK AND SEEMS TO HOLD ALOT OF DIFFERENT SPECIES	FISH ROOM IS HIDDEN FROM CASHIERS VIEW F CANT SEE WHAT ANYONE IS DOING IN THERE. AND IF THE NEED HELP THEY HAVE TO COME UP FRONT.
GROOMING ROOM IS INCORPORATED WITH THE STORAGE. SEEMS SMALL.	THE GROOMING ROOM NEEDS TO BE ALOT LARGER. MORE ROOM FOR KENNELS IN BACK AND MORE SHELVING.
INTERIOR SPACE IS BROKEN UP BY THE LARGE BIRD ROOM IN THE CENTER OF THE PLAN.	THAT ROOM HINDERS MY SIGHT TO THE BACK OF THE BLDG. IT SHOULD OF BEEN PUT UP AGAINST A WALL.

Figure 5-36 Walk-Through Observation/Interview.

Credit: Perry Vettraino, 1987. Program for Retail Pet Shop. Permission: School of Architecture, Arizona State University

SPACE INVENTORY

After the initial walk-through is complete, it is important to make arrangements to return to the walk-through area to review the information obtained and then to make an inventory of the space, furnishings, and equipment. It is best to do this after a typical day, but before janitors or maintenance personnel have come in, so you can observe where objects are actually used. If available, take appropriately scaled plans and elevations of the area on which to sketch furnishing and equipment arrangements. If plans and elevations are not available, take a clipboard to obtain the same information. It is also important to have a tape measure to obtain sizes of objects and distances between the objects and the surrounding walls, and to take a camera to provide photo documentation of the space. Polaroid or digital cameras are excellent for this purpose, because you can determine if you obtained a satisfactory picture before leaving the space.

Space inventory categories include:

1. Dimensioned plan of space

2. Furnishings and equipment shown to scale on plan

3. Annotated elevations or perspective views (photographs or sketches)

4. Key to trace evidence of use and misuse of the space

5. Identification of key issues, good solutions, and problem areas

The site developed space inventory sheets will vary according to the nature of the space and the information available about it. The adjoining are typical student developed on-site space inventory sheets (Fig. 5-37). Similar on-site space inventory sheets by the author can be found in Appendix A-2.

The initial sheets can be refined to make a more systematic and handsome presentation of the space inventory information (Fig. 5-38).

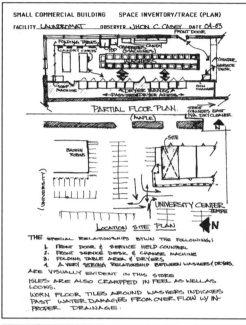

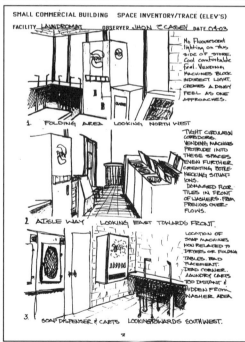

Figure 5-37 On-Site Space Inventory Sheets.

Credit: Jhon C. Casey, 1987. *Coin Operated Laundry Program.*
Permission: School of Architecture, Arizona State University

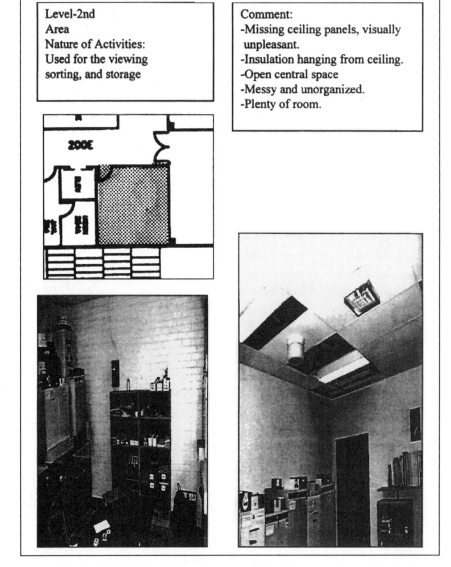

Level-2nd
Area
Nature of Activities:
Used for the viewing
sorting, and storage

Comment:
-Missing ceiling panels, visually
 unpleasant.
-Insulation hanging from ceiling.
-Open central space
-Messy and unorganized.
-Plenty of room.

Figure 5-38 Finished Space Inventory Sheet.

Credit: Jennifer Keaton and Erik Peterson, 1997. Section 1. Second Year Design Studio. *Architecture Expansion Program.* College of Architecture, The University of Arizona

Professional programming firms will often develop space inventory forms to expedite information gathering and to ensure that what will be needed later is included (Fig. 5-39).

The space inventory can be an important adjunct to other information gathering techniques. It is rarely covered in programming and research texts, perhaps because its need is not so obvious

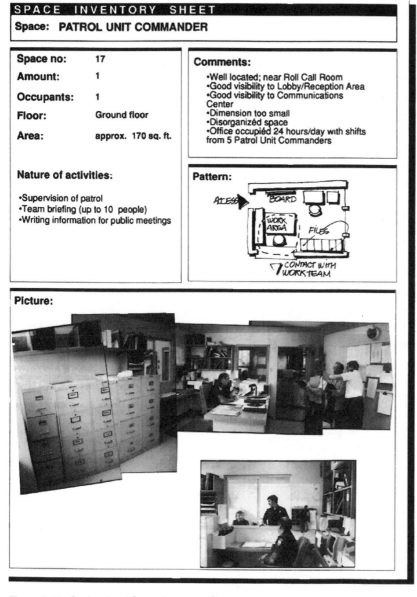

SPACE INVENTORY SHEET

Space: PATROL UNIT COMMANDER

Space no: 17	**Comments:**
Amount: 1	•Well located; near Roll Call Room
Occupants: 1	•Good visibility to Lobby/Reception Area •Good visibility to Communications Center
Floor: Ground floor	•Dimension too small •Disorganized space
Area: approx. 170 sq. ft.	•Office occupied 24 hours/day with shifts from 5 Patrol Unit Commanders

Nature of activities:

•Supervision of patrol
•Team briefing (up to 10 people)
•Writing information for public meetings

Pattern:

Picture:

Figure 5-39 Professional Space Inventory Sheet.

Credit: Raymond Bertrand (1993). Permission: Wolfgang F. E. Preiser

and the methodology appears to be so simple. Yet, it is often an important step in developing an architectural program. Simply put, the space inventory involves the physical measurement, photographic documentation, listing, and counting of the materials, equipment, and furniture in the interior and exterior spaces of the client's existing building(s) that will be affected by the plans for expansion or relocation. It can also involve similar documentation of other comparable facilities thought to be more adequate than those currently occupied.

This type of inventory serves as a kind of checklist for the programmer to make certain that nothing is forgotten in the new facility. It also serves as the primary basis for the client and users to estimate what will be needed to serve them in the new facility. Using the information from the inventory, they are able to see and easily understand what they currently have, compare it with similar facilities, and then project what they will need for the new facility.

TRACE OBSERVATION

Observation of physical traces is a very good and unobtrusive way of gathering information about how an existing facility has been used and abused, and can often be accomplished as an adjunct to the space inventory effort. It involves observation of evidence left behind by users (Zeisel 1981).

Throughout the diagnostic observation process, the observer should not only be aware of the interactions of people and their environment in an overall or global sense, but should also look carefully to see if clues about the human and environment interaction have been left by previous users. Signs of rearrangement or remodeling can be important to diagnosis. What areas of the building have already been subjected to a number of changes in use? It may be likely that such areas will continue to be rearranged and modified given their previous history. If chairs or tables are located in different places each time a room is visited, it may indicate that the room is used for more purposes than those indicated in an interview with the client. Signs in unusual places may indicate some inadequacy in the original design. For example, door signs such as "Do Not Open Quickly" or "Door Swings Out," or pavement markings as shown in Fig. 5-40, may indicate a major problem in door location.

Wear and tear on furnishings, floor surfaces, wall surfaces, and the like are good indicators of use, providing excellent clues as to how the architect could

Figure 5-40 Door Swinging into a Walkway.

improve design. Are there marks on the walls where the backs of chairs have rubbed against them? Perhaps a wainscot or a thicker base or base shoe is needed to keep the chair backs away from the wall, or another chair should be selected for the new building. Signs of pedestrian traffic, such as worn spots and smudge marks on carpets, can show where and how they have been used. Broken light fixtures and windows or spray paint on walls may indicate areas of high vandalism where concerns for building security should not be underestimated. Freezing and thawing can cause very noticeable abrasion on brick faces, especially at exposed edges and corners (Fig. 5-41).

Figure 5-41 Abrasion on Masonry Steps.

Abrasion also frequently occurs because of traffic in areas not intended for heavy use. Bicyclists on a university campus, for instance, like to go everywhere that pedestrians go. If adequate provisions are not made, they will often make trails through grassed or garden areas to reach their destinations (Fig. 5-42).

Figure 5-42 Bicycle Ramp by Stairs.

There may also be examples of accretion rather than abrasion. This frequently happens on doors where inadequate space has been provided to post notices (Fig. 5-43).

However, as shown on the next page, if a conveniently located bulletin board is covered by a locked glass door, there are few people who will get permission to have their notices posted there. They will simply post them on the door (Fig. 5-44)!

Look for locations where the paper piles up at the end of the day, both on the desk and in the wastebasket. Are there adequate work surfaces, filing spaces, and trash receptacles? Examine an architect's environment after a major charrette! Look in the rest rooms. Are there redundant paper dispensers and waste receptacles? This may

Figure 5-43 Accumulation of Notices.

Figure 5-44 Notices in Convenient Location.

Figure 5-45 Paper Dispensers and Receptacles.

Figure 5-46 Debris at Trash Enclosure.

indicate the inadvisability of providing built-in containers when the owner is going to hire a supply firm to put in their own system (Fig. 5-45). It would be better to save the money for use elsewhere.

Are there similar problems outside? Is there an accumulation of debris at the trash enclosures (Fig. 5-46)?

Or what if the architect forgot to include a mailbox in a design? One could show up just outside of the school door (Fig. 5-47).

Unlike the more descriptive space inventory, the purpose of trace observation is to discover relationships explaining how people behave in and use spaces. Just as the good physician does with a patient, it is necessary to look very closely to make the correct diagnosis, so proper treatment or intervention can be prescribed. For example, in the programming for the College of Architecture and Environmental Design at Arizona State University, the programmers documented numerous situations that indicated problems with existing spaces. The faculty offices were found to be much too small to accommodate all of the storage space needed for books and oversized documents and models (Fig. 5-48). As a result, the program called for larger offices and better provisions for storing oversize materials.

The accumulation of furnishings and equipment near a required exit from the Architecture Library at The University of Arizona indicates a need for more space and attention to safety issues (Fig. 5-49).

Similarly, heavy barricading and bolting of the rear exit door of a gun shop is probably a very good indicator that there are serious problems with burglary and theft that must be dealt with during design (Fig. 5-50).

Figure 5-47 Mailbox near School Entry.

Figure 5-49 Library Exit Area.

Figure 5-48 Typical Faculty Office.

Credit: Greg Daugherty, Marianne Dziki, and Leanne Streit, 1986. Permission: School of Architecture, Arizona State University

Figure 5-50 Rear Door of Gun Shop.

Credit: Ethan Hine, 1987. *Gun Shop Program.* Permission: School of Architecture, Arizona State University

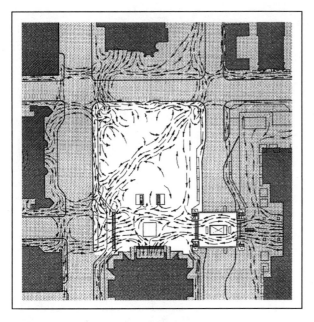

Figure 5-51 Solar Oasis Pedestrian Circulation.

Credit: Richard Larry Medlin and NBBJ/Gresham Larson, 1988. *Program for the Arizona Solar Oasis*, Phoenix, Arizona. Permission: Richard Larry Medlin

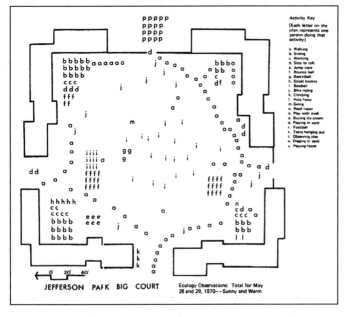

Figure 5-52 Jefferson Park Behavioral Map.

Credit: Hester, Randolph T. Jr. 1975. *Neighborhood Space*. Stroudsburg, PA: Dowden, Hutchinson & Ross Inc. Permission: Randolph T. Hester Jr.

BEHAVIORAL MAPPING

Behavioral mapping is a technique developed by social scientists to obtain a better understanding of how people use various public spaces (Ittelson et al. 1970; Cook and Miles 1978). It typically involves the use of a map or plan of the space or place being studied. The observer takes this map to the site and records where people are located and codes what they are doing. This is done throughout an entire time cycle, often at different times of year, in order to get a good idea of how the space or place is used. The frequency counts can reveal heavily used areas, seldom used areas, paths of travel, places of conversation, and the like and, hence, can be most helpful to the programmer in coming to an understanding of existing behavior in a space. This is of value when remodeling or adding to an existing space. It is also of value in coming to a general understanding of how people use space. Pedestrian patterns are shown in the following illustration from the programming study for the Solar Oasis in Phoenix, Arizona (Fig. 5-51).

A more specific behavioral map showing a variety of activities occurring in an urban park was conducted by Randolph T. Hester Jr. (1975) in the Big Court of Jefferson Park (Fig. 5-52).

An excellent example of such mapping is shown in the film *The Social Life of Small Urban Spaces* by William Whyte (1988). In this study, Whyte discovered that the key elements in designing a successful urban space included: sun(light), access to street, seating, water, trees, and food vendors as important elements, and a combination called "triangulation" as key to attracting users. Studies by Downs, Stea, and others (Downs and Stea 1973) have revealed similar insights for both outdoor and indoor environments.

A simplified version of the same technique can be used in mapping existing circulation systems when programming for the expansion of existing facilities. It is also useful in studying places of particular congestion or importance, such as the nursing station in a hospital or the cooking and serving areas of restaurants, in order to determine the space or arrangements required to relieve traffic congestion or especially inconvenient movement in these kinds of situations (Fig. 5-53).

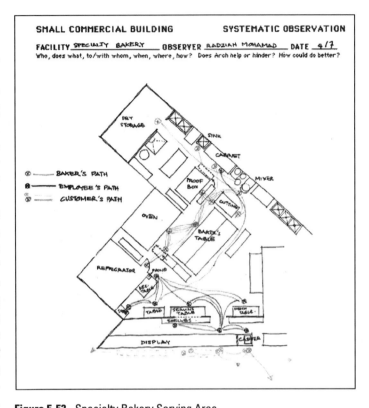

Figure 5-53 Specialty Bakery Serving Area.

Credit: Radziah Mohamad, 1987. *Specialty Bakery Program.* Permission: School of Architecture, Arizona State University

SYSTEMATIC OBSERVATION

- Problem Oriented
- Multiple Focuses
- Time/Scale Sampling
- Statistical Analysis

Systematic observation as used in programming differs from other types of observation in several respects. First, it is planned or structured to obtain specific information about previously identified problems in the relationships between buildings and their human content, their physical surroundings, and elements of the buildings themselves. Second, it is structured to minimize bias and preconceptions by making certain that the observer takes into consideration all factors that may be influencing a particular environmental situation. It is an important supplement to the other forms of observation when some question about conflicting findings needs to be resolved.

• *Problem Oriented:* In programming, systematic observation should be conducted only to answer specific questions raised or to test specific hypotheses developed from the results of the other five forms of observation, the initial interviews, and the literature search and review activities. If the interviews conflict with the observations relative to how some space is used, it may be advisable to set up a specific study to discover the actual behavior in a space.

For instance, if doctors and nurses have different perceptions of where they spend their time and on what kind of hospital activities, it may be possible to set up a situation in which the doctors and nurses can be observed systematically over a period of time to confirm or disprove the other findings. This would be important, of course, only if the results could make a design difference and impact on some important human values. In the above example, this could involve the time it takes the doctor or nurse to get to a patient who suddenly is discovered to be in a life threatening situation—the survival value comes into play. How far can the nursing station or the doctor's parking area be from a patient room and still maintain an acceptable margin of safety? Functional values could also be involved. How many times can nurses go between the nursing station and a distant patient's room in an eight-hour shift without compromising their effectiveness due to exhaustion?

The problem to be studied should be one that is considered important relative to the design of the facilities to be programmed and for which the previous evidence regarding requirements is inconclusive.

• *Multiple Focuses:* In order to ensure that all parts of the particular problem are considered, it is usually wise to alternate the focus of observation between people, places, tasks, and objects.

　- *People* If people are the primary focus, the observation activity may involve the tracking of people to see what they do during the course of a workday. This would include following them about and recording what they do, with whom they interact, how and when certain interactions take place, what furnishings or equipment support the interaction, and on. This was accomplished very well by Roslyn Lindheim in a hospital study titled "Putting Research to Work" (Lindheim 1966). It allowed her to diagnose which areas in a hospital had essential relationships with each other (Fig. 5-54)

- *Places* If places, or settings, are to be the focus, then the observation will involve staying in one place and noting all of the people who use the place, why they use it, when they use it, whether they do it singly or in groups, and again what furnishings or equipment tend to support the interaction (Barker 1968). For example, careful observation of multiple patient rooms in special care facilities for the elderly has led researchers to the conclusion that a single person will occupy the room (Fig. 5-55), and that the others will be absent as often as possible (Pastalan and Carson 1970).

- *Tasks* A focus on tasks would result when someone has identified the importance of a particular activity, and the designer must know how many and what kinds of people are involved in the activity, where and when it takes place, and the props that are used to support it (Moore and Golledge 1976).

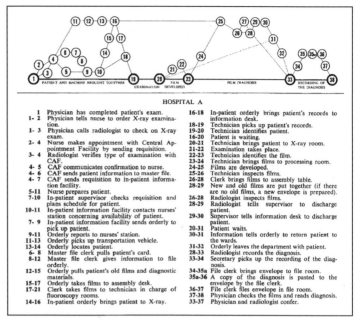

HOSPITAL A

1	Physician has completed patient's exam.	16-18	In-patient orderly brings patient's records to information desk.
1- 2	Physician tells nurse to order X-ray examination.	18-19	Technician picks up patient's records.
1- 3	Physician calls radiologist to check on X-ray exam.	19-20	Technician identifies patient.
2- 4	Nurse makes appointment with Central Appointment Facility by sending requisition.	16-20	Patient is waiting.
		20-21	Technician brings patient to X-ray room.
3- 4	Radiologist verifies type of examination with CAF.	21-22	Examination takes place.
		22-23	Technician identifies the film.
4- 5	CAF communicates confirmation to nurse.	23-24	Technician brings films to processing room.
4- 6	CAF sends patient information to master file.	24-25	Films are developed.
4- 7	CAF sends requisition to in-patient information facility.	25-26	Technician inspects films.
		26-28	Clerk brings films to assembly table.
5-11	Nurse prepares patient.	28-29	New and old films are put together (if there are no old films, a new envelope is prepared).
7-10	In-patient supervisor checks requisition and plans schedule for patient.		
10-11	In-patient information facility contacts nurses' station concerning availability of patient.	26-28	Radiologist inspects films.
		28-29	Radiologist tells supervisor to discharge patient.
7- 9	In-patient information facility sends orderly to pick up patient.	29-30	Supervisor tells information desk to discharge patient.
9-11	Orderly reports to nurses' station.	20-31	Patient waits.
11-13	Orderly picks up transportation vehicle.	30-31	Information tells orderly to return patient to the wards.
13-14	Orderly locates patient.		
6- 8	Master file clerk pulls patient's card.	31-32	Orderly leaves the department with patient.
8-12	Master file clerk gives information to file orderly.	28-33	Radiologist records the diagnosis.
		33-34	Secretary picks up the recording of the diagnosis.
12-15	Orderly pulls patient's old films and diagnostic materials.	34-35a	File clerk brings envelope to file room.
		35a-36	A copy of the diagnosis is pasted to the envelope by the file clerk.
15-17	Orderly takes films to assembly desk.		
17-21	Clerk takes films to technician in charge of fluoroscopy rooms.	36-37	File clerk files envelope in file room.
		37-38	Physician checks the films and reads diagnosis.
14-16	In-patient orderly brings patient to X-ray.	33-37	Physician and radiologist confer.

Figure 5-54 Uncoupling Spatial Systems.

Credit: Lindheim, Roslyn, 1966. *Putting Research to Work*. AIA Journal. February: 46–53. Reprinted with permission from ARCHITECTURE, February, Copyright 1966, BPI Communications, Inc.

Figure 5-55 Multiple Patient Room.

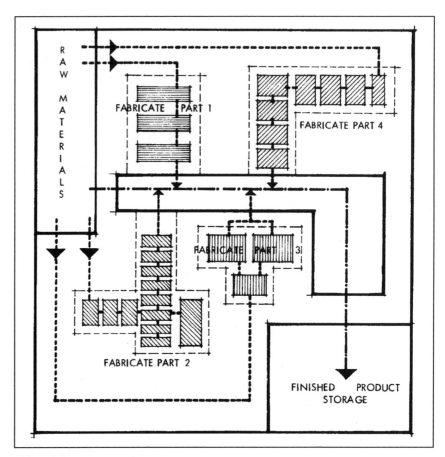

Figure 5-56 Layout of Manufacturing Facility.

Credit: Mostafa Shalaby, 1968. Dissertion: Optimum Layout of Manufacturing Facilities, The University of Pennsylvania. Permission: Mostafa Shalaby.

- *Objects* Focus on objects is crucial if the observer is to comprehend such things as an assembly line cycle. An understanding of what happens to a particular manufactured item, from the raw material entering the facility to the finished product leaving the facility, could effectively determine the optimal spatial layout of a manufacturing plant (Fig. 5-56).

• *Time/Scale Sampling:* It may not be readily apparent, but it is true that we all live in different worlds. For almost any individual, the world changes day by day. For various individuals, the scale of environmental focus can be drastically different. One person may visit a place and concentrate on how the site impacts the buildings placed upon it; another person may visit the same place and concentrate on how the buildings impact the surrounding community; still another person may concentrate on the views from the site. In systematic observation it is important to vary the scale of observation to ensure that a complete understanding of the design problem will result.

Scale is particularly important as we consider the various phases of programming. If the programming is for master planning, attention to the site and its surroundings is most important. It would be necessary to establish interrelationships of various buildings and other features both on and off the site. If, on the other hand, the intent is to produce a program for schematic design of a particular building after the master plan has been established, then the focus will be narrower and relate to the content of the building to be designed as well as to its interaction with the immediate external environment. For purposes of design development, the focus will be almost exclusively on details, materials, equipment, and furnishings to see how they are used and how they hold up. In all cases, it is important to sample from at least the next higher and next lower scales to obtain a better understanding of the nature of the design problem.

The various scales of place focus include:

- Region
- Community
- District
- Neighborhood
- Site Surroundings
- Site
- Buildings
- Zones within Buildings
- Rooms
- Spaces within Rooms

Time of observation is also of considerable importance. What a person observes at one time of the day, week, month, or year may have little to do with what would be seen at another time. In the life of most businesses, Monday morning is a time of considerable interaction and confusion. In the life of a church, nothing happens early Monday morning, because the big occasion was the day before. The observer must carefully sample from the times when it will be most fruitful to observe. This can be based on what the clients and users have said about various periods of use or by random or systematic sampling of all possibilities. In programming, however, because of the typical lack of time and money to conduct a study, it is usually necessary to concentrate on what the client/users consider to be the crucial times. For any kind of retail business, this might include the peak periods, the slow times, and the typical or average times. In a restaurant, the crucial times would be similar; however, these periods might occur and be rather different three times each day at meal times.

However accomplished, systematic observation must cover the complete cycle or cycles of use to obtain an accurate understanding for program diagnosis. Such studies could have a crucial impact on the size of the facility, possibilities for outside overflow, for one-person staffing at slow periods, or other such factors.

It may also be useful to understand the frequency and duration of use. What are the peak periods of use? How frequently do they occur? How long do they last? These are important questions when it comes to planning ingress and egress from a site. Will a traffic light be required? How much backup space will be needed to minimize congestion and accidents? The same is true for interiors. How much room is required at a nursing station in a home for the elderly? (Fig. 5-57) If observation of several such facilities reveals that these places are typically congested at certain times of the day because many of the wheelchair bound and other elderly gather to observe the activity of the nurses, even when plans of the building suggest that the residents should be elsewhere, the programmer needs to understand why this is the case. The client may wish to enlarge the area around the station or to locate a dayroom adjacent to it in or-

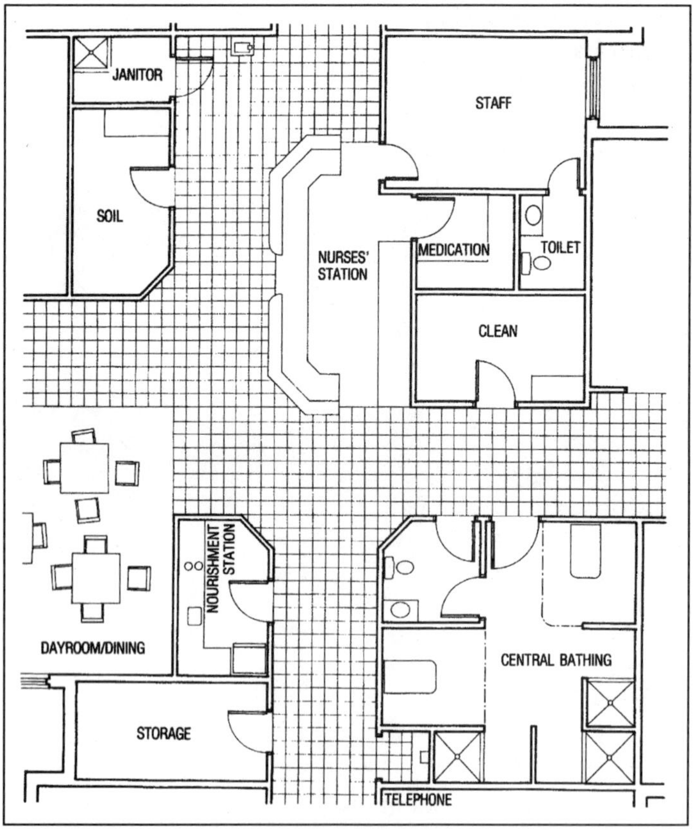

Figure 5-57 Nursing Station and Dayroom.

Credit: (AIA Task Force on Aging 1985), 113. Permission: American Institute of Architects

der to accommodate this typically unprogrammed activity, rather than allowing it to interfere with important nursing functions (AIA Task Force on Aging 1985).

Duration of an activity may be of equal importance. If one major activity overlaps with another major activity, it could create serious spatial problems. For instance, if people are coming to park for one event before people attending another event have departed, there may be a considerably increased need for parking for the few minutes of overlap. How is this accounted for in the existing facilities or other exemplary facilities? If a facility is only used periodically or seasonally, problems of shutdown and startup may be very important. Seasonal variation of activities may be pronounced, even for a continuously operating facility. These variations should be accounted for, even if the period for observation must be confined to only one season. It may require further literature search and/or interviewing to fill in the needed information.

These are all important issues that could have major impacts on design requirements. Systematic observation, coupled with trace observation and archival research for times or events that cannot easily be observed, can prove most useful in uncovering important information that can make a design difference.

• *Statistical Analysis:* Systematic observation should be organized to allow for easy analysis when information gathering is complete. If the expected cost of error is not great, this may involve the simple counting of events and other descriptive statistics to show the frequency, magnitude, and distribution of various events. The results of such counting and averaging can be shown in histograms, pie charts, graphs, and tables (Figs. 5-58 through 5-61). The development of such statistics is discussed in detail in a number of books written by social and behavioral scientists (Siegel 1956; Blalock 1960; Rosenbaum 1979; Weisberg et al. 1996).

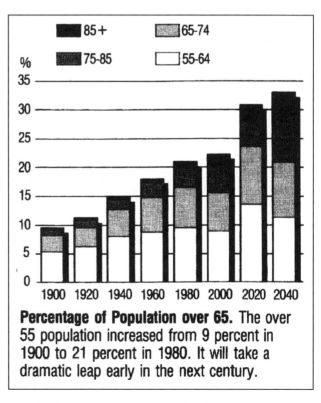

Percentage of Population over 65. The over 55 population increased from 9 percent in 1900 to 21 percent in 1980. It will take a dramatic leap early in the next century.

Figure 5-58 Histogram: Percent over Age 65.

Credit: (AIA Task Force on Aging 1985), 2. Permission: American Institute of Architects

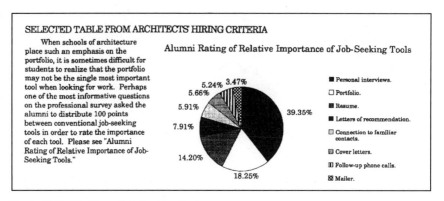

Figure 5-59   Pie Chart: Job-Seeking Tools.

Credit: Daniela Fruenfelder, 1993. Master's Thesis, Decoding Architect's Hiring Criteria and Students' Perceptions of the Job-Seeking Process, in Communication, College of Architecture, The University of Arizona, 21 July 1993, 2. College of Architecture, The University of Arizona

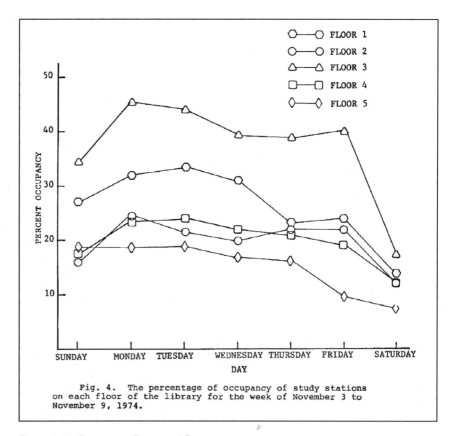

Figure 5-60   Frequency: Percent of Occupancy.

Credit: Robert Cass, Fred Marks, and Steve Sedor, 1974. *Research Study on Use of Existing and Future Space in Hayden Library*. Permission: School of Architecture, Arizona State University

QUESTIONNAIRE SUMMARY – PART 1	CHANDLER TEACHERS	FIGURE 12	
No.	QUESTION	Windowed	Windowless
1	I like to be in this room.	Pos	Pos
2	I find it easy to teach in this room.	Pos	Pos
3	I like to spend the entire day in this room.	Neutral	Pos
4	This room gets too cold.	Pos	Neutral
5	This room gets too hot.	Neutral	Pos
6	This room doesn't get enough ventilation.	Pos	Neutral
7	It's too bright in this room.	Pos	Pos
8	It gets too noisy in this room.	Neutral	Pos
9	I feel confined in this room.	Pos	Pos
10	There isn't enough privacy in this room.	Pos	Pos
11	This room makes me feel tired.	Pos	Pos
12	This room is depressing.	Pos	Pos
13	The students are easily distracted in this room.	Pos	Pos
14	The students are anxious to get outside.	Neutral	Pos
15	This room needs more tack space.	Pos	Pos
16	I feel that I don't have control over temperature conditions in this room.	Pos	Neg
17	I feel secure leaving valuables in my room overnight.	Neutral	Neutral
18	I like the way this building looks.	Pos	Pos

Figure 5-61 Table: Windowed versus Windowless.

Credit: Patricia Partridge, Tony Rodriguez, Barbara Sacks with Professor Robert Hershberger, Advisor, 1983. *Windowed vs Windowless Schools: An Analysis of Economy Behavioral and Academic Effectiveness.* Post Occupancy Evaluation. Permission: School of Architecture, Arizona State University

If the costs of error are likely to be very high, as with a frequently repeated element such as the patient room in a hospital, a space station environment, or even a building to be repeated many times across the country, then the client may be satisfied with nothing less than a study in which the probability of an error occurring might be as little as .001 percent. In other words, this would

Bldg. _____ Rm. _____ Date _____

Who (principal characters)

Does What (activity, task)

To/With Whom (others)

How (with what objects)

Where (place, setting)

When (time, frequency, duration)

Does architecture help or hinder? Why?

Could it be better designed? How?

Figure 5-62 Observation Form #1.

involve setting up an experimental or quasi-experimental situation involving significance tests using inferential statistics. In such cases, the beginning programmer would be advised to associate with an environmental scientist familiar with the conduct of such studies to make certain that the probability of an event can be predicted accurately. The development of such studies is the subject of complete textbooks and will not be covered here (Bechtel et al. 1987).

Observation Formats

A number of different observation formats have been developed for systematic observation studies (Zeisel 1981). One approach is to take the various focus categories and develop a holistic information listing (Fig. 5-62) to be certain that a complete observation has been taken and recorded (Lindheim 1966).

The first six categories are capable of observation and are descriptive in nature. The final two categories are the subjective interpretation and diagnosis by the observer, as well as suggestions or prescriptions by the client for possible treatments or interventions that would improve the situation. These categories help to develop understanding of the relationships between human activities and the architectural environment. The description alone means little unless it results in an accurate diagnosis of the problem, so that an appropriate remedy can be proposed.

Some observers are comfortable with such a structured matrix. Others prefer to keep the eight categories in their heads or only at the top of the first recording sheet, to allow for more freedom of response and recording in each of the focus categories. The remainder of the sheet can remain blank for recording a series of observations, taking as much space as needed, including additional pages. The important thing to remember is to cover all of the focus categories listed at the top of the sheet. It is hard to tell when observing what information will prove to be useful during analysis (Fig. 5-63).

Another format used in the walk-through observation and by experienced observers for systematic observation involves creasing the observation sheet near the center and reserving the left side for observations and the right side for commentary, as described on page 251.

In any format, it is important to be clear about what is actually observed and what is inferred from it. The two types of information should not be mixed, so someone else can make sense of the information when it comes time to incorporate it into the program. In other words, observed facts and inferred ideas or concepts should be kept distinct, so that a person interpreting the results does not mistake a fact for an idea, or vice versa.

Depending on the specificity of the research task, it might be necessary to develop a recording format specifically for the observation task. For example, this could include the floor plan of an area to be used for behavioral mapping. It could also involve a series of specific questions or required observations in which a simple count is taken. Such forms must be developed in response to the observation to be undertaken. In any case, the observer should become very familiar with the observation problem(s) to be able to make critical observations, and not to collect a great deal of useless data. In programming, the emphasis should be on gathering only the information necessary to develop an understanding of the design problem, rather than gathering as much information as possible.

Figure 5-63 Observation Form #2.

Photographic Methods

A number of social scientists (Collier 1967) and programmers (Davis and Ayers 1975) are strong advocates of photographic documentation as a primary observation method. There is no substitute for such documentation when it comes to the space inventory. Photographs of rooms showing all of the principal elevations, the furnishings within the room, the type and spacing of light fixtures, and the like are invaluable as the programmer begins work on space requirement sheets for the new or expanded facility. It is impossible to remember all of the details of the existing spaces unless they have been documented. Photographs are undoubtedly the most accurate and efficient way to document everything in a space.

Various programmers advocate different film types for this job. Polaroid shots have the advantage of letting you know immediately if you have recorded the needed information and allow coding of room, orientation, and special commentary as you proceed. It is, however, quite tedious to use this procedure on large projects. An alternative for the competent photographer is to use high-speed color print film and either a log or previously prepared plan of the building on which to show the location of each shot by number. Additional information such as room name, furnishing, or ceiling heights can also be recorded in any of these formats. Digital cameras are becoming popular and have the advantage of direct transfer into the program documents. It is rather easy to document trace evidence using any of these methods. Photographic images make very convincing evidence of findings when included as part of a programming report (Fig. 5-64).

Photographic techniques for systematic observation are much more complicated

Display of gum as well as last minute items are by cash registers. Signage of Pharmacy easily readible. Adequate lighting A lot of visual merchandise.

3. VIEW OF CASHIER CHECK OUT - FACING NORTH

Areas appear to be cluttered with merchandise Better organization of merchandise would be helpful to define aisles

4. View of sundries aisle and Front of Store.

Figure 5-64 Annotated Photograph: Drug Store.

Credit: Marcia Morris, 1987. *Drug Store Program*. Permission: School of Architecture, Arizona State University

and expensive (Webb 1981). They often involve time-lapse photography to cover the full spectrum of use of a facility. As with other systematic methods, this approach is most fruitful when a hypothesis has been generated. It is important to generate actual counts to determine if what was observed at a certain time was really characteristic of a total situation. This allows repeated observation of the same place, so that information missed the first time can be picked up later. The approach is especially valuable when some important architectural feature, such an escalator or conveyor, is going to be used in a major public building and there is concern about how well existing ones work.

5.4 Questionnaires and Surveys

- Relationship to Other Methods
- When to Use the Questionnaire
- Planning Is Essential
- Understanding
- Questionnaire Preparation
- Steps to Prepare a Questionnaire
- Logical Order of a Questionnaire
- Question Types
- Sampling
- Bias
- The Survey
- Data Analysis
- Cost of Error

A questionnaire is an instrument that employs a predetermined set of questions to be answered by a respondent. A survey is the administration of the questionnaire to a group of respondents. It can be administered by an interviewer who records the responses, or given to the respondents to answer at their convenience (Blalock 1960; Berdie et al. 1986; Weisberg et al. 1996).

Relationship to Other Methods

The questionnaire/survey is different from diagnostic interviewing, primarily because it relies on pre-established questions, which each respondent is asked to answer. The questions typically are closed, that is, having a limited rather than an open-ended response format. The respondent is required to follow both the line of questioning and the line of answering predetermined by the persons preparing the questionnaire. Unlike observation, both interviews and questionnaires treat the respondent as a subject rather than as an object. They are also more intrusive than observation in that they require the respondent's full attention. The self-administered questionnaire is somewhat less intrusive than the interview, because the respondents can answer the questions at their at a time and place of their own choosing. However, the questionnaire requires respondents to answer questions developed by the programmer in the order presented—to accept the programmer's agenda rather than discussing areas of greatest personal interest. As a result, the diagnostic interview tends to be more effective in discovering issues of importance to the respondent, while the questionnaire is usually more effective in obtaining factual information about specific facility and equipment needs.

The questionnaire can also be very effective in determining whether or not most respondents share the viewpoints of those initially interviewed. Like the interview, and unlike observation, the questionnaire can be used to get at why people do what they do, what they think works well or poorly, and how they think something might be done better—but only within the limits of the alternatives actually provided in the questions. Just how effective the questionnaire is in this respect depends on the proficiency of the programmer in preparing, administering, and analyzing the results of the questionnaire.

When to Use the Questionnaire

A questionnaire should not be used in architectural programming until after literature review, diagnostic interviewing, and diagnostic observation have been completed. Even then, it should be used only if it would be more expensive to obtain additional needed information by continuing with the other information gathering techniques. For most small- to medium-sized programming commissions this is rarely the case. It is usually quicker and less expensive simply to go back and ask someone for additional information or to count or measure something to obtain the missing data.

The time and effort to prepare, administer, and analyze a major questionnaire intended to obtain information about respondent values, goals, needs, and ideas is warranted only when programming facilities for very large or complex organizations. On those occasions, it is advisable to employ a survey specialist to assist in developing and administering the questionnaire to ensure its reliability and validity. It is, however, important for the programmer to understand the purposes of the questionnaire and the procedures to be followed in order to provide guidance to the specialist. It is also important for the programmer to be able to develop and administer more limited questionnaires focusing only on specific facility, furnishing, and equipment needs for mid-size projects for which funding for professional survey consultants may not be available.

Planning Is Essential

While casual (unplanned) observation and interviewing are both reasonably effective ways of obtaining useful information about issues of importance to various user groups, there is no such usefulness to casual questionnaires. The effective use of questionnaires requires more preparation than any form of interviewing and most forms of observation. The programmer must first establish what information is needed, and then use the questionnaire only if the information cannot be more easily obtained by searching the literature or through interviewing and/or observation. Having established that a questionnaire will be required, the programmer must determine the specific questions that should be asked to obtain the needed information. It must also be established who will receive the questionnaires and whether the selected respondents can provide reliable and valid answers. It should also be determined if there is enough budget and time available to administer and analyze the questionnaire.

The medical analogy might once again be of some use, even though it breaks down in several respects. Most physicians have developed a medical history form, a questionnaire that they use to ask each patient (or parent) to complete prior to interviewing or observing the patient. Such questionnaires ask about basic demographics: name, address, occupation, age, sex, and the like.

They also ask about previous illness (even in the patient's family), if related persons are still alive, current medications, allergic reactions to drugs, and so on. You might wonder why such a standard questionnaire is not appropriate in architectural programming? The answer is that most people are very much alike in terms of their basic anatomy, physiology, and types of medical problems. Most buildings are not! Each building type has fundamental differences in organization and structure as well as specific space needs. The doctor is trying to diagnose problems within a group of similar entities. The architectural programmer is trying to diagnose the nature of the entity itself, an entity which as yet does not exist, albeit an entity nowhere near the complexity of the human body.

There are, however, instances in which the medical analogy is appropriate regarding the use of questionnaires in architectural programming. If an architectural programmer has done numerous programs for a particular type of facility (offices, hospitals, schools), there are likely to be recurring questions. Questionnaires developed to provide such information on previous projects might be adapted for use on each new project. Such repetition has the advantage of developing some standards of comparison and eventually, perhaps, of developing some generalizable knowledge about the nature of a particular institution, user group, or activity area.

In any case, the time and effort required to develop an appropriate questionnaire for each new commission should not be expended until the programmer has a good idea of the nature of the specific architectural problem. This can usually be determined through literature search and review, diagnostic interviewing, and diagnostic observation. If information is still needed, a questionnaire can be developed to test preliminary conclusions or to uncover additional facts about the user, context, climate, etc., that would be too time consuming and costly to generate through additional diagnostic interviewing or observation (Fig. 5-65).

Name _____ Position _____ Date _/_/_

1. Please check all of the equipment needed for your workstation: 3'×4' desk ___ or 3'×5' desk ___; typing return ___, left side ___ or right side ___; secretary chair ___, with arms ___ or without ___; side chair(s) ___, with arms ___ or without ___; table lamp ___, telephone ___, computer ___ (model type and number, if known _____ _____); filing cabinet(s) (indicate number of each) 2 drawer ___, 3 drawer ___, 4 drawer ___; shelves ___ (indicate linear feet _____); other ___ (please name each item) _____

Figure 5-65 Typical Checklist Questionnaire.

Understanding

The purpose of the entire programming process is to obtain and communicate the information needed to help the designer obtain a correct understanding of the architectural problem. The intent is not to generate a large quantity of descriptive data. The questionnaire is different from diagnostic interviewing in that its primary use in programming is to obtain supporting evidence: facts, opinions, and needs to enrich understanding, rather than to obtain a broad understanding of the issues and activities important to the client and user groups.

Questionnaire Preparation

The process of preparing a good questionnaire is quite involved and time consuming (Berdie et al. 1986; Weisberg et al. 1996). It is similar to when a professor prepares an "objective" test using true-false and/or multiple choice answers. It is time consuming and even exasperating to develop a series of "objective" questions to test the broad issues and understandings that an instructor hopes the student has obtained. Such "objective" tests do not lend themselves to questions about broad issues or areas of understanding. Rather, they tend to force the teacher to ask about facts: names, dates, and formulas which the student must memorize. However, if the instructor is able to develop a satisfactory set of questions, the answers can be placed directly on a computer coding sheet by the student and machine graded, thus taking virtually no time on the part of the instructor to analyze the results. On the other hand, if the instructor chooses to administer a "subjective" short answer or essay test, the problem is reversed. It may not take long to develop a set of satisfactory questions, but the reading and evaluation of the answers will be time consuming and fraught with subjectivity as the grader tries to determine if the students really understood the material on which they were being tested.

In programming, the way out of the dilemma is obvious. Use the diagnostic interview to get at the broader conceptual issues. Use the questionnaire to confirm or refute what has been discovered using the other information gathering methods, but more particularly, to obtain information on the specific space and equipment needs of the individual respondents. In a large organization, obtaining this type of information could be very time consuming, hence expensive, to obtain in any other way.

The literature review, diagnostic interview, and diagnostic observation activities serve as the basis for determining what should be asked in the questionnaire. They help the programmer understand the nature of the problem and reveal what detailed information is still required. There are ten basic steps required in the preparation of a questionnaire. They are sequential in the sense that they usually occur in the order shown below. However, it must be understood that there will be recycling or minor loops within the ten steps, and when completed, there will quite often be major recycling from the beginning to the end of the entire list.

Steps to Prepare a Questionnaire

- List the goals and objectives of utilizing a questionnaire
- Determine who should be answering the questions: client, users, others
- Prepare a schedule for the types of questions to be asked
- Develop specific questions for each part of the questionnaire
- Analyze the questions to see if any can be combined or eliminated
- Answer the questions as if you were in each respondent group
- Revise the questions to make them clearer
- Attempt to tabulate the answers and summarize the results
- Revise the questions to make tabulation possible
- Pre-test the questionnaire with your peers and members of the respondent group(s)

LIST THE GOALS AND OBJECTIVES OF UTILIZING A QUESTIONNAIRE

List in general terms what information is needed. Are there specific hypotheses (propositions that need to be confirmed) about how the organization should operate? Would the client like to know how the majority of users feel about certain issues and be willing to modify the program to accommodate their preferences? Are there facts about specific furnishing or equipment needs that are still unknown? Write this information down and review it with the client and designer (if available). They should be able to determine which hypotheses, issues, and facts are important enough to warrant the use of a questionnaire. The following is a short list of issues and requirements that served as the starting point for developing a questionnaire on how to improve the architecture building at The University of Arizona (Fig. 5-66). Determine who should be answering the questions: client, users, others.

1. Shop facilities are completely inadequate and poorly located.

2. Studio spaces are not large enough to provide adequate student stations at the sophomore and junior levels.

3. The lecture room is unattractive, noisy, and cramped, with uncomfortable seating. Its lighting controls are very difficult to use effectively, especially by visiting speakers. It is also difficult for visitors to find.

4. The slide library is much too small and crowded.

Figure 5-66 Key issues and requirements.

There is no sense asking a question of someone who has no idea how to answer it, or who may provide irrelevant or inappropriate answers. Should there be one overall questionnaire to be answered by everyone, or should there be two, three, or more different questionnaires to be answered only by those capable of answering particular questions? Would it be easier to go back to certain key individuals and ask them some of the questions? Just as information should be provided to those who need to know, information should be sought from those who do know. The chances are that a number of questions will be dropped from the questionnaire as a result of this analysis and re-addressed by diagnostic interviewing or observation. A number of other questions will be asked only to subsets of the respondents.

PREPARE A SCHEDULE FOR THE TYPES OF QUESTIONS TO BE ASKED

Organize the needed information so a systematic way of asking the questions can be developed. Will demographics come first? Will opinions on organizational issues come second? Will controversial issues follow? Will detailed personal equipment needs come last? How can each of these question types be best asked? Can each question within a group be asked using the same format? If not, should a subset be formed to allow two or more different question types?

DEVELOP SPECIFIC QUESTIONS FOR EACH PART OF THE QUESTIONNAIRE

Write down each question as clearly as possible using simple terminology. Consider at all times what the designer really needs to

1. In addition to the equipment currently in the shop, which of the following should be in the new shop? Check all that apply.

    a. ____ metal working and welding equipment
    b. ____ plastic working and molding equipment
    c. ____ ceramic working and finishing equipment
    d. ____ miniature model making tools
    e. ____ painting booth
    f. ____ other _____
    _____

or

Rank order from 6 (most needed) to 1 (least needed)

    a. ____ metal working and welding equipment
    b. ____ plastic working and molding equipment
    c. ____ ceramic working and finishing equipment
    d. ____ miniature model making tools
    e. ____ painting booth
    f. ____ other _____
    _____

Figure 5-67 Checklist versus Rank Order.

1. How does Room 103 function as a classroom?

    excellent ___ good ___ fair ___ poor ___ very poor ___

    Why? _____

2. How does the T.M. Sundt Gallery function?

    excellent ___ good ___ fair ___ poor ___ very poor ___

    Why? _____

Figure 5-68 Rating Scale with Explanation.

know to make design decisions. Will a simple "yes" or "no" answer suffice? Are there several options that allow for a multiple choice response? Can the question be an inventory list, where the respondent simply checks off the appropriate categories? Or does there need to be a ranking of items in terms of priority? Should the answer involve rating, such as from "highly desirable" to "highly undesirable?" Should the question be open-ended, requiring the respondent to fill in a blank area with his/her own words?

Try to ask the question in a way that will get the needed information in as clear and understandable a manner as possible, so that the answers can be easily coded, tabulated, and computer analyzed (Fig. 5-67). Would a simple checklist or a rank ordering be better?

Would the ranking questions yield important information not obtainable by the checklist questions? Or would a rating question be more desirable and easier to analyze? Would it be desirable to know why (Fig. 5-68)?

After a series of questions has been formulated, it is relatively easy to see if some questions are asking the same thing and, thus, might be combined or the least effective ones eliminated. By reviewing the questionnaire goals and the question categories, it is also possible to see if an essential question has been left out, or that a question, as phrased, will not obtain the desired information. Revise the questions as necessary to arrive at the needed information (Fig. 5-69).

Does including "why" provide the programmer with essential information? Will there be enough analysis time for the programmer to code and tabulate all of the "why" answers, especially if they are diverse? Would it be better to ask more detailed questions about each room (Fig. 5-70)?

In the previous example, would it be important to add a follow-up question such as in Fig. 5-71.

Rate how each space functions

	excellent	good	fair	poor	very poor
a. Room 103	—	—	—	—	—
b. Room 204c	—	—	—	—	—
c. Room 302	—	—	—	—	—
d. Conf. Room	—	—	—	—	—
e. Sundt Gallery	—	—	—	—	—
f. 1st flr studio	—	—	—	—	—
g. 2nd flr studio	—	—	—	—	—
h. 3rd flr studio	—	—	—	—	—
i. Grad studio	—	—	—	—	—

Figure 5-69 Combining Questions.

ANSWER THE QUESTIONS AS IF YOU WERE IN EACH RESPONDENT GROUP

Can the people you will be questioning really answer your questions? Will the answers be as you expected? For example, in a multiple choice format, the respondent may wish to choose two or three answers, or think to herself, "Well, sometimes it's this way, and other times it's that way, now which should I check?"

1. Evaluate the effectiveness of Room 103 on the following scale

	excellent	good	fair	poor	very poor
a. size	—	—	—	—	—
b. sight lines	—	—	—	—	—
c. seating	—	—	—	—	—
d. acoustics	—	—	—	—	—
e. lighting	—	—	—	—	—
f. lighting control	—	—	—	—	—
g. ventilation	—	—	—	—	—
h. slide proj.	—	—	—	—	—
i. video	—	—	—	—	—
j. overhead proj.	—	—	—	—	—
k. chalkboard	—	—	—	—	—
l. floor surface	—	—	—	—	—
m. HC access	—	—	—	—	—

Figure 5-70 More Detailed Questions.

Indicate the most needed improvement(s) _____
_____
_____
_____

Figure 5-71 Follow-up Question.

Can the question be phrased to avoid these difficulties? Or, quite often people in one respondent category simply will not have the understanding necessary to answer the question. For example, first-year students who have not yet been admitted to a professional program in architecture will not know how well the upper division studios work. If you asked them that question, they might respond, but how much confidence would you have about the answer? Similarly, questions relating to the desired size of a space or object are often very difficult for laypersons to answer. They may be able to tell you what they do and what equipment and/or furnishings they need, but few can tell you the size of space that will be required. That is something that the programmer will have to figure out from the answerable questions and the wealth of information that can be obtained in other ways.

REVISE THE QUESTIONS TO MAKE THEM CLEARER

This is an iterative, laborious process. The questions have to be just right or you receive practically nothing of worth for your effort. You cannot probe, answer the respondent's questions, or give examples of what you mean if you are not there to do so. This, of course, is a good reason to have an interviewer administer the questionnaire. Even so, if it becomes clear after a number of persons have already responded that a question has been poorly written, what should be done with their answers? It is much better to spend the time and energy beforehand to be certain that problems will not occur that could invalidate some responses.

The story is told about one of the early Kinsey Reports on the sex lives of Americans of a question that asked: "Do you think that new babies should be sterilized?" The majority of respondents said "Yes." Apparently these people thought the question related to keeping babies clean or in a clean environment. Others who responded "No" apparently thought the question dealt with sexual sterilization. But could anyone be certain? Because there could be no follow-up, as in the diagnostic interview, there was no way to tell what the respondents really did mean, so the question had to be discarded. There was no reliable way to interpret the result. The same frequently happens with much less controversial topics such as those found in architectural programming.

ATTEMPT TO TABULATE THE ANSWERS
AND SUMMARIZE THE RESULTS

If only one or two persons in the organization can answer a question, ask them! There is no sense in asking everyone. Most organizations are not truly democratic. The opinion of the boss will be far more important than that of a temporary employee. But if you need a majority opinion or to summarize or average the answers from some particular group, can it be done with the type of answers you will be receiving? Can these answers be easily analyzed by computer? Will you have enough time and money to hand code and tabulate the answers? If not, you may need to reformulate the questions so that the answers can be more easily tabulated. Or you may wish to reassess your strategy and be satisfied with the results of additional interviews with a few key people.

REVISE THE QUESTIONS TO MAKE TABULATION POSSIBLE

Does the question really need to be answered? Can the programmer figure out the answer from the literature review, interviewing, and observation activities? Are there standards available and little reason to suspect that the current situation is really unique? Could a different question be asked that would confirm the standard or reveal the few ways in which the situation is unique? Many questions simply need not be asked. It might be interesting to know, but in truth it is not likely to make even a minor design difference!

Why burden the respondent with the question and the programmer with the work of tabulating and trying to make sense of such answers? There is rarely time or budget to waste in programming. But for those questions that remain to be answered in a questionnaire, it is important to make it as easy as possible to administer, code, tabulate, and analyze the results.

PRE-TEST THE QUESTIONNAIRE WITH YOUR PEERS
AND MEMBERS OF THE RESPONDENT GROUP(S)

The pretest is an essential part of the preparation of any questionnaire. It involves a small number of respondents who are asked to complete the questionnaire and to comment on its merits and faults. It lets the programmer know if the questions are presented in a reasonable order, phrased in understandable terms, and if the answers generated will be useful to the designer.

The programmer also learns how long it takes for a respondent to complete the questionnaire and sees if it is possible to make sense of the answers. Indeed, it allows the programmer to check if all previous steps were well carried out.

At least two pretests should be conducted. In the first pretest, it is desirable to ask other members of your peer group, particularly the persons most likely to be involved in the design and design development of the project, to pretend to be respondents as they complete the questionnaire. There are five typical steps in a pretest:

1. Ask the respondents to complete the entire questionnaire while you keep track of the time it takes them to do so.

2. Ask them to critically review each question, the order of the questions, and the length of the questionnaire.

3. Go through their answers with them to see if they answered appropriately.

4. Ask them to offer suggestions to improve the questionnaire.

5. Try to tabulate the answers to determine if the results will be understandable.

Have you asked the most important questions? Were they in a logical order? Was the questionnaire too long? Did you ask leading questions? Did you use jargon that could not be understood by some respondents? The answers to these questions might prove embarrassing if your colleagues are highly critical of the questionnaire. However, as a professor once said (Ackoff 1967):

Better to be a fool among your peers than before the world.

If you cannot take the constructive criticism of your colleagues, it will be worse from members of the respondent group. Actually, most respondents will be very guarded in their criticisms and suggestions to the detriment of helping you improve your product. Because your colleagues and friends have your best interests in mind, they are likely to be more aggressive, hence more helpful, in their criticisms and suggestions.

After you have repeated steps one through nine of questionnaire preparation in answering the criticisms rendered in the first pretest, it is time to conduct a pretest with members of the respondent group(s). This pretest should involve two or three persons from each of the actual subgroups relating to the facility for which the program is being prepared and should be conducted using the same three steps as in the first pretest.

Again, this pretest must be followed by a careful review of the results to make certain that the answers given can be coded, tabulated, and analyzed in a satisfactory manner. Will the answers be useful to the designer? Will they provide information that will help the designer obtain a better understanding of the problem? Indeed, it may be necessary to iterate through the entire 10 steps several times to refine the final questionnaire. If this appears to be a very time consuming and tedious procedure, rest assured that it is! However, it will be worth the initial time spent in terms of overall time saved.

Students reading this material will no doubt recall midterm or final examinations in which certain questions were phrased in a very confusing way, or dealt with areas that had hardly been covered in the course, or were about trivial issues, when important issues had been covered. Unfortunately, it is difficult for a professor to pre-test an examination because of the distinct possibility that the questions will leak to the remainder of the class, invalidating the test. And how would the instructor grade the students selected for the pretest? Fortunately, with a questionnaire there is no such problem, so validation of its potential effectiveness through pretesting can be done to the great benefit of the questionnaire.

Logical Order of a Questionnaire

- Interest the Respondents
- Discover Who They Are
- Proceed from General to Specific
- Save Personal Questions Until Last
- Allow for Explanation or Justification
- Tell the Respondents What to Do When Finished with the Questionnaire

The above listed order works well for questionnaires associated with architectural programming. It is not necessarily the ideal order for other kinds of questioning situations, particularly those where a person might feel uninvolved, as with a public opinion survey or with the evaluation of colleagues relative to organizational change. The programming questionnaire can go directly to the desired information so long as the order is understandable

HMO: FACILITY REQUIREMENTS

Name _____ Position _____ Date _/_/_

This questionnaire is aimed at discovering the specific furnishing and equipment needs of the staff of HMO Company. It is important that you respond to all questions so that your needs can be determined and the designer be required to provide you with adequate space. Please take the time necessary to respond to each question thoughtfully and accurately. Thank you very much for your help?

Figure 5-72 Introduction to a Questionnaire.

and the answers to earlier questions do not set an inappropriate framework for answers to later questions.

INTEREST THE RESPONDENTS

This activity is best accomplished with a statement at the very top of the questionnaire or in a brief cover letter that explains the questionnaire's purpose and, especially, why it is important that respondents complete it. Usually, it is best to be straightforward about its purposes as in Fig. 5-72.

There is no need to labor this introduction. Practically anyone knowing that his/her facilities are about to be improved will cooperate fully.

DISCOVER WHO THEY ARE

This section is on the demographics of the respondents. Who are they? What is their role in the organization? What characteristics do they have that might cause the designer to do something differently? Will you want to sort out questionnaires based on this information? Will you want to come back to some respondents to ask more particular questions depending on their responses? Here, again, ask only what you really need to know. Is it important to know the respondent's sex or age? Maybe not! If you do want to separate the responses based on age, be sure to use large enough age groups so that you do not appear unnecessarily personal in asking the question. You need to know the respondent's name only if you want to be certain who has completed the questionnaire to be able to make a new request of those who fail to complete it, or if you have the need, time, and money to follow up on specific or unusual answers.

The most likely reason to ask demographic questions is to be able to separate subgroups to discover their special preferences or needs. For example, if you were commissioned to program a major public housing project involving several ethnic groups and age groups, you would probably want to separate the responses during analysis into age, sex, and ethnic groupings in order to draw conclusions about the needs and preferences of each of the subgroups.

If the demographic questions are limited in number and were not considered to be overly personal in the pretest, it works well to put these questions at the beginning of the questionnaire. People typically like to think about themselves, and if the response categories are obvious and broad enough, most respondents can provide reliable answers with little effort. They are thus off to a good start with the questionnaire and in an appropriate mind-set relative to stating their personal ideas about the desired information (Fig. 5-73).

The first question could be an important one on which to separate the questionnaires to see if there are significant differences in housing preferences and needs for various ages of adults. No difference may appear between some adjoining categories, but differences may become evident between several categories, e.g., under fifty and over fifty. This category might also be interactive with other categories such as sex and marital status. Single women over fifty living alone are likely to have different housing preferences and needs than married women over fifty living with a spouse, and than married women under fifty living with a spouse and children. There may also be differences relating to housing preferences between persons of different ethnic groups owing to their cultural backgrounds.

Note that it was not considered important in the above questionnaire to discover if the single person was divorced, widowed, or never married. The reason for asking only if single or married

PHOENIX DOWNTOWN INFILL HOUSING QUESTIONNAIRE

The Phoenix Housing Authority is in the process of developing plans for over a thousand low cost infill housing units to be placed in the southwestern section of the city. Because you have indicated an interest in relocating into this housing when it becomes available, the authority is most interested in your preferences and needs. Please take a few minutes to consider carefully what you feel would be the most satisfactory housing for you. Be assured that the housing authority will be responsive to the results of the questionnaire.

PART ONE (Please respond to each question by underlining the appropriate answer)

1. Your age?   Under 20   20–29   30–39   40–49   50–59   60–69   Over 69
2. Your sex?   Male   Female
3. Ethnic background?   Caucasian   Black   Asian   Mexican   Native American   Other
4. Marital status?   Married   Single (includes divorced, widowed, never married)
5. Number of adults living in household?   One   Two   Three   Four   Over four
6. Number of children living in household?   One   Two   Three   Four   Over four
7. Ages of Adults?   18 thru 29   30 thru 49   50 thru 69   Over 69
   (Underline as many as currently apply.)
8. Ages of Children?   Under 6   6 thru 12   13 thru 18
   (Underline as many as currently apply.)
9. Current monthly rent?   Under $200 $200–$300 $300–$400   Over $400
10. Affordable monthly rent?   Under $200 $200–$300 $300–$400   Over $400

Figure 5-73 Introduction and Demographics.

rather than being more detailed might be to avoid appearing to be too curious about personal matters such as cohabiting unmarried men and women. It might be embarrassing or threatening for a respondent to admit to cohabiting in such a questionnaire. Indeed, it is problematic whether question four should have been included at all, since marital status can have a serious negative impact on public assistance. It might have been better to leave out the question entirely, and simply to determine with later questions if two or more adults living in a household prefer arrangements that make cohabitation possible. The designer does not need to know if the relationship has been officially sanctioned by the state. It is important, however, for the designer to know how many adults and children are likely to be living together in the same household and how many, if any, are willing to sleep in the same bedroom.

It is also important to know the ages of the children and adults, because the implications for neighborhood support facilities vary for different age groups. Interestingly, however, if most of the children of prospective tenants are young, there is a good possibility that the housing and support facilities will have to adapt as the children grow older, unless it can be determined that families typically move out of such housing as the children age. The final two questions about financial ability may be crucial in determining the size and quality of housing and support facilities that can be built.

Do you think that there are other demographic questions that should have been included? Could some of these questions be left out without sacrificing necessary information? These are the types of questions that must be dealt with when preparing a questionnaire. Remember, unless the information requested could actually impact how something might be designed, it should not be asked (Fig. 5-74)!

Would this shortened list provide the demographic information necessary to design housing for the group of respondents? If not, what would need to be added?

PART ONE (Please respond to each question by underlining the appropriate answer)

1. Number of male adults living in household?
   One   Two   Three   Four   Over four
2. Number of female adults living in household?
   One   Two   Three   Four   Over four
3. Ages of Adults?   18–29   30–49   50–69
   Over 69
   (underline as many as currently apply)
4. Number of children living in household?
   One   Two   Three   Four   Over four
5. Age of Children?   Under 6   6–12   13–18
   (underline as many as currently apply.)
6. Ethnic background?   Caucasian   Black
   Asian   Mexican   American Indian   Other
7. Affordable monthly rent?   Under $200
   $200–$300 $300–$400   Over $400

Figure 5-74 Simplified Demographics Section.

PROCEED FROM GENERAL TO SPECIFIC

You cannot assume that a respondent shares your concerns about a particular problem, or even that he or she is concentrating on the questionnaire or thinking about what it will accomplish. It is far more likely that he or she will be thinking about personal affairs. Hence, the questionnaire has to be structured to get the respondent into the programmer's mindset. The introduction and demographic questions begin this process. But the first few substantive questions really set the tone and serve to get the respondent thinking about architectural issues (Fig. 5-75).

The first question gets right to the heart of matter. Which type of housing would be preferred by the respondent? Here it is important not to offer an option that could not be made available because of cost, density requirements, or other limits. The designer needs to know what

1. Which type of housing would meet your needs best? Rank in order of preference:
   1 most preferred to 4 least preferred.

   a. Single Family detached
      (one or two stories) _____
   b. Single Family attached
      (duplex, triplex, row) _____
   c. Multiple Family walkup
      (up to three stories) _____
   d. Multiple Family elevator
      (up to ten stories) _____

2. Once into your unit could your family live comfortably in a two story unit?
   yes _____ no _____ (check one)

   If you answered "no", is someone in your household disabled in some way?
   yes _____ no ___. Please describe: _____
   _____
   _____

Figure 5-75 General to Specific.

will help him/her make intelligent design decisions within the various constraints imposed by site, climate, client, economics, etc. Was this a good lead question? Could it have been asked more clearly? What first substantive question might you have asked instead of the one shown?

More specific questions that follow might relate to the number of bedrooms or baths. Although here again the type of housing, or more precisely society's willingness and/or the tenant's ability to pay, may limit the number of bedrooms even for large family groups: one for the cohabiting adults, one for single males, one for single females, regardless of age. A low-income family will likely have to share one bathroom regardless of the size of the household. In any case, only questions to which the architect can actually respond should be asked.

SAVE PERSONAL QUESTIONS UNTIL LAST

Any question that seems very personal in nature is best located toward the end of a questionnaire. Otherwise, the respondent is likely to feel that the questionnaire is being unnecessarily inquisitive,

9. Would you be willing to accept gang-type showers in the locker room if the number of toilet stalls could be increased?
yes ____; no ____.

or more elaborately

9. Limited school budgets normally preclude supplying toilets or urinals beyond the minimum required by code. However, if gang-type showers in both the men's and women's locker rooms were acceptable to the users, it would be possible to provide two additional toilet stalls in the women's toilet rooms and two additional urinals in the men's toilet rooms. Would this be a desirable tradeoff as far as you are concerned?
yes ____; no ___; not sure ____.

Figure 5-76 Personal Questions.

and may not complete it or may give inaccurate responses—either of which makes the overall results of the questionnaire less useful. An example would be the provision of showers in schools and other public facilities. In the past, it was assumed that men were willing to share gang-type showers, while women required individual stalls. It would be useful to discover if most women today would gladly give up the privacy provided by shower stalls in order to have a greater number of toilet stalls. A question that could get at this issue might be phrased somewhat like that in Fig. 5-76.

How many other ways could this question be asked? The objective in writing the questionnaire is to get at important design issues in an easily understood way. The first question may be too short and brusque. Will the respondents understand what gang-type means? The second question may be too long. How could each question be better phrased?

If nearly all of the men respondents replied yes and most of the women respondents said yes, what should the designer do? What about the opinion of the minority? Perhaps they have an extremely valid reason for saying no. Here is a case where it would be important to allow for amplification or justification of the answer, and quite possibly to encourage the designer to allow for choice. It may be that a number of both men and women would prefer individual shower stalls.

The same may be true for other situations relating to issues such as personal territory, privacy, and safety. A variety of options can be discovered and provided for in design, if questions are phrased in such a way that an appropriate variety can be determined.

ALLOW FOR EXPLANATION OR JUSTIFICATION

It might be useful to state at the beginning of the questionnaire that the respondent should feel free to explain any answer, and to include a blank line after each question or a final blank page for this purpose (Fig. 5-77). This way, no one should feel unduly constrained by the questionnaire. Such amplification is often useful to the designer. On the other hand, if the questionnaire is to go to several hundred respondents, it may become financially impossible to code and tabulate all possible answers, so such amplification may in fact be wasted.

The person(s) preparing the questionnaire must assess the time and money available to analyze the questionnaire. If the time and money are not available for proper analysis, do not ask the question(s).

TELL THE RESPONDENTS WHAT TO DO WHEN FINISHED WITH THE QUESTIONNAIRE

The respondent must know what to do with the questionnaire when it is completed. This can often be stated as part of the introductory section or in a cover letter. However, this information should also be provided at the end of the questionnaire after a salutation such as in Fig. 5-78.

Question Types

- Dichotomous
- Nominal
- Ordinal
- Interval
- Short Answer
- Open-Ended

9. Please explain your answer:

_____
_____
_____
_____

or if you prefer to be more specific

9. If you answered "no" to the above question, please explain your answer. This will be of great help to the designer.

_____
_____
_____
_____

Figure 5-77 Supplemental Questions.

Thank you very much for completing this questionnaire!

Please fold the questionnaire in thirds along the dotted lines shown on the back sheet and insert it in the pre-addressed, stamped envelope attached to the questionnaire.

Remember, the questionnaire must be returned no later than Friday, April 12, 1998, to be useful to the designer.

Thanks again for your help!

Figure 5-78 Instructions at Ending.

There are a number of different types of questions that may be used in a questionnaire. They vary from simple checklists to open-ended free-answer questions (Blalock 1960; Bradburn et al. 1979). As mentioned before, the simpler the response, the easier it is to code and analyze the results. Also, the simpler and clearer the question, the less problems there are with reliability; that is, the more likely the respondents will provide the same answers under slightly different circumstances of time or place. The answers must also be valid. Validity in this sense means answers that are both true and important relative to design. If you repeatedly ask a group of uninformed or misinformed people a question, you might get consistent (reliable) answers, but they would be misleading, hence invalid. Similarly, if you ask a question requiring answers that are more detailed or precise than the respondents are capable of providing, the results are likely to be imprecise at best. Some respondents will leave the question blank, indicating they do not know, while others will venture a guess, providing answers that are neither reliable nor valid. In any case, the effort should be made to ask questions to arrive at the needed information in the most reliable and valid way possible. This generally means that the questions must be phrased simply and clearly relative to the particular respondent group's understanding of the problem, and that the possible answers be equally simple and clear for the benefit of analysis. This is easy to say, and difficult to accomplish.

DICHOTOMOUS (TRUE/FALSE AND YES/NO QUESTIONS)

These questions usually involve an assertion that the respondent must determine to be true or false, or with which they agree or disagree (Fig. 5-79).

Such answers can be coded onto computer answer sheets and analysis would involve only counting the number of positive and negative answers. If the demographics allow separating the answers into respondent groups, it may be possible to determine if opinions vary for different groups. For example, women faculty, staff, and students may have different attitudes in this regard. Perhaps only the faculty/staff toilets require additional stalls. Male respondents would have no basis on which to respond to the above questions, nor would they be affected, so they should not be asked to respond. It might be better to rephrase the question to omit "women's" so that both men and women could respond relative to their own experiences, and then to separate out the answers for analysis based on sex, so as to be able to determine if the need

5. There are an insufficient number of toilets in the women's rest rooms in the College of Architecture. True ____ False ____

or

5. It would be desirable to increase the number of toilets in the women's rest rooms in the College of Architecture. Yes ____ No ____

Figure 5-79 True/False and Yes/No Questions.

for more stalls is general, or applies only to one or the other of the sex groups (Fig. 5-80).

NOMINAL (SINGLE WORD, CHECKLISTS, MULTIPLE CHOICE)

This type of question is often a variation of the dichotomous question, which requires only a check for affirmative (or negative) answers. It is particularly effective when there are long lists of similar questions. The most common lists in programming typically deal with furnishings and equipment. Another such list might relate to activities of the respondent.

These are easy to code directly onto computer coding sheets for analysis, which can be as simple as computing the total number of checks for each answer for a particular respondent subgroup. The answers in the final column below would, of course, have to be hand tabulated and considered on the merits of the justifications offered. Here, it might be important to know the names or titles of the specific respondents to determine if there is actually a smaller subgroup than the demographic data indicates. In any case, the total number of checks allowed should be reasonable and based on information gained in the previous literature review, diagnostic interviewing, and diagnostic observation activities (Fig. 5-81).

The multiple choice question is a variation where there are more choices than yes/no, but usually only one answer is permitted, as the following question indicates (Fig. 5-82).

This question would, of course, only be applicable for a person who had previously indicated a need for a secretarial desk.

5. There are an insufficient number of toilet stalls in restrooms in the College of Architecture. True ____ False ____

or

5. It would be desirable to increase the number of toilet stalls in restrooms in the College of Architecture. Yes ____ No ____

Figure 5-80 Reworded Dichotomous Questions.

6. Please place a check in the appropriate column for furnishings needed in your office.

item & number	0	1	2	3	4	More
			indicate if more than 4			
a. executive desk	—	—	—	—	—	—
b. secretarial desk	—	—	—	—	—	—
c. executive chair	—	—	—	—	—	—
d. secretarial chair	—	—	—	—	—	—
e. side chair	—	—	—	—	—	—
f. conference table	—	—	—	—	—	—
g. conference chair	—	—	—	—	—	—
h. 4 drawer filing cabinet	—	—	—	—	—	—
i. 2 drawer filing cabinet	—	—	—	—	—	—

Figure 5-81 Nominal Questions (Checklist).

7. Your preference for a secretarial desk is which of the following? (check one)

    a. left side typing surface   _____
    b. right side typing surface   _____
    c. typing surface on both sides _____
    d. other (explain)   _____

_____

_____

_____

Figure 5-82 Multiple Choice Questions.

10. Please rank the following in terms of their importance to you.
    (1 as most important to 7 as least important)

    a. Functional Relationships   _____
    b. Response to Climate   _____
    c. Relationship to Existing Building _____
    d. Structural Expression   _____
    e. Initial Cost   _____
    f. Operating Costs   _____
    g. Aesthetic Image   _____

Figure 5-83 Rank Ordering Questions.

Please rate the following questions from: 1. (extremely important), 2. (moderately important), to 3. (relatively unimportant).

8. How important to you is each of the following relative to the addition to the College of Architecture? (Check the appropriate blank)

	1	2	3
a. Functional Relationships	__	__	__
b. Response to Climate	__	__	__
c. Relationship to Existing Building	__	__	__
d. Structural Expression	__	__	__
e. Initial Cost	__	__	__
f. Operating Costs	__	__	__
g. Aesthetic Image	__	__	__
h. Safety/Security	__	__	__

Figure 5-84 Rating Scales.

ORDINAL (RANK ORDERING)

Ordinal questions can be used to discover a particular respondent's preferences for almost anything. However, it is difficult to summarize results from a number of respondents (Fig. 5-83).

A problem can occur if a respondent feels that two or more of the possible answers are of equal importance. Another problem is the coding and analysis of the results. About all that can be done is to add up the responses to each subquestion and divide by the number of respondents to come up with the average rating for each category. This can be rather deceptive if some respondents give several items the same ranking or leave out some items because they cannot decide where they rank. It is not easy for most respondents to make clear decisions relative to rank ordering. It may require the presence of an interviewer to be certain that the question is completed correctly. Hence, it is generally best to avoid this kind of question in a distributed questionnaire.

INTERVAL (RATING SCALES)

Questions requiring ratings are somewhat more complex than true/false or checklist questions. They are similar to multiple choice and rank order questions, except that they deal with a continuum of attitudes or preferences for each subquestion (Fig. 5-84).

Unlike rank ordering, this type of question is easy to answer and code, even on computer coding sheets, to allow easier sta-tistical analysis. It is possible to calculate totals, means, and distributions for the several possible answers to each question. It is also possible to establish the rank order for a question for the whole group. In the above case, the highest rank would be given to the category with the lowest total score, and the lowest rank being given to the category with the highest total score. It is also possible that some categories may rank the same, or nearly the same (Fig. 5-85).

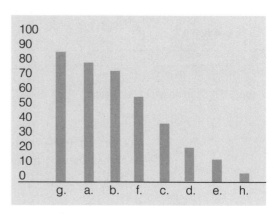

Figure 5-85 Histogram Showing Rank Ordering.

SHORT ANSWER

These questions are necessary when more specific information is needed than could reasonably be provided using a finite number of categories. Questions asking for a person's name, address, and telephone or identification number are examples of short answer questions for which simple categorization is rarely appropriate. These are all demographic questions and are nominal in nature. Questions asking a respondent what he or she thinks are important design issues, or for suggestions as to how to solve a problem, may also prove difficult to cover with a limited set of alternatives. It may not be appropriate to assume that you have thought of all of the alternative ideas. A short answer may be required (Fig. 5-86).

The problem with the short answer is coding. Each answer must be content analyzed and coded by a person, which takes time and money. If the possible answers are seemingly endless or approaching infinity, then coding simply breaks down to the most frequently mentioned categories and the rest are grouped under an "other" category. This may be useful for an exploratory questionnaire when interviewing to accomplish the same purpose would be difficult or impossible. However, the diagnostic interview is better suited to finding answers to such questions. If some doubt exists about whether the persons interviewed are representative of the group, additional interviews can be conducted until sufficient understanding of the categories of response can be established.

14. What are the three most important issues for the design of a new architecture building?

  a. _____

  b. _____

  c. _____

Figure 5-86 Short Answer Questions.

Please explain

Figure 5-87 Short Answer Clarification.

The most common short answer question that should be used in a questionnaire is the request for amplification, clarification, or insertion of nominal information for "other" categories. Here again, the value of this information is questionable, unless there is sufficient time and budget for the survey team to analyze the results. When this is possible, a number of insights can be gained that would otherwise have been missed (Fig. 5-87).

OPEN-ENDED

Use of open-ended questions in a questionnaire can be problematic. It is difficult to count or summarize the variety of answers likely to be obtained from a large number of individuals, but it is possible to read through the responses to gain a feeling for the sentiment of the group. However, this approach to analysis is fraught with uncertainty about how much the reader brings from past experience to the conclusions reached. It is, of course, possible to do a complete content analysis in which certain groups of answers are identified and their instances counted, but this is a very time consuming activity. In either case, the wisdom of using open-ended questions in a questionnaire is doubtful, because the same information could more easily be obtained through diagnostic interviewing.

Sampling

As with the methods of information gathering discussed earlier, sampling is extremely important when using questionnaires (Blalock 1960; Ackoff 1962). If the wrong persons are asked to respond, the answers may be useless. It is, therefore, important to develop a careful sampling plan. So who should be included? The people who are likely to know the answers! Depending on the role they fill in an organization, the people questioned may have very different, but possibly equally valid, answers. It is important to identify all of the different categories of people likely to be affected by the design solution and to survey a sample from each of these groups. For example, a questionnaire relating to the expansion of an architectural building may need to be responded to by each of the following groups: student majors, other students, faculty, staff, administrators, and maintenance personnel. Probably, however, only the student group would be so large as to require that a questionnaire be used. A representative sample or even the entire group of persons in other categories could be interviewed.

In the case of the students, it might make sense to survey a sample from each class level (freshmen through senior undergraduate, first- and second-year graduate, non-majors using the building, etc.). If there are 50 or more students at each year level, perhaps only ten need to be surveyed to obtain a reasonably accurate understanding of student attitudes, needs, and ideas. This is a type of stratified sampling procedure. Selections within each group might involve further stratification (e.g., by age, sex, ethnicity, place of residence) or perhaps by random selection. If a need exists to project from the small sample to the population (group) the sample represents, it is probably advisable to utilize a random sampling procedure, so the probability of the sample being unlike the overall group can be estimated. This can be done rather easily by identifying every member of the group, assigning a unique number to each, then utilizing a table of random numbers to select the persons to be given the questionnaire. This approach becomes more important as the population of the group to be surveyed increases (Fig. 5-88).

Note that a somewhat different questionnaire may be necessary for some of the groups surveyed. For instance, if you wish to survey users who are not employees, but perhaps frequent or occasional visitors or customers, they will not be able to provide the same depth or detail of information as a staff member. It is also possible to utilize a single survey instrument with directions to respondents to skip over certain portions of the questionnaire, depending upon earlier answers.

Typically, sampling for programming questionnaires involves stratification of the entire population of users or potential users of the facility to be designed. Thus, the sample is referred to

Dean	Director of Architecture	Director of Planning
Associate Dean	Graduate Program Director	Administrative Assistant
Administrative Associate	Administrative Assistant	
Business Manager		Planning Faculty
Development Officer	Architecture Faculty	First year grad students
Administrative Assistant	First year students	Second year grad students
Receptionist	Second year students	Third year grad students
Shop Superintendent	Third year students	Graduate Assistants
Librarian	Fourth year students	
Archivist	Fifth year students	
Head Custodian	First year grad students	
	Second year grad students	Director of Landscape Arch.
Provost	Third year grad students	Administrative Assistant
Advisory Council Pres.	Graduate Assistants	
AIA President		Landscape Faculty
Campus Planning Dir.	Library Visitors	First year grad students
Facilities Director	Lecture Visitors	Second year grad students
Facilities Management	Gallery Visitors	Third year grad students
		Graduate Assistants

Figure 5-88 Persons to Survey in Architecture.

as a stratified sample. The stratification is usually done with respect to the role the persons play in the facility so that all legitimate needs are accounted for in the survey. Within each strata, the sample should be random to ensure that various types of individuals have an equal chance of being represented: young, old, male, female, minorities, and so on. If it is possible to identify each member of the population and to assign them numbers, then a simple random sample can be made using a table of random numbers. If a random sample is taken for each subgroup, the sampling procedure is referred to as a stratified random sample. If the strata involves only a few persons, such as the maintenance staff, it may be possible to question the whole population so that there will be no need to worry about representation within the strata. Finally, since the opinions held by some members of an organization may be considered more important than those held by other members, for instance, management versus staff, there is often an agreed or imposed weighting of some strata. In this case, the sampling design might be referred to as a weighted stratified random sample.

If it is not possible to identify each of the members of a strata, such as expected visitors to the facility, it might be necessary to use a systematic random selection procedure, that is, choosing the first respondent using random selection, then selecting every tenth (or another number) person to respond to the questions. The sample would then be referred to as a systematic stratified random sample. This turns out to be a relatively complicated procedure, and there are entire books on the topic (Rosenbaum 1979). If the organization is large and/or complex, it would be highly desirable to work with professionals in developing the survey. However, if the organization is simple or small, common sense can go a long way toward developing an adequate plan. Here again, our earlier discussions of cost of error should not be forgotten.

Bias

- Sampling
- Questioner
- Respondent
- Situation
- Technique

A key problem of survey research is bias. This problem has been considered at great length by social scientists involved in survey research (Blalock 1960). A brief summary here will help the reader understand several of the areas where problems of bias can develop. Persons concerned with the impact of such problems are advised to consult with people who have spent their lives developing the skills necessary to conduct research that avoids these biases.

SAMPLING

If the sample leaves out certain population subgroups or clearly admits a disproportionate number of another group, the results are likely to be biased toward the interests of the represented groups. As already mentioned, however, programming research is typically biased toward the interests of the management group, since they pay the bill. Other people are surveyed to be certain that their legitimate needs are satisfied.

QUESTIONER

This is the most common bias in programming research. It involves such things as leading questions. These are questions that look for a certain answer: "Don't you agree that more toilet stalls are needed in the women's toilet room?" "Most educated people now desire a bidet in addition to the normal toilet stool. What is your preference?" If a question looks as if it is leading toward a certain answer, it probably is not a good one. Another problem is vague or confusing questions: "What do you do each day?" This question is simply too broad.

Classic examples of confusing and leading questions are found in the political literature. For example, a recent survey by a political action committee asked respondents to rate issues of importance. One issue was to "Eliminate *obsolete* [my italics] federally funded programs." It would be unusual for any reasonably intelligent person to answer that we should keep "obsolete" programs. Another question asked: "Do you believe *everything* [my italics] you hear or see from the media?" It is hard to imagine many persons saying "yes" or "not decided" to this one. The same questionnaire asked: "Are you committed to fighting the liberal bias in the news media?" (Quayle 1996). No matter how you answer this question, you can be counted as agreeing that there actually is a "liberal bias" in the news media. Perhaps.

The language in a questionnaire must be absolutely clear to the respondent, because there is no opportunity to probe or ask for clarification. The respondent reacts only to what he or she understands the question to ask.

RESPONDENT

This can be a problem in both interviews and questionnaires. In this case, the respondent tries to say what he or she thinks the questioner, or perhaps management, wants to hear. This is particularly true when the respondent's answers can be identified as belonging to the respondent. If this is a problem, it is sometimes necessary to have the questionnaire returned in an unmarked envelope. But even with this precaution, a person in a unique role may easily be identified by their concerns. Rarely, however, is a question asked in architectural programming that might cause major problems between supervisors and subordinates.

SITUATION

This can also be a major source of error in surveys. If the respondent is asked to complete a questionnaire when busy, you can be sure that not much thought will be given to the endeavor, even if the questionnaire is completed. Or if a work environment questionnaire is administered away from a person's workstation, it is likely to result in guesses based on poor recollection or visualization. Both the time and place to administer a questionnaire should be carefully chosen.

TECHNIQUE

The way of asking questions can also introduce bias. As already mentioned, it is difficult to discover a person's unique values, goals, and ideas with any "objective" question in which all of the possible answers have already been identified. Multiple choice or checklist questions confine a person's answers to those available.

The Survey

Ultimately, the time comes to administer the questionnaire—to conduct the survey. Will it be affordable to have a person administer each of the questionnaires? Will it be possible to send or deliver the questionnaires to each of the respondents to complete and return? If the required sample is large, it may be very expensive to have someone visit every respondent. Indeed, if this much time can be made available, perhaps a series of diagnostic interviews would be a more appropriate use of available time!

Sometimes arrangements can be made to have all respondents come to a central place, as with an examination, where general instructions can be given to everyone and questioners can be available to answer specific questions as they occur. This can be efficient, ensure a reasonably good understanding of the questions, and enable the programmer to get the questionnaires back very quickly. It does not, however, allow the respondents to refer to their own environments to obtain the requested information. Like a closed book exam, it requires that the person recall all of the information requested. Most people are not very good at recalling environmental information, so chances are that answers will be neither reliable nor valid.

The most common procedure, where a building programming activity is concerned, is to prepare a cover letter with the signature of the client, to be sent either to department heads for distribution, or directly to a preselected sample of administrators and employees as appropriate. The letter should briefly state the purpose of the questionnaire, by what date it must be completed, and how and where it must be returned. It is also important to stress the questionnaire's importance in obtaining a satisfactory building for the respondent's particular needs, so respondents will have a personal interest in completing the questionnaire (Fig. 5-89).

Once returned, the questionnaires can be collated as appropriate and then the job of coding the data onto appropriate data forms can begin. Whenever possible, this should be done on computer answer sheets, so that the entire analysis can be done by computer. When this is not possible, a carefully preplanned sheet for manual tabulation can be used to tabulate and summarize the results. Once summarized, the format should be

INDUSTRIAL GROUP OF AMERICA
11 EAST EDGE STREET,
CAMBRIDGE, MA 10238

May 17, 1997

Roger Grand, Director of Development

Dear Roger:

The enclosed survey from the architect of the new plant needs to be completed and returned to the Personnel Office no later than May 24, 1997. It is crucial that you take the necessary time, consulting appropriate staff, to complete and return the questionnaire on schedule.

We value your continuing service to the company very much and hope that you are as excited as we are about the opportunity to greatly improve our working environment.

Sincerely,

Charlotte Mead, President

Figure 5-89 Cover Letter.

such that the results are readily apparent; that is, they should make sense to the designer. Otherwise, the entire survey effort will have been a waste of everyone's time.

Data Analysis

If the questions have been carefully written to allow ease of coding and an appropriate sampling plan has been developed and followed, analyzing the results is a relatively straightforward problem. Clerical staff can be instructed how to code the limited number of short answer responses. The programmer or designer can be given the longer open-ended answers to try to obtain an overall view of the respondents' answers. The balance of the answers can be transferred to computer coding sheets and the data fed to the computer to develop specific information such as totals, averages (means), distributions, and other statistics.

For most programming commissions, simple descriptive statistics such as those mentioned above are appropriate. If the number of persons questioned is a substantial proportion of the total, there is very good reason to believe that they will be representative, especially if they were chosen randomly. Simply illustrating the results by tabulations or visually with tables, pie charts, or histograms will be enough to let the designer know what is needed (Fig. 5-90).

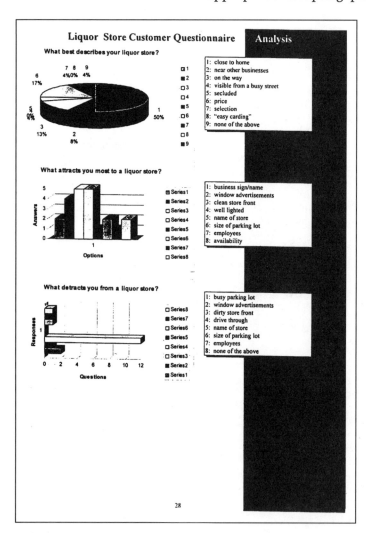

Figure 5-90 Questionnaire Results.

Credit: Jeffrey Burns, Malcolm Calvin, Mitch Dodge, and Paul Johnson, 1996. *U of A Liquors Building Program.* College of Architecture, The University of Arizona

If, on the other hand, the population from which the samples were taken is very large in comparison to the samples, it may be necessary to test the significance of the results using some combination of descriptive and inferential statistics. A very common social science technique is to develop means and variances for various distributions of data and to use t-tests, analysis of variance, or some other appropriate parametric or nonparametric test of significance. If it comes to this, both social scientists and statisticians should be involved in the development of the questionnaire, sampling plan, and statistical analysis. The discussion of these research procedures is beyond the scope or intent of this text. Those interested in pursuing these approaches should refer to such books as Methods in Environmental and Behavioral Research (Bechtel et al. 1987).

Cost of Error

It should be added that cost of error is a factor to be weighed in the development and analysis of any information gathering activity (Ackoff 1962). If the information was not gathered at all, would there be a cost if the designer was allowed to design and construct an inappropriate building? Very likely there would be large costs. The various rooms within the building might be of the wrong size or shape, so the intended activities could not take place within the rooms. The cost of error may involve lost efficiency of production, and thus an overpriced product. Or it might involve the cost of a complete remodeling of the building to make it usable. The building might project an inappropriate image to the community, so that the intended users will not enter. The building may let in maximum sun in the hot summer months and minimum sun in the cold winter months, so the utility costs would be very high. The building might greatly exceed the client's budget, causing bankruptcy for the client, who might sue the architect for damages.

Clearly, in the case of no information gathering, the costs of error can be high. What about the case of minimum information gathering—the case where the client provides a brief and the architect begins to design? In this case, the cost of error depends on how good the client is as a programmer. In many cases, the client will not be very good. Client programs are often reactions to inadequate present facilities. In an effort to oil squeaky parts, the client may forget what kind of business he or she is really involved in. Clients often have a very poor sense of size, so they tend to over- or underestimate the sizes of needed spaces. The client may tend to be overly conservative or even redundant in what is wanted.

Most laypersons have not been educated on the environmental possibilities for flexibility, adaptability, incremental growth, or other areas where an architect has knowledge. The costs of error can be quite high if laypersons are left to do their own programming. They may give up on program needs, thinking they cannot get everything they want, when in fact they could with careful programming for multiple use, growth, and so on. They may also get a facility that is appropriate for the past when their organization is moving toward the future. The costs in such cases are often substantial, but difficult to measure precisely.

So what about a program prepared by an architectural firm in consultation only with the owner/client? Here again it depends on the programming qualifications of the architectural firm and how well the owner/client represents the users. If the architectural firm has done similar buildings before, it may be able to design a satisfactory building with very low costs of error. However, if the client/user is unlike those of previous commissions by the architect, then some preconceptions will be inappropriate and the resulting architecture is likely to impose costs on the client that could have been avoided.

But what if the architectural programmer has done a careful literature review, conducted extensive diagnostic interviews, and observed both the organization and the new site carefully, but has not administered and analyzed a carefully planned questionnaire according to a scientific sampling plan? What will be the cost of error? This depends on the specific problem. It is, however, the author's experience that many master planning and schematic design programs can be developed quite adequately without administering a questionnaire of any kind. Literature search and review, interviews, observation, and client/user work sessions (see Chapter 6) provide sufficient information to convey an understanding to the designer that allows development of a building design meeting the needs of clients and users alike. Very few errors result, and those that do occur are easily remedied through minor furniture rearrangement or organizational change. Hence, the cost of error is usually minimized.

However, with very new, large, or complex institutions where change is a constant or is highly unpredictable, or for facilities for user groups for whom the architect or perhaps even the client has had little previous experience, the development and administration of a carefully constructed questionnaire may prevent misconceptions developed in the initial interviewing sessions from going forward into the program. If important issues that have the potential to affect design cannot be fully explored within the framework of interviews and observation, then broad distribution of a questionnaire will save money in the long run.

Similarly, when a great deal of factual information from a large number of subgroups is needed to establish the minimum or even optimal size of a great number of repetitive spaces, obtaining this information in a detailed manner may allow incremental savings in terms of convenience, stress, or building or furniture costs, which will be very substantial when totaled. Here, the time and cost associated with developing and administering a questionnaire may be warranted. Each situation will dictate what needs to be done. The programmer must be alert to discover what is appropriate. For example, organizations such as the Disciples of Christ often develop self-report questionnaires, allowing individual congregations to accurately determine their facility needs (Fig. 5-91).

7. Educational Space Requirements

The projection of future numbers of classes should take into consideration not only the growth expected in church school attendance, but the changing or advancing age of present and future class members. Particular attention should be given to the need for adult classes for entirely new groups of young adults which will be expected to come into a growing church. New congregations will need to consider starting at least one new adult class every year for the first five years.

			NEEDED NOW (First Unit)			FUTURE/MASTER PLAN		
	Age	Sq. Ft. Per Pupil	Avg. Attend.	*Space Needed For Avg. Attend. + 20%	*Space Pro-vided	Avg. Attend.	Space Needed	Recomm. Students Per Room
**Infants		3 Ft. Betw'n Cribs						4-10
**Toddlers	1	25-35						4-10
**Nursery I	2	25-35						6-10
**Nursery II	3	25-35						8-12
**Kind'grn	4	25-35						10-12
**Kind'grn	5	25-35						10-20
Grade 1	6	20-30						
Grade 2	7	20-30						
Grade 3	8	20-30						
Grade 4	9	20-30						12-25
Grade 5	10	20-30						
Grade 6	11	20-30						
Grade 7	12	15-25						
Grade 8	13	15-25						
Grade 9	14	15-25						
Grade 10	15	15-25						12-25
Grade 11	16	15-25						
Grade 12	17	15-25						
Post High		12-20						
Adults I		12-20						
Adults II		12-20						
Adults III		12-20						12-25
Adults IV		12-20						
Adults V		12-20						

*Space listed does not include restrooms, storage, stairways, hallways, etc., 25%-30% should be added to total educational space for these areas. The minimum recommended room size is 300 square feet.
**In many instances there will be more children in preschool and nursery rooms during worship than during church school. Include the number which is the largest attendance if it is during the worship hour.

27

Figure 5-91 Disciples of Christ: Questionnaire.

Credit: Board of Church Extension of Disciples of Christ, 1990. *Strategic Planning & Building Planning for New Congregations.* Permission: Board of Church Extension of Disciples of Christ

5.5 Site and Climate Analysis

• Site Considerations

• Site and Climate Analysis

Site and climate analysis is a part of architectural programming that is conducted parallel to the several information gathering activities covered in this chapter. It is not an information gathering method like the others. Rather, it is a specific application of literature search and diagnostic observation. It is included in this chapter on information gathering because of the particular nature of the application and because it often precedes the development of the programming matrix covered in the next chapter.

The analysis of site and climate during architectural programming is dependent on several conditions, the foremost being that a site has been identified and is accessible for analysis. If a single site has been identified or is already owned by the client, then conducting a complete site and climate analysis is essential to the preparation of an architectural program. If several sites have been identified but none actually selected or purchased, then the analysis of each site might initially be limited to the information necessary to make the selection. Indeed, the architectural programming process may be held aside while a more limited site suitability study is conducted.

Although the principal human issues, specific user needs, and the space program for a facility can be studied in the absence of a specific site, a comprehensive architectural program covering environmental, cultural, technological, temporal, economic, safety, and aesthetic issues is usually dependent on the identification of a specific site. The topography, geology, hydrology, size, exposure, configuration, views, and vegetation of a site are all likely to have a significant impact on what will be designed, so these areas of information need to be developed. The macro- and microclimatic conditions will have an impact on what functions can occur outdoors and may impact the orientation and configuration of the facilities to be designed. Code and ordinance requirements and deed restrictions relating to the specific site will have an impact on design, as will the existing community fabric. Locally available materials, construction techniques, and market conditions are also likely to affect what can be designed. Even the desired image of a facility is likely to change from an urban to a suburban to a rural site. If the site is on a hill, next to water, between two existing buildings, or with major day or nighttime views, these conditions will strongly affect how a building should be designed. Time issues are also difficult to address when a site has not been selected.

Site Considerations

- Regional Conditions

- Local Conditions

- Site Conditions

The analysis of a site for programming purposes should be both systematic and comprehensive. It can include more subjective site evaluations dealing with the various "moods" or "qualities" of the site as experienced by the programming group. If included, this would not relieve the building designer of the normal responsibility to confirm the program and, hence, to review the factual site information and to visit the site to determine if the more subjective information corresponds to his/her own evaluations. As with the rest of the information contained in an architectural program, the site and climate data serve only as a beginning point for the designer.

REGIONAL CONDITIONS

Every site is located within a larger regional context. It may be on the south slope of a major watershed subject to periodic flooding or subterranean water flow. The same topography may result in nocturnal weather cycles or periodic weather anomalies. For instance, a location at the midpoint of a southern slope may create a generally warmer nighttime condition than a location either in the lowest drainage areas or at the top of the sloped area. The site may be located near a major geologic fault and be subject to earthquakes. If the site is on a broad alluvial fan in a river basin, the river could change course during a period of major flooding and destroy any improvements. If the site is downwind from a major source of air pollution or in the flight pattern of a military or commercial airport, there may be problems with air or noise pollution, and even the possibility of a disaster threatening the lives of the building occupants. Any information of this type relating to the region in which the site is located should be developed and included in the programming document, because it could have a major effect on what is designed (McHarg 1969).

LOCAL CONDITIONS

The context of the site is also important. What currently exists near the boundaries of the site? Are there existing buildings, streets, rivers, forests, or other important features? What are the likely future uses? What is the current zoning on all sides of the property? Does the municipality have a history of making zoning changes or granting use variances? Or does it have a history of not deviating from earlier zoning and other regulatory decisions? Is there an orderly process available whereby arguments for change can be heard and a rational decision made? Is the site in a designated zoning district or at its fringes, where change is more likely? Are the surrounding buildings of a consistent character and quality to which the proposed facility should conform, contrast, or respond in some fashion? What existing city services or utilities are available at the site: water, sewer, electrical, gas, telephone, trash pickup? Are the services all beneath grade or are some at grade or above grade? What kind of traffic passes by the site? Is the major access road divided so that a median break would be required to gain access to the site? Are there streetlights and pedestrian crossings at existing corners? Any or all of these may have an impact on design (Fig. 5-92).

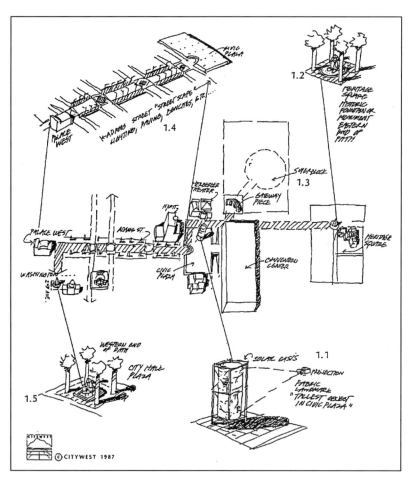

Figure 5-92 Pedestrian Path System.

Credit: City West, 1987. Downtown Pedestrian Core Path. *The Phoenix Public Arts Master Plan: Preliminary Observation.* Permission: Bill Morrish

SITE CONDITIONS

The conditions of the site itself are of great importance to the designer. The site's shape and dimensions, primary orientation and views, topography and geology, microclimate, flora and fauna, natural and built features, and other peculiarities are all needed to begin and complete the design. These, like the broader local and regional conditions, must be discovered and set forth in the architectural programming document so that the programmer can understand the context to which the facility requirements must relate.

Site and Climate Analysis

- Literature Search
- Site Surveys
- Photographic Documentation
- Other Procedures

The methods and techniques of site and climate analysis during programming vary depending upon the nature of the particular problem. Literature search, interviewing, observation, and photographic documentation are all used to collect information about the site and climate. Engineered site surveys, hydrological surveys, and even archeological studies are often required. Detailed coverage of site analysis procedures are included in a number of books specifically addressing site analysis and planning (Lynch 1971; Rubenstein 1987). The student of architectural programming is encouraged to obtain such books and to learn the approaches covered. Only a cursory examination of the various methods, techniques, and tools of site and climate analysis will be provided in the following paragraphs.

LITERATURE SEARCH

Much of the important data on regional and local conditions can be obtained from existing public documents available in public libraries, private bookstores, and the archives of governmental or quasi-governmental agencies. Access to these information sources varies from place to place but generally is not difficult to achieve, because everyone who develops projects in a particular region or locality has need for this type of information. U.S.G.S. topographic maps are readily available in map stores, outdoor sporting

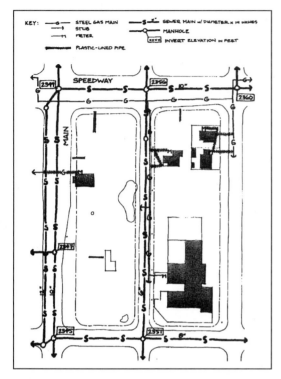

Figure 5-93 Site Utility Information.

Credit: Fourth Year Design Studio, Professor Poster, 1990. *Salvation Army Homeless Facility: Program and Site Analysis.* College of Architecture, The University of Arizona

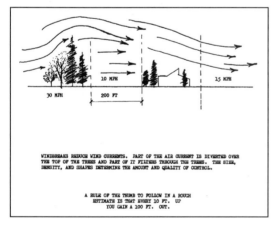

Figure 5-94 Air Current Diagram.

Credit: Bradley Graham, 1978. Main Library for Flagstaff. Permission: School of Architecture, Arizona State University

goods stores, and often in blueprint shops. Watershed information is often available in local libraries, Army Corps of Engineers offices, and within city and county engineering offices. Climate data can be obtained from most local or university libraries as well as from the National Weather Service offices, often located in or near municipal airport facilities. With the advent of a number of computer programs dealing with energy efficient design, data banks on weather are available in association with energy analysis programs used by architectural and engineering firms. Maps of existing utilities (water, sewer, gas, power) and public streets, sidewalks, and curbs are often available in the engineering or public works divisions of local municipalities. Existing ownerships and legal descriptions of property, including easements and deed restrictions, can be found in the offices of the county recorder or in large real estate and title insurance offices. In short, there is often a large body of site and climate information available in local libraries, archives, and other repositories of information (Figs. 5-93 and 5-94).

SITE SURVEYS

The type of topographic and geologic information contained in public documents such as those described above are often enough to meet the needs of architectural programming, particularly for master planning a site. However, before proceeding with schematic design, it is wise to develop more specific site information. An architectural site survey including setting of corner stakes, locating all site features (major outcroppings, trees, existing structures), and public utilities (water, sewer, gas, electricity, telephone, cable, etc.), and establishing site contours with suitable vertical intervals is generally a requirement for design. Similarly, it is important to determine the soil conditions, including bearing strength and expansiveness of the soil, before making design decisions. Although required by the designer, the site survey and soil analysis often are not a direct part of the architectural program (Fig. 5-95).

PHOTOGRAPHIC DOCUMENTATION

It is also possible to obtain primary information, such as aerial photographs, of many sites in municipalities where aerial photography companies operate. These images are made at various engineering scales and show the precise location of major geographic, geologic, building, and landscape features. They often are oriented so as to contain information about topographical conditions, and may even include contour lines superimposed on the photograph. These are of great value to the designer and may be included as folios in an appendix to the program document.

Direct photography of the site and its immediate context by the programming group is also of great value to the designer when included in the program or its appendix (Figs. 5-96 and 5-97).

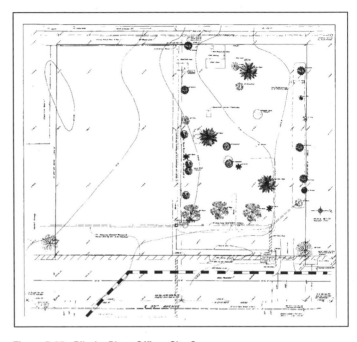

Figure 5-95 Pilgrim Plaza Office: Site Survey.

Credit: Robert Hershberger and Ernest Nickels , Par 3 Studio, 1974. *Pilgrim Plaza Office Building Site Survey*

Figure 5-96 Aerial Photo: Downtown Tempe.

Photo credit: Landiscor

WEST

SOUTH

EAST

NORTH

Figure 5-97 Composite NSEW Views.

Credit: Bradley Graham, 1977. Main Library for Flagstaff. Permission: School of Architecture, Arizona State University

OTHER PROCEDURES

Walking and observing the site and sur-roundings; making comparisons with other known sites; holding discussions with local residents about microclimates (weather, prevailing breezes, etc.), air quality, noise pollution, flooding, and other potential problems; sketching base maps; and noting significant features and views are other ways of evaluating a site (Figs. 5-98 and 5-99). Detailed discussion and representa-tion of these procedures are included in various books on site analysis. The student who has not had the opportunity to take a course on site analysis should review one or more of these books (Lynch 1971; White 1983; Rubenstein 1987).

5.6 Exercises

Literature Search and Review

1. Go to the library and find at least two books and three articles on architec-tural programming. Hint: the topic is not listed in the subject catalog.

2. Find three references for program-ming a preschool. How does it differ from a day-care center architec-turally?

3. Discover the basic ways that park-ing structures work. Consider a va-cant site nearby. What system would work best?

4. Find where all of the utilities are lo-cated servicing a specific site near your home: water, gas, power, tele-phone, cable.

5. What are the basic exiting require-ments for an auditorium in a type 3 building according to the Uniform Building Code (UBC)?

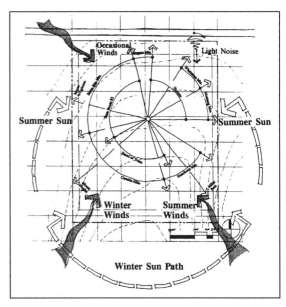

Figure 5-98 Site Analysis Sketch.

Credit: Line and Space, 1990. Building Program for a New Elementary School, Sonoita Elementary School District #35. Permission: Line and Space.

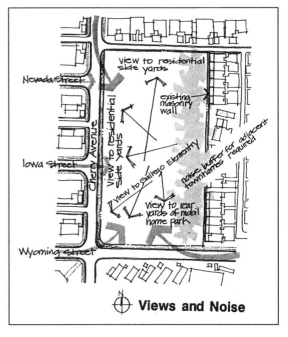

Figure 5-99 Site Analysis Sketch.

Credit: Arquitectura Ltd, 1988. *Pre-Design Workbook, Verde Meadows Recreation Center.* Tucson, Arizona. Permission: Arquitectura Ltd.

6. Your client wants a steeply pitched roof, but is unsure of the material to use. How many different generic types of roofing material can you find in the product literature that would be appropriate to use?

Diagnostic Interviewing

1. Choose a partner and an observer. Then try to sit facing the partner for one minute without communicating anything! Have the observer check the time and whether you or your partner communicated anything.

   You will find that a minute of silence is a long time. You will also find that it is practically impossible not to communicate! Even if you say nothing, much will be communicated non-verbally. Ask the observer what he/she saw.

2. Stay in the same grouping with two persons playing the roles of interviewer and interviewee by facing each other at a comfortable distance. Decide on a current design topic to be discussed. Then try to use only non-verbal acceptance skills (nodding, uh-huhs, smiles, openness, eye contact) to keep the other person talking. Then add verbal acceptance skills. Have the observer explain what he/she saw.

3. Switch roles and add two active listening skills (reflection, clarification). Switch roles again and add the management skills (amplification and redirection). It will take some practice to become comfortable using all of these appraisal skills.

Practice these skills in private conversation. Try to get another person to do all of the talking. You will be amazed at how interesting the person will find you to be, when he/she does all of the talking!

4. Also practice the diagnosis skills. In succinct phrases, try to interpret the essence of what you have heard. After a period on the same general topic, summarize to obtain some affirmation that you have captured the interviewee's point of view.

5. Plan an interview to include the six steps outlined in the chapter (introduction, appraisal, diagnosis, recording, review, open ending).

6. Following the above plan, role play a complete interview on an architectural topic of interest using a three-person group (interviewer, interviewee, observer).

7. Follow up with two or three actual interviews for a current project. Bring along an observer to tell you how well you do.

Diagnostic Observation

1. Tune up your observational abilities by looking at familiar places, varying focus from people, to places, to tasks, and to objects.

2. Conduct a walk-through of a familiar facility with a user to learn how their perceptions differ from yours. Use a recording sheet similar to one of those described to record your observations, the user's comments, and your own thoughts.

3. Take a space inventory of two different spaces used for the same general purpose, like two faculty offices or classrooms. Use all of the techniques described to make the inventory. Then try to determine through the use of trace evidence how the rooms have actually been used.

4. Take a map of a well known public space and conduct a one-day session mapping the behavior of all users to see if the conclusions of other researchers appear to be confirmed.

5. Take a problem in your environment and plan a systematic observation to cover all people, places, tasks, and objects over a certain time period. Vary the scale of your observation from area to room, materials, and furnishings. Set up your observation to involve counts of various elements at specified time intervals so that simple descriptive statistics can be developed and a pie chart or histogram used to summarize the findings.

Questionnaires and Surveys

1. Using the 10 steps of questionnaire preparation, develop a questionnaire to administer to your colleagues to determine the human/functional needs for a completely up-to-date design studio. Use each of the first five question types outlined in the text.

2. Accept the criticism of your peers in a pretest and reconstruct the questionnaire in a logical order and with more appropriate questions.

3. Identify the different categories of persons who can provide insights about your organization, and select a small representative sample of persons to fill out your questionnaire.

4. Administer the questionnaire to the sample, tabulate the answers, and analyze the results.

5. Analyze and evaluate what you have learned in the exercise about:
   a. Questionnaire preparation
   b. The logical order of questionnaires
   c. Advantages and disadvantages of question types
   d. Problems of sampling
   e. Problems of answer analysis

6. Identify the various forms of bias that have become apparent and restructure your questions to avoid this bias.

7. Have you discovered information that would have been difficult to uncover with literature review, interviewing, or observation? What types of information?

8. Did you find it difficult to discover some types of information that would be needed to redesign your facility? What types of information?

Site and Climate Analysis

1. Go to the offices of a local or regional planning agency and request information on a specific site within their area of jurisdiction. Request general plans, area plans, topographic maps, aerial photographs, legal subdivision plans, road plans, and utility plans including sewer, water, power, telephone, gas, etc. Were these all available in one place? If not, what other agencies did you have to visit in order to obtain the requested information?

2. Using the same site, attempt to perform a thorough regional, local, and site analysis. Keep track of the time you take to uncover the needed information in each area. Develop a diagramming system in which all of the information can be presented effectively in a program document.

3. Search the local library or visit the nearest weather bureau or weather station to obtain weather information that applies to the above site. Add some of this information to the site analysis with notes and diagrams.

4. Refer to textbooks and other references on regional, local, and site analysis methods and techniques. Do the same for climate analysis. There is much to be learned in these areas.

5.7 References

Ackoff, Russell L. 1962. *Scientific Method: Optimizing Applied Research Decisions*. New York: Wiley.

_____. 1967. Class lecture in operations research at the University of Pennsylvania, Philadelphia, Pa.

AIA Task Force on Aging. 1985. *Design For Aging: An Architect's Guide*. Washington, D.C.: American Institute of Architects.

American Institute of Architects. 1994. *Architectural Graphic Standards*, edited by John Ray Hoke. New York: John Wiley.

Bardens, Dennis. 1969. Churchill in Parliament. South Brunswick, N. J.: A. S. Barnes.

Barker, Roger. 1968. Ecological Psychology; Concepts and Methods for Studying the Environment of Human Behavior. Stanford, Calif.: Stanford University Press.

Bechtel, Robert, Robert Marans, and William Michelson. 1987. *Methods in Environmental and Behavioral Research*. New York: Van Nostrand Reinhold.

Berdie, Douglas R., John F. Anderson, and Marsha A. Niebuhr. 1986. *Questionnaires: Design and Use*. Metuchen, N.J.: Scarecrow Press.

Bertrand, Raymond. 1993. The Role of the Programmer as Interpreter and Translator. *In Professional Practice in Facility Programming*, edited by Wolfgang F. E. Preiser. New York: Van Nostrand Reinhold.

Blalock, Hubert M. Jr. 1960. *Social Statistics*. New York: McGraw-Hill Book Co. Inc.

Blosser, Fred. 1992. *Primer on Occupational Safety and Health*. Washington, D.C.: Bureau of National Affairs.

Board of Church Extension of Disciples of Christ. 1990. *Strategic Planning and Building Planning for New Congregations*. Indianapolis, Ind.: Disciples of Christ.

BOCA. 1990. *The BOCA National Building Code*. Country Club Hills, Ill.: Building Officials and Code Administrators International.

Bradburn, Norman M., Seymour Sudman, and Edward Blair. 1979. *Improving Interview Method and Questionnaire Design*. San Francisco: Jossey-Bass.

Bradfield, Valerie J., ed. 1983. *Information Sources in Architecture*. Boston: Butterworths.

Callender, John, ed. 1982. *Time-Saver Standards for Architectural Design Data*. New York: McGraw-Hill.

City of Tucson. 1972. *Tucson Historic Districts: Criteria for Preservation and Development*. Tucson, Arizona: Department of Community Development, Planning Division.

Clark, Roger, and Michael Pause. 1996. *Precedents in Architecture*. New York: Van Nostrand Reinhold.

Collier, John Jr. 1967. *Visual Anthropology: Photography as a Research Method*. New York: Holt, Rinehart and Winston.

Cook, R., and D. Miles. 1978. *Plazas for People: Seattle Federal Building Plaza: A Case Study*. New York: Projects for Public Spaces, Inc.

Davis, Gerald, and Virginia Ayers. 1975. Photographic Recording of Environment and Behavior. In *Behavioral Research Methods in Environmental Design*, edited by William Michelson. Stroudsburg, Pa.: Dowden, Hutchinson & Ross.

Deasy, C. M., and Thomas Lasswell. 1985. *Designing Places for People*. New York: Whitney Library of Design.

De Chiara, Joseph, and John Hancock Callender, eds. 1973. *Time-Saver Standards for Building Types*. New York: McGraw Hill Book Co.

Diercks, Janet E., ed. 1998. *Architects' First Source For Products*. Atlanta, Ga.: Architects' First Source.

Downs, Roger, and David Stea, eds. 1973. *Image and Environment; Cognitive Mapping and Spatial Behavior*. Chicago: Aldine Pub. Co.

France, Kenneth, and Michelle Kish. 1995. *Supportive Interviewing in Human Service Organizations: Fundamental Skills for Gathering Information and Encouraging Productive Change*. Springfield, Ill.: Charles C. Thomas.

Frisch, David, and Susan Frisch. 1998. *Metal Design and Fabrication*. New York: Watson-Guptill Publications.

Harris, David A. 1981. *Planning and Designing the Office Environment*. New York: Van Nostrand Reinhold.

Hester, Randolph T. Jr. 1975. *Neighborhood Space*. Stroudsburg, Pa.: Dowden, Hutchinson & Ross.

International Conference of Building Officials. 1994. *Uniform Building Code: Administrative, Fire- and Life-Safety, and Field Inspection Provisions*. Volume 1 of Uniform Building Code. Whittier, Calif.: ICBO.

_____. 1994. *Uniform Building Code*. Whittier, Calif.: ICBO.

Ittelson, William H., Leanne G. Rivlin, and Harold M. Proshansky. 1970. The Use of Behavioral Maps in Environmental Psychology. In *Environmental Psychology: Man and His Physical Setting*, edited by Harold M. Proshansky, William H. Ittleson, and Leanne G. Rivlin. New York: Holt, Rinehart and Winston.

Kirk, Stephen J., and Kent F. Spreckelmeyer. 1988. *Creative Design Decisions: A Systematic Approach to Problem Solving in Architecture*. New York: Van Nostrand Reinhold.

Kumlin, Robert R. 1995. *Architectural Programming: Creative Techniques for Design Professionals*. New York: McGraw-Hill.

Lindheim, Rosyln. 1966. Putting Research To Work. *AIA Journal*. 66(2), 46-53.

Lynch, Kevin. 1971. *Site Planning*. Cambridge, Mass.: M.I.T. Press.

Marans, Robert, and Kent Spreckelmeyer. 1981. *Evaluating Built Environments: A Behavioral Approach*. Ann Arbor: Survey Research Center, University of Michigan.

McGraw-Hill Construction Information Group. 1997. *Sweet's Catalog File*. New York: McGraw-Hill.

_____. 1997. *Sweet's General Building & Renovation Catalog File*. New York: McGraw-Hill.

McHarg, Ian. 1969. *Design with Nature*. Garden City, N.Y.: Natural History Press.

Moore, Gary, and Reginald Golledge. 1976. *Environmental Knowing: Theories, Research, and Methods*. Stroudsburg, Pa.: Dowden, Hutchinson & Ross.

Palmer, Mickey A. 1981. *The Architect's Guide to Facility Programming*. New York: Architectural Record Books.

Pastalan, Leon A., and Daniel H. Carson. 1970. *Spatial Behavior of Older People*. Ann Arbor: Institute of Gerontology, University of Michigan; and Wayne State University.

Peña, William, and John W. Focke. 1969. *Problem Seeking: New Directions in Architectural Programming*. Houston, Tex.: Caudill Rowlett Scott.

Peña, William, Steven Parshall, and Kevin Kelly. 1987. *Problem Seeking: An Architectural Programming Primer*. 3rd ed. Washington, D.C.: AIA Press.

Peponis, John, Craig Zimring, and Yoon Kyung Choi. 1990. Finding the Building in Wayfinding. *Environment and Behavior*. 22(5): 555-590.

Preiser, Wolfgang F. E., ed. 1978. *Facility Programming: Methods and Applications*. Stroudsburg, Pa.: Dowden, Hutchinson & Ross.

_____. 1985. *Programming the Built Environment*. New York: Van Nostrand Reinhold.

Quayle, Dan. 1996. *Election Year Survey on Politics and the Media*. Alexandria, Va.: Media Research Center.

Rae, Leslie. 1988. *The Skills of Interviewing: A Guide for Managers and Trainers*. Aldershot, Hants.: Gower.

Reznikoff, S. C. 1986. *Interior Graphic and Design Standards*. New York: Whitney Library of Design.

Ripley, Robert. 1980-85. Classroom lectures and demonstrations in active listening in the architectural programming class at Arizona State University, Tempe, Arizona.

Rosenbaum, Sonia. 1979. *Quantitative Methods and Statistics: A Guide to Social Research*. Beverly Hills: Sage Publications.

Rubenstein, Harvey M. 1987. *A Guide to Site and Environmental Planning*. 3rd ed. New York: Wiley.

Sanoff, Henry. 1977. *Methods of Architectural Programming*. Stroudsburg, Pa.: Dowden, Hutchinson & Ross.

Shalaby, Mostafa. 1988. *The Optimum Layout of Single Story Manufacturing Areas*. Ph.D. diss., The University of Pennsylvania, Philadelphia.

Siegel, Sidney. 1956. *Nonparametric Statistics for the Behavioral Sciences*. New York: McGraw-Hill.

Sommer, Robert. 1974. *Tight Spaces; Hard Architecture and How to Humanize It*. Englewood Cliffs, N.J.: Prentice-Hall.

Sullivan, Louis. 1949. *The Autobiography of an Idea*. New York: Peter Smith.

Trites, David, Frank Galbraith Jr., Madelyne Sturdavant, and John Leckwart. 1970. "Influence of Nursing-Unit Design on the Activities and Subjective Feelings of Nursing Personnel." *Environment and Behavior*. 2(3): 303-334.

Webb, Eugene T. 1981. *Nonreactive Measures in the Social Sciences*. Boston: Houghton Mifflin.

Weisberg, Herbert F., Jon A. Kronsnick, and Bruce D. Bowen. 1996. *Introduction to Survey Research and Data Analysis*. Thousand Oaks, Calif.: Sage Publications.

White, Edward T. III. 1983. *Site Analysis: Diagramming Information for Architectural Design*. Tucson, Ariz.: Architectural Media.

Whyte, William H. 1988. *The Social Life of Small Urban Spaces* [video recording]. Los Angeles, Calif.: Direct Cinema Limited.

Wilson, Forrest. 1984. *A Graphic Survey of Perception and Behavior for the Design Professions*. New York: Van Nostrand Reinhold.

Yao, Wimberta. 1987. Literature Search Steps. Unpublished manuscript. Arizona State University, Tempe.

Zeisel, John. 1981. *Inquiry by Design: Tools for Environment-Behavior Research*. Monterey, Calif.: Brooks/Cole Publishing Co.

Work Sessions

The final method for gathering and analyzing information for architectural programming is the work session. This is a type of show and tell activity in which the programmer presents the previously gathered information to the client/user group on a large wall-sized matrix with the intention of defining the whole problem when completed. The client/users are asked to confirm or refute what is presented, to generate new information, and to reorganize the information to improve the matrix. It is a very effective method for filling in gaps left after using the other information gathering techniques. It is also effective in getting the client/user to make decisions regarding which of the previously suggested values, goals, facts, needs, and ideas should be retained in the architectural program.

Work sessions are the heart of any client/user group programming process where agreement with the program is considered essential. They are both the final step of information gathering and the first step of program preparation.

As an information gathering process, the work session is similar to diagnostic interviewing as discussed in Chapter 5. It is similar in that the programmer is attempting to get the clients/users as a group to articulate what they think is important information for architectural programming. The same active listening skills utilized in the diagnostic interviewing process are helpful in getting the clients and users to identify their areas of concern. It is different from the diagnostic interviewing sessions in that the programmer will typically be presenting information obtained from the other information gathering methods with the intent of securing agreement from the client/user decision makers as to its accuracy and importance. To do this effectively, skills in appropriate presentation of information and negotiation of agreement are essential.

Value areas that were identified in the literature search, interviewing, observation, and questionnaire/survey phases of information gathering need to be presented and discussed. Do the decision makers agree that the preliminary list of values is complete? If an order of importance was identified earlier, do the decision makers agree with the order? Are the specific project goals appropriate? Are the decision makers willing to spend money to accomplish them? Which goals must be accomplished? Which could remain unaccomplished and not seriously reduce the effectiveness of the organization? Are the previously identified goals, facts, or needs statements really important or just someone's pet project, which the organization as a whole is unwilling to support?

In other words, the work session is a time for both active presentation and listening by the programmer and the client/user decision makers. If the first five areas of information gathering could be considered as primarily objective in their intent, simply to obtain the data, this phase could be considered as primarily subjective. It is a time for group decision making, a time for sorting out what is important from what is not. It is, as Peña and Focke (1969) said, a problem seeking situation, a time to resolve and agree on the design problem. Presentation, interaction, and negotiation of agreement are the essential methods.

The effectiveness of work sessions is at least partially due to the presentation of everything that has been discovered in a clearly organized format, such that the whole problem can be seen and understood by those present. It is also essential that the method of presentation be flexible, to allow for change and augmentation by the work session participants.

6.1 Client/User Work Sessions

- Composition
- Presentation
- Interaction
- Negotiation
- Agreement
- Wrap-Up

Composition

The client/user work session should involve all of those persons who have a stake in the project. This, of course, would involve virtually everyone who will ultimately use the facility. In most cases this is impractical, so a representative group must be assembled. Typically, this group will consist of the leadership of the organization, division and department heads, perhaps section leaders, and representatives from each of the employee or user types. The intent, on one hand, is to be democratic, so that no one in the organization will feel left out of the process—indeed, so that every person can talk about their values, goals, needs, and ideas with someone who will attend the work session. On the other hand, and equally important, the intent is to not leave anyone out who can shed important light on the needs of the facility.

For a college of architecture building addition, the client/user work sessions may involve the dean, each department chair, elected representative faculty (design, technology, history, etc.), elected representative classified staff, elected representative students (from each year level), development officer, librarian, media specialist, shop superintendent, head custodian, and any other person likely to have a unique perspective on the project. Such a group could easily number 25. For a church, the programming group would likely involve the senior minister, each associate minister in charge of a particular area (contemporary worship, education, youth, music, fellowship, outreach, etc.), choir director, organist, elected chairs of various committees (staff parish, deacons, trustees, finance, worship, music, education, missions, foundation, etc.), appointed representatives of various age groups (children, youth, young singles, married, older singles, etc.), head custodian, etc. Here again the number can easily reach 25 or more. The same will be found to be true for most other organizations. For large corporations, there will be even more persons that may have a stake in a major building project. In such cases, it can be important to conduct parallel sessions relating only to parts of the project, so that a manageable number of persons can be involved in each session.

It is also possible, when conducting the sessions in the client's facilities, to invite all interested persons in the organization to stop by during lunch breaks and after hours to review the progress of the work, so as to be able to communicate items of importance that seem to have been missed by the participants. Occasionally, this will bring out someone with a particular point of view or expertise who can contribute to the overall process and improve the program.

"The Salvation Army, founded in 1865, is an international, religious and charitable movement organized and operated on a quasi-military pattern and is a branch of the Christian church. Its membership includes officers (clergy), soldiers/adherents (laity), members of varied activity groups and volunteers who serve as advisors, associates and committed participants in its service function.

"The motivation of the organization is love of God and a practical concern for the needs of humanity. This is expressed by a spiritual ministry, the purposes of which are to preach the gospel, disseminate Christian truths, supply basic human necessities, provide personal counselling and undertake the spiritual and moral regeneration of all persons in need who come within its sphere of influence regardless of race, color, creed, sex or age.

Figure 6-1 Mission of Salvation Army.

Credit: Fourth Year Design Studio Professor Paster, 1990. *Salvation Army Homeless Facility, Program and Site Analysis*. College of Architecture, The University of Arizona

We are here today to begin to formulate the goals and requirements for a new wing of the residential unit. This wing will allow our organization to accommodate an additional thirty women and their children for long enough periods to allow the women to be trained for and to receive suitable employment.

Figure 6-2 Purpose of the Project.

Credit: Fourth Year Design Studio Professor Paster. 1990. *Salvation Army Homeless Facility. Program*

Presentation

When the group session begins, the programmer typically presents a brief overview of the organization's mission, the purpose of the project, the proposed budget, and the expected schedule as determined in an earlier meeting with the executives of the organization (Figs. 6-1 through 6-4).

If there has been little or no information gathering prior to the initial work session, the programmer must indicate how the session is to proceed. This could involve pointing to a wall containing signs for values, goals, facts, needs, and ideas spaced along the top of the wall, then explaining the programmer's intent to develop information under each of these categories during the work session, beginning with values and working through to ideas. The process could then follow the CRS system (Peña et al. 1977) with members of the programming staff preparing and posting cards for each of the suggestions made by the group (Fig. 6-5). An alternative would be to have several easels with grid paper, on which the programmer could write the suggestions and then post them on the wall as each sheet becomes full of information (Fig. 6-6).

If there has already been a substantial effort at information gathering, the programmer will explain how the preliminary matrix was developed. This could involve a brief review of the value categories along the left side of the matrix and the goals that have thus far been articulated, perhaps identifying those which seem most important. The programmer could then discuss the facts, needs, and ideas that have been uncovered in a similar fashion. This verbal presentation of the

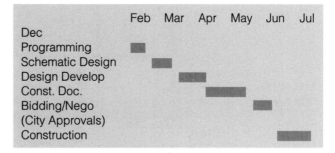

The total budget for the project is one million dollars. With expected overhead costs, architect/engineer fees, furnishing costs and the like, the construction budget will be in the neighborhood of eight hundred thousand dollars.

Figure 6-3 Project Budget.

Figure 6-4 Project Schedule.

Figure 6-5 Matrix Development with Cards.
Photo Credit: Richard Brittain

Figure 6-6 Matrix Development with Grid Paper.

visual matrix helps to ensure that everyone (client, user, programmer, designer) understands what is being presented. This is
a very effective system of presentation with many additional benefits that will be discussed in the following sections.

Interaction

As soon as the programmer has concluded his/her initial presentation of the results of the information gathering phase of
programming, it is time for the client/users to begin reacting
and interacting. Is the statement of purpose for the new facility
appropriate? Is the initial program statement as presented on
the matrix correct? If taken seriously by the designer, would the
resulting building meet the important goals of the organization
and serve the actual needs of the users? This is the time for
feedback from the client and users (the subjects of the interviews and the objects of observation). Did the programmer discover the design problem, or is it yet to be adequately defined?
Are the most important issues covered? Chances are that the
various information gathering methods have resulted in only
partial understandings of the problem. The group session will

be important in correcting misunderstandings and filling in missing information.

The group session at this point tends to be synthetic, that is, to be involved in bringing together all of the findings to get a picture or better understanding of the whole problem. Are the values presented in the correct order? What is the highest priority for design? Is it function, form, economy, time? Is it image, context, life cycle costs, user needs? Are all of the presented values really of importance to the organization? Has some value area been completely left out as the interviewed individuals have considered the nature of the problem? Are the goals attainable? Are they attainable by means of architecture, or are they a matter of reorganization or economics in general? Are the facts valid, or are they someone's idiosyncratic statements? Are there other facts that need to be stated? Are there specific needs or ideas for solution which have not been revealed, or are those thus far stated inappropriate in some manner? This is what the interaction of the work session is all about.

The client/users are expected to confirm or refute what has been presented and to add any material that has been omitted. This requires the programmer to use the interviewing skills discussed earlier (acceptance, reflection, clarification, amplification, redirection, interpretation, and summary), but now they must be applied with each and every participant who has something to say during the work session. The participants must understand that they are free to state what is on their mind. It should also be clear that what is being presented is what the programmers have discovered so far, and that it might be inaccurate in many respects. The group must understand that the programmers have no vested interest in the presented information and are looking for the client/users to set them straight while it is still inexpensive to do so, rather than after the architectural firm begins design or, worse yet, after construction has begun.

If it appears that a few people want to dominate the work session, it may be appropriate to have different echelons of people in at different times, with the key decision makers reserved for first and last (see 6.2 Executive Work Sessions). Or within groups, it may be necessary to be systematic, to go around the group in one direction, asking for input from each person, possibly for each category of information.

Leading a work session is a very subjective activity and requires a good deal of sensitivity to be done effectively. When a person says something, a simple verbal acceptance or reflection may be appropriate to assure the person that their participation is appreciated and was heard. If it is unclear whether they are talking about goals, facts, needs, or even ideas, a simple question asking for clarification in this regard may be appropriate. If the programmer thinks he/she really understands what is being suggested, it is appropriate to offer a diagnostic statement or an interpretation such as:

> *An important image goal is to communicate concern for the user in the quality of the building.*

If the person nods his/her head in the affirmative, then the programmer should say something like,

> *If others agree,* (pause) *I will record the idea and place it in the matrix. Okay?*

If someone disputes the idea of another participant, then the programmer must go through the same process to determine what the new person is concerned with, using the various stages of active listening as required, until the new person's thoughts are fully articulated. Here again the programmer must see if the first person has accepted the new argument. If so, then the new idea should be put on a card (or grid paper) and tacked up for all to see. If others still disagree, then the procedure must be continued until a consensus is reached, or both ideas can be left up as unresolved issues for the chief decision maker(s) to decide at a later date. The work session must not be allowed to deteriorate into extended conflict between opposing parties.

Negotiation

Negotiation between persons with strongly held opposing points of view is not easy to handle. Sometimes it reflects personal animosities or power struggles that have very little to do with programming a new facility, but the work session becomes a forum for the disagreements to surface. The programmer should try to remain neutral in such arguments, never actively taking one side or another. The programmer may, however, serve as a kind of neutral analyst, sharing insights based on professional experience.

Rules of conduct can sometimes help in this situation. It might be stated, for instance, that "this group is here because the owner feels that each person in the group has something important to contribute. Let's really listen to each person's ideas to be sure of the point that is being made."

It might also be stated, for the first part of the session, that the rules of brainstorming will apply, e.g., that no suggestion can immediately be challenged (Rawlinson 1981). Challenges will be recognized only after the initiator has had time to articulate fully the idea and its rationale, and until after each person in attendance has had an opportunity to present his or her ideas. This later condition has the pleasant effect of removing the author of an idea from the criticism, because criticism offered later can be directed at the idea, rather than at the person who suggested it.

If there is a challenge to any idea after this initial go around, that challenger should be asked to articulate his/her thoughts, then others should be asked how they feel, or if there is still another alternative. The author of the original idea can remain somewhat anonymous if he/she wishes, or even join in trying to improve the new statement. The final intent of negotiations of this type should, wherever possible, be a win-win situation (Hall 1993). The group should be looking for a statement that addresses the legitimate concerns of all parties. If possible, a consensus should be reached, recorded, and placed on the matrix.

If a consensus cannot be reached, it may be possible to obtain agreement to list both ideas and to let the designer grapple with the problem. This often is an appropriate resolution of conflict. It is akin to Robert Venturi's "both/and" philosophy rather than an "either/or," "black/white," mentality (Venturi 1977).

The author, for instance, once conducted a work session with a church building committee in which some of the members insisted that the church seating be in the round so that all worshipers could gather around the communion table as evidence of their being a "community of believers." Another group of the members insisted that a more traditional church with chancel at one end, seating in rows between, and the narthex at the other end was the only appropriate solution. Because the groups were nearly evenly divided and firmly set in their opinions, the programmer asked if it had to be one way or the other, that perhaps the designer could figure out a way in which each group could sit in the manner they desired.

The members of the church's programming group could not see how this could possibly be done, but were relieved to pass the problem on to the architect, who found it very easy to resolve by

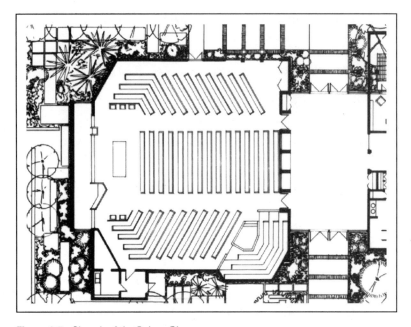

Figure 6-7 Church of the Palms: Plan.

Credit: Robert Hershberger and Ernest Nickels, Par 3 Studio

arranging the main section of seating in a traditional manner, but with side sections angled and brought forward to surround the communion table. The building committee, which had been so divided, accepted the solution unanimously. When the church was built, those who preferred one way always sat in "their" section, and those who felt the other way sat in "theirs." Everyone was happy, not only that their needs were satisfied, but that the other group's needs were satisfied as well (Fig. 6-7).

Agreement

Once agreement has been reached, the suggestions should be recorded on cards or grid paper and placed on the wall so that everyone can see and affirm that the programmer's understanding is agreeable to all. When working on a complex building type, this process can take several hours, even days, as numerous values, goals, facts, needs, and ideas are discussed, modified, refined, and finally agreed upon as being appropriate to include in the program.

If the project is small, or there are only two or three decision makers involved, then such an elaborate procedure would be inappropriate. Simply preparing a preliminary programming report on 8½" × 11" paper of what has been discovered, circulating it to the persons concerned along with a request for review and comment, followed by a meeting around a small conference table, may be all that is necessary to come to agreement as to the nature of the architectural problem.

Wrap-Up

When the matrix appears to be complete or everyone is exhausted by the process, it is time to wrap up the session. A very brief review of what is before the group, emphasizing only the most important points, is usually appropriate. This should be followed by an open ending, in which the programmer indicates what will be done with the information, when the participants can expect to see the results in another work session or in preliminary report form, and what they should do with it when they receive it. Here again it is wise to ask everyone to review the preliminary program promptly, and to let the programming group know immediately if they have any problems with it. This has two important benefits:

1. It allows the conscientious participants to help in proofreading and confirming that the programming report is an accurate reflection of the agreements reached in the session.

2. It is a good way to keep the less conscientious (or more critical) from arguing that they did not have a chance to review and comment on the program before it was adopted.

It is important to let everyone have an opportunity to comment at a time when changes are still easy to make!

6.2 Executive Work Sessions

Special work sessions with the top leadership of an organization can be used effectively both before and after the larger client/user work session(s). The first executive work session with top leadership should be used to gain an understanding of the mission and structure of the organization, to establish the purpose of the project, and to set forth budget and schedule guidelines. It is important to present this information at the beginning of each client/user work session to set a framework in which the participants can work. The second executive work session is important for refining and prioritizing all of the programmatic information advanced from the client/user work sessions, in confirming the project schedule, and in agreeing on specific square footages to be allocated to various functions while exploring the budget and expected project costs.

The reason for working with a more select group for these sessions is quite simple. Decisions relating to project purpose, size, schedule, and budget should be made by those who will be held accountable for them. Peña's axiom that "those who will be held responsible must have authority" clearly applies here (Peña and Focke 1969).

These later work sessions may include trading off earlier established required spaces, sizes, or desired materials and finishes in order to bring the building size or quality into line with the financial capabilities of the organization. There could be trade-offs of earlier established needs in order to meet other requirements such as project schedule. For instance, this might be done to avoid disruption of the client's ongoing operations. The executive group might also discard some programmatic concepts or design ideas that they feel could threaten the successful continued operation of the organization, even though other people in the organization feel strongly about including them.

The approach described above may seem undemocratic to some readers, but there are very few organizations where everyone involved is of equal status. The people at the head of the organization are clearly the ones who will be held responsible for the success or failure of the overall organization and, therefore, must claim authority to make decisions of this magnitude. On the other hand, the head of a particular division within the organization should have authority concerning specific program requirements for the spaces allocated to that division. Similarly, the secretarial staff should have some authority over the furnishings for and arrangement of their individual workspaces, and the janitors or maintenance personnel should have some say about how the janitors' closets and work areas are arranged as well as about maintenance problems associated with particular materials, furnishings, and equipment.

All of the people in the organization should have input into the areas of the program affecting them. Superiors in an organization who avoid or ignore this input risk failure in part of the organization. However, superiors are generally in their positions because they have a broader view of the needs of the organization, and ultimately will be held responsible if their area or division is not effective. They must, therefore, be able to make final decisions as to what goes and what stays, particularly if the organization has a limited ability to provide all of the desired amenities.

Ultimately, it is the strongly held values of the executive leadership of an organization, set up against the realities of budget and schedule, that will determine the allocations of space and the construction quality for the project. The tradeoffs that may be necessary can rarely be accomplished successfully solely by the chief executive officer. They are generally the result of work sessions in which the advantages and disadvantages of each decision are openly discussed by those with responsibility for various areas of the organization. In this way, the final decisions will provide the most beneficial overall distribution of resources. Often these decisions will be by consensus of the decision makers, but usually over the objection of someone who feels disadvantaged.

Sometimes the final allocations of space and other resources will be over the objection of one or more persons who feel that their area of responsibility is not receiving sufficient attention. This is simply a fact of decision making responsibility and authority. The programmer should serve as an unbiased catalyst or mediator who allows, indeed insists, that the client resolve these disputes, so that the designer is not asked to do the impossible! The programmer should not be drawn into making decisions about client operational needs, or worse, to serve as an arbitrator who makes the decision. The programmer can often mediate the differences and offer advice based on personal or professional experience. If the programmer has sufficient experience, and particularly if the designer is part of the team, it may be possible to allow some programmatic indecision or ambiguity, knowing that appropriate design decisions can accommodate the difficulty.

In some areas, such as the net-to-gross ratio (efficiency) or the current level of construction costs for a particular building type, the programmers must be knowledgeable and hold their ground, because they will be held responsible if the building cannot be designed within the gross square footage allocated or built for the stipulated budget. In other words, there are some areas where the programmer must have or develop special expertise. It is a rare client that has sufficient understanding or expertise in these areas, so the client should not be expected to make the final decisions in these areas. If the programmer is also the designer or if the designer is a part of the programming team, then he or she should have something to say about the probable construction costs, costs of particular materials, appropriate space sizes, building efficiency expectations, building configurations, and so on. The designer should also have input on the project schedule. He or she ought to have the most to say about aesthetics, building form, fire safety, accessibility, and other areas in which the designer ultimately will be held responsible for failures.

Clearly, a variety of work sessions will be necessary to establish all of the project parameters. The programmer must develop an understanding of the nature of an organization and make certain that the persons who will be affected by programming decisions are included in the appropriate work session(s).

6.3 Work Session Setting

The work sessions should, ideally, be on the client's premises in a room large enough to accommodate all of the participants and the presentation materials. For major programs, the room should be available all day long and into the evening hours for one or more days. For smaller projects, the work session might take place in a three- to four-hour time frame, with a few days in between two or three such sessions. In this way the programmer will have time to refine and re-present information before each session.

The work session room should have at least three walls that will accept tacks or tape, several work tables, and seating for all participants. The lighting level should be quite high for easy visibility, and there should be good sound isolation from the rest of the building. Ideally, the room should have a separate thermostatic control and adequate ventilation for long sessions, which may involve more than the normal number of occupants of the room.

The programming matrix for a card-based presentation is typically set up along one wall of a large room. For a grid paper presentation, more than one wall will likely be required. In either case, the initial presentation can be set up prior to the group meeting using the value categories, goals, objectives, ideas, and needs statements identified during information gathering and/or the first executive work session. Related information such as the mission statement, organizational chart, purpose of the project, preliminary space allocations, preliminary relationship matrices, sketch relationship diagrams, preliminary cost estimates, and tentative project schedules can be set up on the remaining wall(s).

If wall space is at a premium, the organization's mission and organizational chart could be presented at the beginning of the meeting by slide or overhead projection, preferably the latter, so that they can remain visible or be shown again as needed during the session.

Such a format for presentation allows everyone in the work session to see and act upon the same information at the same time and to make group decisions as to the true nature of the architectural problem. So, while the work session is the last stage of information gathering, it is also the first stage of presenting the program to the client, users, and designer.

The two floor plan diagrams show typical room arrangements for work sessions involving 20 to 30 participants in a standard classroom of approximately 32 feet by 40 feet (Figs. 6-8 and 6-9).

The first plan shows an open room with chairs arranged in an arc facing the matrix wall. This arrangement has the advantage of being easily changed to allow all participants to face the wall currently being used. It also allows participants to move around and come and go. The second plan shows an arrangement using eight 30" by 96" tables to form a u-shaped plan. This has the advantage of providing each participant with a place to take notes and lay out their materials. It also allows the programmer to move around the center area to show everyone detailed information. It makes moving in and out of the session more difficult. Also, some of the participants will have their backs to some of the posted materials at all times.

6.4 Matrix Development

- Values
- Goals (intentions, objectives, aspirations)
- Facts (constraints, conditions, opportunities)
- Needs (requirements)
- Ideas

Values

As discussed in Chapters 2 and 3, the focus of value-based programming is to discover the key values that should become issues as the

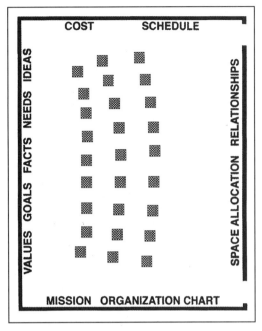

Figure 6-8 Typical Work Session Room Plan.

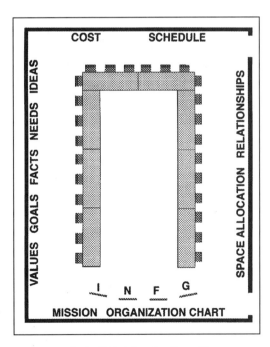

Figure 6-9 Typical Work Session Room Plan.

designer attempts to create architecture. The programmer must discover and enumerate the values associated with the purpose(s) of the organization for which facilities are to be designed. The programmer should also identify other important values of the client, users, community, and designer (if already selected). Typically these value areas can be remembered using the acronym HECTTEAS: human, environmental, cultural, technological, temporal, economic, aesthetic, and safety. However, it must be remembered that the important value categories are likely to change from project to project.

The alternative acronym TEST EACH reinforces the notion that there is not a pre-determined number or order for the value categories. After the initial values have been identified or confirmed in the client/user work session(s), the programmer should "test each" of the unused HECTTEAS values to determine if some were inadvertently left out. For example, a client/user group may not mention safety concerns as they focus on the primary mission of an organization, but if mentioned as a possible issue, they may say "oh yes, this is very important, particularly in the ___ areas." Safety could then be added as another value area. On the other hand, the client/users may say this is not a major concern, and it would not be added as a value area. Thus, programming matrices in value-based programming might vary from one project to the next, as illustrated in the following sample programming matrices, with the values listed down the left side of each matrix (Fig. 6-10).

The last programming matrix is composed essentially of the eight HECTTEAS areas outlined in Chapter 3, but with some slightly different words that might relate better to how a particular client/user group thinks about their design problem. The idea in value-based programming is not to use the list of eight value areas for every project, but to come up with the most appropriate value areas for the problem at hand, especially categories that are easily understood by the client, users, and architect.

The programmer should TEST EACH of the HECTTEAS value categories to be certain that no value of importance is left out, and thus to be sure that the whole problem will be adequately defined. As with the CRS system, it is a tremendous advantage to be able to define the whole problem in a limited, easy-to-remember set of categories, so that both direction and flexibility of inquiry can be maintained. Values are easy to recognize because they typically can be represented by single words.

Values can be expanded upon with broad statements suggesting appropriate goals for a facility. This was done as part of the programming activities for the new building for the College

Values	Goals	Facts	Needs	Ideas
Image				
Function				
Environment				
Technology				
Economy				

Or the programming matrix may be very similar to that advanced by CRS.

Values	Goals	Facts	Needs	Ideas
Function				
Form				
Economy				
Time				
Context				

Another programming matrix may approximate the HETTEAS categories.

Values	Goals	Facts	Needs	Ideas
Human				
Environmental				
Cultural				
Systems				
Time				
Finance				
Aesthetic				
Safety				

Figure 6-10 Sample Value-Based Programming Matrices.

Aesthetics:	The building should be of award winning quality, teach about design, identify the College purposes, relate to the campus context and existing building, be as good inside as outside, and be lasting...not the latest fashion.
Education:	The purpose is high quality design education: teaching, research and service. Requires adequate facilities, state of art equipment, administrative support, and outstanding faculty and students.
Community:	Want a unified College, sense of community, lots of interaction, interdisciplinary activities. Bring departments together, all students in buildings, faculty near students, central focus areas where all can come together: galleries, commons, courtyards.
Openness:	Accessible to all people, clear circulation system, flow from floor to floor, space to space, interior to exterior, new building to old building.
Security:	Adequate, yet controlled entry. Ways to allow 24 hours of activity, safety of persons and property.
Environment:	Respond to local climate with orientation, shading, daylighting, useable exterior spaces, and roof top solar research. Relate to campus context in scale, colors and materials.
Service:	Need adequate service areas and short-term parking.
Technology:	Lead the profession with computer infusion all areas, electronic studio, intelligent building, state of art research laboratories, solar and daylighting systems.
Time:	Should be flexible, adaptable, expandable to allow for unforseen growth and change.
Economics:	Must stay within space budget of 100,000 gross square feet and 75% efficiency guidelines.

Figure 6-11 Architecture Building Expansion.

Permission: School of Architecture, Arizona State University

of Architecture and Environmental Design at Arizona State University (Fig. 6-11).

Goals (Intentions, Objectives, Aspirations)

When the programmer has identified the overall value areas that are most appropriate for a particular problem, attention is then directed to identifying specific goals relating to each of the values. The goal statements are placed in the second column next to the value to which they relate. Goals may relate to more than one value. If so, try to place the goal next to the value to which it is most closely related. It is also possible to have several goals for each value area. Indeed, there are often subvalues or issues (Duerk 1993) that relate to each of the main value areas. For example, if "environment" were one of the value areas, goals might include preserving topography and flora in site development, being a good neighbor to surrounding development, and orienting for solar penetration or for views.

> *Goals are those aspirations, intentions, or objectives that bring focus to the programming and design project.*

What is it that the client wants to accomplish by building? If there is a concern that the appropriate image be projected for a small commercial facility, "image" should be used as a value category, and following it there should be one or more project goal statements such as:

> *To communicate the nature of the business through the designed form*
>
> *To provide dominant verbal/graphic signs to identify the business*

If, on the other hand, functional efficiency is very important, then "function," "efficiency," or "functional efficiency" would be a value category, and there could be one or more related project goals such as:

To minimize the number of persons needed to operate the shop

To define separate areas to be used by customers and staff

As previously mentioned, there should be at least one project goal for every value area. If there is not, then the programmer should question if the value area is really worth noting. Perhaps the value relates primarily to organizational structure, administrative assignments, or activities that are not affected by the design of the facility, and thus should not be part of the architectural problem statement. Or perhaps the value is a "lip-service goal," as Peña et al. (1977, 58-59) state, important to everyone, but not something anyone is willing to do anything about.

Goals are usually general, and thus difficult to measure relative to accomplishment. As statements, they are easy to recognize because they usually begin with the words "we need" followed by an infinitive such as to have, to communicate, to achieve, to define, or to organize. Sometimes the "to" is left off and the goal statement begins with a verb. Both types of statement are seen in Fig. 6-12.

Some goals will be very lofty or global in nature, others more

```
TEMPE CENTER FOR THE HANDICAPPED    ARCHITECTURAL PROGRAM

VALUES

Institutional Values

1.    Handicapped  are individuals with the potential for  growth
      and development.

      Goal:    To help the handicapped trainees reach their
      potential

2.    Handicapped  as individuals have the right to self  respect
      and deserve  the opportunity to be  contributing members of
      society.

      Goal:    To provide individualized rehabilitative and voca-
      tional  training to  help the  handicapped develop  work
      skills.

      Goal:    To provide paid work opportunities for handicapped
      individuals within the community or in a sheltered setting.

Human Values

1.    Safety of Clients (and Staff).

      Goal:    Meet all of the handicapped and health  and safety
      requirements of  applicable codes,  especially  providing
      clear means of egress.

2.    Comfort of Clients (and Staff).

      Goal:    Provide clean, well lit, conditioned  environment
      with individually taylored work space/surface.

3.    Efficiency of Operations.

      Goal:    Reduce client  distraction,  provide  orderly flow
      of materials and  appropriate work  environment for clients
      and staff.

      Goal:    Maintain adequate staff and support facilities for
      operations.

Aesthetic Values

1.    Welcoming/Friendly Appearance

      Goal:    Maintain same  character as existing building  so
      that everyone will continue to feel this is a good place.
```

Figure 6-12 Goal Statements Sheet.

Credit: Elaine Cesta, for Par 3 Studio, 1976. *Program for Tempe Center for the Handicapped*, Tempe, Arizona

particular. Some will be very important in expressing the nature of the institution, others in solving particular problems. It is not important to differentiate between the types of goals early in the programming process, but later it may be necessary to sort them out on a priority basis and keep only those with broad implications for design as goals and to convert others that are more specific, or more directly measured in terms of accomplishment, into appropriate need statements.

In the above regard, it should be understood when the matrix is being developed in a programming work session, that the process is not entirely ordered or predictable. If someone offers a goal statement that has little or no relationship with earlier stated values, the goal is placed in a new bottom row of the matrix. Once placed, the participants will inevitably state a new value to which the goal statement relates. The same will be true for facts, needs, and ideas statements. The programmer can try to keep everyone focused on an area, but the participants will contribute in areas where they have knowledge and/or interest. In a matrix without preestablished value categories, it is possible to add information, even when it is offered at an inappropriate time.

Facts (constraints, conditions, opportunities)

After the project goals are identified, it is much easier to know where to focus attention in discovering facts and establishing needs.

Facts are reliable pieces of information about the existing and future situation involving the design project.

Typically, facts relate to specific conditions, constraints, and opportunities that should influence design. There will be facts that relate to each of the earlier identified value areas. There will be facts about the human purposes or activities to be accommodated, cultural concerns, legal requirements, environmental context, economic situation, time factors, available technology, safety regulations, and aesthetic preferences. But which facts to search out and at what level of detail will depend on the importance of the particular values and related project goals—what the client hopes to accomplish with the building project.

If the building must accommodate a specifically defined activity such as a basketball court or a less-defined but still known activity, such as "socializing," many facts can be discovered about the size, shape, and relationships of the physical environment that will support these activities. The size and characteristics of basketball courts are well established and can easily be discovered in reference books such as *Ramsey/Sleeper: Architectural Graphic Standards* (Ramsey 1994). There is also information on appropriate sizes and distances relating to most social activities from conversation to dancing. If functional efficiency is considered important, the literature can be searched to discover facts about exemplary facilities; the currently occupied facilities can be observed to identify areas that are most and least efficient; and time can be taken to visit similar facilities to obtain comparable information. *Time-Saver Standards for Building Types* (De Chiara and Callender 1990) contains numerous facts regarding most standard building projects.

If views are valued and a goal to capture particular views has been established, then special attention can be given to identifying the precise direction and nature of the desired views in the program document. These are facts. The illustration below from the Desert House project at The University of Arizona shows both the desirable and undesirable near and far views from the site. It also indicates wind direction and solar angles at various times of the year (Fig. 6-13).

Facts such as shown above are not likely to be discovered during a work session. Rather, in value-based programming, they will be found in the information gathering stage of site analysis that precedes the work session. Thus, these facts are developed before and often presented during the work session. They are extremely useful to the designer when presented in diagram form, because they can be pinned up at the designer's desk for ready reference as the design is being developed.

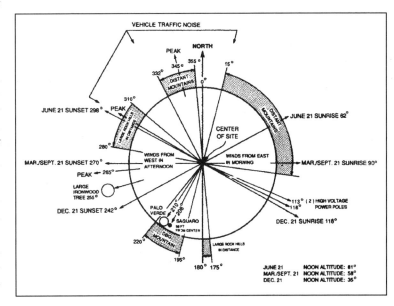

Figure 6-13 View/Wind/Solar Diagram.

Credit: Richard Brittain, Martin Karpiscak, Fred Matter, and Kennith Foster, 1988. Desert House: A Water/Energy Conservation Demonstration and Research Project Final Report. College of Architecture, The University of Arizona.

```
PROGRAMMING MATRIX:  FACTS

1.  a.  Handicapped access required for all galleries.

2.  a.  All gallery exhibits should be easy to assemble,
        disassemble and store.

    b.  Main gallery should function as a display area for
        both student and professional work.

    c.  Satellite galleries to provide additional display
        space for student work.

3.  a.  Energy efficient lighting is cost effective over
        time.

4.  a.  Higher qualities of material are more cost effective over
        time.

    b.  Effective lighting enhances work displayed (North Light)
        and the quality of space.

5.  a.  Exhibits are valuable and should be protected.

6.  a.  Quality gallery space will enhance work exhibited.

7.  a.  Extremes of temperature and humidity can harm art work.

8.  a.  Student work, being a product of the college, should be
        displayed.
```

Figure 6-14 Gallery and Exhibition Facts Sheet.

Credit: Walter Bullock, Dagnall Folger, and Timothy Bade, 1986. Building Area 11, Gallery and Exhibition Spaces, *Architecture Building Expansion Program*. Permission: College of Architecture and Environmental Design, Arizona State University

During the client/user work session, it is more likely that the programmer will discover facts about client/user operations and activities. This is particularly true relative to the merits and faults of the existing facility. But it is also true for expectations of the new facility. Adjoining is a list of the facts gathered during a work session relating to a gallery and exhibition space (Fig. 6-14).

Facts can be easily distinguished from goals and needs because they are not something the clients or users either want or do not want. They simply are statements or diagrams expressing or showing what exists, what is known to work in other situations, or what is likely to exist in the future. Facts are located in the third column of the matrix and are placed in the row of the goal to which they most closely relate. They are recorded and placed in the matrix whenever they are pointed out and agreed upon during the work session.

Needs (requirements)

Once the important values, goals, and related facts have been identified, it is important to establish and agree with the client/users upon project needs. Needs, like goals and unlike facts, relate to the future facilities, not simply to the present or future situation in which the future facilities will exist. In preparing the matrix, the programmer should not worry about whether the needs statements relate to performance or design features. The programmer should record them simply as needs by using short clear phrases and/or visual representations as appropriate.

Needs are requirements that must be satisfied in the design of the project.

When placing needs in the programming matrix, it may be difficult to differentiate needs from goals. An example given in the goals section earlier was: "to define separate areas to be used by customers and staff." The goal could as easily have been stated as a requirement: "provide separate areas for customers and staff." If an item makes just as much sense when stated as a need, change it to a need. Goals should be broader in nature. For example, it is not as easy to restate the other goal statement made earlier as a needs statement: "to minimize the number of persons needed to operate the shop." Even if the "to" is removed and the statement reads like a requirement: "minimize the number of persons needed to operate the shop," there is no clear directive to the designer as to what should be done to accomplish this. It thus remains a goal: something desired, but with no clearly defined performance or feature required.

The programmer should not seek requirements where they do not exist! If the client is looking to the architect for a creative new way to achieve a goal, it makes little sense to set forth strict performance or design criteria. It may be better left as a goal. However, if a particular performance or feature really is required, it should be stated. Figure 6-15 shows the list of needs from the matrix for the Gallery and Exhibition Space in the previous illustration.

In a programming matrix, the same general information can appear as both fact and need. For example, certain site or climate conditions can be

1. a. One loading zone approximately 500 sq. ft. to accomodate medium size trucks or vans for loading and unloading exhibits.(Main Gallery only)

   b. Easy access to visitor and temporary parking.(Main Gallery only)

   c. Ramps and elevators to be required unless the gallery is located at grade.

   d. Student galleries should be located adjacent to circulation.

2. a. Movable partitions based on a modular system so that the partitions can be combined to create larger display surfaces.

   b. Easily adjustable, minimal heat gain, even lighting and glare reduction.

   c. Electrical outlets at various spacings. Standard spaced wall outlets, Cieling outlets spaced one per every 200 sq. ft., Floor outlets spaced one per every 100 sq. ft.

   d. Storage to accomodate 25, 12-15 sq. ft. display partitions, 15 display stands, and 5 locking display cases, along with 200 sq. ft. of space for storing short term visiting exhibits. (Main Gallery only)

   e. Double doors at all entries to accommodate access to large exhibits. (Main Gallery only)

   f. Visual connection from exterior circulation to interior of gallery.

   g. Storage for each satellite gallery should accomodate; 6, 12-15 sq. ft. display partitions, and 3 display stands.

Figure 6-15 Gallery and Exhibition Needs Sheet.

Credit: Walter Bullock, Dagnall Folger, and Timothy Bade. Permission: College of Architecture and Environmental Design, Arizona State University

said to exist as fact. Necessity to account for these facts in design can be stated as needs. This is often very confusing to clients and users, especially if the programmer appears to be confused about it. Student programmers frequently cannot decide whether some items are actually goals, facts, or needs. It helps if the work session proceeds from left to right across the matrix, going from the global values, to broad goals, to related facts, and finally to needs in a logical progression from general to specific. The programmers should remember, however, that there will be opportunity to reorganize or restate the information when they prepare the program document. They should not be overly concerned if the matrix is not completely correct. If all of the cells have been filled with useful information, it is likely that the overall problem has been fairly well defined. Correct placement can occur later in a less public forum.

Ideas

Ideas relate to how the design problem might be solved. They can fall into the category of programmatic concepts as defined by CRS (Peña et al. 1977) and involve such notions as "centralized versus decentralized," which may have a great deal to do with how the organization is structured but may not necessarily have strong physical design implications; or perhaps to design ideas such as "compact versus dispersed," which have very direct physical form implications. These can often be represented by conceptual diagrams (Figs. 6-16 and 6-17).

There might also be ideas expressed about how the building might appear. These might include pictures of other buildings that the client or users find attractive, which they bring forward. This frequently occurs for house commissions, where the husband and wife have been collecting a file or scrapbook of houses that they like in anticipation of having a new house designed for them-

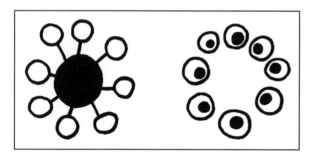

Figure 6-16 Centralized versus Decentralized.

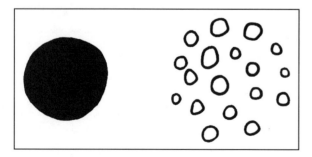

Figure 6-17 Compact versus Dispersed.

selves. These images should not only be welcomed by the programmer, but should be discussed at length to develop an understanding of the underlying values being expressed. All images of this kind should be retained in an appendix of the program.

The reason for collecting both programmatic and design ideas is primarily because both kinds of ideas frequently occur during programming. Clients, users, and architects all come to the programming process full of preconceptions—things they would like to see occur somewhere, sometime, perhaps in this particular project. The ideas will be expressed and should be recorded, because they might be useful to the designer.

There may also be ideas for a functional solution to a particular user problem, to meet particular city or governmental requirements, or to respond to site and climate conditions. There may be ideas for particular spatial solutions to the problem. It is only natural when confronted with a problem to develop ideas of how to solve it, even if one is not an architect. These ideas should be encouraged, but recognized for what they are—preconceptions based on an incomplete definition of the problem. However, they may be good ideas and potentially important form generators. The designer should be informed about what the client and occupants think would be appropriate design solutions, as long as the ideas are not stated as requirements.

When ideas come up during the development of the matrix, they can be expressed verbally, with a simple diagram, or both ways. Peña et al. (1969, 1977, 1986) refer to such diagrams as "programmatic concepts" and caution not to include "design concepts." Another author, Edward T. White (1972), refers to all such diagrams a "precepts." This author prefers to refer to all such diagrams, sketches, and photographs simply as "ideas", so as to not give any idea more status than another (Figs. 6-18 through 6-20).

Regardless of how they are labeled, value-based programming deals with

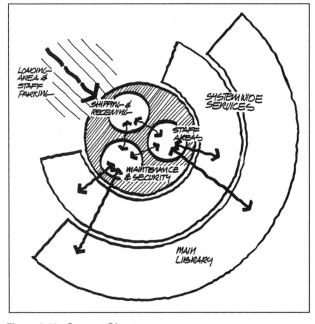

Figure 6-18 Concept Diagram.

Credit: Anderson DeBartolo Pan, Inc, 1986. Architectural *Program for the City of Tucson Main Library*. Tucson, Arizona. Permission: ADP Marshall

Figure 6-19 Precept Diagram.

Credit: Brooks & Associates AIA, Architects and Planners, 1985. *Design Program and Site Analysis for Morris K. Udall Regional Park and Recreation Center.* Tucson, Arizona. Permission: Albanese-Brooks Assoc. PC

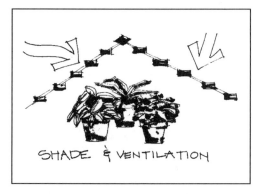

Figure 6-20 Design Idea.

Credit: Kuzuhiro Baba, 1985. *Duck and Decanter Program.* Permission: School of Architecture, Arizona State University

all of the ideas brought forward by the client/ users. The ideas should be recorded as they occur during information gathering and placed in the matrix during the work sessions. Like all of the information inserted in the matrix, the ideas should be evaluated by the programming group relative to their appropriateness for the particular design problem. Those ideas that are obviously inappropriate should be discarded. Those ideas that are relevant should remain in the ideas column.

The purpose of the large visible matrix set up in one room is to set forth the whole problem for all participants to see, to comment upon, to modify, and ultimately to accept as a correct representation of the design problem. With this definition more or less complete, the initiative again returns to the programming team to further refine the information—to develop space projections and relationship digrams, and to prepare cost estimates and schedules based on the information developed in the matrix.

6.5 Presentation Methods

- 5" × 8" Cards
- Grid Paper
- Other Techniques
- Electronic Methods

5" × 8" Cards

The best known method of presenting program information was developed by William Peña et al. (1969, 1977, 1987) of CRS. This system involves the use of horizontally placed, unlined 5" × 8" cards on which one goal, fact, concept, need, or problem statement is presented visually and verbally. These cards are tacked or taped to a wall surface organized into the firm's standard information matrix: function, form, economy, and time down the left side and goals, facts, concepts, needs, and problem statement across the top.

The same approach can, of course, be used by any programming firm and with whatever information categories they deem to be appropriate. Thus, the card system is an effective method to use in value-based programming.

The following are reproductions of a number of "fact" cards prepared during a programming session by CRS (1971) for a Community Mental Health and Retardation Center (Figs. 6-21 through 6-23).

Note how the preformatted cards include simple diagrams with a few descriptive words developed during the programming session, previously prepared site information modified to point up particular facts, and occasionally cards with only words on them.

Because CRS did a large amount of their work on facilities similar in type and size, they often found comparable goals, facts, and needs and reoccurring concepts that could be represented in a similar way. This allowed the members of the firm to become very efficient and skilled in developing new cards. They kept these cards very simple and straightforward, which gave their presentations a sense of continuity and quality. It takes time to learn these skills of summary and restraint, as will be evident in the following cards by students.

Figures 6-24 through 6-27 are representative of 5" × 8" cards prepared by students in the School of Architecture at Arizona State University over several years. As can be seen the cards can be as varied as imagination, time, and talent allow.

Cards with a small amount of text and simple diagrams seem to be the most easily read and understood during a programming session. But it is not easy to come up with crisp statements or meaningful diagrams in the heat of a programming session (Fig. 6-28).

For most students, it is much easier to develop text-based cards during the actual work session (Fig. 6-29).

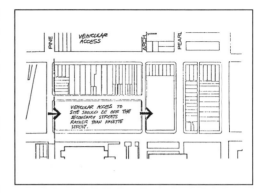

Figure 6-21 Form Fact.

William Peña, HOK

Figure 6-22 Economy Fact.

William Peña, HOK

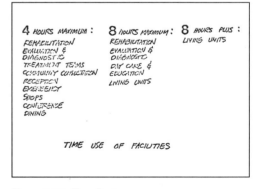

Figure 6-23 Time Fact.

William Peña, HOK

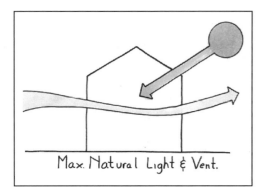

Figure 6-24 Goal Card.

Credit: Les Partch and Marcello Cardenas. Permission: School of Architecture, Arizona State University

Figure 6-25 Fact Card.

Credit: M. Arnold and Curtis Clark. School of Architecture, Arizona State University

Figure 6-26 Need Card.

Credit: Vince Dodd and Richie Poole. School of Architecture, Arizona State University

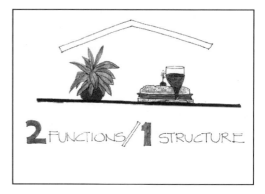

Figure 6-27 Idea Card.

Credit: Rich Potosnak and Paul Price. School of Architecture, Arizona State University

Figure 6-28 Text and Diagram Card.

School of Architecture, Arizona State University

Figure 6-29 Text-Based Card.

School of Architecture, The University of Arizona.

Text-based cards have the advantage of simple recording at a scale that is easier for the group session participants to read and react to from a distance. However, they lack the visual icon to which persons can readily attach and remember the meaning of the card.

All of the previous cards by students were developed during actual work sessions and represent some of the best cards made over several years in the work session setting. However, the development of uniformly attractive and meaningful cards during a work session is difficult, especially when several unequally talented students are producing the cards. Therefore, the author has encouraged students to refine the cards after the work session in order to have a more attractive and meaningful matrix to review at the next work session (Figs. 6-30 through 6-32).

Note how the text-based approach, as shown above, has the advantage of leaving enough room on the same card for amplification of the key words or phrases with smaller lettering. In this case, key words for the basic idea are printed so as to be easy to read when up on the wall, but additional information clarifying and amplifying the idea can also be included in small print. This tends to overcome the fact that only those involved in the programming session have any idea about the true meaning or intent of the pictures and short phrases.

A number of professional programmers also use text-based cards during work sessions (Fig. 6-33).

Like CRS, many firms use a combination of small diagrams with short verbal descriptions. This is an effective way to combine the advantages of pictures and words, without some of the problems (Fig. 6-34).

Developing effective visual and/or text-based cards during a work session is very difficult because of the speed at which they must be produced to keep up with the session. It is desirable, therefore, to produce as many cards before the

Figure 6-30 Refund Card.

Credit: Jennifer Da Ros, Will Pew, Adam Sprenger, and Lauren Watson. College of Architecture, The University of Arizona.

Figure 6-31 Refund Card.

Credit: Jennifer Da Ros, Will Pew, Adam Sprenger, and Lauren Watson. College of Architecture, The University of Arizona.

Figure 6-32 Refined Cards.

Credit: Jennifer Da Ros, Will Pew, Adam Sprenger, and Lauren Watson. College of Architecture, The University of Arizona.

Figure 6-33   Text-Based Card.

Credit: Anderson DeBartolo Pan, Inc. Permission: ADP Marshall

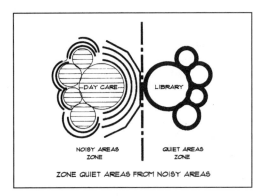

Figure 6-34   Text and Diagram Card.

Arquitectura Ltd.

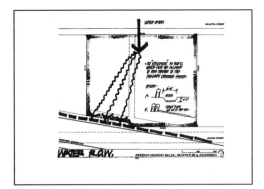

Figure 6-35   Site Data Card.

Credit: Anderson DeBartolo Pan, Inc. Permission: ADP Marshall

session as is possible. Such cards can be prepared based on all of the previous information gathering activities. They can be done at the student's workstation or in the architect's office over a period of time. This is particularly true for all of the zoning, site, utility, and climate data cards (Fig. 6-35).

Regardless of how or when the cards are produced, an essential element of the card matrix is the notion of "carding" and "discarding" (Peña et al. 1969, 1977, 1986). When the card is first placed in the matrix, it is done with the implied or actual questions: Is this okay? Does the card represent what has been said? It is offered in a similar way as the interpretation in diagnostic interviewing. If accepted in interviewing, the idea is recorded. If accepted in the work session, the card is kept in the matrix.

After a card has been up for a time, it may become evident that it is not quite right. In this case, the card may be modified or taken down (discarded). If further discussion has shown that the card is inappropriate, or its need has been eliminated by similar cards, it will stay down. In other cases, a new card will be made and put in its place.

It may also be discovered that a card is or seems to be in the wrong cell of the matrix. Now the programmer must decide if this is the case, often with competing opinions being expressed by the work session participants. As mentioned previously, what originally appeared as a goal may later appear to be a need. It may be necessary to develop two or even three cards. For instance, an original goal might be "to stay within the overall project budget." A fact might be that the overall project budget cannot exceed "four million dollars." The need would then be "to stay within the overall project budget of four million dollars." An appropriate card could be placed in each of the three cells relating to the economic value category.

The author has found it better to have some seemingly redundant cards in the matrix, rather than being drawn into an argument
as to where a card belongs. It is often possible for a programmer to
devise an appropriate replacement card while other areas are being
discussed. It is also possible to resolve such things in the quiet of
the programmer's office after the work session (Fig. 6-36).

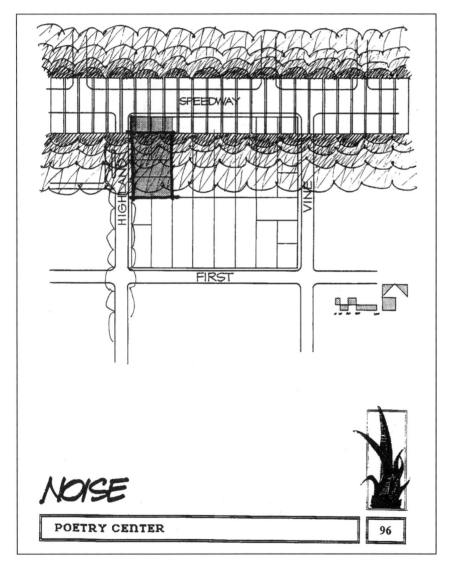

Figure 6-36   Site Data on 8½" × 11" sheet.

Credit: Corky Poster, W. Kirby Lockard, Chris Evans, Kim Kuykendall, Scott Pask, and Donna Sink. Permission:
Architecture Laboratory, Inc.

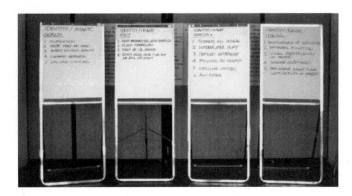

Figure 6-37 Grid Paper on Easels.

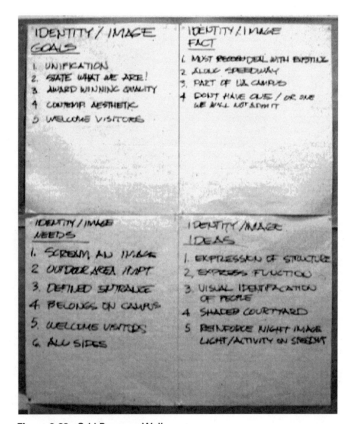

Figure 6-38 Grid Paper on Wall.

Grid Paper

Another group session presentation technique involves the use of standard flip chart pads of 1" cell, 28" × 38" grid paper on which to record the program information. In this form of presentation, a single programmer uses four easels on which to record goals, facts, needs, and ideas for each value area. As the sheets become full, they can then be removed from the easels and placed on the walls of the room in an arrangement similar to the card system (Fig. 6-37). This can be done by a member of the programming team or a member of the work session group.

It is also possible to begin with a number of partially completed sheets tacked or taped to the walls of the room that list the previously identified value areas, followed by specific project goals, key facts relating to the goals, preliminary statements of needs, and even ideas for partial solution of the problem. The completeness of this presentation, of course, will depend on the completeness of the earlier information gathering processes (Fig. 6-38).

Because information is recorded at a larger scale than on cards, this system requires more wall surface than the card system. The author uses two or more walls of a room beginning on the left side with the first value, which is listed at the top of the first sheet and with goals placed directly under as they are presented. This sheet is set high enough on the wall to allow a second sheet to be hung below it. To the right of the value/goal sheet is hung a fact sheet, then a need sheet, and finally an idea sheet. At 28" wide, the four sheets take up nearly 10 linear feet of room width. This allows a matrix with as many as four value areas along a 40-foot wall. It would, thus, require at least two such walls to accommodate the eight HECTTEAS value areas.

Because there are several rows of information on each sheet, the sheets cannot be as easily modified as can the cards. Incorrect information can be corrected by inserting words above or below the original statement. This can look messy. If much change is required, the original information can be crossed out. New or substitute information can be added after the last statement on the appropriate sheet (Figs. 3-39 and 3-40).

When the sheets on the walls are full, the programmer prints on the grid paper on the four easels. When filled, these are taped on the wall below the ones already there for all to see and review. The programmer can also add information to the posted sheets if there is room.

It is important to use markers designed specifically for easel paper or to tack up double thicknesses of the sheets to prevent the markers from flowing through to the wall behind. A more foolproof system is to tack or tape brown butcher paper across each of the walls first, and then to tape the grid paper sheets on top of the butcher paper. This has the advantage of providing a uniform background for the presentation, even when the room walls are of a variety of colors or surfaces. It is also easy to roll up

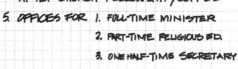

FUNCTION - GOALS

1. CHURCH TO GROW TO 250-300 MBRS
2. AUDITORIUM TO SEAT 200-250 PEOPLE & FELLOWSHIP H.   200 AT TABLES
3. UNCOVERED "COURTYARD" FOYER
4. EXTERIOR COVERED/PAVED AREA FOR AFTER CHURCH FELLOWSHIP/COFFEE
5. OFFICES FOR 1. FULL-TIME MINISTER
                2. PART-TIME RELIGIOUS ED.
                3. ONE HALF-TIME SECRETARY
6. SUPERVISED LIBRARY/MULTI-USE
7. KITCHEN - POT LUCKS, COFFEE, PRE-SCHOOL L.
8. S. SCHOOL CLASSROOMS -CHILDREN 0-14
9. MEETING SPACE - HIGH SCHOOL STUDENTS
10. SUPPORT FACILITIES - ALL OF ABOVE

Figure 6-39 Goals on Grid Paper.

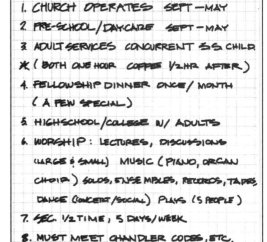

FUNCTION - FACTS

1. CHURCH OPERATES SEPT - MAY
2. PRE-SCHOOL/DAYCARE SEPT - MAY
3. ADULT SERVICES CONCURRENT S.S. CHILD
   * (BOTH ONE HOUR COFFEE 1/2 HR AFTER)
4. FELLOWSHIP DINNER ONCE / MONTH
   (A FEW SPECIAL)
5. HIGH SCHOOL /COLLEGE W/ ADULTS
6. WORSHIP : LECTURES, DISCUSSIONS
   (LARGE & SMALL) MUSIC (PIANO, ORGAN
   CHOIR) SOLOS, ENSEMBLES, RECORDS, TAPES,
   DANCE (CONCERT/SOCIAL) PLAYS (5 PEOPLE)
7. SEC. 1/2 TIME, 5 DAYS/WEEK
8. MUST MEET CHANDLER CODES, ETC.
9. PRESENT FACILITIES - AUDITORIUM INADEQ.
   (SIZE & SHAPE) KITCHEN BAD LOCATION

Figure 6-40 Facts on Grid Paper.

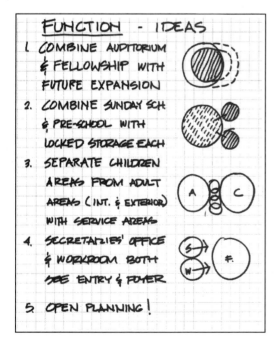

FUNCTION — NEEDS

4 SUNDAY SCHOOL ₐGₑ PHASE I - 2
#   #
a. BABIES/TODDLERS (1-3)   3-5   8-10

b. PRE-SCHOOL (3-5)   8-12   15-20

c. PRIMARY (GRADES 1-3)   8-12   20-25

d. INTERMEDIATE (GRADES 4-6)   8-12   20-25

e. JR. HIGH (GRADES 7-8)   5-8   10-15

f. SR. HIGH (GRADES 9-12)   5-8   10-15

g. PRE-SCHOOL (AGE 3-5, SOME   30-40   50-80
   OLDER AFTER SCHOOL, SHARE
   b, c, d, e, f ?)

h. TOILETS (DIRECT ACCESS (3-5)) CODE   CODE

i. LOCKED STORAGE RE. IN PS. REQ'D   REQ'D

j. PARKING DROPOFF/PICKUP   6 SP.   6 SP.
   (SHARED ON SUNDAY)

Figure 6-41 Needs on Grid Paper.

FUNCTION - IDEAS

1. COMBINE AUDITORIUM
   & FELLOWSHIP WITH
   FUTURE EXPANSION

2. COMBINE SUNDAY SCH
   & PRE-SCHOOL WITH
   LOCKED STORAGE EACH

3. SEPARATE CHILDREN
   AREAS FROM ADULT
   AREAS (INT. & EXTERIOR)
   WITH SERVICE AREAS

4. SECRETARIES' OFFICE
   & WORKROOM BOTH
   SEE ENTRY & FOYER

5. OPEN PLANNING!

Figure 6-42 Ideas on Grid Paper.

the entire presentation for easy transportation to and from the work session. Be certain to get permission from the client for whatever system is used if working in their facilities. Some clients are very particular about having their walls marred by tack holes, tape pulls, or flow pen marks.

Note that the grid paper system requires that the session participants focus on one value area at a time. Otherwise, each sheet of grid paper would have information on mixed value areas and could be quite confusing. If the work session participants decide that they need to discuss another value area, the programmer must move to the other value area. Or if it is a new area, then it may be necessary to flip the paper over the top of the easel to expose clean sheets below. The new information can be recorded on these sheets and later placed on the wall.

Typically, the grid paper procedure is text-based and does not use visual illustrations or diagrams such as those contained on the cards in the CRS programming process. It is possible to include a sketch diagram on the grid paper to make an idea clear to the participants. But this might be used only five or 10 percent of the time, rather than for every piece of information (Figs. 6-41 and 6-42).

Site and climate information can be presented on prints of surveys or aerial photos, or on 8½" × 11" sheets. The client's mission, purpose, and organization chart can be similarly presented, or if too small to read from across the room, can be transferred onto grid paper for the work session.

Other Techniques

Possible alternatives to the above matrix presentation techniques could involve the use of other size cards, 8½" × 11" sheets of paper, newsprint paper on easels, or the use of large chalk or white boards. Another option might involve presentation of the material using slides, overhead projection, or possibly the distribution of the information to each of the participants in small packets of 8½" × 11" paper, or some combination of the above. However, remember that the intent at this point is to be very flexible—to be able to gather and change the information in accordance with the desires of the work session group. Any approach that interferes with this flexibility should be avoided.

The use of 8½" × 11" sheets has the advantage, particularly with the variety of fonts and drawing programs available on personal computers, of allowing the development of easy-to-read information including sufficient detail and, perhaps, graphic material in a form that can be affixed to a wall, but which can also be stapled and circulated to those who could not attend the work session. A computer and a small ink-jet printer in the work session room may allow a member of the programming team to prepare sheets during the session, in the same manner as for cards. It may be tempting, however, to place more than one idea on each 8½" × 11" sheet. This would make individual sheets difficult to discard during the work session. However, if not done, it would tend to double the size of the matrix. In the author's experience, the use of standard 8½" × 11" sheets works best when programming with a very small client/user group, all of whom can sit around a table and easily see, discuss, and modify the sheets as appropriate.

The use of chalk or white boards presents a number of difficulties. Usually the boards are not large enough to hold all of the matrix information at once, so, as changes are made, erased information is lost. Or if much information is provided in one area there may not be enough space left to add to it. Similarly, if some new rank ordering is desired, there is no easy way to reorder. Also, when the session is finished, the information must be transcribed, or it will be lost when erased. If boards are already available in the work session room, usually on only one wall of the room, they can be used more effectively to show and modify the project schedule or the project budget during the later stages of the work session.

After the initial presentation by the programmer, it is essential that all program information remain visible and changeable. The card system is most flexible in this regard. The 8½" × 11" paper system can work for small groups. The grid paper system is sufficiently flexible that it can also work. In fact, where a single programmer is involved, grid paper is practically the only way to present the program effectively to a medium- to large-size group, because development and placement of cards and 8½" × 11" paper sheets requires at least two programmers—one leading the discussion, the other preparing the cards or paper sheets. With the grid sheets a single programmer can both lead the discussion and put the notes on the sheets.

The use of slides or overhead projection for recording information in a work session is very awkward. Not only is it difficult to modify erroneous information in a timely way, but it is not possible to place all information in front of the group at one time. A projected Microsoft PowerPoint presentation would make it easier to modify information during the session, but it is still not possible to place all information in front of the group at one time. This leaves the participants uncertain if everything has been suitably considered and modified. Thus, slides and overhead projection should be reserved for introductory or background material on the client group's mission, history, organizational structure, and purpose for the project, or for final presentation of program materials where only minimum interaction and/or modification is expected.

Electronic Methods

Collaborative groupware technologies are being used by business organizations for developing mission, vision, and strategic planning documents. Recent developments in interactive computer technologies also hold considerable promise for programming. Methods of group decision making (Delbecq et al. 1975; Linstone and Turoff 1975) using various brainstorming techniques are particularly adaptable to collaborative electronic environments. For example, programmers from the College of Architecture and the Center for the Management of Information at The University of Arizona (Mittleman 1995; Doxtater and Mittleman 1996) have adapted existing computer software to support structured on-line programming sessions for large groups, with each group member seated at a computer console in one of several collaborative laboratories on campus.

The assembled group members make suggestions about values, goals, facts, needs, and ideas using their individual computer keyboards. These suggestions are immediately shown to the entire group on their individual monitors and on several large screens at the front of the room. This process stimulates ideas from others to the point where a large number of suggestions can be generated in a very short period of time. The suggestions are shown in the order presented and anonymously, so that no participant need fear that someone else in the work session will dislike their idea and negatively identify the suggestion with the person making it (Figs. 6-43 and 6-44).

Figure 6-43 Electronic Work Session Leader.

After the initial suggestions have been made, the group can use a discussion format to comment on other ideas. They can also place the suggestions into appropriate categories and prioritize them by simple voting procedures. This is an effective method of generating a large amount of valuable information in a short period of time. Indeed, the method is so effective that it can virtually eliminate the need to conduct interviews with any of the individuals participating in the work session.

The information can be electronically tabulated and represented in the after-voting format for all to review. The group can again be asked to suggest refinements in an open-ended electronic discussion session until all parts of a potential information matrix have

Figure 6-44 Electronic Work Session Participants.

been covered. This information can be saved electronically, printed, and distributed during or immediately following the session.

The only apparent drawbacks to the system are:

1. The need to assemble all of the participants into a space away from their own workplaces for an extended period of time

2. The relatively high cost of renting the collaboration facilities and facilitators.

If the entire programming group can be so assembled this method has the advantages of:

1. Avoiding normal workplace interruptions during the session.

2. Generating a tremendous amount of information in a short period of time.

3. Being able to assimilate and reorganize the data during the session.

4. Allowing all suggestions to remain anonymous.

5. The savings in manpower costs, because of the efficiency of the process, are likely to more than offset the cost of renting the space.

Where decision laboratories are available, the author highly recommends their use, especially on complex or controversial programming projects. Note that personnel in the Center for the Management of Information at the University of Arizona are currently working on Internet software that will allow collaborative work sessions to take place on computers located throughout a client's organization. When this software becomes available, it will eliminate the need to assemble a group at a remote location. Indeed, it may eliminate the need to have a group assemble at all. The participants could remain at their personal workstations and the collaborative work session could occur in a so-called virtual environment (Fig. 6-45).

Most Important Issues (Vote)

Voting Results
Agree/Disagree (5-Point) (Allow bypass)
Strongly Agree (SA), Agree (A), Neutral (N), Disagree (D), Strongly Disagree (SD)
Number of ballot items: 12
Total number of voters (N): 22

Mean

Mean	Item
4.43	1. function
4.38	2. image
4.24	3. Location
4.15	4. meeting customer and employee needs
4.14	5. Accessability
3.95	6. Catering to Students
3.81	7. Fitting in with college neighborhood!
3.67	8. Safety of patrons and employees
3.52	9. advertisement
3.52	10. theft prevention
3.24	11. Attractive signage as well as varied seating options for different user types within the general university crowd
2.71	12. values

Number of Votes in Each Rating

	SA (5)	A (4)	N (3)	D (2)	SD (1)	Total	STD	n
1. function	12	7	1	1	0	93	0.81	21
2. image	10	9	2	0	0	92	0.67	21
3. Location	12	5	2	1	1	89	1.14	21
4. meeting c	8	9	2	0	1	83	0.99	20
5. Accessabi	9	6	6	0	0	87	0.85	21
6. Catering	9	6	4	0	2	83	1.24	21
7. Fitting i	6	7	7	0	1	80	1.03	21
8. Safety of	5	10	3	0	3	77	1.28	21
9. advertise	4	7	6	4	0	74	1.03	21
10. theft pr	6	7	3	2	3	74	1.40	21
11. Attracti	6	5	3	2	5	68	1.58	21
12. values	4	0	10	0	7	57	1.45	21

Figure 6-45 Prioritized Values Summary Sheet.

Credit: Daniel Mittleman. Permission: Center for the Management of Information, The University of Arizona

6.6 Requirement Sheets

- Brown Sheets
- Other Formats

A second work session is used to expand upon and clarify the needs information to make it more useful. The various facility needs stated on the matrix during the first work session are developed into lists of required interior and exterior spaces, including the projected size of each. Matrices and diagrams showing relationships between spaces are developed for focused consideration. Tables showing the proposed project schedule and estimates of project costs are also developed or refined during this session. Ideally, agreement on the lists is obtained from the client/users before ending the session.

All of this information is typically developed in tabular form, independent of the information matrix, at a large enough scale for all work session participants to see. The information is sometimes developed from scratch as a final stage of a work session, but an initial tabulation is more frequently prepared in the programmer's office prior to the final work session. This preliminary tabulation is based on the results of the other information gathering activities including reference to standards and the results of earlier work sessions with the executive group of the organization.

It is wise to use enough space (wall and paper) and a flexible system so that initial space, size, time, or cost projections can be revised several times throughout the presentation, negotiation, and agreement process, until everyone is satisfied that each space is of sufficient size to accommodate its intended uses, and that the size and scope of the project does not exceed the proposed budget and schedule. This can take time to work out to everyone's satisfaction. Indeed, it is often a good idea not to prepare the information matrix and the various tabular sheets at the same work session. It is probably better to schedule two or more separate sessions, so that everyone will be reasonably fresh for each session. This is especially true for the programmer, who must demonstrate the same leadership through all of the sessions.

Requirement sheets cover such areas as space identification and allocation, relationship matrices and diagrams, room program sheets, project schedule, and project cost analysis. While the development of information in each of these areas can begin during the executive work session(s) and the client/user work session(s), the final documents are typically developed in the programmer's office, usually on the computer. This information is returned to the user for confirmation and editing as needed to obtain final agreement.

CRS developed the concept of brown sheets of butcher paper that can be taped up on the work session room walls and printed on with colored chalk (Peña et al. 1969, 1977, 1986). This allows for erasing and modification of data as the work session(s) progress. It is an effective, if somewhat messy, technique for developing this type of information. Kumlin (1995), on the other hand, recommends the use of 30" × 40" sheets and stick-on notes, or white boards. The author uses grid paper, usually on a dedicated easel. When reasonably complete, each of the sheets is transferred to a wall to free up the easel for another area of information.

In the interest of avoiding redundancy, the detailed discussions of space identification and allocation, relationship matrices and diagrams, space program sheets, cost analysis, and project schedule are contained in Chapter 7. The discussion in this section will be confined to the various methods of presenting this information during the work session.

Brown Sheets

As stated earlier, the space allocations, relationship matrices, project schedule, and project cost analyses are first developed during the work session on rolls of brown butcher paper. These sheets are rolled out and taped horizontally across an entire wall. Colored chalk is then used to identify the various spaces, number of each type, and the appropriate square foot allocations. The space types are often listed in accordance with the existing or proposed departmental structure of the organization, so that subtotals of the areas required can be tabulated.

All of the identified spaces can be listed on another sheet and a matrix developed to show how the various spaces relate to each other. Simple relationship diagrams can also be shown. The same sheet can be used to show how the project schedule is likely to develop as well as to develop a matrix to estimate project costs (Fig. 6-46).

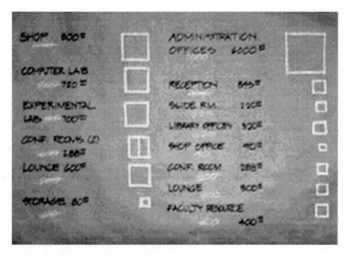

Figure 6-46 Typical Brown Sheet.

The obvious advantages of the combination of the large brown paper sheets and chalk are that all of the spaces and sizes can be shown at once and can be revised repeatedly in place until everyone is satisfied that all assignable spaces have been identified and that appropriate square footages have been recorded for each. The same is true for relationships, schedule, and costs. At the end of the session, the programmer needs only to roll up the brown sheets and take them to the office to transcribe the information into the program document. This is an efficient and effective way to develop and obtain agreement on the spatial allocations, relationships, schedule, and costs for medium-sized to large and complex projects. The primary disadvantage of the brown sheets is the mess created by the chalk. The paper can also look very messy after a few erasures. In addition, in order to see the sheets effectively, it is usually necessary to supplement the chalk with black flow pens. This, of course, makes changes of categories difficult to make.

Other Formats

It is also possible to use 30" × 40" sheets of print paper or 26" × 32" sheets of grid paper on which to develop the tabular information on requirements (Fig. 6-47). The 30" × 40" sheets have the advantage of being larger than any other alternative to the brown sheets. The grid paper sheets have the advantage of taking up less room than brown sheets or 30" × 40" sheets, so that easels can be used while developing and initially displaying the information.

In both of the above cases, the material is confined to a much smaller area than when using rolls of brown butcher paper, so that only limited information can be contained on an individual sheet. It is also more difficult to modify the number of spaces or square

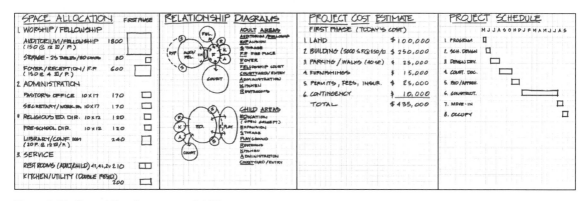

Figure 6-47 Posted Requirements on Grid Paper.

foot sizes required, particularly if markers are used to record the information. A number can be crossed out and replaced only a few times before the entire sheet becomes too messy to understand. The use of stick-on notes for areas and costs can help mitigate this problem, but it does not allow space names to be changed or shifted. Both of these alternative methods are obviously more appropriate for smaller or less complex projects, where it is less likely that a great amount of space will be needed and where the number of changes to the presented information is likely to be small.

The use of simple 8½" × 11" sheets can be appropriate for a table-top discussion with client(s) for a small project or in any situation where it is not possible to have a group work session to work out differences. The use of a laptop computer and spreadsheet program with a small ink-jet printer can be effective in allowing automatic tabulation as areas and costs change.

For larger projects, it may be possible to use the computer and spreadsheet program along with a digital projector to allow all participants to see what is being changed. Otherwise, it may be necessary to circulate the preliminary space allocation table, the relationship matrix, the tentative project schedule, and the project cost projections to everyone concerned for their review and suggestions before and after the work session. Once reviewed, these allocations could be modified and then returned to the respondents until a point is reached where everyone is satisfied with all of the proposed allocations. Obviously, the use of a work session involving all of the decision makers would be more efficient and appropriate for most organizations.

The easel-size grid paper sheets have the advantage of being easy to see for use in the work sessions. With large format photocopy machines, they can easily and inexpensively be reduced to 8½" × 11" sheets for inclusion in a program report. Where funding for programming is small, this has the distinct advantage of saving personnel costs, which can be substantial in transcribing brown sheets.

The one-inch grid has the added advantage of helping the programmer line up rows and columns to provide a common format from sheet to sheet. They also provide appropriately sized module on which to draw graphic representations of the required square footages at a scale that all session participants can see and use to make comparisons of their relative sizes. The same, of course, would be true for 8½" × 11" grid paper sheets for small groups sitting together at a table (Figs. 6-48 through 6-51).

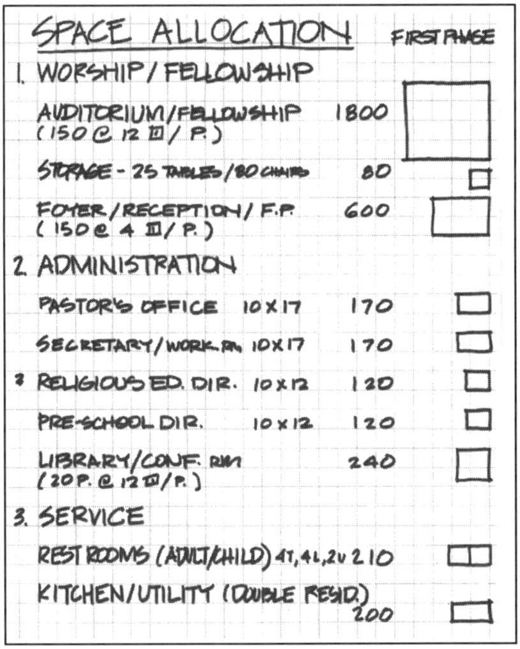

Figure 6-48 Space Allocation on Grid Paper.

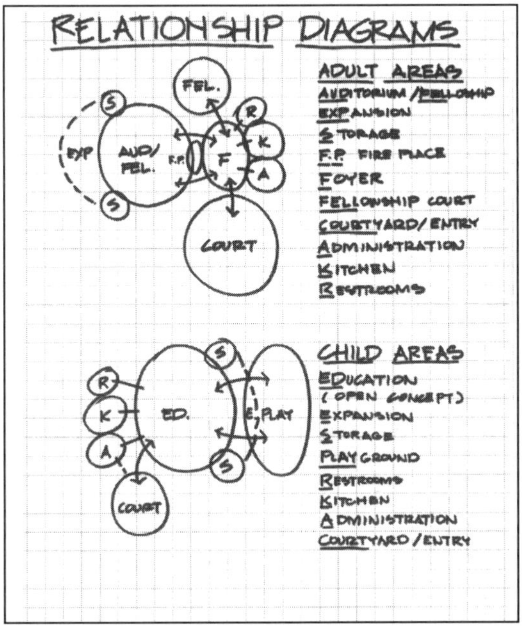

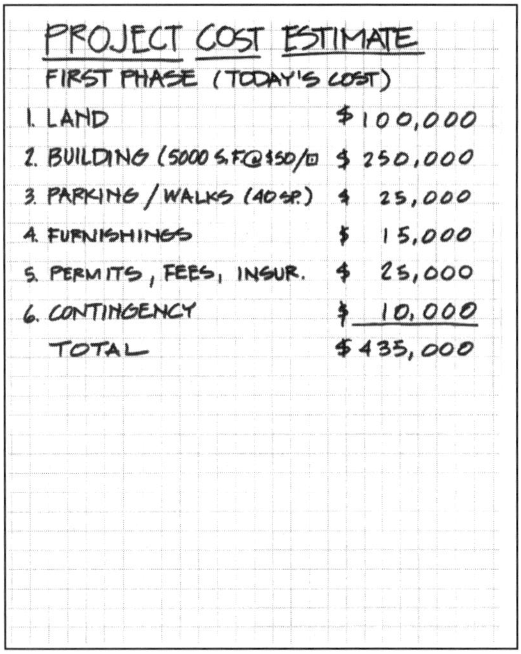

Figure 6-50 Project Cost Estimate on Grid Paper.

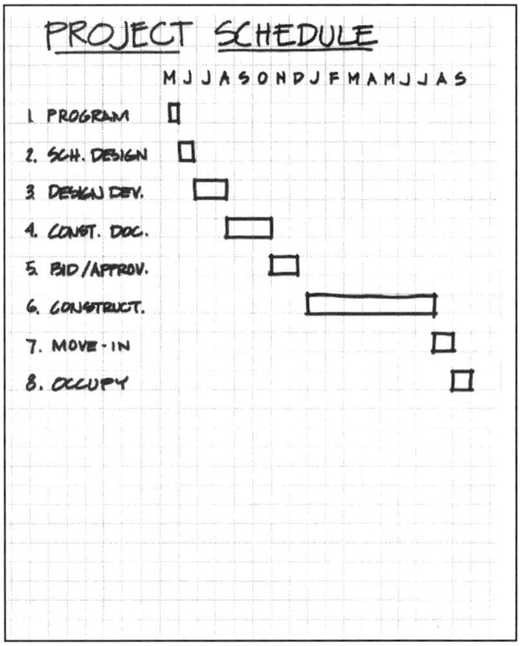

Figure 6-49 Relationship Diagrams on Grid Paper.

Figure 6-51 Project Schedule on Grid Paper.

6.7 Exercises

1. Pretending to be a client or user, develop the following information for the top three value areas of a simple design problem.
   a. Decide on the three value areas.
   b. Develop three to six appropriate goals.
   c. List several facts relating to the design problem.
   d. Write at least three design requirements for the top priority goal statements.
   e. Note and/or diagram several design ideas.

   Discuss your results with a colleague. Do they make sense? Do they help your colleague understand the design problem?

   Note that in a real programming situation with a client and users, it should be possible to discover this information! Conjuring up goals, facts, needs, and ideas would not be appropriate.

2. Analyze a program document by someone else, possibly found in the library or in an architect's office, and answer the following questions:
   a. What are the primary values and goals for this project? Are they clearly stated?
   b. Does the program provide clear criteria for evaluating the success of the design?
   c. Does the document illustrate design ideas or concepts? If so, are they presented in such a way as to allow the designer freedom to design, or are they already pointing toward a specific design solution?

3. Select a few colleagues to participate in an executive work session to set forth the mission of the your school or office, to decide on a building project that would meet perceived needs of the organization, to develop a clear statement of the purpose of the project, and to establish a preliminary budget and project schedule. Also have them enumerate the values, goals, facts, needs, and ideas for such a project.

4. Organize the information collected during earlier exercises on a card-based, wall-mounted programming matrix similar to the ones described in this chapter. Then conduct a work session with a larger group of volunteers

from the organization, asking them to modify and expand the information presented on the matrix and requirement sheets.

5. Ask the groups to critique both the matrix used to present the data and the developed data. Ask them how the information could better be obtained and presented. Also ask them to critique how you handled the work session. How could your performance be improved? How could the card maker's performance be improved?

6. Use the grid paper presentation system and proceed through the two questions above with the same groups or different groups from the same organization, asking them at the end of the session which method worked best. Also ask them if and how each method could be improved.

7. Consider alternative ways of obtaining data from large groups of individuals. Could the information gathering methods described in Chapter 5 replace the group sessions? For what type or size of projects would only work sessions be needed? For what type or size of projects would both the information gathering methods and the work sessions be required? Is there an alternative way to obtain the information?

6.8 References

CRS. 1971. Community Mental Health and Retardation Center Program. State of Maryland Department of Public Improvement. Baltimore, Md.

De Chiara, Joseph, and John Hancock Callender, eds. 1990. *Time-Saver Standards for Building Types*. New York: McGraw-Hill.

Delbecq, A. L., A. H. Van de Ven, and D. H. Gustafson. 1975. *Group Techniques for Program Planning: A Guide to Nominal Group and Delphi Processes*. Glenview, Ill.: Scott, Foresman.

Doxtater, Dennis, and Daniel Mittleman. 1996. "Creating a New Campus Setting for S.A.L.T.: Facilitation Design Processes by Linking Kinds of User Knowledge with Electronic Decision-Making in Groups." In *Proceedings of the 3rd Design & Decision Support Systems Conference*. Held at Spa, Belgium, August. 81-116.

Duerk, Donna P. 1993. *Architectural Programming: Information Management for Design*. New York: Van Nostrand Reinhold.

Fisher, Roger, and William Ury. 1981. *Getting to Yes: Negotiating Agreement Without Giving In*. Boston: Houghton Mifflin.

Hall, Lavinia, ed. 1993. *Negotiation: Strategies for Mutual Gain: The Basic Seminar of the Harvard Program on Negotiation*. Newbury Park, Calif.: Sage.

Kumlin, Robert R. 1995. *Architectural Programming: Creative Techniques for Design Professionals*. New York: McGraw-Hill.

Linstone, H. A., and M. Turoff, eds. 1975. *The Delphi Method: Techniques and Applications*. Reading, Mass.: Addison-Wesley.

Mittleman, Daniel David. 1995. *Architectural Programming Tool Box: Using Group Support Systems Technology to Increase the Effectiveness of User Participation in Architectural Programming*. Ph.D. diss., The University of Arizona.

Peña, William, and John W. Focke. 1969. *Problem Seeking: New Directions in Architectural Programming*. Houston, Tex.: Caudill Rowlett Scott.

Peña, William, William Caudill, and John Focke. 1977. *Problem Seeking: An Architectural Programming Primer*. Boston, Mass.: Cahners Books International.

Peña, William, Steven Parshall, and Kevin Kelly. 1987. *Problem Seeking: An Architectural Programming Primer*. 3rd ed. Washington, D.C.: AIA Press.

Ramsey, Charles George. 1994. *Ramsey/Sleeper: Architectural Graphic Standards*. New York: J. Wiley.

Rawlinson, J. G. 1981. *Creative Thinking and Brainstorming*. New York: Wiley.

Venturi, Robert. 1977. *Complexity and Contradiction in Architecture*. New York: Museum of Modern Art.

White, Edward T. III. 1972. *Introduction to Architectural Programming*. Tucson, Ariz.: Architectural Media.

CHAPTER
7

Program Preparation

After gathering and analyzing information about the various issues in architecture, it is necessary to process and organize this information so it can be communicated effectively to the client and to the designer. It is important to inform the client and designer of the findings both to help them understand the nature of the architectural problem and to obtain their concurrence that the program document is correct as presented.

Programs are prepared for at least three different design phases: master planning, schematic design, and design development.

Programs for each of these design phases should contain the information that the designer needs to make informed design decisions for that phase. Frequently, programming and design for a master plan is completed prior to beginning schematic or detailed programming for specific buildings. Some architects and programming firms advocate that only the information required for schematic design be included in the initial program for a building, so as to avoid confusing the designer with detailed information before it is needed (Peña et al. 1969, 1977, 1986; Duerk 1993). Often, however, a comprehensive architectural program containing the information required for all three design phases is prepared at the beginning of a major project. There are advantages to each approach relative to efficiency and cost of information gathering that need to be assessed on a project-by-project basis.

For ease of explanation, this chapter deals with a comprehensive architectural program covering all three phases of programming, but when appropriate indicates to which design stage the information typically relates.

7.1 Program Form

A variety of presentation formats are used in architectural programming. Most often the final architectural program is produced as a bound paper publication. Typical sizes include 8½" × 11" vertical or horizontal and 8½" × 14" or 11" × 17" horizontal. They are generally bound at the left edge with a plastic comb or three-ring binder, so that the document can be opened and laid flat for easy use by the designer. In addition to cover stock, they often have a transparent film cover to protect the booklet. The larger programs are placed in three-ring binders because of their added strength and flexibility of use.

Note that the format of the sheets can be varied to allow incorporation of illustrations and to promote easier reading. The vertical format works well with single columns and illustrations or a combination of double columns and half- or full-page illustrations. The horizontal format can accommodate three or four columns per sheet with illustrations either one or two columns wide and with possible sidebar usage. The choice is usually a decision of the programmer and often depends on the programming budget and word processing capability of the programming firm. The 8½" × 11" format is best for placing on book shelves and for filing, which is a significant advantage (Fig. 7-1).

7.2 Program Content

The content of programs varies, depending on what the programmer considers to be the most important information about a project. If the programmer is preoccupied with functional considerations and/ or budget, then these ar-

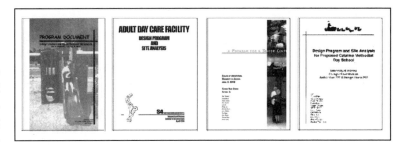

Figure 7-1 Typical Program Covers.

Credit: Students of the Architectural Programming class at The University of Arizona, Spring Semesters of 1998. College of Architecture, The University of Arizona, Tucson, Arizona

eas are likely to receive the most attention in the program. If site and climate analysis are major concerns, then these might receive emphasis. If the programmer is oriented toward the overall values and goals for the project, then these might receive the most attention. If facility needs are the objective, then these might be treated in greater depth. A balance is needed when programming for architecture.

The designer surveys the programming document and attempts to find information relevant to a particular stage of design. Thus, if the program is to be most helpful in the pursuit of architecture, it should be organized so that the designer can first discover the major issues and goals, then the facts and needs, and lastly the more detailed information on how to develop the design.

The level of development and detail should increase and become more focused at each stage of the programming and design process. If too much detail is included in the first stage, it may have a negative impact on design by confusing important formative information with relatively unimportant information. On the other hand, if too little information is provided, the designer may make erroneous decisions based on incomplete information. The programmer must be able to ascertain the important information for each stage of design and present it in a way to be of maximum benefit to the designer.

A complete architectural program is likely to have five to eight major sections including an executive summary, values and goals, design considerations, specific project requirements, budget, schedule, and an appendix of relevant materials. The reader should understand, however, that the varying nature of design problems will affect how each program is structured, so that a slightly different format can be expected for every program.

TABLE OF CONTENTS

Figure 7-2 Typical Table of Contents for an Architectural Program.

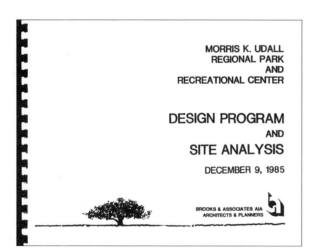

Figure 7-3 Plastic Comb-Bound Program Cover.

Permission: Albanese-Brooks Assoc. PC

A program for a small project may combine several of the sections into a single section. A very large program for a hospital or major government building complex may have several more sections and be in several volumes. However, the basic structure of the program is likely to remain similar to the one illustrated in Fig. 7-2.

7.3 Preliminaries

- Cover Sheets
- Transmittal
- Acknowledgment
- Directory
- Methods
- References

Cover Sheets

The typical architectural program document includes heavy paper or plastic cover sheets with the essential information on the front cover. These include the name of the project, the owner/client organization, the name and address of the programming group, logos, photographs, publication date, and any other information that helps identify the contents of the document.

The document shown in Fig. 7-3 is typical of a horizontally composed document. The plastic comb binding is important to allow the document to lay flat when open.

Transmittal

The cover sheet is sometimes followed by a letter of transmittal from the programmer to the client indicating the nature of the document and its intended uses. Often this letter is used only as an accompanying transmittal and is not included in the program document (Fig. 7-4).

Acknowledgment

Some programs include a section acknowledging help received in developing the program. This section is important to include in order to give credit where it is due. It can be an effective public relations tool. However, if used, it is important to understand the politics of the organization, to make certain that the acknowledgments do not leave out someone important or associate the project with someone who has lost credibility in the organization (Fig. 7-5).

Directory

September 24, 1982

Wesley Veatch, Minister
Bellevue Christian Church
105th Avenue, S.E. and S.E. 25th
Bellevue, Washington 98004

Dear Wes:

I am pleased to submit this report of the Architectural Consultation at the Bellevue Christian Church.

The Long Range Planning Committee did an excellent job of establishing the direction of your church and identifying specific facility needs. This report is an architectural reflection of the identified needs. The two phase proposal is in recognition of the highest priority items and budgetary restraints. Accomplishments of phase one should promote the growth necessary to proceed quickly into phase two.

I hope the suggestions I have made will receive your serious consideration and serve as a basis for ultimate development of your site and facilities.

I surely did enjoy meeting with you, your wife and the several church members in the Long Range Planning and Design Committees. Please give them my regards and keep me posted on developments.

Cordially,

Robert G. Hershberger

Figure 7-4 Typical Transmittal Letter.

To recognize the contributing energies of all involved people would produce a list far too long to print. Special thanks, though, must go to Allen Arebalo (Program IV Director) and Mary Wagner (Program IV Psychologist). They took a great deal of time away from their daily schedule to provide information, leads and access throughout the complex hospital environment. Jay Farbstein gave direction and feedback throughout the project. Gene Schultheis contributed valuable energy to initial research and development.

© Copyright August 1977
Michael Feerer

Figure 7-5 Short Acknowledgment.

Credit: Michael Feerer., 1977. *Family* Services Ward, *Environmental Architectural Program for Atascadero State Mental Hospital.* Atascadero, California. Permission: Michael Feerer

If there are persons that the design team should contact relative to specific areas of design, a directory can be included that lists the areas of concern, name, position, address, telephone, and e-mail for the appropriate persons. Inclusion of the directory can be an important time saver for the designer(s), particularly during design

Organization Name, Address, Phone, FAX
  Owner/CEO
  VP (in charge)
  Department Officer 1
  Department Officer n
  Building Manager
Architect Name, Address, Phone, FAX
  Partner (n charge)
  Project Programmer
  Project Architect
  Project Designer
Consultant(s) Name, Address, Phone, FAX
  Contact Person(s)
Regulatory Agency, Address, Phone, FAX
  Contact Person(s)

Figure 7-6 Directory Categories/Information.

PROCESS

The contents of this report were developed through a series of user interviews and Library Administration reviews held at the offices of Anderson DeBartolo Pan, Inc. during the weeks of April 14th - 18th and April 21st - 25th. Further work sessions were held during the week of April 28th - May 2nd with the City of Tucson Library Planning Consultant, Richard L. Waters; and the Architect's Space Planning Consultants, David and Andrea Michaels, to refine the results of the User Interviews Space Needs Tabulations and to establish spatial requirements and criteria for a balanced budget.

Following these work sessions a Preliminary Program Report containing the results of the Space Needs Tabulations was developed and reviewed by all parties involved in the programming process. The Spatial Needs Summaries included herein have incorporated the comments and modifications suggested in those revisions.

Figure 7-7 Typical Methods Section.

Credit: Anderson DeBartolo Pan, Inc. 1986. *City of Tucson Main Library Architectural Program.* Tucson, Arizona. Permission: ADP Marshall

development when detailed information may be required for specific areas of the project. The designer will use the directory to contact persons who can provide needed information (Figs. 7-6).

Methods

If the program is a major one, such as for a governmental agency planning a large facility or for numerous replications of the same facility, a separate section on programming methods may be useful. This section typically includes a summary of the information gathering and analysis procedures used to produce the program document, so that subsequent users have a trail to follow when challenging conclusions or trying to acquire additional information for a specific installation (Fig. 7-7).

References

It is also appropriate to acknowledge reference materials that could be useful to the designer for particular aspects of the project. This list could occur in an appendix (Fig. 7-8).

7.4 Executive Summary

- Purpose
- Format

Purpose

The executive summary serves several important purposes. As the name suggests, it allows the executive to take only a few minutes to read and understand the nature of the architectural problem.

If the summary appears to be an adequate reflection of the overall needs of the organization, the executive can accept the program without spending valuable time reading through all of the detail that may be important to subordinates, but of no special concern to the executive. The executive can delegate to others the task of reviewing detailed information in specific areas. In the same way, the executive summary allows the designer to obtain an understanding of the entire design problem before digging into all of the supporting information necessary to develop a successful design. Indeed, it reveals to anyone reading the document the key issues to look for as they continue through the document.

```
We gratefully acknowledge the following publications:

American Institute of Architects.  General Conditions of
the Contract, Washington, D.C.: American Institute of
Architects, 1976.

Dell 'Isola, Alphonse.  Value Engineering in the Construc-
tion Industry, New York, NY: Van Nostrand Reinhold
Company, 1982.

Kitchell CEM.  Planning A Successful Contruction Project,
Sacramento, CA: Kitchell CEM, 1986.

Kitchell CEM.  Security Testing Glazing Program and
Recommendations (prepared for the California Department of
Corrections), Sacramento, CA: Kitchell CEM, 1985.

State of California, Youth and Adult Correctional Agency,
Board of Corrections (prepared by Farbstein/Williams and
Associates).  Corrections Planning Handbooks, Sacramento,
CA: Board of Corrections, 1981.

National Institute of Justice
Construction Information Exchange
Box 6000
Rockville, MD 20850
(800) 851-3420 or (302) 251-5500

NOTE:  Refer particularly to the following NIJ publi-
cation: DeWitt, Charles, B.  National Directory of
Corrections Construction (First Edition), Washington, DC:
U.S. Department of Justice, National Institute of Justice,
1986.
```

Figure 7-8 Typical List of References.
Credit: Kitchell CEM, 1986. More for Less: Jail Construction Cost Management Handbook. State of California, Board of Construction Cost Management.Kitchell CEM

Format

The executive summary typically is only a few pages in length and contains information about all program areas. It should briefly state:

- The organization's mission/purposes
- How the project will serve these purposes
- The principal values or issues
- Specific goals to be achieved
- Important constraints or opportunities
- Special user needs
- Overall sizes and relationships

- The quality level of materials and systems
- The project schedule
- The project budget and preliminary cost estimates.

If it is for a speculative building, it might also include summaries of market conditions or financial feasibility studies. These are simply very condensed versions of the sections that follow, but with emphasis on the overall goals, requirements, schedule, and costs.

The executive statement may also indicate that some requirements of the program may change as the design progresses, and, if so, that a change in the scope of services and compensation may be required. If such a statement is included in the summary, it gives the programmer and architect a measure of protection if later developments require extensive changes in the work (Fig. 7-9).

It may not be possible to get everyone to sign off on a disclaimer such as the one shown in the adjoining executive summary; however, it is an excellent idea. The preliminary design is in some sense another restatement of the program, often containing compromises relative to goal accomplishment, variations from the program in the actual size or relationship of spaces, and other characteristics that do not conform exactly to the original program document. This is to be expected and should not come as a shock to anyone. It should be understood by all parties that the program is not immutable; that more will be learned about the program during the design process; and that this new knowledge might necessitate deviations from the original program (Robinson and Weeks 1984).

EXECUTIVE SUMMARY

The following program is an initial understanding of the primary goals used to develop a small commercial building to accommodate a retail camera store. The total building square footage of the retail camera store is expected not to exceed 1200 s.f.. This may allow the possibility for additional commercial retail or office space, depending on the site size and local codes.

The main issues of this program are to: communicate store type and image through store front design, provide a welcome environment and easy access for the client, provide an open plan with 90-95% of merchandise displayed and the flexibility of interior spaces to simplify circulation, provide adequate interior lighting that will effectivly display mechandise, be cost effective while in accordance with local codes.

The proposed site is locate in the Central Commercial District of downtown Tempe, Arizona, on the north side of seventh street between Mill Ave. and Maple Ave.. The site is presently vacant and rests next to a historical warehouse on the west side and a single story commercial building on the east side.

The Owner/Client, Programmer, and Designer understand and agree that this is a preliminary program document, and acknowledge that further design exploration may reveal additional opportunities or constraints which might necessitate adjustments in program requirements. If such adjustments have any major effects on the issues stated in this program, it may be necessary to renegotiate fees to reflect the increased scope of architectural services.

Total Budget: Low $50211.00   Med $71729.00   High $83246.00

Owner/Client_____ Date_____

Programmer_____ Date_____

Architect_____ Date_____

Figure 7-9 Short Executive Summary.

Credit: Michael Kummer, 1987. *Retail Camera Shop Program.* School of Architecture, Arizona State University

On the other hand, if the owner changes the project requirements substantially after the program has been accepted and especially after design has commenced, or even when the building is at some stage of completion, it should be clearly understood that such changes will serve as a basis for the architect to renegotiate fees. A disclaimer in the program, or as part of the agreement for professional services, might help avoid unnecessary disputes and delays during the design process. This is especially important if the client decides that substantial additional space is needed or that an upgrade in material or system quality is essential, but wants both within the original design and construction budget. This is not an unusual situation! Clients often change their minds as they gradually develop an understanding of the design implications of the program. Some are also very forgetful as to what they had agreed upon earlier. Many clients are unrealistic about what they want, compared to what they can afford.

7.5 Values and Goals

After the executive summary should come a section in which the information developed in the programming matrix is refined for the program document. A direct reproduction of a wall-sized matrix is not possible in an 8½" × 11" document, so it must be presented in another way. The author has found that first presenting the values and goals in simple phrases or sentences is an effective way to bring the designer up-to-date on the crucial issues to be dealt with in schematic design. This section can be followed in logical order with a design considerations (facts) section to show the context in which the values can be expressed and the goals met. This section can be followed by an extensive project requirements section in which master plan, schematic design, and design development requirements can be systematically covered. Finally, the ideas generated for the matrix can be presented.

The primary values and goals of the client/user articulated in the programming matrix should be identified and amplified as necessary to show the designer what is important to accomplish in the design. The importance of this section in setting an appropriate framework from which to structure the rest of the program and to begin design cannot be overstated.

As covered extensively in Chapters 1 through 3, values and issues uncovered in an architectural program will include several major areas such as the HECTTEAS areas: human, environmental, cultural, technological, temporal, economic, aesthetic, and safety. What is the mission of the particular institution for which the program is being prepared? What special considerations should there be for the human users? Is function a very important consideration? Are there users with handicaps or other special needs? Is it important to communicate a certain image to the community? Does the community have important urban design objectives or guidelines which the individual building must support and enhance? Similarly, there are often values and goals relating to the natural environment, to available technology, to time, to economic conditions, and to aesthetics. The important goals for the project should be enumerated with each appropriate value.

In value-based programming, the values should be placed in order of importance, with specific goals or objectives listed and discussed beside each value heading. The goals should also be ranked relative to importance from essential, to important, to desirable, or some similar listing. Prioritization of values and goals is of help to the programmer when budget constraints require reductions in program requirements. It also helps the designer know where to focus design efforts.

It is important in this section of the program to provide the designer with an opportunity to develop a clear understanding of what must be accomplished and what would be desirable to accomplish if various constraints allow. There is no point in cluttering the designer's mind with constraints until a clear understanding of what the client hopes to accomplish has been attained (Fig. 7-10).

Design Goals and Objectives

Chapter 2 of this program contains a detailed list of design goals and objectives. Major goals are summarized below:

Economics. Maximum value for investment (best ratio of quality to cost). Minimize maintenance, repair and replacement costs.

Operational Efficiency. Efficient layout and flow. Minimize staffing requirements. Access for the handicapped.

Control, Security and Safety. Excellent visual surveillance and physical control.

Timing. Occupancy by the end of September, 1984. Maintenance of current operations. Accommodation of long term development, including flexible interior layouts and an eventual separate commercial crossing point.

Energy and Environment. Comfort throughout the facility with energy efficiency. Special attention to canopies and booths. Adequate, glare-free light; acoustic controls.

Image and Esthetics. A quality design reflecting the dignity, vigor and stability of the U.S. government. Response to local climate and culture. Welcoming.

User Perception and Wayfinding. Sensitivity to user/visitor problems of access, information needs, communications as well as extreme contrasts of light and heat.

Workplace Quality. A pleasant, comfortable, attractive place to work, with the ability of workers to control certain aspects of their environments.

Figure 7-10 Values and Goals Summary.

Credit: Farbstein/Williams & Associates, Inc., 1983. Border Station San Luis, Arizona, Pre-Design Program. United States Government, General Services Administration, Region 9, San Francisco, Project Number: NAZ01000-Am. Permission: Jay Farbstein and Associates

7.6 Design Considerations (facts)

- Human (activities and characteristics)

- Environmental (site and climate)

- Cultural (traditions, laws, codes, and ordinances)
- Technical
- Other

Programmers present the design considerations generated during the programming process in a variety of ways. Some programmers, such as William Peña of CRS, preferred to present them in the same format as found in the programming matrix that his firm uses (Peña et al. 1969, 1977, 1986). The "facts" section of the program matrix needs only to be taken down from the wall and reproduced in program format. Generally, however, Peña and other programmers using the card system will reduce the card size in the program and add verbal description to make them more understandable to persons who were not at the work sessions (Fig. 7-11).

By re-presenting the cards, this approach avoids the possibility that information will be included in the programming document that was not actually presented to and considered and accepted by the group during the work sessions. Programmers using verbal cards or grid paper are more likely to transcribe the information into a typed format and, thus, to produce a somewhat more dense and information rich set of facts. This is particularly true if their intent is to provide information not just for schematic design, but for design development as well (Fig. 7-12).

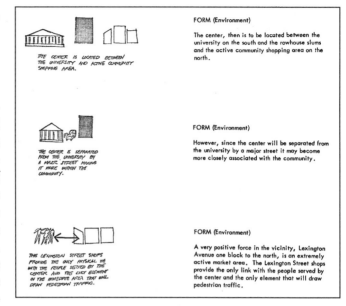

FORM (Environment)

The center, then is to be located between the university on the south and the rowhouse slums and the active community shopping area on the north.

FORM (Environment)

However, since the center will be separated from the university by a major street it may become more closely associated with the community.

FORM (Environment)

A very positive force in the vicinity, Lexington Avenue one block to the north, is an extremely active market area. The Lexington Street shops provide the only link with the people served by the center and the only element that will draw pedestrian traffic.

Figure 7-11 Facts Page of a CRS Program.

Credit: CRS, 1971. *Community Mental Health and Retardation Center* Program. Permission: William Peña, HOK

```
1.  Current  main  entry  is confused with back entry.(Main  entry
    does not face community.

2.  Presently  there  is  only 1 elevator that is  inadequate  in
    speed and accessibility.

3.  At this time,  the rear stairwells serve as both a  vertical
    circulation  system  and ingress/egress,  which  causes
    major  conjestion,  and  threatens  emergency  exiting
    procedures.

4.  The  handicapped  access is limited to front  entry  through
    gallery  and secondary basement entry.  Gallery  entrance  is
    locked after 5 pm,  and basement entry  is  locked  many
    times also, therefore denying handicapped access to elevator.

5.  Currently,  students  are  unaware of other  students  work
    within the different levels of the college.(Pre-proffession-
    al included.

6.  Existing information tack boards can only be accessed during
    administraion office hours which limits student awareness.

7.  Presently,  there  is  only 1 soft drink machine  which  is
    inconveniently  located in the basement,  and is many times
    empty.
```

Figure 7-12 Facts Page of a Text-Based Program.

Credit: David Sandvig, Rob Darney, and Chris Caroselli, 1986. *Program for the New Architecture Building.* Permission: School of Architecture, Arizona State University

ZONING / ISSUE CHART

	DAY USE	NIGHT USE	PUBLIC	PRIVATE	STAFF	YOUTH
Outdoor Space	●		●			●
Storage	●				●	
Public Bathroom	●		●			●
Youth Bath - Girls		●				●
Bedroom - Girls		●				●
Youth Bath - Boys		●				●
Bedroom - Boys		●				●
Foyer	●			●		●
Director's Office	●			●	●	
Counseling	●			●		●
Multi - Purpose	●		●			●
Laundry	●		●			●
Linen Closet	●		●		●	
Staff Office	●				●	
Staff Bath	●				●	
Kitchen	●		●			●
Pantry	●				●	
Dining / Study	●		●			●

Day Uses: Youth are permitted in these area between the hours of 7a.m. and 10p.m.

Night Uses: Youth are only permitted in these area between the hours of 10p.m. and 7a.m.

Public: The activities in these spaces should not interfere or disrupt the activities in the private spaces

Private: The nature of these spaces demand privacy from all public spaces

Staff: These spaces are primarily used only by the staff. The youth are only permitted with permission

Youth: These spaces are used primarily by the youth with staff supervision

Figure 7-13 Summary Zoning/Issue Chart.

Credit: Zachary Burns, Roger Dong, Stacy Kluck, Kean Ong, and Marc Soloway, 1995. *Open-Inn Runaway Center Program*. College of Architecture, The University of Arizona

It is also possible to condense some of the factual information onto charts or graphs to make it easier to understand and compare (Fig. 7-13).

It makes sense to present the facts that should impact design in a format similar to the matrix of values developed earlier in the programming process. Typically there will be facts (constraints and opportunities) relating to each of the value areas identified.

Human (activities and characteristics)

Often something needs to be said about the particular nature of the organization and its activities before specific requirements for spaces and relationships are set forth. It is most helpful for the designer to know the organizational structure as well as the major human functions that the existing and future facilities will accommodate. Information about the organization's mission and goals is also useful. If particular social relationships are encouraged or discouraged, this should also be pointed out. Special needs of the current and prospective users may also be included. Are very old, very young, handicapped, or other non-typical people frequent users of the building? If so, what are their particular characteristics and physical needs? All of these facts should be stated so the designer can acquire a better understanding of the design constraints and opportunities relating to the human content of the facility (Fig. 7-14).

Environmental (site and climate)

The development of a good understanding of the environmental context of a design problem typically or logically begins with a description and appropriate visual illustrations of the location of the project: the city or region in which the site is located, its immediate environmental context, the characteristics of the site, the climate and microclimate, and any other information on sues of the design problem. Typically, information about a site is overlaid and annotated on a plan of the site (Fig. 7-15).

Factual information about local climate conditions can be obtained from the United States Weather Bureau publications. It is often represented in charts and diagrams (Fig. 7-16).

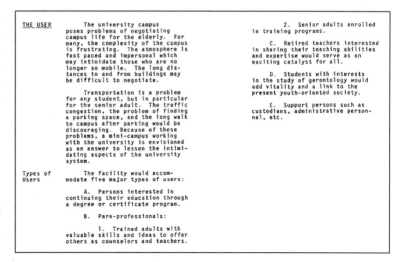

Figure 7-14 Human Fact Statements.

Credit: Carmelita Apodaca, Elaine Cesta, Linda Congreve, Marley Porter, Bob Krikac, and John Jakob, Associate Professor, 1980. *Program for Sachel: Senior Adult Community for a Higher Education Lifestyle*, Tempe, Arizona. Permission: School of Architecture, Arizona State University

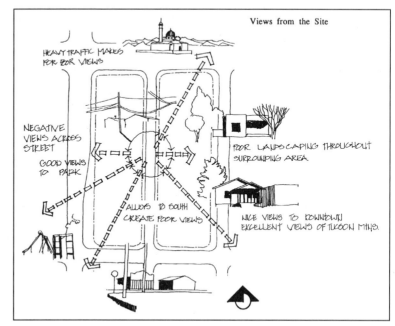

Figure 7-16 Site Information.

Credit: Fourth Year Design Studio, Professor Poster, 1990. *Salvation Army Homeless Facility, Program and Site Analysis*. College of Architecture, The University of Arizona

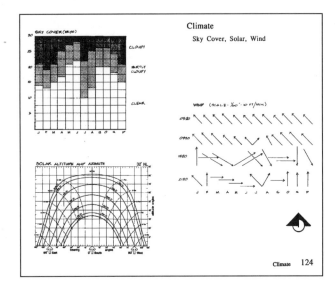

Figure 7-16 Climate Information.

Credit: Fourth Year Design Studio, Professor Poster, 1990. *Salvation Army Homeless Facility, Program and Site Analysis.* College of Architecture, The University of Arizona

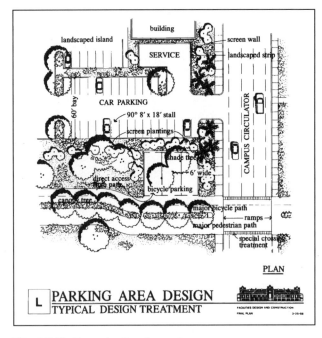

Figure 7-17 Screening Requirements.

Credit: *Comprehensive Campus Plan,* 1988. The University of Arizona, and the Arizona Board of Regents. Permission: The University of Arizona

Cultural (traditions, laws, codes, and ordinances)

An explanation of the cultural context of the problem is also important. What are the community traditions? Are there particular expectations relative to the building type to be designed? Is there a community fabric to which the designer should be sensitive? Can the project help the community achieve some of its urban design objectives? If so, these facts should be pointed out to give the designer an opportunity to fit the design within this larger framework. This section should also point out whether the community has adopted ordinances or special review procedures relating to site, building, or landscape appearance. A description of how and where the designer can obtain the ordinances and review procedures should be included in this section along with information about key or unusual provisions of the ordinances or procedures. For instance, some communities and institutions have restrictive sign control and landscaping requirements while others have few or minimal restrictions. The designer needs to know what the requirements are before commencing design (Fig. 7-17).

Technical

There may also be facts about physical or technical aspects of the facility which should be pointed out in the program. Do the occupants or equipment for this type of facility typically need closely controlled temperature or humidity? Are particular materials or finishes used in order to meet the requirements of occupants or maintenance objectives of the organization? This type of information should be included if it is likely to impact upon design decisions.

The programmer must be careful when presenting facts. There is a danger of implying that the future solution must be similar to the existing when, in fact, the owner would like to entertain alternative approaches. It should be made clear to what extent the included information relates to the existing facility, to characteristics of other similar facilities, or even to historical prototypes. These are not facts about the facility that has yet to be designed. If there are physical or technical requirements for the future facility, they should be set forth in the section on project requirements.

Other

There could, of course, be design considerations relating to any of the other HECTTEAS areas or to any other value areas agreed on during programming. There could be facts relating to the image of the facility, to signage, even to form or color. There may be facts relating to energy conservation and other similar concerns which arise during programming. There could be facts relating to safety, accessibility, or to any other value area discovered in the programming process that constrain or provide opportunities for design. The above sections on human, environmental, cultural, and technical design considerations are only examples of the types of information typically covered in the design considerations section of the program.

It is also appropriate to set forth facts about budget and time constraints in the section on design considerations. Many programmers, however, prefer to discuss facts about budget and schedule in separate sections of the program, because these areas are of such great importance for the successful completion of a project. There is also a problem of deciding if such information should be a design consideration (fact) or a requirement (need). The client's budget is a fact with which the designer must be familiar because it sets limits or constraints on what can be done. It is also a requirement in the sense that design decisions must be made that will keep the cost of the facility within the stated limits.

The same is true for project schedule. There may be a specific date when the client must vacate existing facilities. This is a fact. But the schedule to vacate may also set a requirement for when the new facility must be ready for occupancy. For these reasons it is best to include information about budget and schedule in separate sections of the program to highlight their crucial importance to the successful completion of the project.

7.7 Project Requirements

- Needs
- Performance Requirements (PRs)
- Design Requirements (DRs)

Project requirements will vary considerably depending on the nature of the project under consideration. If the program includes master planning for the entire site, then there will be a section on master plan requirements. If it includes programming for a specific building project, the program will list requirements appropriate for schematic design including tabular information on space allocation, room relationships, relationship diagrams, project schedule, and project cost analysis. If it is a comprehensive architectural program involving design development, the program will also include requirements for individual spaces and for building systems. Requirement statements will be developed from the needs cards or short phrases of the programming matrix. They will be refined into performance requirements or design requirements, or distilled into tabular form showing required space allocations, space relationships, project schedule, and project costs:

- Master Planning Requirements
  - Site Design (circulation, parking, drainage, retention, utilities)
  - Building Layout (overall building relationships, sizes, location, orientation, future expansion)

- Schematic Design Requirements
  - Building Design (building organization, size, orientation, image, growth, change)
  - Interior Design (user needs, activities, sizes, relationships, conditions)
  - Space Identification and Square Footage Allocation
  - Relationship Matrices and Diagrams

- Design Development Requirements
  - Space Program Sheets
  - Building Systems Requirements (materials, systems, processes)

If a program is intended to serve only one of these design phases, then information relating to the other phases might be left out of the document. For instance, if the master planning has already been accomplished, perhaps by another design firm, then the program could focus only on the specific building to be designed. Elimination of material from earlier or later sections of the program would be appropriate if the purposes of the program were so limited.

Needs

In many poorly developed programs, a simple listing of the required spaces is the program. The client or novice programmers set forth what space they think is needed, without any systematic consideration of the institutional purposes to be served, values to be expressed, project goals and objectives to be met, environmental or cultural context, special users, client/user design ideas, or any other such considerations. They fail to develop the context of values, goals, and facts from which needs should be derived. This is unfortunate and confusing to the designer, and tends to reduce design to a puzzle-solving exercise, rather than a creative endeavor in which design solutions are the result of keen insight into the nature of the design problem.

On the other hand, when the preliminary sections of the architectural program contain complete information on the client's and user's values, goals, and objectives as well as on factual constraints and opportunities, the project requirements (or needs) section of the program will be easy to develop and can be lean and straightforward. It can focus on the required performance and facility needs without further discussion of the key issues, explanation of important facts, or other considerations, because they will already have been covered.

The space needs developed in the value-based programming matrix are presented in much the same way as for goals and facts. Programmers using cards in the programming matrix will often group the cards on pages of the program and augment them with verbal descriptions (Fig. 7-18). Those using verbal cards or grid paper are more likely to accumulate the needs into lists relating to each of the respective value areas (Fig. 7-19).

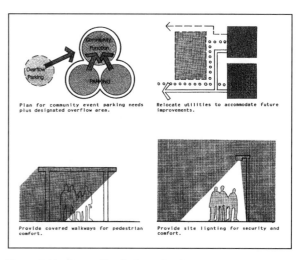

Figure 7-18 Space Needs Page: Cards.

Credit: Brooks & Associates AIA, Architects and Planners, 1988. Vail Middle School Master Plan & Program. Vail School District No. 20. Vail, Arizona. Permission: Albanese-Brooks Assoc. PC

```
┌─────────────────────────────────────────────────────────────┐
│ FORM NEEDS                                                    │
│                                                               │
│ 1. Complete screening of parking from Warner Road.            │
│                                                               │
│ 2. Parking and pedestrian access from both Warner and Pennington. │
│                                                               │
│ 3. Overflow parking at retention panhandle.                   │
│                                                               │
│ 4. Earth berms to integrate and insulate building.            │
│                                                               │
│ 5. South facing windows are for passive heating and daylighting (Use │
│    fixed insulated units owned by church).                    │
│                                                               │
│ 6. North facing windows for view and daylighting.             │
└─────────────────────────────────────────────────────────────┘
```

It is worthwhile to consider how need statements can be reformulated after the work sessions, because how needs are stated can have an important effect on design. There are two kinds of needs statements included in an architectural program: performance requirements and design requirements (Duerk 1993).

FORM NEEDS

1. Complete screening of parking from Warner Road.

2. Parking and pedestrian access from both Warner and Pennington.

3. Overflow parking at retention panhandle.

4. Earth berms to integrate and insulate building.

5. South facing windows are for passive heating and daylighting (Use fixed insulated units owned by church).

6. North facing windows for view and daylighting.

CONTEXT NEEDS

1. Large patio for 150 standing people for coffee & BBQ?

2. Small patio for 35 people & BBQ?

3. Adequate lighting for parking and patios.

4. Filtered light for patios on north.

5. Exterior places for table tennis, baseball, volley ball.

6. Exterior places for pre-school and older children (in view).

7. Access to trash at alley.

8. Short time parking near pre-school for drop off and pick up.

9. Overflow parking in handle of retention.

FUNCTION NEEDS

	Phase 1	Future
1. Auditorium/Fellowship		
a. Auditorium/Fellowship - to seat for services	125-150 p.	200-225 p.
b. Auditorium/Fellowship - to seat for potlucks	150 p.	225 p.
c. Foyer/courtyard to stand for coffee	125-150 p.	200-225 p.
d. Storage for round tables seating six persons	25 t.	38 t.
e. Storage for folding/stacking chairs	75 ch.	150 ch.
f. Space in auditorium for modular stage/risers	—	—
g. Space in auditorium for piano, organ, audiovisual control, art	—	—
h. Conference/library/bride/etc. (See administration area)	—	—
i. Kitchen to serve potlucks/lunchs	5-6 p.	6-8 p.
j. Rest rooms (Male/female)	Code	Code
k. Parking (code-projected)	38-60 sp.	57-100 sp.

Figure 7-19 Space Needs Page: Text.

Credit: Hershberger Kim Architects, 1982. *Valley Unitarian Universalist Church, Architectural Program and Master Plan Study. Chandler, Arizona.*

Performance Requirements (PRs)

Performance requirements are statements of how some aspect of the organization or design should perform. They are a small step below goals, and in traditional terms could be referred to as objectives—specific ways that a goal can be met. Performance requirements can relate to the building occupants, spaces, systems, and materials, and typically are stated in such a way that it is possible to measure their accomplishment. The measurement can be:

1. A simple binary or dichotomous judgment by the designer, owner, or experts—yes or no, accomplished or not accomplished.

2. An acceptable range of values that can be physically measured, such as in inches, decibels, lumens, or degrees. The achievement of a goal may require accomplishment of one or several performance requirements.

The following are examples of goal statements followed by performance requirements:

1. Goal: To have excellent seating for theatrical performances.

   PR: Provide an unobstructed view of at least three-quarters of the stage from all seats.

   PR: Provide sound to each seat at the same level and quality as if the seat were 20 feet from the stage.

2. Goal: To utilize daylighting strategies to reduce energy consumption.

   PR: Provide 75% of the daytime lighting load with daylighting.

3. Goal: To have safe access from parking and residential units to a commons room.

   PR: Provide a minimum illumination level of two foot-candles on the walking surface at exterior circulation ways.

   PR: Circulation ways must at all points be visible from at least two adjacent living units.

4. Goal: To communicate the bank's purposes to the public.

   PR: 95% of passing motorists must be able to recognize the building as the First Service Bank.

   PR: Access points to parking, drive-through teller, and automatic teller must be evident to passing motorists.

Achievement of each of the above performance requirements can be measured or estimated. In the first example, it is possible to draw sight lines from every seat to determine whether or not three-quarters of the stage can be seen. It is also possible with a sound system to calculate and to measure (when completed) if the same level of sound is being provided at every seat as that provided to seats 20 feet from the stage. If a certain level of illumination is required, the foot-candles or lumens can be calculated during design using performance data for expected daylighting conditions as well as for specific lighting fixtures. The same is true for ventilation, heating, cooling, and acoustical performance.

Expected levels of human performance can also be estimated during design (and measured after occupancy). If a person must be able to reach a certain control switch, anthropometric data can be used to determine if this will be possible. If a person must be able to exit from a room in two alternative directions, this can be observed by inspecting the drawings. A required image or quality of space or form, on the other hand, may require professional judgment to determine if the need will be met. While not as precise as other measures, this still allows appropriate evaluation before proceeding to build a project.

Note that measured accomplishment of the performance requirements does not ensure that a goal will be achieved at the highest level. It only helps to ensure that the goal will be accomplished, perhaps at a minimum level. For instance, achieving a goal of "excellent seating" certainly requires unobstructed sight lines and proper acoustics. But it also requires comfortable seating and adequate leg room, good accessibility to the seats, proper ventilation and air conditioning, and acoustical and lighting separation from other parts of the building. An almost endless list of performance requirements would have to be developed for each and every space to ensure a high level of goal achievement. It is best to state only those performance requirements that are considered to be unique or crucial to the proper functioning of a facility.

Design Requirements (DRs)

Design requirements, like performance requirements, are more specific and measurable than goal statements. However, they refer directly to the physical characteristics of the building to be designed, rather than to the performance of the occupants, spaces, systems, or materials. All statements, numbers, or diagrams specifying the size, shape, physical characteristics, and relationships of various spaces are design requirements. Specifications of particular furnishings, equipment, materials, and finishes are also design requirements.

In value-based programming, all needs should be given in terms that allow accomplishment in the design to be measured in some way. This is usually easy to do if a certain product is specified. It is either provided or it is not. A binary measure (yes, no) or a simple count can be used to determine if the required number of spaces or pieces of furnishing or equipment have been provided. It may be necessary to read a label on the drawing or in the specifications to determine if a particular piece of equipment has been provided. Square footage requirements can be verified by measurement and calculation. Accomplishment of required relationships can be verified by observation and even measurement of the drawings.

Design requirements for the goal statements listed above illustrate the difference between performance and design requirements. The part of the sentence in parentheses indicates the related performance requirement.

1. Goal: To have excellent seating for theatrical performances.

   DR: Offset and vary the width of seating (to allow persons to see between persons seated in front of them).

   DR: Provide a minimum three-inch rise between rows of seats, and raise the stage three feet above first row (to allow people to see over the people seated in front of them).

   DR: Provide a distributed electronic sound reinforcement system (to provide the same level and quality of sound at each seat).

   DR: Provide a minimum of 6,000 square feet for the seating area (to provide ample seating for 600 people).

2. Goal: To utilize daylighting strategies to reduce energy consumption.

   DR: Provide a clerestory lighting system (to provide 75% of daytime lighting load).

3. Goal: To have safe access from parking and residential units to a commons room.

   DR: Provide walk lights at 20 to 30 feet on center (to provide no less than two foot-candles of light at the walking surface).

   DR: Design kitchen window in housing units to overlook all pathways (to be certain that circulation ways are visible from no less than two adjacent living units).

4. Goal: To communicate the bank's purposes to the public.

   DR: Provide free-standing, lighted signs with minimum four-inch-high letters with name and logo of the bank at each street frontage and at street faces of the building (to be certain that 95% of passing motorists can recognize the building as a branch of First Service Bank).

   DR: Provide same color brick, covered teller canopy, and entrance canopy as currently exist on all other branch banks (to be certain that 95% of passing motorists can recognize the building as a First Service Bank, even if they do not see the signs).

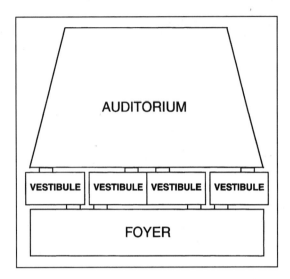

Figure 7-20 Vestibules as Light/Sound Locks.

It is easily seen from the above illustrations that design requirements are actually second order requirements. A performance requirement is almost always used (explicitly or implicitly) to arrive at the design requirement. For example, a performance requirement to meet the goal "to produce an excellent auditorium" might be "that no light or sound should be introduced into the auditorium from any adjacent public circulation area." If left at this level, the designer would be free to devise any system that would ensure that this performance requirement would be satisfied. On the other hand, experience with numerous theaters and auditoriums has led to the repeated use of vestibules as light and sound locks between the auditorium and the surrounding circulation ways (Fig. 7-20). It may be more likely, therefore, to require that vestibules be provided (to ensure that light and sound not penetrate into the auditorium).

Another design requirement for an auditorium might be that the seating be "fully upholstered theater type seating" or even that the seating be "fully upholstered theater seating by Theater Seating Company A." This might relate to acoustical performance, audience comfort, accessibility to interior seats, or to maintenance requirements. A client may want a specific seat by a particular company and will settle for nothing less, because in lengthy experience the client has found no other satisfactory seat and does not want to take a chance on poor quality seating! This approach may seem unduly restrictive to a designer who wishes to select or even to design the seating, but if an owner group has had previous negative experience with many seating systems and positive results with only one model, they may not be willing to consider performance requirements. They will want a design requirement—the specification of a particular product. Sometimes, however, it is possible for the programmer to convince a client to define the performance desired and, thus, to allow a more creative design or selection procedure.

In some cases the client may wish to state only the goal, and let the designer try to meet it by her/his own creativity, knowledge, and experience. The architect can always refer to recognized design for guidance when requirements are not included in the program (Fig. 7-21).

It is generally best to provide a combination of goals, performance requirements, and design requirements in a program. This allows the client, programmer, and designer to obtain a better understanding of the design problem. The goals allow everyone to see what the organization hopes to achieve. The performance requirements provide an understanding of how important aspects of a facility must work. Design requirements ensure that certain minimum needs are satisfied in crucial areas. Together they help the programmer make projections of the overall size of the facility and estimate the probable construction cost.

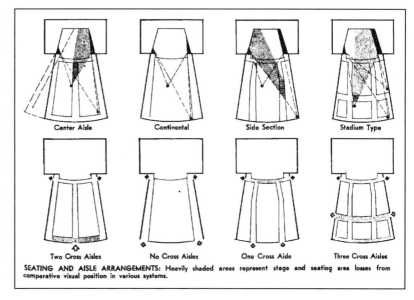

Figure 7-21 Auditorium Sight Lines.

Credit: Joseph De Chiara and John Hancock Callendar, 1973. *Time Saver Standards for Building Types.* McGraw Hill Book Co., NY, NY, p. 677. Permission: McGraw-Hill

The programmer should not seek or develop requirements where they really do not exist. If the client and users are looking to the architect for a creative new way to achieve a goal, it makes little sense to set forth a number of strict requirements. However, if a particular performance is required, it should be stated in the program. If a particular design feature is required, it also should be stated in the program.

Requirements for a project can also be expressed in tables consisting of lists, associated numbers, and diagrams. These are efficient ways of stating needs, but unlike typical needs statements, performance requirements, and design requirements, do not provide any amplification or justification as to why something should be done. They are simply efficient ways to show the overall size of spaces and cost of the facility to be designed. The primary uses of tabular presentation of needs are covered in sections 7.8, 7.9, 7.11, and 7.12.

7.8 Space Identification and Allocation

- Tabular Presentation
- Leadership
- Iconic Representation
- Building Efficiency

Tabular Presentation

In the work session, the spaces identified as required in the programming matrix are listed in tabular form on brown sheets, grid sheets, or another format for everyone to see. This promotes focused group consideration and discussion of the number of required spaces and the appropriate size for each space. Thus, the square footages are listed to the right of each of the listed spaces to form a simple table. The same form is carried into the program document for the convenience of the designer.

Leadership

It is common for the programmer to lead lengthy work session discussions regarding the number of persons who will be using various spaces, the activities in which they are likely to engage, and the type and amount of furnishings and equipment that will be needed. The programmer will also point out norms or standards for space sizes as found in the literature, in comparable facilities, and for existing spaces in facilities of the client/user group. This is done to help the client/user group come to an understanding and agreement as to what size each space must be to accomplish the purposes of the organization. Clients and users generally have little or no idea how big the spaces are that they use or will need in the future. The programmer must be the expert in this area.

All of the information gathered during the work session should be recorded by a member of the programming group as it is brought forth, because it will be useful in developing the space program sheets discussed in section 7.10. At this point, however, it is important to list all of the required spaces and to record their respective sizes, so that an assessment can be made of the overall scope of the project.

Iconic Representation

An effective adjunct to listing the square footage of each required space with numbers is to illustrate it with small rectangular figures at the same scale, i.e., at ¹⁄₁₆" = 1'O". This system is effective in showing laypersons the comparative size of spaces. It can also be helpful to the designer during initial analysis of the design problem. The numbers may not be as effective as the illustrations, since most client/users have little or no understanding of the numerical sizes of the spaces in which they live or operate, but they can see the relative differences in the sizes of various spaces in the graphic illustrations. Similarly, designers are often more comfortable with iconic rather than numeric imagery. If one space looks excessively large relative to another space, the participants will be quick to point this out to the programmer.

Because this information is generally developed in a tabular form during the work session(s), as discussed in Chapter 6, it is necessary only to upgrade the presentation of the material for the program document. Simple word processing combined with the use of presentation software will allow the programmer to develop a quality presentation of this vital information (Fig. 7-22).

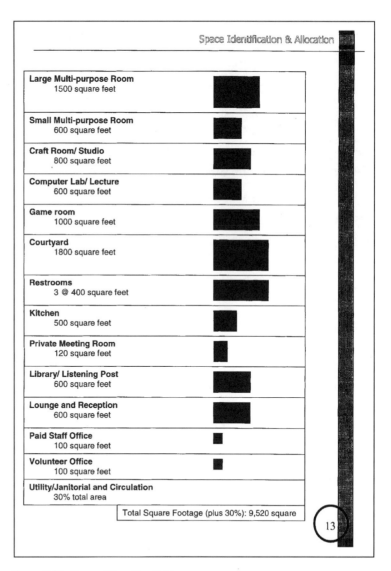

Figure 7-22 Space Allocation Table.

Credit: Architecture 202, Section 3, Professor Hershberger, 1998. A Program for A Senior Center. Permission: College of Architecture, The University of Arizona

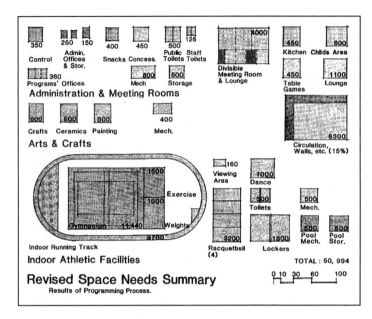

Figure 7-23 Space Allocation Table.

Credit: Brooks & Associates AIA, Architects and Planners, 1985. *Design Program and Site Analysis for Morris K. Udall Regional Park and Recreational Center.* Tucson, Arizona. Permission: Albanese-Brooks Assoc. PC

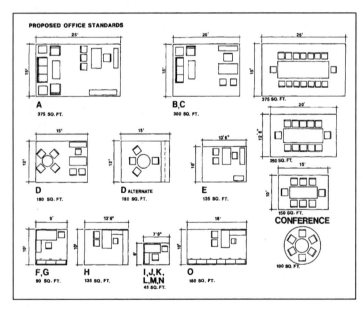

Figure 7-24 Typical Office Standards.

Credit: Martha O'Mara, 1985. The Programming of Office Interiors in *Programming the Built Environment*. Ed. W. F. E. Preiser. New York: Van Nostrand Reinhold. Permission: Wolfgang F. E. Preiser

This information can also be presented in a more diagrammatic form, rather than in a list with the areas shown to scale as in the above illustration. The following illustration shows the effect of a carefully drawn diagram as an alternative method of presenting the space allocation information in the program document (Fig. 7-23).

Using either of the above approaches, the initial space allocation sheets from the work sessions can be reorganized in the quiet of the programmer's office. Logical groupings of spaces can be made and tabulations of subtotals, efficiency factors, and totals can be prepared.

It is also possible to develop more detailed illustrations of some of the required spaces. This is sometimes done for offices, with size variations and furnishing differences for various personnel, from the chief executives to the secretarial staff. If used, the preliminary standards developed by the programming group will need to be reviewed in an executive work session to be certain that they are acceptable before being incorporated into the programming document (Fig. 7-24).

Building Efficiency

When all of the required spaces have been identified and square footages assigned, it is necessary to estimate the amount of additional square footage that will be required to account for unprogrammed space, including circulation spaces, walls, mechanical and electrical rooms and chases, janitor's closets, rest rooms, and miscellaneous storage. This amounts to a very substantial percent of the building area, and must be figured into the overall size of the facility and subsequently to its cost. This is referred to in programming as the "net-to-gross ratio" or "building efficiency" and varies significantly for different building types. If it is accounted for incorrectly, particularly on the low side, it can have a significant negative impact on building quality.

So, what are some expected net-to-gross ratios? A warehouse or simple storage building may have a very high net-to-gross ratio. The assignable area would be the warehouse or storage space. The unassigned area would include only the exterior walls, assuming that mechanical equipment could be placed on the roof, electrical service placed on outside walls, and janitorial equipment simply placed within the warehouse area. Even so, a 50' × 100' building of this type would not have 100 percent efficiency because the exterior walls would take up unassigned space. Assume for simplicity that the walls were one foot thick and that the exterior was exactly 50' × 100'—then the net-to-gross ratio would be 4,704 net square feet divided by 5,000 gross square feet, a building efficiency of 94 percent. If the building were larger or the walls thinner the efficiency would be even higher, perhaps 95 percent. The "grossing factor"—the percentage difference between the net and gross square feet—in this case would be 5 or 6 percent (Fig. 7-25).

In fact, most simple warehouses will include an office or two, at least one restroom, a janitor's closet, some office storage, a reception area, and a short hallway to connect them to the warehouse. Interior partitions will be required to create these separations. As a result, the expected efficiency of

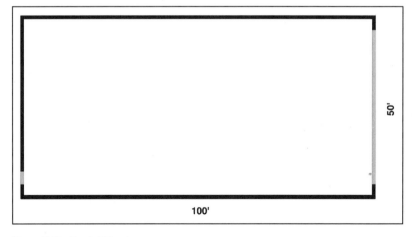

50'

100'

Figure 7-25 Basic Warehouse.

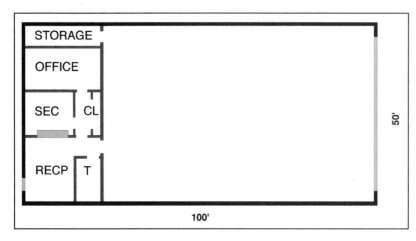

Figure 7-26 Warehouse with Office Space.

1. Circulation	15–25%
2. Mechanical	05–10%
3. Walls, Partitions, Structure	07–10%
4. Toilets (public)	1.5–2.5%
5. Janitor Closets	0.2–1.0%
6. Unassigned Storage	0.3–1.5%
Total	30–50%

Figure 7-27 Unassigned Space Variations

Adapted from: (Peña et al., 1987), 109. Permission: American Institute of Architects and HOK

Administration	55%
Student Center	60%
Science Building	60%
Dormitory	60%
Auditorium	60%
Museum	65%
Library	65%
Academic	65%
Physical Education	70%
Building Services	75%

Figure 7-28 Typical Building Efficiencies

Adapted from: (Peña et al., 1987), 110. Permission: American Institute of Architects and HOK

most simple warehouses would be closer to 85 or 90 percent (Fig. 7-26).

For most building types, the efficiency is not nearly as high as for a warehouse. Academic buildings, for instance, will often have an efficiency of between 60 and 70 percent, and this does not allow for spacious entryways, corridors, or, especially, two- or three-story interior spaces. Two-story spaces are less efficient than one-story spaces. Not very surprising, perhaps, but often forgotten by beginning programmers and designers, who try to ignore that such spaces require higher walls, use space from the level above, and often require greater circulation and wall space at the upper level. Arizona State University, for instance, requires that all two-story volumes be counted as one and one half times their actual assignable square foot area to account for the added costs related to the decrease in building efficiency.

A major public building such as a civic auditorium or city hall may have an efficiency as low as 50 percent to allow for development of major circulation areas, multiple-story halls, major atriums, or other similarly grand spaces. The following charts indicate the probable range of unassigned space and efficiencies for various building types (Figs. 7-27 and 7-28).

It should be clear at this point that the grossing factor is, in fact, an educated guess based on experience. It is of great importance to educate the client of its reality and importance. As a programmer, it is better to err toward the less efficient so that the associated costs can be built into the preliminary cost analysis. Clearly, the cost of a building can vary 10 to 30 percent or even more based on unassigned space. It is better, therefore, to estimate on the low side of efficiency and try to determine the relative importance or priority of some program requirements, so that if something must be eliminated or reduced in size to achieve a satisfactory design solution, no one will be needlessly surprised or the design quality unnecessarily compromised.

Calculation of efficiency during programming is rather simple: net square feet divided by expected efficiency equals gross square feet:

$$\frac{Net\ Square\ Feet}{Efficiency} = Gross\ Square\ Feet$$

Detailed discussions of this topic are contained in Peña et al. (1987) and Kumlin (1995). This author would recommend both sources as essential reading to programming practitioners who need to be aware of the differing ways of counting efficiency used throughout the building industry.

7.9 Relationship Matrices and Diagrams

- Relationship Matrices
- Relationship Diagrams

Understanding relationships is a very basic and important part of architectural programming.

There are at least three distinct levels at which relationships are important. The first is the relationship of activities within an organization. The second is the relationship of activities to objects or places. The third is the relationship between different objects and/or places. All three types of relationships are important to the architectural designer. They will be discussed briefly before showing how such relationships can be described through the use of matrices and diagrams.

Does food preparation normally have a close/essential relationship with eating? What about eating with food preparation?

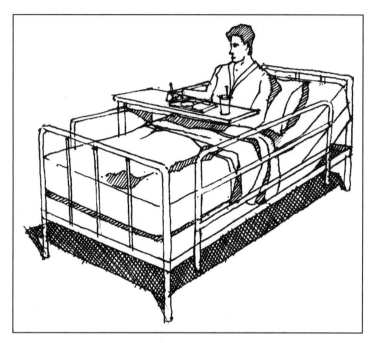

Figure 7-29 Person Eating in Bed.

Credit: Carl Okazaki

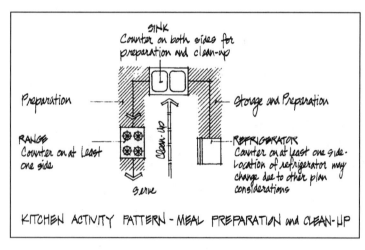

Figure 7-30 Plan of Kitchen Triangle.

Credit: See (Green et al 1975), 74. Permission: Michigan State Housing Development Authority

In most household situations, the obvious answer would be "yes" to both questions. What about in a restaurant? Or what about for a picnic? Or for vending machines? The answers to these questions are less clear. Does food preparation have a close/essential relationship with sleeping or bathing? Probably not. What about breakfast in bed? Some people look forward to this luxury. Some hotels advertise it as a special service to attract visitors. People in hospitals often eat in bed. However, they usually do not eat while they sleep—unless they are being fed intravenously. In every case there is a different relationship between food preparation and the point of consumption. The programmer must discover the actual relationships and not make assumptions based on limited past experience (Fig. 7-29).

Maybe a better question is: "Where are all the places that a person in this organization eats?" This would be the second important level of relationship that should be understood by the designer—the relationship of activities to objects or places. A particularly good example of the importance of the relationship of activities to objects is found in the kitchen, where most cooks like to have a logical, efficient, and timesaving arrangement in order to conserve effort (Fig. 7-30).

A final type of relation-
ship would be the relationship between the different
objects or places. Does the
dining room relate to the
kitchen? Does the kitchen
relate equally or identically
to the dining room? Does
the dining room relate to the
bedroom? Does the bed-
room relate to the kitchen?
These rooms do or do not
relate to each other based on
the activities they contain. A
programmer can make rela-
tionship diagrams by un-
derstanding their individual
relationships (Fig. 7-31).

Important relationships
between defined spaces or
areas are initially shown on

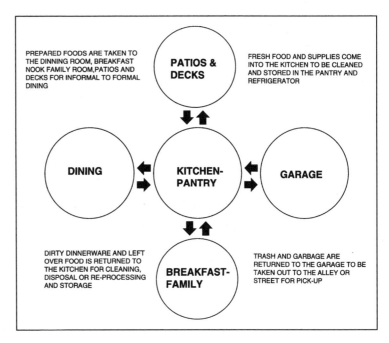

Figure 7-31 Kitchen Relationship Diagram.

brown sheets or grid paper during work sessions, as described in
Chapter 6. However, it is the underlying activity to place relationships that must be understood to define the space relationships.

In fact, the programmer needs to have a good understanding of
all of the relationships between activities, objects, and places in
order to know which activities and objects can and should be separated into distinct spaces or rooms, and which will work better
in one common area. For example, the arguments continue between the merits of open office arrangements and offices in separate rooms. The fact is that some office activities can occur in the
same space, while other activities must be separated to be most
effective. What is the nature of separation needed? Visual? Aural?
Olfactory? Thermal? Perhaps the secretary or even a whole group
of secretaries and their furnishings and equipment need only be
visually separated from the circulation space to avoid distraction
by passersby.

Someone who needs to concentrate on a difficult mental task,
however, may need acoustical separation from everyone else, to
be able "to hear oneself think!" An officer or manager who deals
with personnel matters may need both visual and acoustical separation to provide a higher degree of privacy. Heat generated by

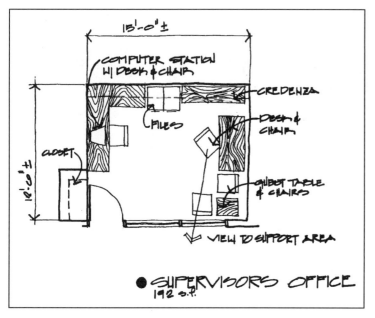

Figure 7-32 Annotated Plan of an Office.

Credit: Arquitectura, 1990. Program for Tucson Water Eatside Water Satellite Operations Facility. Tucson, Arizona. Permission: Arquitectura, Ltd.

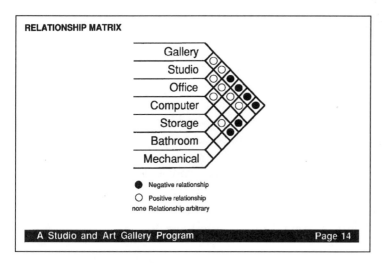

Figure 7-33 Simple Relationship Matrix.

Credit: Chris Barta, Kevin Camp, Dan Clavin, and Shauna Herminghouse, 1992. *A Program for the Design of an Artist's Studio and Art Gallery*. College of Architecture, The University of Arizona

some computing equipment or perhaps by groups of people in meetings may necessitate separate spaces in order to maintain adequate thermal control. Noise generated by copy machines, and the people that use them, may dictate separation for acoustical reasons. Whoever decides spatial relationships must understand the relationships of the activities and objects to be housed in each of the spaces in order to make appropriate decisions (Fig. 7-32).

Relationship Matrices

A system frequently used to develop and show how various spaces relate is the relationship matrix. In this case, every identified space is located vertically along one side of the matrix. Lines at a 45-degree angle to the end of each identified space extend to provide one cell connecting each space to every other space. A simple distinguishable code can be used to show the nature of the relationship between the spaces (Fig. 7-33).

Preparation of such a matrix can be even more helpful if there are a large number of individual spaces and/or complex relationships. Each line of cells can be followed to see how each space relates to every other space. If large numbers of spaces have no essential relationship with most other spaces, the matrix may reveal some important overall patterns of relationships when completed. For instance, logical departments or work units might be revealed by obvious clusters of related spaces or rooms. However, if the building has a very large number of individual spaces, use of the matrix can be mind boggling. It may require following along with a finger or ruler so as not to jump from one cell to another, and the overall effect can be disorienting, owing to the large number of relationships shown (Figs. 7-34 and 7-35).

The author has found that most clients find this type of relationship indicator to be confusing. These indicators actually work best if developed in the programmer's office as a systematic way of making certain that every possible spatial relationship has been considered. The matrices can then be useful as a step toward developing individual space relationship diagrams that visually show how each space relates to other spaces.

Relationship Diagrams

The basic relationship diagram employs small circles or "bubbles," each of which contains the name of one of the identified spaces. The bubble representing the space under consideration is drawn first, then other spaces relating to it are indicated in additional bubbles placed near the first bubble. Typically, only those spaces that have an important relationship to the first space are included in the diagram. For instance, in a house, the living room may not have an essential relationship to the sleeping areas, kitchen, or garage, so these spaces would not be included in a diagram showing relationships to the living

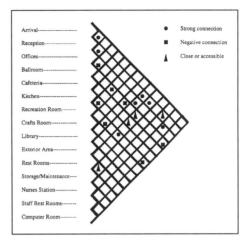

Figure 7-34 Simple Relationship Matrix.

Credit: Fourth Year Design Studio with Professor Hershberger, 1986. *Gilbert Municipal Complex Program. Gilbert, Arizona.* School of Architecture, Arizona State University

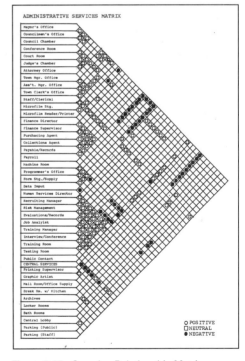

Figure 7-35 Complex Relationship Matrix.

Credit: Fourth Year Design Studio with Professor Hershberger, 1986. *Gilbert Municipal Complex Program. Gilbert, Arizona.* School of Architecture, Arizona State University

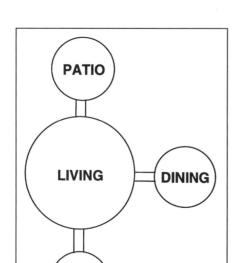

Figure 7-36 Simple Relationship Diagram.

room (Fig. 7-36). Each of the non-dimensional bubbles represents a space identified in the program. The center bubble is the one to which the other spaces are being related. The relationships between the spaces are indicated by simple lines. They could also be shown with different line weights, colors, or other characteristics to indicate the nature of the relationships. This more elaborate system works well for buildings for which there may be a number of different kinds of relationships to express. The lower diagram shows two types of relationships (Fig. 7-37).

For simple buildings, it may also be possible to prepare a diagram which, like the relationship matrix, shows the interrelationships of all interior and exterior spaces (Fig. 7-38).

However, as the building becomes more complex, it is difficult to prepare such a diagram without implying some relationships that may not exist. In this case, it may be necessary to relate only the established major zones of the building (Figs. 7-39).

When the bubbles are kept separate, heavy-, medium-, and light-weight lines can be used as a code to indicate strong, moderate, and weak relationships. Or the code can be more specific and even indicate visual, auditory, olfactory, and thermal relationships. The code should be clearly indicated and relate to what the designer needs to know to provide an adequate environment for the activities to be accommodated.

For purposes of architectural programming, relationship diagrams should be kept very simple so as not to confuse real relation-

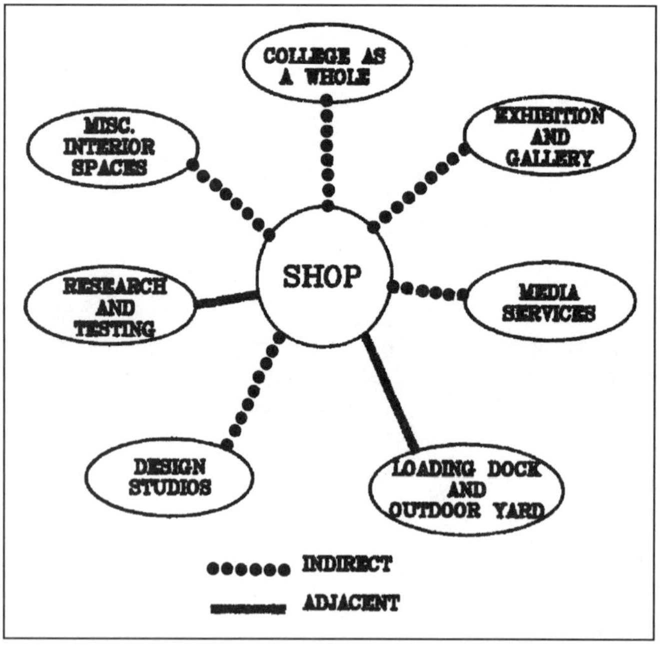

Figure 7-37 Simple Relationship Diagram.

Credit: Tim Bjella, Randy Jones, and Neil Urban, 1986. *Program for the New Architecture Building.* Permission: School of Architecture, Arizona State University

ships with circumstantial ones. This can be ensured if the initial diagrams are developed for one space at a time and do not go beyond its relationships with other spaces. In other words, the programmer should not begin with one large diagram in which every activity/space is related to every other activity. Unlike the relationship matrix, this will distort relationships, because bubbles placed in close proximity to other bubbles may appear to be more related when they actually are only artifacts of a spatially organized diagramming system (Fig. 7-40).

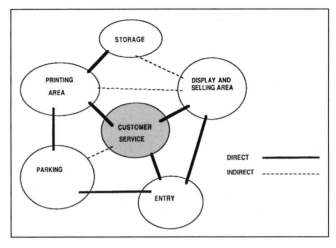

Figure 7-38 Overall Relationship Diagram.

Credit: Sing Kuai Ng, 1987. *Program for a Blue Print Shop*. Permission: School of Architecture, Arizona State University

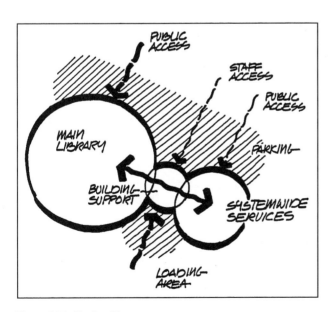

Figure 7-39 Zoning Diagram.

Credit: Anderson DeBartolo Pan, Inc, 1986. *City of Tucson Main Library Program*. Tucson, Arizona. Permission: ADP Marshall

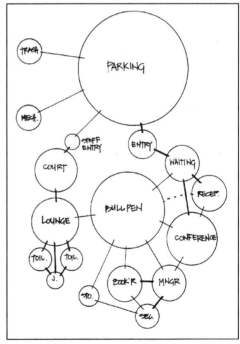

Figure 7-40 Complex Relationship Diagram.

Credit: Mark Poppe, Dave Truman, and Ed Binkley, 1985. *Architectural Program for a Real Estate Office*. Permission: School of Architecture, Arizona State University

LOCATION CRITERIA

FIRST LEVEL

space	entry	street	campus	service	daylight	view	outdoor	hours
Atrium	●		●		●	●		24
Hearth	●		●		●	O	O	24
Copy Center	O	●		O				14
Newsstand	●							14
Student Lockers	o	●			×	×		24
Student Mailboxes	o	●		●				24
Super Bathrooms					×	×		24
Student Development	O	●			●	●		8
Center Management	o	●			●	●		14
Facilities/Event Planning	o	●			●	●		8
CAC Desk	●		O					14
Collegium 5 & 6	O		●		●	●	O	24
Conversation Nooks	●		●		●	●	o	24
Center for Leadership	O		O		●	O		8
Pathways & Wellness Ctr	O		O		●	O		8
Meeting Room	O		O		O	O		24
Poster Area	o	o			o			24
ASSU	O		O		●	●		24
Student Clubs	O		O		O	O		24
Vending Machine Area				●				24

Code		Hours	
●	= Extremely Important	8	= 8 am - 5 pm
O	= Very Important	14	= 8 am - 10 pm
o	= Important	24	= all day
	= No Relationship		
×	= Negative Relationship		

Figure 7-41 Locational Criteria.

With a large or highly inter-related facility, there could be so many overlapping lines between related bubbles that the diagram would become very complex and confusing. Efforts to reorganize the diagram to make it less confusing could embody preconceptions about the final design. Thus, it may be more helpful to the designer to use a separate diagram for each space, department, or zone. Sometimes the use of a chart is more effective in conveying complex zoning information (Fig. 7-41).

It is actually quite difficult to devise a clear and easily understood system of diagrams, codes, and charts to explain all the kinds of relationships which should be accommodated in design. Thus, a combination of diagrams, charts, and text is often required. Basic proximate relations can be illustrated in a relationship diagram and the specific types of sensory separations or connections can be covered beneath the diagram using short descriptive phrases.

The programmer should avoid initiating diagrams that have design preconceptions built into them. However, if a client group insists that a particular design idea or approach is mandatory, it certainly makes sense to communicate this to the designer, so that he/she will at least consider the preconception during design. The designer always has the prerogative of challenging such preconceptions and of trying to convince the client to accept a different design resolution.

It may be possible and desirable to develop relationship diagrams in which whole groups of spaces are combined, as with the distinct departments of a large organization. It is important, however, not to make such diagrams until it is clear from earlier relationship analysis that the departments or activities actually exist and should be maintained as distinct spatial units. For instance, every organizational department of a major office building may indicate a need for good access to photocopying equipment. Does this mean that every department will need to have its own reproduction space, or that a single reproduction space should be conveniently located to all departments? A good understanding of the organization is necessary to make such decisions. Similarly, would a client want to organize the administrative offices in a separate department, or

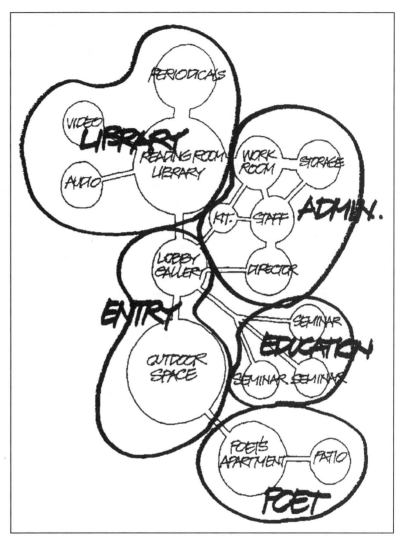

Figure 7-42 Zoning Relationship Diagram.

Credit: Corky Poster, W. Kirby Lockard, Chris Evans, Kim Kuykendall, Scott Pask, and Donna Sink, 1988. University of Arizona Poetry Center, Building Program and Site analysis. Permission: Architecture Laboratory, Inc.

distribute these offices among the various departments? Only when activity areas or organizational units are known to be spatially distinct should overall diagrams be utilized. When such information is known, diagrams can be useful in revealing the overall conceptual organization appropriate for design (Fig. 7-42).

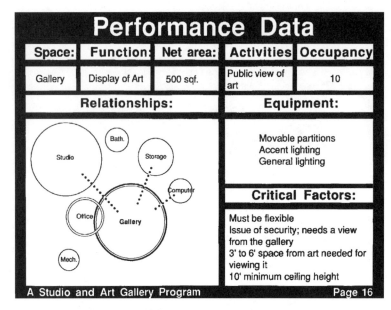

Figure 7-43 Space Program Sheet.

Credit: Chris Barta, Kevin Camp, Dan Clavin, and Shauna Herminghouse, 1992. *A Program for the Design of an Artists Studio and Art Gallery.* College of Architecture, The University of Arizona

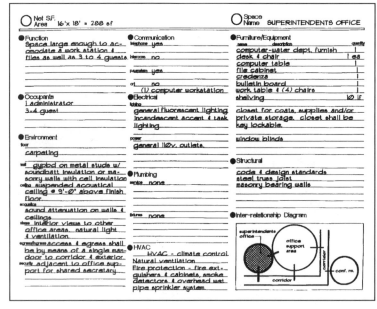

Figure 7-44 Space Program Sheet.

Credit: Arquitectura, 1990. Program for Tucson Water Eastside Water Satellite Operations Facility. Tucson, Arizona. Permission: Arquitectura Ltd.

7.10 Space Program Sheets

A very effective way to illustrate specific design requirements for a building is to include a space program sheet for each identified space. These sheets typically include statements regarding the purpose, the square foot allocations, and the important relationships for each space. They also include information about the types and numbers of people who will use the space; the activities in which people will be engaged at various times of the day, week, and year; furnishing and equipment needs; and any other requirements that can help the designer make decisions about configuration and layout of the particular space. Figures 7-43 through 7-46 show space program sheets from several programming firm and student projects.

As can be seen from the previous illustrations, space program sheets can have a great deal of variability in format and content. But their purpose remains essentially the same—to provide a complete miniature program for the space covered. They are usually pre-

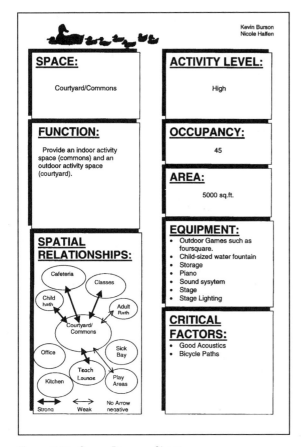

Figure 7-45 Space Program Sheet.

Credit: Kevin Burson and Nicole Halfen, Arch. 202, Section 1, 1998. *Catalina United Methodist Day School program*. College of Architecture, The University of Arizona

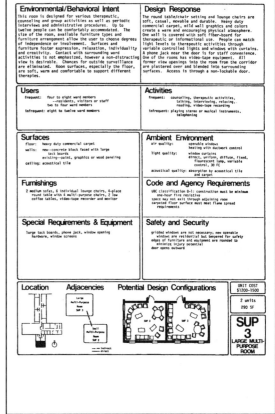

Figure 7-46 Space Program Sheet.

Credit: Michael Feerer, 1977. Family Services Ward Environmental/Architectural Programming for Atascadero State Mental Hospital, Atascadero, California. Permission: Michael Feerer

pared in the programmer's office, based on all of the information gathering activities including the client/user work sessions. The sheets are then included in the final draft copy of the program document, which can be circulated throughout the client's organization for review, comment, and correction. The space program sheets will be of greatest interest to those most likely to use the space, and will be subject to their scrutiny. The results of review can be an important fine tuning of project requirements, which may save considerable designer time and energy. It is important that the designer know about the particular requirements of each space even during schematic design. A careful programming effort is likely to turn up all of the needed information.

After receiving the marked-up space program sheets, it may be necessary to have another work session to sort out the importance of various suggestions. Here again the decision makers within the client's organization will need to listen to the arguments for additional space, equipment, furnishings, and the like from various divisions of the organization and decide what they can support or not support, based on the budget and various other important issues set forth in the program.

7.11 Budget and Cost Analysis

- Owner's Budget
- Construction Costs
- Project Costs
- Life Cycle Costs

Owner's Budget

If the construction budget is fixed, this should be stated clearly in the program. If it can vary depending on the quality and character of the design, this should also be made known. If market conditions or specifics of financing are crucial areas of concern, then these should be covered in the program or in a companion document prepared by specialists in these areas. This should be an integral part of programming, so that the stated requirements will be for a facility that the client can afford to build. It makes little sense to prepare a program ignoring the realities of the client's budget. The budget will almost always be an area of client concern and will be included as a primary value area (Fig. 7-47).

Construction Costs

Clients generally have a good idea of what they can afford to spend on the construction of a new facility. If not, they will develop this information early in the programming process as they begin to realize the

Preliminary Opinion of Probable Construction Cost

Fees
- Basic Design Services — $ 24,000
- Bidding & Construction — 7,000
- Additional Services — 28,600
- Reimbursable Expenses — 16,800 : $ 76,400 total fees

Construction
- Site Development — 300,000
- Building & Furnishings — 600,000 : $900,000 total construction

Construction Budget for Phase One : $350,000

$350,000 ÷ $80.00 per square foot : Approximately 4,400 s.f. of construction 1st phase

Figure 7-47 Budget Card from Matrix.

Credit: Arquitectura, 1988. *Pre-Design Workbook, Verde Meadows Recreation Center.* Tucson, Arizona. Permission: Arquitectura Ltd.

financial implications of what they are trying to achieve. What clients likely will not understand is how much building they can get for their money. If they are interested in building a new house, they probably have been talking with others who have built new houses in recent years, or have been looking at prices of developer houses in their locality. Unfortunately, this cost information may have little relationship with the actual cost of constructing a new, custom-designed house. The owner's figures for custom housing may be several years out-of-date and not account for inflation, while the figures for developer housing will reflect cost savings attributable to size of operation. In the Tucson metropolitan area, for instance, most developer houses were being built for between $60 and $70 per square foot in 1995, but custom houses by architects were running from $90 to over $200 per square foot, depending on the quality of materials and treatments specified. The costs of custom houses also appeared to be inflating at a greater rate than developer housing. Similarly, speculative industrial buildings could not exceed $25 to $30 per square foot, or they would price themselves out of the market. It was possible to use only a few highly competitive building systems and configurations to keep the cost in this range. The same financial reality impacts nearly every kind of building construction activity.

Construction cost data for buildings in the United States is readily available for most building types. The current versions of the Means Square Foot Costs and Marshall Valuation Service are good examples (Fig. 7-48 through 7-50). These sources

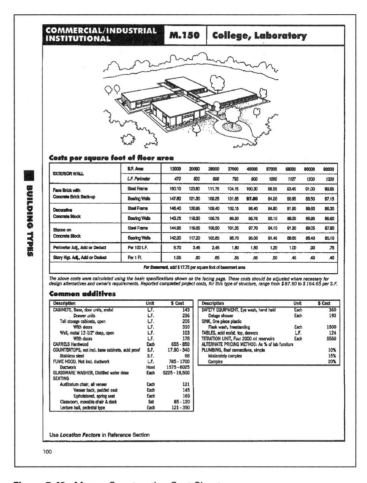

Figure 7-48 Means Construction Cost Sheet.

Commercial/Industrial/Institutional Section

Table of Contents

Figure 7-49 Means Construction Cost Contents.

From *Means Square Foot Costs 1996.* Copyright R.S. Means Co., Inc., Kingston, MA, 617-585-7880, all rights reserved.

Figure 7-50 Marshall Evaluator Cost Data Sheet.

Credit: Marshall & Swift, L.P., 1995. *Marshall Valuation Service.* Los Angeles, California: Marshall & Swift, L.P. Permission: Marshall & Swift, L.P.

can be very useful in architectural programming because they contain average costs for various building types. The most useful ones for programming separate the costs into high, medium, and low averages; show the kinds of construction systems that lead to these various averages; and provide factors to modify the costs for particular regions of the country. The programmer can use this information to project a probable range of construction costs for the facility even before any design studies have begun, based on the projected square footage and desired quality of materials and systems. The ability to do this with reasonable accuracy is very important. If it appears that the costs will be too high, then the program can be modified in terms of size, quality, or both.

It is better to confront budgetary problems at this early stage of the building development process than to keep the client happy for the moment, suggesting that he/she can have everything desired, when, in fact, it is evident that the budget is not sufficient to construct the building. When this happens no one wins. The programmer appears incompetent, the designer appears inadequate, and the owner, belatedly, has to find additional money or reevaluate the program and decide which requirements are really important. This is a difficult and sometimes bitter and costly process which may include costs for extensive redesign and even of litigation to establish who is responsible for underestimating costs. All such situations can be avoided by early recognition and resolution of potential budgetary problems).

The LMRector Corporation publishes a bimonthly magazine, Design Cost Data, that contains similar current information (Fig. 7-51).

Sources such as the ones discussed above can be obtained in some public and university libraries, and in the offices of architects, contractors, and real estate professionals who use them on a daily basis to estimate the costs of projects. They should be obtained and utilized by the architectural programmer to estimate the range of possible costs for the buildings being programmed.

ARCHITECT
HOLABIRD & ROOT
300 West Adams Street
Chicago, IL 60606-5174

FILE UNDER
EDUCATIONAL
Palos Hills, Illinois

GENERAL CONTRACTOR	**W.E. O'Neil Construction Co.** 2751 N. Clybourn Avenue Chicago, IL 60619
STRUCTURAL ENGINEER	**Holabird & Root** 300 West Adams Street Chicago, IL 60606-5174
ELECTRICAL ENGINEER	**Holabird & Root** 300 West Adams Street Chicago, IL 60606-5174
MECHANICAL ENGINEER	**Holabird & Root** 300 West Adams Street Chicago, IL 60606-5174
LANDSCAPE ARCHITECT	**Gary R. Weber Associates** 615 West Front Street Wheaton, IL 60187
ACOUSTICAL CONSULTANT	**Yerges Acoustics** 5209 Lee Avenue Downers Grove, IL 60515

GENERAL DESCRIPTION

SITE: N/A.
NUMBER OF BUILDINGS: One; 800-seat mainstage & 150-stage black box theater; seating capacity, 311; eight classrooms at 32 seats, one classroom at 55 seats.
BUILDING SIZES: Basement level, 7,400; first floor, 42,511; second floor, 30,196; penthouse, 4,000; total, 84,107 square feet.
BUILDING HEIGHT: Basement, 11'; first floor, 15'; second floor, 15'; fly tower, 75'2"; penthouse, 18'4"; total, 75'2".
BASIC CONSTRUCTION TYPE:
FOUNDATION: Concrete spread footings, concrete foundation walls.
EXTERIOR WALLS: Precast concrete, brick, curtainwall.
ROOF: Single ply membrane, ballasted.
FLOORS: Terrazzo, glass ceramic mosaic tile, wood, VCT, carpet.
INTERIOR WALLS: Drywall, CMU, ceramic tile.

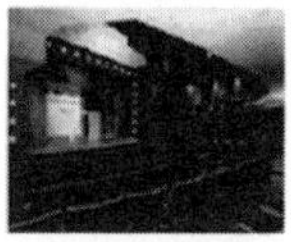

FINE & PERFORMING ARTS CENTER, MORAINE VALLEY COMMUNITY COLLEGE

Date Bid: Mar 1992* · Construction Period: Apr 1992 to Dec 1993 · Total Square Feet: 84,107

C.S.I. Divisions (1 through 16)	COST	% OF COST	SQ.FT. COST		SPECIFICATIONS
BIDDING REQUIREMENTS	94,876	0.85	1.13		Bonds & certificates.
1. GENERAL REQUIREMENTS	1,165,723	10.42	13.86	1	—
3. CONCRETE	1,430,798	12.79	17.01	3	Formwork, reinforcement, accessories, cast-in-place, curing, precast.
4. MASONRY	1,030,581	9.21	12.25	4	Masonry & grout, accessories, unit.
5. METALS	1,184,829	10.59	14.09	5	Structural framing, fabrications.
6. WOOD & PLASTICS	229,740	2.06	2.73	6	Rough carpentry, finish carpentry.
7. THERMAL & MOIST. PROTECT.	171,722	1.53	2.04	7	Waterproofing, dampproofing, firestopping, manufactured roofing, membrane roofing.
8. DOORS & WINDOWS	863,728	7.72	10.27	8	Metal doors & frames, special doors, entrances & storefronts, metal windows, hardware, glazed curtainwalls.
9. FINISHES	752,227	6.72	8.94	9	Lath & plaster, gypsum board, tile, terrazzo, acoustical treatment, resilient flooring, carpet, painting, wall coverings.
10. SPECIALTIES	—	—	—	10	—
11. EQUIPMENT	594,363	5.31	7.07	11	Theatre & stage.
12. FURNISHING	—	—	—	12	—
13. SPECIAL CONSTRUCTIONS	—	—	—	13	—
14. CONVEYING SYSTEMS	94,868	0.85	1.13	14	Elevators.
15. MECHANICAL	2,231,202	19.94	26.53	15	Fire protection, plumbing, HVAC.
16. ELECTRICAL	1,344,603	12.02	15.98	16	—
TOTAL BUILDING COST	**11,189,060**	**100%**	**$133.03**		
2. SITE WORK	471,117			2	Dewatering, excavation support systems, paving & surfacing, sewerage & drainage.
LANDSCAPING & OFFSITE WORK	119,027				Landscaping.
TOTAL PROJECT COST	**11,779,204**	*(Excluding architectural and engineering fees)*			

UPDATED ESTIMATE TO JANUARY 1997: $152.85 PER SQUARE FOOT

*Fast Track, three bid packages: Pkg. 1, Jan. '92; Pkg. 2, Mar. '92; Pkg. 3, May '92.

29

Figure 7-51 LMRector Design Cost Data Sheet.

Credit: LMRector Corporation. Jan/Feb 1997. *Design Cost Data*. Volume 41, Number 1. Permission: LMRector Corporation.

Project Costs

Many owners and architects get into trouble by thinking that the construction cost is the bottom line for a building project. In reality there are other costs which increase the overall or project budget well beyond the construction cost. These costs include the cost of the land, taxes, and debt retirement during construction, and fees for architectural programming, financial feasibility studies, architectural and engineering services, governmental approvals, and permits. They also include costs for site surveys and soils tests, archeological surveys where required, landscape

- Building Cost (gross sq. ft. ¥ sq. ft. cost)
- Fixed Equipment (5% to 25% of A)
- Site Development (5% to 25% of A)
- Total Construction Cost (A + B + C)
- Site Acquisition/Preparation (check with appraiser/contractor)
- Moveable Equipment (5% to 25% of A)
- Professional Fees (5% to 15% of D)
- Contingencies (5% to 15% of D)
- Administrative Costs (1% to 10% of D)
- Total Project Cost (Add D through J)

Figure 7-52   Project Cost Estimating Categories

Adapted from: (Peña et al., 1987), 115. Permission: American Institute of Architects and HOK

and interior design services, site and off-site development, moveable furnishings and equipment, additional staff to monitor the project, and the financing costs to secure a mortgage.

These and all other costs associated with the project can add up to an amount substantially greater than the construction cost. They must be factored into the cost picture, or the client could end up with a project costing well beyond the available funds. It is necessary, therefore, to include all such costs in the architectural program. If the total project cost exceeds the funds available, it will be necessary to reassess the program to determine what can be reduced to bring the project within budget. A project cost estimate can be developed using the categories shown in Fig. 7-52.

The question, then, is how does the programmer determine each of the above costs? It is not simple or automatic. Some of the cost figures are contained in the aforementioned estimating guides and in the *R. S. Means Company's Means Estimating Handbook* (1990). Others can be found in Peña et al.'s book *Problem Seeking* (1987) and Kumlin's book *Architectural Programming* (1995). Most other books on construction cost estimating contain the more detailed estimating done by contractors and are not usable at this early stage of the project.

It is advisable to provide a range of estimated costs because many of the areas of cost are not known at this early stage of a project. The architect/engineer fees may not have been established. The building configuration, materials, and systems have not been established. Where the building is sited and how it is configured will have a major impact on site development costs. Costs of fixed and moveable equipment vary considerably based on quality and quantity of items purchased. If the site has not already been acquired, only local realtors and appraisers will be able to predict the cost of acquisition. Even then, a property owner may want considerably more (or less) than market value for the desired land parcel. Administrative costs, while normally one to two percent of the cost of the project, may reach as high as 15 percent in some institutional settings where elaborate facilities planning, construction, and management programs are partially supported by building projects.

The percentage factors for site development, equipment and furnishings, architectural fees, and contingency are likely to vary from one locality to another, with the size of the site, from one building type to another, and from one architect to another. At the programming stage it is possible at least to develop a realistic range of these costs (Fig. 7-53).

The following is an estimate prepared during programming for a small high-bay workshop addition to the College of Architecture at The University of Arizona utilizing the above system of cost estimating. Note the considerable differences between the low, medium, and high estimates (Fig. 7-54).

Providing for a range of costs will allow the client to set the project budget at the level needed to obtain the quality of building materials, systems, site development, furnishings, and equipment desired. It is very important that the cost estimate be realistic, and especially not unreasonably low, so that the designer can produce a design of suitable quality within the budget. In this regard, the program

	Low	Med	High
A. Building Cost	—	—	—
B. Fixed Equipment	—	—	—
C. Site Development	—	—	—
D. Construction Cost (A+B+C)	—	—	—
E. Site Costs	—	—	—
F. Moveable Equipment	—	—	—
G. Professional Fees	—	—	—
H. Contingencies	—	—	—
J. Administrative Costs	—	—	—
K. Total Project Cost (D+E+F+G+H+J)	—	—	—

Figure 7-53 Project Cost Estimating Form

Adapted from: (Peña et al., 1987), 115. Permission: American Institute of Architects and HOK

BUILDING SQUARE FOOTAGE
Net Square Footage = 6,235
95% Efficient
Gross Square Footage = 6,547

	LOW AVERAGE	MED AVERAGE	HIGH AVERAGE
Building Cost	$229,145	$294,615	$392,820
Fixed Equipment	5% $11,457	6% $17,677	7% $27,497
Site Development	5% $11,457	10% $29,462	20% $78,564
Total Construction	$252,059	$341,754	$498,881
Movable Equipment	10% $22,915	10% $29,462	10% $39,282
Professional Fees	8% $20,165	10% $34,175	12% $59,866
Contingencies	5% $12,646	10% $34,175	15% $74,832
Administrative Costs	1% $2,521	2% $6,835	3% $14,966
Total Budget Required	$310,306	$446,401	$687,827

Figure 7-54 Small Project Cost Estimate.

Appendix

COST ESTIMATE

Art Gallery and Studio   **1945 gross sqf**

		High	Medium	Low
A.	Building Cost	116,700	106,975	97,250
B.	Fixed Equipment	5,835	4,279	2,917
C.	Site Development	4,668	3,209	1945
D.	**Total Construction**	**127,203**	**114,463**	**102,112**
E.	Site Acquisition/Demolition	—		
F.	Moveable Equipment	23,340	19,255	15,560
G.	Professional Fees	12,720	11,446	10,211
H.	Contingencies	8,904	6,867	5,105
I.	Administration Costs	1,272	1,144	1,021
J.	**Total Budget Required**	**$173,439**	**$142,877**	**$134,010**

A Studio and Art Gallery Program   Page 23

Figure 7-55   Small Project Cost Esimate.

Credit: Chris Barta, Kevin Camp, Dan Clavin, and Shauna Herminghouse, 1992. Program for a Studio and Art Gallery. College of Architecture, The University of Arizona

might state some caveats explaining that actual design configuration, building efficiency, material and system selection, inflation, and the like will have a significant impact on costs, so that the final costs to build the facility may differ from the estimate provided in the program document. A contingency allowance of 5 to 10 percent of the construction estimate is also advisable and usual in most sophisticated programming documents to account for unexpected cost increases (Fig. 7-55).

The ranges for construction costs can be found in the Means and Marshall estimating literature. The estimates for the other items are generally based on firm experience. In this text we will use the experience of CRS as contained in Peña et al. (1987) to arrive at the possible range of project costs (Fig. 7-56).

In addition to the costs shown in Fig. 7-56, it may be necessary to consider the costs for interim and permanent financing of the project and for cost escalation should the project schedule cover a lengthy time period. These can be added as separate categories following category "K." They will be somewhat like those shown in Fig. 7-57 on the following page.

Still other costs are shown in a project cost budget included in the competition program for the new architecture building at Arizona State University (Fig. 7-58). Note that this estimate contains a number of the project costs noted above as well as a number not mentioned. This is to be expected. Every project will have its particular environment and associated costs. The programmer must make certain that all of the anticipated costs are included in the project budget/cost estimate.

A. Building Cost
Net Area ÷ Efficiency Ratio = Gross Area
Gross Area × Unit Cost = Building cost

Example:

12,000 Net SF ÷ .60 = 20,000 Gross SF
20,000 Gross SF × $140/SF = $2,800,000

B. Fixed Equipment

Percentage of Line A

Low	5%
Medium	10–15%
High	20%
Very High	30%

Commercial Office	.5–7%
Sports Center	5%
Elementary School	6–10%
Secondary School	8–12%
University Academic Bldg.	7%
Civic Center	8%

Housing Project	7–10%
University Average Building	14%
Jail	12–15%
School of Medicine	15%
Hospital	18–20%
University Science Bldg	20%
Civic Auditorium	20–25%
Heavy Industrial Arts	30%
Teaching Dental Laboratory	30%
Church/Synagogue	5–15%

C. Site Development

Percentage of Line A

Low	5%
Medium	10–15%
High	20%
Very High	30%

Urban Site	5%
Elementary School	6–12%
Secondary School	10–15%
Suburban Site	14–15%
Hospital	10–15%

Secondary School	20%
Special Conditions	30%
(rock excavation, steep slopes, etc.)	

D. Total Construction Cost

Sum of A + B + C

E. Site Acquisition and Preparation (real estate appraiser, contractor)

F. Movable Equipment

Percentage of Line A

Low	5%
Medium	10–15%
High	20%

Elementary School	6–10%
Secondary School	8–12%
College	10–15%
Library	15%

Medical Office Bldg.	15%
Hospital	18–20%
Vocational School	20%
Church/Synagogue	5–10%

G. Professional Fees (including consultants)

Percentage of Line D
Varies from 5% to 15% (See Figure 7-71)

H. Contingencies (Percentage of Line D)

Low	5%
Medium	10%
High	15%

J. Administrative Costs

Percentage of Line D varies from 1% to 10%

K. Total Budget Required

Sum of D + E + F + G + H + J = K

Figure 7-56 Calculation of Project Costs

Adapted from: (Peña et al., 1987), 104–105. Permission: American Institute of Architects and HOK

L. Interim Financing Cost
Percentage of Amount Borrowed (1.5% to 2.5% above prime per year
of construction)

M. Permanent Financing Cost
Percentage of Amount Borrowed (varies from 1% to 2.5% above prime)

N. Cost Escalation
Percentage of Line K (has varied from under 3% to over 10%)

Figure 7-57 Additional Project Costs.

D. Preliminary Construction Budget:

Construction Cost

a. New construction (100,000 s.f. gross)	$ 7,600,000
b. Remodelling/Renovation (including connection to existing building)	90,000
c. Special fixed equipment (including lecture hall seats, audio and solar testing equipment)	400,000
d. Telecommunications distribution	150,000
e. Site development (site preparation)	250,000
f. Utilities extensions	150,000
g. Other	0
Subtotal: Construction Cost	**$ 8,640,000**

Miscellaneous

a. Furnishings and equipment: movable	800,000
b. Contingency (4%)	377,600
c. Inflation adjustment (15 mo. x .0042)	594,720
d. Parking replacement (60 spaces x $800)	48,000
e. Telecommunications equipment	100,000
f. Surveys and tests	67,000
g. Move-in costs	15,000
h. Planning overhead	0
I. Fees and competition cost	857,600
j. Other	0
Subtotal: Miscellaneous	**$ 2,759,920**
PROJECT TOTAL	**$11,500,000**

Figure 7-58 Preliminary Construction Budget.

Credit: Competition Program, 1986. ASU Project #125-2E. Permission: College of Architecture and Environmental Design, Arizona State University

Similarly, a plan involving major additions and renovations to an existing church facility required two separate estimates, because construction was to be phased over several years. In this case, the systems and materials of the new work were well defined during the consultation so that the construction cost and other project costs could be accurately estimated (Fig. 7-59).

Note that it is possible to be more precise in a number of areas, as the particular nature of a project becomes evident. For example, the Means Estimating Handbook has charts showing the average costs for architectural and engineering fees for a variety of project types (Figs. 7-60 and 7-61).

Life Cycle Costs

If operating or maintenance costs are important considerations, and they are with most clients, then performance requirements relating to energy consumption of the various mechanical and electrical systems, as well as heat loss and gain from the building systems, may need to be spelled out. Likewise, the costs to maintain the building and systems in proper working order and projections of their useful lives (how often they will have to be replaced) may also be important.

Some owners are willing to pay more for the building initially, if it means that the continuing costs of operations and maintenance can be reduced. In fact, nearly all construction costs are financed over a period of years, so that they are covered by the continuing receipts of the organization. These costs, which are often fixed, are accompanied for the life of the building with operations and maintenance costs, which are not fixed. In recent years the operations and maintenance costs have escalated rapidly to the point where they often exceed the mortgage costs. If this is an area of concern, the owner may wish to spell out a strategy whereby the initial costs are increased in order to reduce the potentially high costs later on. This activity is referred to as life cycle costing, and can be a very important consideration in programming.

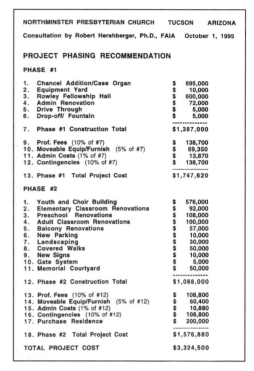

Figure 7-59 Project Phasing Cost Estimate.

7.12 Project Schedule

When time is of the essence, a project schedule is included as a brief separate section of the program, so that it will not be lost in the text and possibly be seen as unimportant by the designer. This schedule should address every phase of the project to be most effective—programming, design, construction, and occupancy. If the owner must vacate present facilities on a specific date, or the building must be completed by a certain time to meet bonding or other financial requirements, an achievable schedule should be set forth indicating what the client and architect must accomplish by a certain time to complete the design and construction documents on schedule. A similar schedule should indicate when various phases of construction must be complete to allow the scheduled occupancy to take place (Figs. 7-62 and 7-63).

Architectural Fees for project sizes of:	
Up to $10,000	15%
to $25,000	13%
to $100,000	10%
to $500,000	8%
to $1,000,000	7%

The listed fees are approximate for smaller projects, such as repair work and/or remodeling existing structures.

Figure 7-60 Architectural Fees for Small Projects.

Permission: From *Means Estimating Handbook.* Copyright R.S. Means Co., Inc., Kingston, MA, 617-585-7880, all rights reserved.

Building Type	Total Project Size in Thousands of Dollars						
	100	250	500	1,000	2,500	5,000	10,000
Factories, garages, warehouses repetitive housing	9.0%	8.0%	7.0%	6.2%	5.6%	5.3%	4.9%
Apartments, banks, schools, libraries, offices, municipal buildings	11.7	10.8	8.5	7.3	6.7	6.4	6.0
Churches, hospitals, homes, laboratories, museums, research	14.0	12.8	11.9	10.9	9.5	8.5	7.8
Memorials, monumental work, decorative furnishings		16.0	14.5	13.1	11.3	10.0	9.0

In this figure, typical percentage fees are tabulated by project size, for good professional architectural service. Fees may vary from those listed depending upon the degree of design difficulty and economic conditions in a particular area.
Rates can be interpolated horizontally and vertically. Various portions of the same project requiring different rates should be adjusted proportionally. For alterations, add 50% to the fee for the first $500,000 of project cost and add 25% to the fee for the project cost over $500,000.
Architectural fees tabulated above include Engineering Fees.

Figure 7-61 Architectural Fees for Larger Projects.

Permission: From *Means Estimating Handbook.* Copyright R.S. Means Co., Inc., Kingston, MA, 617-585-7880, all rights reserved.

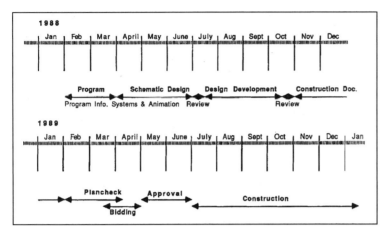

Figure 7-62 Project Schedule.

Credit: Larry Medlin and NBBJ Gresham Larson, 1988. *Program for The Arizona Solar Oasis at the Phoenix Civic Plaza.* Phoenix, Arizona. Permission: Richard Larry Medlin, Architect

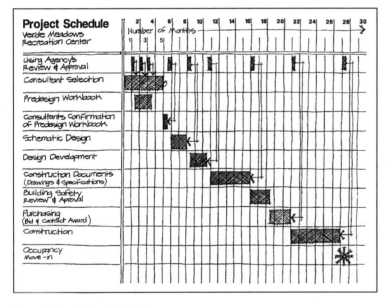

Figure 7-63 Project Schedule.

Credit: Arquitectura, 1988. Pre-Design Workbook, Verde Meadows Recreation Center. Tucson, Arizona. Permission: Arquitectura Ltd.

As can be seen from the above two examples, a project schedule can be shown in different ways. Probably the most common way is the bar chart as shown above.

If the schedule is very tight, it may be necessary to prepare a crucial path schedule to ensure that everything can be accomplished by a certain deadline. In this case, items that simply must be accomplished before others can proceed are placed on the crucial path. Other items that can take place at several different times or throughout one phase of the project fall out of the crucial path (Fig. 7-64).

Such a tight schedule can have a profound effect not only on how the work is processed, but also on the final design character of the building itself. The designer must carefully choose systems that can be placed in a very systematic way to avoid unplanned delays in construction.

It may be necessary to fast track a project in order to reduce the time from beginning to completion. This process involves major overlaps of what are normally discrete phases of the work. For example, it might require initial development of a master plan program followed by design, development, and construction of the infrastructure of roads, utilities, and landscaping of a major project; leaving only undeveloped sites for construction of specific buildings. While the design of the master plan is proceeding, the programming for schematic design of specific facilities will begin. While the foundations are being built, the schematic design of the buildings will be taking place. If the deadline for completion is tight, construction documents for the foundations and utility services to the building will be prepared, even before the design of the superstructure is complete. Similarly, the shell of the building may be under construction even before design development programming and detailed design of the interior are complete (Fig. 7-65).

The above theoretical example indicates how the foundations could be fast tracked such that when the rest of construction is bid, the foundations would already be in place and ready to receive the superstructure of the building.

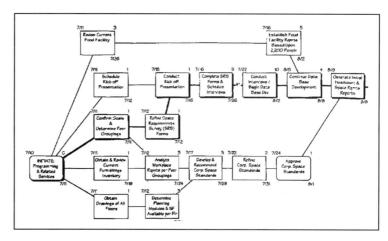

Figure 7-64 Crucial Path Schedule.

Credit: Richard C. Maxwell and David J. Wyckoff, 1993. Interior Programming, Stacking, and Blocking for Society National Bank. *Professional Practice in Facility Programming*. Wolfgang F.E. Preiser, Ed, NY: Van Nostrand Reinhold. Permission: Van Nostrand Reinhold

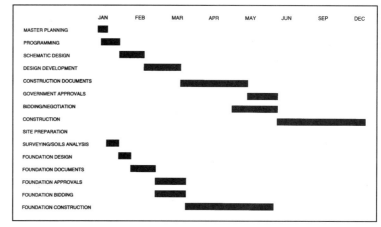

Figure 7-65 Fast-Track Schedule.

Clearly, when such a collapsed process is undertaken, assumptions must be made about the probable character of yet unprogrammed or designed facilities. In the master plan, enough room must be left and services provided for the anticipated buildings.

Table at left is average construction time in months for different types of building projects. Table at right is the construction time in months for different size projects. Design time runs 25% to 40% of construction time.

Type Building	Construction Time
Industrial Buildings	12 Months
Commercial Buildings	15 Months
Research & Development	18 Months
Institutional Buildings	20 Months

Project Value	Construction Time
Under $1,400,000	10 Months
Up to $3,800,000	15 Months
Up to $19,000,000	21 Months
Over $19,000,000	28 Months

In order to estimate the General Requirements of a construction project, it is necessary to have an approximate project duration time. Duration must be determined because many items, such as supervision and temporary facilities, are directly time variable. The average durations presented in this chart will vary depending on such factors as location, complexity, time of year started, local economic conditions, materials required, or the need for the completed project.

Figure 7-66 Design and Construction Time.

Permission: From *Means Estimating Handbook*. Copyright R.S. Means Co., Inc., Kingston, MA, 617-585-7880, all rights reserved.

When footings are constructed before design is complete for the building, the designers must correctly anticipate the configuration and loads of the superstructure. Almost inevitably, this leads to master plans with locations for discrete building units and to simple buildings with open, free-span floor areas, which will allow any of the anticipated but yet unprogrammed uses to fit reasonably well. Typically this involves both simplification of form and over-sizing of spaces and services. Thus, it becomes an important influence on the design, having a profound effect on building form. It also may have an effect on the project budget, increasing design costs, but possibly reducing construction and financing costs. If such a tight schedule is mandatory, all of the potential costs and savings should be given careful attention, to make certain that the job will remain within the project budget.

Relative to construction time requirements, Means has some helpful guidelines related to the time it takes to construct several different types of buildings. It also indicates that design time typically runs 25 to 40 percent of construction time (Fig. 7-66).

Programmers should develop an accurate record of time spent on the various phases of the design and construction process on every commission so that over a period of time they will be able to make reasonably accurate predictions as to the time (and personnel resources) that will be necessary to accomplish each phase of the work. This can be of great help to the client and architect as they move forward with a project.

7.13 Design Analysis

- Client Ideas
- Precedents
- Programmatic Concepts
- Design Precepts

- Design Concepts
- Design Exploration

There may also be ideas about an appropriate design solution that the client, user, or programmer wants the architect to consider when designing the project. These are not usually considered requirements for design, simply ideas which have come up in the course of the diagnostic interviewing or work sessions. If they seem to be good ideas to the client and programmer, they are probably worth including in the program, not as design requirements, but as possible directions for the designer to explore when formulating the design solution.

The ideas about design should be kept in a separate concluding section of the program or in the appendix, for they are a beginning of the architectural design process rather than an integral part of architectural programming. The fact that design ideas come forward while people are considering the nature of a problem should not seem unusual. It is human nature to consider solutions when defining problems. It should be recognized, however, that these ideas are preconceptions, not design concepts or solutions. Indeed, as the design problem is explored, it will be found that some of the ideas are not at all appropriate and must be discarded, while other ideas are very good and can be incorporated into the overall design. In any case, ideas that are set forth at any time during the programming process should be recorded and summarized in this section of the program document.

Client Ideas

The classic case of design ideas being offered during programming, perhaps, is that of the couple who has collected a whole scrapbook of ideas from Better Homes and Gardens, Sunset, and other magazines that they think are nice and could be incorporated into the design of their new house. Clients in corporations, businesses, and institutions may also have design ideas, perhaps based on trade journals or on personal experience with particularly effective or ineffective building arrangements. Some novice architects may prefer to ignore such ideas, feeling they are threats to the architect's need for personal design expression, but many experienced designers and programmers will encourage the client to collect and preserve this material as a data bank of design ideas. There is every reason to believe that the persons who use a

Entry Gate

Island and Beams

Wood Vegas

Decorative Stair

Curved Walls

Window Trim

Curved Wall

Window Trim

Shaded Patio

Figure 7-67 Magazine Clippings from a Client.

COLLEGE OF ARCHITECTURE AND ENVIRONMENTAL DESIGN EXPANSION

Student Group _DAVID SANDVIG_   _ROB DARNEY_   _CHRIS CAROSELLI_
(name of each student)
Building Area _15_   _MISC INTERIOR SPACES_
(1-16) Name: (College as a whole, School of Architecture... Design Studios)

PROGRAMMING MATRIX: IDEAS

1. Provide a large formal entry for visitors/public and an informal, efficient access, for student/faculty.

2. If another elevator is required in the new expansion facility, it should be of adequate size to accommodate large scale models, and have direct access from drop-off area.

3. Create a hierarchy of stairwells distinguishing major vertical circulation from emergency exits. (A good example of this is Noble Library.)

4. Locate handicapped access conveniently to elevators.

5. Install lockable display cases adjacent to studios for viewing of current student work.

6. College could rent out space to manufacturers which would offset the cost of the additional square footage and possibly create revenue for student activites.

7. Document the best student work in the form of slides, microfisch, prints, or originals, so that it can be displayed and also referenced by students/faculty. It could possibly be incorporated as a branch of the library.

8. Provide 1 main information tack wall for display of scholarships, competitions, job opportunities, class schedules, etc.. Also provide secondary tack boards throughout circulation paths for advertisement of activities, lectures, and announcements.

9. Locate soft drinks and vending machines adjacent to secondary circulation path.

Figure 7-68 Design Ideas from Program Matrix.

Credit: David Sandvig, Rob Darney, and Chris Caroselli, 1986.
College of Architecture and Environmental Design Expansion.
Permission: School of Architecture, Arizona State University

facility will have at least some good ideas about the solution to particular aspects of a design problem. The question is how best to present these ideas and not have them become design preconceptions with which the designer is forced to work. The author feels that to treat them simply as design ideas rather than design concepts is the proper approach (Fig. 7-67).

If the ideas are taken from magazines or other published documents, they can be photocopied and included with footnotes crediting the source and indicating why the idea was considered appropriate for the design solution.

If a client or user recognizes that the programmer has accepted and recorded their ideas, they are much more likely to be sympathetic with the final design solution, even if some or even most of their ideas were not incorporated into the design.

If the client or user suggestions are given verbally, they should be recorded and included in the programming matrix under the ideas category. If they seem to be important ideas, the programmer should develop suitable sketches or precept diagrams to make the ideas more clear (Fig. 7-68).

Desired images observed by the programmers in the client's existing establishment are shown in Fig. 7-69.

Precedents

Information about similar buildings collected during the literature review phase of architectural programming should be included in the appendix. However, particularly relevant features of these buildings or typological constants should be included in the ideas section of the program for the designer to consider. The programmer should try to ascertain from the previous solutions if a cultural norm exists or if a very logical arrangement has come to characterize the particular building type, and whether departures from the norm are likely to compromise the effectiveness of the design solution. In other words, if the logical solution for a particular building type has already been demonstrated, the architect's design task may not be to rediscover this essential typology, but rather to adapt it to the particular problem and site at hand and in such a way as to meet the goals and satisfy the requirements of the particular program.

A contemporary example of this is the L-shaped corner shopping center that characterizes so many major intersections in developing areas of the United States. This pattern recurs ad nauseam, to the point where nearly everyone wishes something more unique or creative could be achieved. Yet, when unique approaches are tried, they apparently fail to attract the same intensity of use, so developers return again and again to the same prototype (Fig. 7-70).

The developers of a shopping center in Tempe, Arizona, on the other hand, turned the typical "L" around and created a successful shopping area with the parking behind the buildings rather than in front of them. This approach seems to have worked in this situation; however, the arrangement precludes having a back door service area for the shops, limiting the types of

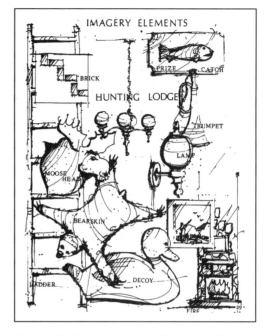

Figure 7-69 Design Ideas from Observation Study.

Credit: Robert Osier, Donald Kidder, and Blair Saville, 1985. *Program for DAX Clothing Sotre*. Tempe, Arizona. Permission: School of Architecture, Arizona State University

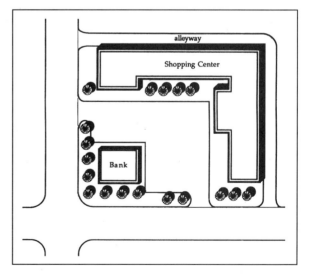

Figure 7-70 L-Shaped Shopping Center.

Credit: Anthony Amidei, Student Assignment, 1993. Permission: College of Architecture, The University of Arizona

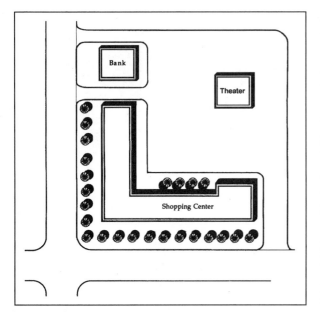

Figure 7-71 Reverse L-Shaped Shopping Center.

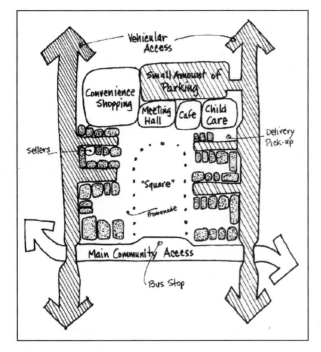

Figure 7-72 Community Market Diagram.

Credit: See Silverstein, Murray and Max Jacobson (1985). Permission: Wolfgang F.E. Preiser

shops that can be located in the center (Fig. 7-71).

On the other hand, some architects and other urbanists long for the pedestrian-oriented shopping streets and squares that typify cities and villages throughout Europe and some pre-automobile cities and communities in the United States. Murray Silverstein and Max Jacobson (1985) make a cogent argument for an alternative program for a community market (Fig. 7-72).

Other contemporary architects and planners advocating for a "new urbanism" have made similar pleas for pedestrian-oriented streets and shopping areas (Kelbaugh 1989; Katz et al. 1994).

Similar arguments for alternative approaches to many building types are presented in Alexander et al.'s *Pattern Language* (1977) and *The Oregon Experiment* (1975). Another book, *Precedents in Architecture* by Roger Clark (1985), shows diagrams of various systems for numerous building types. In any case, a careful literature search should reveal some alternative patterns or approaches that can be presented to both the client and the designer for their consideration.

Programmatic Concepts

In *Problem Seeking* (1969, 1977, 1987) William Peña et al. argued for including programmatic concepts in the program document. He defined "programmatic concepts" as those concepts having primarily organizational or operational implications. Figure 7-73 illustrates "integrated" versus "compartmentalized" as programmatic concepts.

Similar programmatic concept cards can be used effectively to visually explain many of the programmatic ideas that are expressed during the programming process (Fig. 7-74).

With many programmatic concepts there are important form implications. For example, in the programs for the expansion of the College of Architecture and Environmental Design at Arizona State University and of the College of Architecture at The University of Arizona, a marked difference in attitude about the nature of design education resulted in different programmatic concepts for the arrangement of design studios. At Arizona State University, it was decided that each design studio should be separate from the others to allow the students to secure their computers and other personal equipment in a locked room. At The University of Arizona, the students and faculty indicated that they wanted large, open, even multiple year and multiple discipline studios to promote social interaction and collaboration between faculty and students. Security of individual workstations and equipment are of secondary importance. Transportable and personally owned laptop computers are encouraged to reduce the potential for theft in an unsecured environment. The above differences are programmatic in nature, but have very strong formal implications.

Such "ideas" can be expressed in diagrams to make them more understandable to the designer than if they were expressed only in words (Figs. 7-75 and 7-76). While such programmatic concept diagrams do not specifically show "how" the studios are to be designed, there are strong formal implications that, if responded to

Figure 7-73 Integrated versus Compartmentalized.

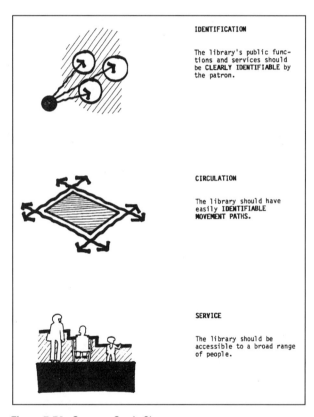

Figure 7-74 Concept Cards Sheet.

Credit: Anderson DeBartolo Pan, Inc. Architects, 1986. Program for the City of Tucson Main Library. Tucson, Arizona. Permission: ADP Marshall

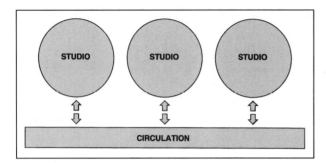

Figure 7-75 Separated Studio Diagram.

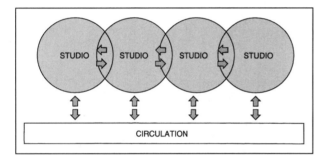

Figure 7-76 Integrated Studio Diagram.

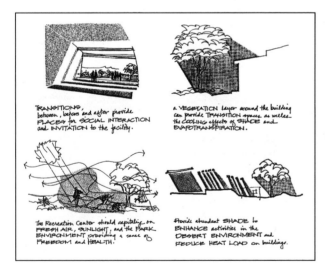

Figure 7-77 Precept Drawings.

Credit: Brooks & Associate AIA, Architects and Planners, 1985. *Design Program and Site Analysis for Morris K. Udall Regional Park and Recreational Center.* Permission: Albanese-Brooks Assoc. PC

by the designer, will produce very different designs (and studio activities).

Design Precepts

Professor Edward T. White (1972) developed the idea of using precept diagrams of partial solutions to design problems as a final step in programming. When the designer is part of the programming team, this is a meaningful way to explore the design impact of various programmatic decisions before attempting to develop an overall design concept.

Three to six concept or precept cards can be reduced in size and shown on one page of the program document (Fig. 7-77). Verbal explanations can be added below or to one side. The reduction is possible because the cards are drawn and lettered at a large scale so as to be easily seen from 10 to 15 feet away in a work session.

Note how precepts can be diagrammatic, physical, or even metaphorical in nature and in how they are presented. This does not matter as long as everyone understands that they are all just ideas—preconceptions about how the final design might respond to the design problem. If they are included in the program document in this way, they give the design architect the benefit of all of the ideas uncovered in the programming process—ideas uncovered in literature review, client and user ideas, and programmer distillation of all of these ideas. If everyone understands that they are only suggestions, not requirements, the designer should benefit from the added insights (Figs. 7-78 through 7-80).

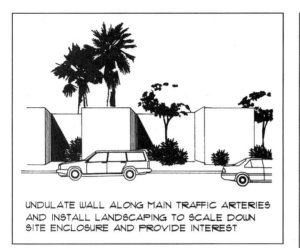

Figure 7-78   Precept Drawing.

Credit: Arquitectura, 1990. Program Document for Pascua Neighborhood Center Growth Master Plan, Tucson Parks and Recreation, Tucson, Arizona. Permission: Arquitectura, Ltd.

Figure 7-79   Precept from Student Program.

Credit: Karin Rosenquist, 1990. Program for the Design of the Department of Agriculture Bee Research Laboratory. College of Architecture, The University of Arizona

AQUARIUM EXHIBITS

The Kelp Forest exhibit has two essential underlying requisites: the surface must be open to receive direct sunlight and the water must be kept in constant motion.

Aquarists will need to use catwalks to access and maintain most of the exhibits. Visitors should not have visual access to any of the support areas.

Figure 7-80   Precepts from Student Program.

Credit: Beri Varol, 1996. Undergraduate Senior Thesis, *The Santa Monica Aquarium*. College of Architecture, The University of Arizona

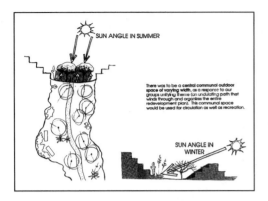

Figure 7-81   Climate-Based Design Concept.

Credit: Elisabet Grajewski, 1992. *Sixth Street Housing Development, Tucson, Arizona.* 5. College of Architecture, The University of Arizona

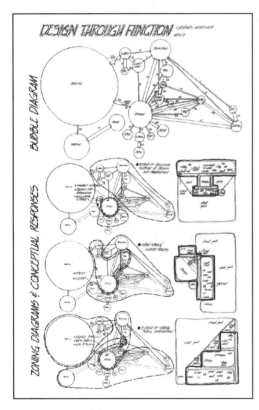

Figure 7-82   Zoning Diagram/Design Concepts.

Credit: Edward T. White, 1990. Concept Sketches for Graphics Workshop. Tucson, Arizona. Permission: Edward T. White

Design Concepts

If the designer is a member of the programming team, it is also possible to begin the development of design concept diagrams as a concluding part of the programming activity. This serves both as a way to confirm the efficacy of the program information and as a way for the client to evaluate if the concept is appropriate for the client's particular facilities problem. It can show, as in the adjacent illustration, how a strongly held value can have a major impact on architectural form (Fig. 7-81).

A process for creating design concepts has been well developed by Professor Edward T. White of Florida A&M University (1990). This analytic approach to developing design concepts focuses on particular issues. The first approach begins with the functional concept diagram. Here, a traditional relationship diagram is generated for the entire building, recognizing from the start that any holistic diagram will be based on certain organizational assumptions. Will one entry serve as reception point for all divisions of the organization or will multiple entries be provided for easier/direct access to each division? Which will serve the client better? What are the staffing implications? Should the program be changed to reflect the new requirements for staffing? Should all of the closed offices be gathered in one area and all of the open offices be placed together in another location? Will this make functional sense? Will it save money in terms of structural and or construction costs?

Very simple bubble diagrams are used to explore the implications of functional arrangements in terms of operations, efficiencies, construction costs, staffing costs, etc. First, White develops the overall relationship diagram. He then decides on alternative ways that the building could be zoned. Finally, he derives several design diagrams based on each of these zoning decisions to see what their implications are for design (Fig. 7-82).

The zoning relationship diagrams and the resulting initial design concepts show how effective such diagramming can be in helping the architect develop a design concept. The example shows that three distinctly different zoning decisions can be made from an identical overall relationship diagram, and that the impact of each approach on the design solution is likely to be very great. The resulting plans are not at all similar in shape or aesthetic potential.

Grouping of functions in zones can also be useful in programming for the reorganization of existing facilities, including related outdoor spaces. In the adjoining illustration, they were proposed by the programming/design consultant as a way to solve programmatic problems (Fig. 7-83).

Whether zoning relationships are appropriate to include in a program document depends on whether they represent programmatic decisions by the client/user, or are, in fact, conceptual ways of approaching the design. In the latter case, the diagram definitely should be left out of the requirements section of the program. It could be included in the ideas section of the program, where it can be evaluated by the designer as an idea rather than as a requirement.

Such analytic diagrams do not have to confine themselves to functional matters. What if the diagram begins with site or context, rather than the functional program? Where would views, access, slopes, special site features, and the like suggest that building entrance, services, or principal spaces be located? Is there another way that the site might better accommodate the facility? If climate, especially solar access, were considered, how would it affect or influence the layout of the building? What if solar access was considered to be the most important issue?

White (1990) goes on to show other diagrammatic ways to develop design concepts that produce different formal relationships than the ones developed from the alternative zoning diagrams, and which require the designer to handle functional relationships in still other ways (Fig. 7-84).

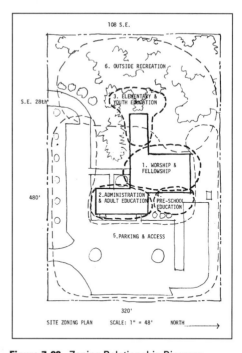

Figure 7-83 Zoning Relationship Diagram.
Credit: Robert Hershberger, Architect, 1982. Consultation for Bellevue Christian Church, Bellevue, Washington.

Figure 7-84 Context Related Design Concepts.
Credit: Edward T. White, 1990. Concept Sketches for Graphics Workshop, Tucson, Arizona. Permission: Edward T. White

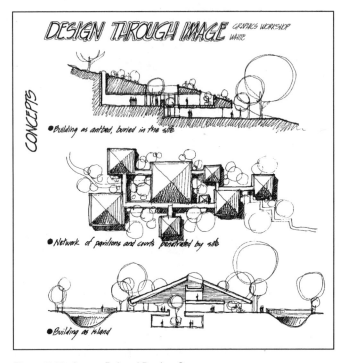

Figure 7-85 Image Related Design Concepts.

Credit: Edward T. White, 1990. Concept Sketches for Graphics Workshop, Tucson, Arizona. Permission: Edward T. White

What if aesthetic values were to be considered first? What should such a building look like, in spite of any functional, site, and climate constraints? This would require a different diagram and a corresponding change in functional layout and relationship to site and climate. What if budget were the most important consideration—the client needs a large amount of space, but has very little money to pay for it? This would have a very serious effect on form. Such diagrams can begin from any of the primary values listed earlier in the program (Fig. 7-85).

Design Exploration

Clearly, most of the above techniques are part of the initial exploratory stages of design. If they are accomplished during programming and the final program is modified to reflect these early design findings, it almost takes the program through the initial schematic phase of design. But it also helps to avoid the problem of the architect having to explain to the owner that certain assumptions of the program were either in error or were unrealistic relative to some of the expressed values and goals.

The author advocates including design exploration in programming only when the designer is involved in the programming process, and even then with some reservations. There are several very good reasons for this recommendation.

The first reason is that confirmation of the client's program typically is the first responsibility of the architect under the normal owner/architect agreement. It is an activity that the architect is prepared to do by training and experience. It is what they expect to do at the beginning of a design problem. Indeed, it is where the value of their extensive education comes into play in the resolution of difficult spatial problems.

The second reason is that the design architect may see other possibilities for problem solution which previous typologies, or the client's, user's, or programmer's limited experience, would not permit to come forward during programming. If the program is based on narrower assumptions than are appropriate given the designer's range of abilities or repertoire of forms, then the program could become an obstruction to a creative solution to the problem—an impediment rather than an implement for the creation of architecture.

Finally, even if the designer is involved in programming, the premature fixing of conceptual ways of solving the design problem may hamper exploration of other alternatives. Indeed, it may require the designer to return to the owner to explain why the earlier adopted design strategy is no longer operational. This is an awkward and sometimes difficult thing to do. The designer, in effect, must prove everyone else wrong.

The programmer should not limit options by imposing constraints which are not inherent in the problem. If the designer is not involved in the programming process, it is preferable to leave all but the most basic design analysis to the designer, recognizing that such analysis may, indeed, necessitate some deviation from the initial program. As long as the client understands and agrees that this is a possibility, it should not be considered a problem of programming, but rather an opportunity which comes from design.

The fact is that programming and design analysis are not really complete until the building is constructed and occupied. Design exploration, schematic design, design development, and even the ultimate occupancy of the building will uncover new ideas, opportunities, and constraints which will make some objectives of the original program difficult to achieve, and often will cause clients to change their minds as to the requirements of the program.

In conclusion, the author would argue that design analysis is the responsibility of the designer and should be under his/her direct supervision. On the other hand, it does not mean that the designer must accomplish the design analysis in a completely singular way. Rather, it is highly desirable for the designer to solicit the participation of the clients, users, and programmers in a common pursuit, as they explore together the design implications of the entire program, including all of the design ideas that have come forward during architectural programming.

Responsibility for the quality of design resides with the designer. Thus, the designer must have authority to make the design decisions.

7.14 Appendix

There is always some material which is of such importance that it should not be lost, because it explains or amplifies some of the information distilled within the program. This information should not be placed in the main sections of the program, but can be placed in an appendix to the program for reference if the need arises.

The only information that should be placed in the body of the architectural program is that which will have a direct impact on design decisions. The programmer should keep the program short and to the point, with essential information relating to design clearly set forth and organized for easy retrieval. As stated previously, "an ounce of explanation is worth a ton of description." Or, to put it another way, "understanding of the program by the designer is inversely related to the amount of material presented." Think about these two sayings when considering the inclusion of material in the program.

The appendix should contain the information obtained from the literature search, observation studies, interviewing, questionnaire/survey, site analysis, and any other data developed during the programming process. If the program is carefully developed, the designer may not even need to refer to the appendix. However, if there is a need to look over this information at some point in the design process, it should be available for reference.

If the program is a large one, the author advocates putting the appendix material in a separate loose-leaf document with tabs to show where each type of material is located. It should be on 8½" × 11" paper so that it can be stored or filed by the designer with the other project materials for ready reference as needed.

7.15 Exercises

1. Utilize the information gained from earlier information gathering and work session exercises to develop a mock architectural program:

   a. Prepare a short "preliminaries" section including transmittal, acknowledgment, directory, methods, and references sections.

   b. Reformulate the programming matrix developed earlier into sections on values and goals, design considerations, project requirements, and design ideas.

      If you used cards to prepare the matrix, try to use the visual materials (diagrams, charts, and sketches) in the program to improve its information content.

      If you used easel-sized grid sheets, either have them reduced to 8½" × 11" by photocopying or re-present them using a word processor. Note how much improvement you make with the grammar and format when you re-present them.

   c. Develop the tabular requirements for space allocation using your understanding of efficiency by providing two-dimensional area representations as outlined in the text.

   d. Prepare a space relationship matrix including all of the interior and exterior spaces. Then prepare space relationship diagrams for every space outlined in the space allocation sheets.

   d. Prepare space program sheets (including relationship diagrams) for all of the spaces identified in the space allocation sheets.

   e. Develop tabular requirements showing project costs using the system and cost factors described in the text.

   f. Develop a project schedule showing duration of all project phases from programming through construction, first for a standard schedule, then for a fast-track schedule.

   g. Prepare the executive summary following the guidelines set forth in the text.

   h. Prepare a cover sheet and bind all of the above into a program document with several copies. Assemble the appropriate appendix material and place it in a three-ring loose-leaf binder.

2. Have the earlier participants in the information gathering and work sessions review the final product.

   Have a meeting with them as a group to discuss the programming process and product, including the contribution of each part of the process and product.

3. Do a design exploration study to see if you have all of the information needed for design.

7.16 References

Alexander, Christopher. 1975. *The Oregon Experiment*. New York: Oxford University Press.

Alexander, Christopher, Sara Ishikawa, and Murray Silverstein. 1977. *A Pattern Language: Towns, Buildings, Construction*. New York: Oxford University Press.

Clark, Roger H., and Michael Pause. 1985. *Precedents in Architecture*. New York: Van Nostrand Reinhold.

Competition Program. 1986. ASU Project #125-2E. *College of Architecture and Environmental Design*, Arizona State University.

Duerk, Donna P. 1993. *Architectural Programming: Information Management for Design*. New York: Van Nostrand Reinhold.

Farbstein, Jay. *Correctional Facility Planning and Design. 2nd ed*. New York: Van Nostrand Reinhold.

Green, Isaac, Bernard E. Fedewa, Charles Johnson, William Jackson, and Howard Deardorff. 1975. *Housing for the Elderly: The Development and Design Process*. New York: Van Nostrand Reinhold.

Katz, Peter, ed. 1994. *The New Urbanism: Toward an Architecture of Community*. New York: McGraw-Hill.

Kelbaugh, Doug, ed. 1989. *The Pedestrian Pocket Book: A New Suburban Design Strategy*. New York: Princeton Architectural Press.

Kumlin, Robert R. 1995. *Architectural Programming: Creative Techniques for Design Professionals*. New York: McGraw-Hill.

Marshall & Swift, L.P. 1997. *Marshall Valuation Service*. Los Angeles, Calif.: Marshall & Swift, L.P.

Moleski, Walter. 1974. "Behavioral Analysis in Environmental Programming for Offices." In *Designing for Human Affairs*, edited by Jon Lang, Charles Burnette, Walter Moleski, and Steven Vachon. Stroudsburg, Pa.: Dowden, Hutchinson & Ross.

Peña, William, and John Focke. 1969. *Problem Seeking: New Directions in Architectural Programming*. Houston, Tex.: Caudill Rowlett Scott.

Peña, William, William Caudill, and John Focke. 1977. *Problem Seeking: An Architectural Programming Primer*. Boston, Mass.: Cahners Books International.

Peña, William, Steven Parshall, and Kevin Kelly. 1987. *Problem Seeking: An Architectural Programming Primer*. 3rd ed. Washington, D.C.: AIA Press.

Rector, Lee. 1997. *Design Cost Data*. Vol. 41, number 1. Tampa, Fla.: LMRector Corporation.

Robinson, Julia, and J. Stephen Weeks. 1984. *Programming as Design*. Minneapolis: Department of Architecture, University of Minnesota.

R. S. Means Company. 1990. *Means Estimating Handbook*. Kingston, Mass.: R. S. Means Company.

_____. 1996. *Means Square Foot Costs: Residential, Commercial, Industrial, Institutional*. 17th ed. Kingston, Mass.: R. S. Means Company.

R. S. Means Company. 1996. *Means Square Foot Costs: Residential, Commercial, Industrial, Institutional*. 17th edition. Kingston, Mass.: R. S. Means Company.

Silverstein, Murray, and Max Jacobson. 1985. "Restructuring the Hidden Program: Toward and Architecture of Social Change." In *Programming the Built Environment*, edited by Wolfgang F. E. Preiser. New York: Van Nostrand Reinhold.

White, Edward T. III. 1972. *Introduction to Architectural Programming*. Tucson, Ariz.: Architectural Media.

_____. 1990. Workshop with Professor Kirby Lockard. College of Architecture, The University of Arizona, Tucson, Arizona.

Methods of Evaluation

A final question about almost any purposeful activity is one of evaluation. How well did we do the job? Does something we created work the way it was intended? Can people accomplish their tasks better than before? Is the building energy efficient? Is it a work of art? At every stage of the design process there is evaluation, as the programmer or designer decides if the work is of sufficient merit to proceed to the next step. There are several key points in the design process when a systematic evaluation should take place:

1. At the conclusion of programming.

2. After each phase of design.

3. At the conclusion of construction.

4. Upon initial occupancy.

5. Sometime after occupancy of the building.

The purposes of each evaluation vary to some extent, but they all tie together as essential elements of effective architectural programming and design. All are needed to advance the art and science of the profession of architecture.

8.1 Program Evaluation

- Process Evaluation
- Simulation Procedures
- Cost of Error

How does one evaluate the architectural program? Is the program simply a hypothesis that will be supported or not supported as the design is developed and the building occupied? To some extent this is true, but if the program is an accurate and complete statement of the design issues and problems, the design will not be a test of the program but rather a response to the issues and problems outlined therein. So how should one evaluate a program? If the program document is agreeable to the client, is that enough? The author would agree that acceptance of the program by the client is the crucial test of the suitability of the program for its intended use, because without this acceptance the project will not go forward. However, there are a number of other useful ways to evaluate the program, both as it develops and after it is completed. The following paragraphs explore some of the ways that evaluation of the program is accomplished.

Evaluation of the program begins with the very first decisions about what to include in the program. Indeed, each decision that is made, whether procedural or substantive, is the result of an evaluative process. The persons involved in programming must decide what needs to be done. What material should the program include? What procedures will be used to collect the needed information? How will the results be presented? These are matters of judgment on the part of the programmer, the client, and others involved in the programming activity. An awareness of the fact that judgments are being made throughout the programming and design process is essential to an informed evaluation of the program. Application of previously agreed upon procedures and criteria for evaluation should increase the program's effectiveness as a design tool.

Process Evaluation

Some criteria that can be applied judgments about the programming process are as follows:

1. Is the program plan comprehensive (Fig. 8-1)? If we follow the plan will we obtain all of the information required to recognize client/user values, accomplish their goals, satisfy their needs, and achieve architecture.

2. Will the information obtained be accurate? Are we using procedures of sampling, data acquisition, and analysis that will produce reliable and valid results?

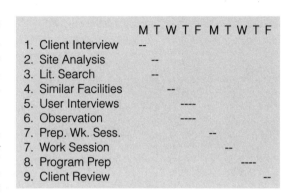

	M T W T F	M T W T F
1. Client Interview	--	
2. Site Analysis	--	
3. Lit. Search	--	
4. Similar Facilities	--	
5. User Interviews	----	
6. Observation	----	
7. Prep. Wk. Sess.	--	
7. Work Session	--	
8. Program Prep	----	
9. Client Review	--	

Figure 8-1 Programming Plan.

3. Will the results help the designer understand the nature of the design problem and related issues? Is the planned program document one in which it will be easy to discover the big issues prior to confronting detail?

4. Will the program result in architecture that can be designed and built within the constraints of the client's budget and schedule? Will the monitoring procedures ensure that projections are achievable within known constraints?

5. Will it be possible to produce the program document within the programming budget? Is enough money available to accomplish the entire program plan?

These and similar questions should be asked early in the development of the program plan, to be certain that all of the programming objectives can be achieved. Inevitably, such questions cause a tightening of programming procedures, which is helpful in producing a quality program. This type of evaluation relies primarily on the judgment of the participants. If, of course, there is very little experience within the programming group, then it might be necessary to involve persons with greater experience.

In the actual collection and analysis of data, some of the standards of research evaluation can be applied. If sampling is necessary because of a very large number of respondents, then a sampling plan conforming to standards set forth in the research literature would be appropriate. Similarly, is data collection being accomplished by methods that have been validated in previous research? Do projections for room sizes and building efficiency conform with known standards for similar facilities? Checking both procedures and data against known criteria and standards is a useful evaluation technique throughout the programming process. Such checking tends to challenge earlier assumptions and conclusions and usually results in refinement of both procedures and data.

Simulation Procedures

- Mental
- Iconic
- Symbolic
- Experimental

It is possible to utilize various forms of simulation as evaluative tools during the programming process.

MENTAL

Mental simulation can be used on a regular basis. What will the effect on traffic be if vehicular ingress and egress are allowed on a major street or near a busy intersection? What would the room size implications be in a hotel if all double beds were to be king size rather than standard size? Will the recommended balcony size allow a small group to sit at a table? Imagine any of these or similar situations. Would the result be acceptable? Virtually every room size has furnishing, equipment, and activity implications. It may be possible simply to consider in one's mind if there will be enough room to accommodate everything. What will be the appearance of the facility? Do we have the same image in mind (Fig. 8-2)?

Figure 8-2 Persons not Sharing the Same Image.

Credit: Kitchell CEM, 1986. *More for Less: Jail Construction Cost Management Handbook.* State of California, Board of Construction Cost Management. Permission: Kitchell CEM

ICONIC

It may be desirable to conduct some type of iconic (image) modeling to determine if program statements are appropriate. A plan for a room showing furniture and equipment may be drawn to scale to determine if its size and shape are adequate to house all required uses. Circulation paths can be drawn with varying widths to indicate volume of use to see if the required activities can occur. If it appears that the required equipment, furnishings, and activities cannot be accommodated, then it might be necessary to increase the size of space, to change its shape, or possibly to re-evaluate if all of the equipment, furnishings, or activities must really be accommodated in the space. In other words, pre-design iconic simulation may be helpful in determining if the initial programmed space allocations are reasonable (Fig. 8-3).

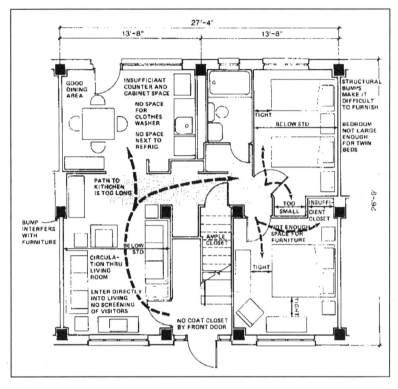

Figure 8-3 Annotated Room Evaluation.

Credit: Walter Moleski and Wallace Roberts and Todd, 1990. *Analysis of Existing Housing Unit, Richard Allen Homes.* Philadelphia, Pennsylvania. Permission: ERG/Environmental Research Group

Two examples from the architectural building competition at Arizona State University illustrate the need for pre-design evaluation, although in this case the evaluations occurred when the competition designs were being reviewed by the client.

First, the university's standard requiring that a 70 percent efficiency be maintained in acade-mic buildings could have been challenged during programming, if most other architectural buildings had been found to have lower efficiencies. This was not done, although everyone involved with the programming felt that the required efficiency was unrealistic for an academic building of this type. The competitors proved the point iconically. None of the design schemes came close to the required efficiency. The floor plan of the winning submission by Alan Chimacoff of the

Figure 8-4 ASU Architecture Building Courtyard.

Photo Credit: Jeff Goldberg, Esto. Permission: Alan Chimacoff, The Hillier Group

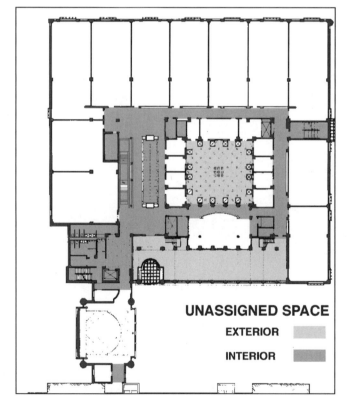

UNASSIGNED SPACE

EXTERIOR

INTERIOR

Figure 8-5 ASU Architecture Building Efficiency.

Credit: Adapted from the floor plan drawing by Alan Chimacoff of The Hillier Group. Permission: College of Architecture and Environmental Design, Arizona State University

Hillier Group, second floor shown below, was the most efficient at about 60 percent, with walls, halls, stairs, chases, toilets, janitors' closets, and the like accounting for 40 percent of the floor area. Unassigned two- and even three-story interior spaces also contributed to a lower efficiency. Unprogrammed exterior spaces, while not directly contributing to efficiency calculations, also increased the quality and cost of the building (Figs. 8-4 and 8-5).

In order to meet the efficiency requirements, the interior hallways of the studio floors were reprogrammed as teaching spaces by locating glassed-in exhibit cases along the hallway walls. Other previously unprogrammed spaces, such as code required rest rooms, were defined as programmed space in order to meet the unrealistic efficiency standards.

Second, the design solution selected by the jury as the winner had long, thin studio spaces. Schematic design analysis conducted by the programmers, after the fact, indicated that an absolute minimum of a twenty-four-feet interior width would be needed to provide the required number of work stations and circulation space within the allocated square footage for the studios. This information was provided to the designer so that there would be no chance that the building would contain studios of the specified square footage size, but in a configuration that would not accommodate the required furnishings (Fig. 8-6).

It is a debatable point as to how much iconic simulation should take place during the evaluation of an architectural program. At what point are decisions about the sizes, shapes, and relationships of the various spaces, furnishings, and equipment going to restrict the range of design opportunity? It is difficult to say. It may be mandatory to develop several alternative solutions during programming in order to establish the minimum size needed to accommodate certain complex program elements. If so, a certain amount of study should be done. But care should be taken not to develop some preconceived notion as to the actual design, because that clearly would be in conflict with the designer's prerogatives to make design decisions.

An example of appropriate use of iconic simulation was accomplished in a programming study by Jay Farbstein for converting an existing space into a dayroom. Several alternative furnishing plans were explored to determine if the space would work for this purpose (Fig. 8-7).

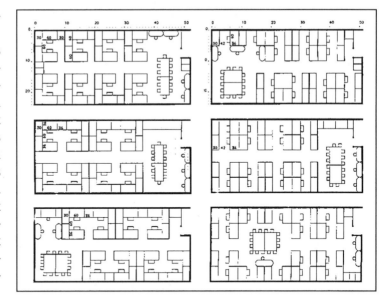

Figure 8-6 ASU Studio Desk Arrangements.

Credit: Tim McGinty, Chair College Building Committee. Permission: College of Architecture and Environmental Design, Arizona State University

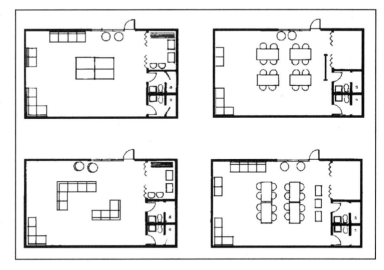

Figure 8-7 Dayroom Furnishing Variations.

Credit: Adapted from Jay D. Farbstein, 1985. Dayroom Furnishing Vriations in "Using the Program" in Wolfgang F. E. Preiser, Ed. *Programming the Built Environment.* New York: Van Nostrand Reinold. Permission: Wolfgang F. E. Preiser

If the programming team includes the designer or design group, then the above question is perhaps moot. It would be appropriate to do as much analysis as necessary for the designers to understand all of the constraints upon design. If the programming activity is being conducted without the participation of the designer, or quite possibly well before the designer has been selected, then some care should be taken to keep the iconic simulations to the minimum necessary to be certain that the projected space sizes will allow the required functions to take place. Care should be taken so that assumptions are not made about the eventual design solution that will restrict the range of creative opportunities for the designer.

SYMBOLIC

It is also possible to utilize mathematical simulations as a basis of program evaluation. Construction cost and financial feasibility analyses involve input of a variety of unit costs, which add up to a buildable or unbuildable project. The same is true for developing the total square footage of a project. These quantifiable items need to be varied until a satisfactory overall size/cost projection is obtained. Scheduling is another program activity that involves manipulation of symbols. The modified preliminary cost estimate for a proposed minor expansion to the College of Architecture at The University of Arizona illustrates the value of mathematical simulation (Fig. 8-8).

Note in the illustration that not only were the square footages reduced in an attempt to bring the project within budget, but the efficiency was increased from 65 percent to 69 percent and the square foot cost was reduced from the average project cost to the low average project cost for buildings on the campus. Both reductions imply a like reduction in the quality of

SPACE ALLOCATION FOR EXPANSION (revised 4-*13*-97)

	NET SQ FT
ARCHITECTURE UNDERGRADUATE	
Fifth Year Design Studio (50 students at 50 sf/p)	2,500
ARCHITECTURE GRADUATE	
Fifth Year Design Studio (20 students at 50 sf/p)	1,000
Administration (director, asst., reception, storage/supply)	~~600~~ *500*
Faculty Offices (4 at 150 sf)	600
PLANNING GRADUATE	
Administration (director, asst, reception, storage/supply)	~~600~~ *500*
Faculty Offices (4 at 150 sf)	600
LANDSCAPE	
Administration (director, asst, reception, storage/supply)	~~600~~ *500*
Faculty Offices (4 at 150 sf)	600
SHARED	
Interdisciplinary Studio(s) (20 arch, 20 plan, 60 landscape)	5,000
Lecture Hall (250 at 8 sf/p)	2,000
Class/Presentation Room (*2* at 500 sf)	*1*,500
Seminar (*3* at 250 sf)	~~750~~ *500*
Small Conf (*2* at 100 sf)	~~200~~ *300*
Graduate Computer Laboratory	~~800~~ *650*
Interdisciplinary Lounge/Exhibit	~~600~~ *500*
Shop/Experimental Laboratory	1,~~500~~ *000*
NET SQUARE FEET TOTAL	~~18,550~~ *17,150*
Efficiency at ~~68~~ *69%* (because of large open spaces)	
GROSS SQUARE FEET TOTAL	~~28~~ *25*,000
Assume ~~medium~~ *low* average project cost at $~~180~~ *160*/sf (same reasons)	
TOTAL PROJECT COST	~~$5,400,000~~ (versus $4,000,000 available)

Figure 8-8　Marked-Up Cost Estimate.

space and materials in the expansion. This is not a good way to achieve quality architecture. As a general rule, the programmer would be wise to project the efficiency toward the lower range and cost toward the upper range when programming for architecture. There is a definite relationship that generally cannot be overcome.

EXPERIMENTAL

Typically, there is very little time or money available during architectural programming to utilize the most precise evaluation strategies. It is a rare instance when it is possible to mock up a particular space, to have it occupied for a time, and to evaluate the results before deciding how the space should be programmed. Yet, however rare, this kind of experimental evaluation does occur (Clipson and Wehrer 1973; Trites et al. 1970). It should occur for large commissions when multiple rooms of the same kind will be programmed and designed. For example, major hotel chains would be wise to mock-up and use new hotel rooms or suites that will be replicated many times. The same is true for major dormitories, special care units, and prison cells. This type of evaluation can save the client a great deal of money and exasperation in trying to overcome problems easily detected by use (including make-up and cleaning).

Examination rooms and patient room layouts in hospitals have been mocked up, and in at least one case entirely new wing arrangements have been built in existing hospital facilities, to explore the results prior to preparing a program for major additions or reconstruction. So, occasionally it is possible to conduct evaluations based on actual experimental research (Figs. 8-9 through 8-11).

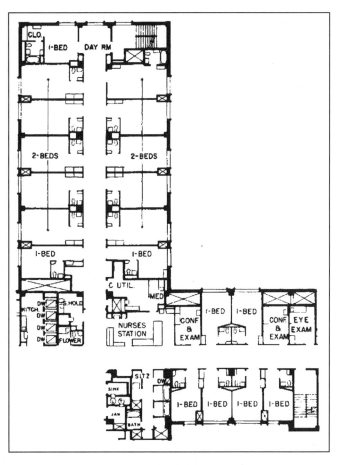

Figure 8-9 Hospital Wing with Single Corridor.

Credit: (Trites et al 1970), 303–334. Reprinted by permission of Sage Publications, Inc.

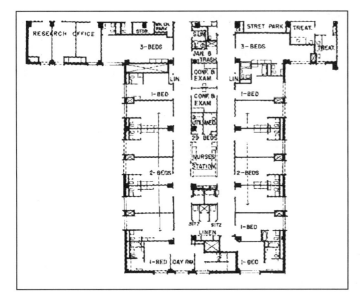

Figure 8-10 Hospital Wing with Double Corridor.

Credit: (Trites et al 1970), 303–334. Reprinted by permission of Sage Publications, Inc.

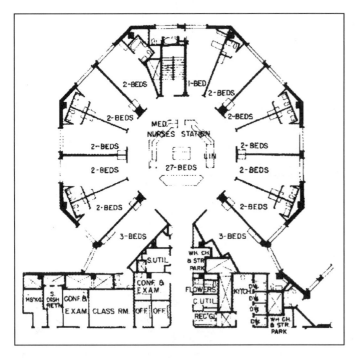

Figure 8-11 Hospital Wing with Radial Plan.

Credit: (Trites et al 1970), 303–334. Reprinted by permission of Sage Publications, Inc.

In this experimental evaluation by Trites et al. (1970), it was found that the radial plan with the nursing unit in the center of the surrounding patient rooms had many advantages over both the double and single corridor plans. Specifically:

- The nursing personnel traveled significantly less.

- Nurses spent more time with patients

- Nurses, doctors, and patients felt the unit enhanced the quality of patient care

- There was lower absenteeism and fewer accidents.

In a sense, housing developers use experimental simulation when they build their model homes. Once built and furnished, the developer can evaluate the effectiveness of the various spaces, materials, and systems and propose changes to prospective buyers that would overcome perceived problems. Developers utilizing repetitive systems would be wise to do the same prior to designing a final product for the mass market. This evaluation option should not be overlooked by the programmer. When warranted, it should be included in the program plan and covered by the agreed upon cost for programming services.

Cost of Error

The expected cost of error is an excellent basis for deciding whether experimental research is warranted during programming. In the case of very expensive and highly repeatable architectural elements, such as might be found in hotel, prison, hospital, or health care bedrooms, or the floor layout for multistory facilities, the cost of error both in budgetary and human terms may be so high as to justify the cost of this type of preliminary evaluation. The programmer should be constantly alert to this possibility and be prepared to request the additional funding and time necessary to conduct these objective evaluations. However, the programmer should also be prepared to deal with the more typical situation in which the client, for whatever reasons, decides that the program must be completed within a certain restrictive budget and time frame, and that the programmer will have to make decisions based on reasoned inferences from studies of similar situations. This, of course, is one of the reasons to conduct a literature search during architectural programming. It allows the programmer to utilize the authority, collective judgment, and actual experimental results of others.

The assumption of the owner/client in many programming situations is that the costs of error of not conducting experimental research is small enough to not warrant the extra time and expense. Whether or not they are correct in making this decision is beside the point. The programmer's response should always be to err in the direction where cost(s) of error are minimized. When it appears that cost of error could be substantial, strategies to mitigate against such costs should be built into the program.

For example, require the designer to provide larger bay spacing and relocatable or easily reconstructed partitions in areas where organizational change is likely to occur, so that dysfunctional areas can be remodeled inexpensively. Increase the space allocation for departments where there is a great deal of uncertainty as to future growth potential or equipment and furnishing requirements. Require design solutions that show future expansion for facilities with uncertain expectations for growth. In other words, when funding is not available to conduct needed simulations or experiments during programming, insist that the architect design a facility in which cost of program error will be minimized.

The final program document will be subject to the collective judgment of the programmer, the client, and others involved in the programming task (Kirk and Spreckelmeyer 1988). The program, thus, will be the best projection of issues and concerns that can be made by these people before design. It is a starting point, not a finishing point—the basis for design, not a rigid prescription. There will be new realizations based on the specific formal character of the design. Some new opportunities will be created that may mitigate some programmatic inadequacies. Give and take may be necessary to obtain the best design solution.

8.2 Design Evaluation

One of the greatest benefits of the carefully conceived architectural program is its use to evaluate design (Spreckelmeyer 1982). How should we evaluate design? If it looks good, is it good? If it follows the most current formal or stylistic trends, is it good? If it is unusual, is it good? These are some of the questions that will be asked and answered by architectural critics, art historians, clients, users, designers, and other architects. The program, however, can serve as the basis for a more objective evaluation of the design. What does the program request? Is it provided? What are the important values to be expressed? Are they expressed? What are the goals to be reached? Were they reached? What are the specific spatial and relational requirements? Have they been met? These are the questions that the program can contribute to the evaluation of design. The program can provide the criteria or standards of evaluation for use by the designer, client, and programmer to judge the design solution.

- Have the values been expressed?
- Have the goals been achieved?
- Have the needs been satisfied?
- Were any of the ideas utilized? If not, why not?

First, having identified the broad issues for design in the program—the values of the client, community, and designer and the specific goals for the project—it should be possible to make judgments about whether the underlying values are being made manifest and the goals are being achieved in the design. Does the design recognize the fabric of the existing community, satisfying the client's to be a good neighbor? Does the design project the image of a place of imagination and inquiry, communicating the value of higher education? Will it allow all of the client's activities to take place efficiently and effectively, recognizing the values of productivity and return on investment? In other words, the program can be effective in reminding the designer of the major design issues and goals for the project. Are the values being recognized, responded to, and expressed? Are the goals being accomplished? Are the most important goals being accomplished very well, and the other goals at least to a satisfactory level? The program can serve as both a guide and a control as the designer begins and continues the quest toward architecture.

The same is true for the design considerations and requirements. Are the important conditions of site and climate being recognized and accommodated? Are code and zoning requirements being followed, or must exceptions be requested? Are special users being recognized and their needs accommodated? Is it going to be possible to meet the construction budget given all of the other requirements that must be met? Are all of the space requirements being satisfied? The various sections of the program can be summarized and used as checklists to evaluate the design. The space allocation sheets can be used, not only to develop the square footage requirements, but also to check if the required number and sizes of spaces have been included in the design. They can also be used to determine if all of the required furnishings and equipment have been provided. The relationship matrices and diagrams can be used in a similar fashion to determine which relationships are most satisfactory and which are not. Have some crucial relationships been ignored? Indeed, the entire program becomes the criteria for evaluating the design, at least from programmer, client, and user perspectives.

If the designer(s) were not a part of the programming group, and thus had no chance to insert personal values into the programming activity, it should be expected that the designer(s) may articulate personal or firm values, associated goals, and even project requirements while confirming the program as outlined in standard architectural services. This is most helpful in establishing if the values and goals of the designer and client are compatible, and may be a basis for modifying some of the program requirements. For instance, if the client and programmer expect too much building for the budget, higher quality materials than the budget will support, or expect the building to be more efficient than reasonably possible, the designer can point this out and insist that adjustments be made to the program so that a satisfactory building can be provided within the budget restrictions. It is desirable to document all such changes and to append them to the program document. This is, of course, essential for subsequent program-based design evaluation to be realistic and effective.

8.3 Building Evaluation

- Tuning the Building
- User's Manual
- Post-Occupancy Evaluation

It is not the purpose of this book to focus on building evaluation, either as the building satisfies the architectural critic in terms of aesthetic qualities or as it fits into one stream of architectural thought or another. Nor is it a concern how well the building relates to the plans and specifications prepared by the designer. These areas of evaluation, while very important, are outside of what architectural programming typically encompasses, except in one very special way. The fact that important design issues have been identified and articulated as values and goals in the program should lead the designer toward more tangible expression of the values and achievement of the goals in the design. In the sense that identification of important values has helped such fine architects as Wright, Le Corbusier, Mies, Kahn, and Venturi to focus their own design efforts, the identification in the program of institutional, client, user, and community values may serve to focus the design energy of other architects to similar accomplishment.

A carefully and thoughtfully conceived program will produce some of the raw material from which creative, thoughtful, indeed, wonderful and poetic architecture can be formed. But it is up to the designer to understand the issues as presented and to respond to them in design. A fine programmatic analysis is an essential ingredient to achieve architecture, but it is not sufficient. An equally fine and creative synthesis of the program elements as assimilated into the architect's design philosophy is necessary to ensure the accomplishment of architecture.

Tuning the Building

Clients often expect their buildings to work perfectly when first occupied—forgetting that buildings are not mass produced objects. Indeed, few other design professionals expect the first prototype to work. They use a prototype to experiment with, to test, to modify, and to change until it works better. They may even make several more prototypes until everything seems to work well. Yet, we have all purchased the so-called lemon on occasion. Given this reality, it is amazing that most newly constructed buildings work as well as they do!

Buildings are so large, require such a major capital investment, sit on various sites in various climates, and respond to different codes and ordinances, it is almost impossible to prepare a full-scale working prototype before constructing the actual building. So the first prototype must work, at least well enough for the client/users to move in and occupy the space. It is not often that a building is "recalled" by the manufacturer because of some defect! But the chance of the initial analysis, the subsequent design, and the actual building construction being without flaw is very slim. There likely will be problems associated with all three.

So what should be done? The client needs to be fully apprised in each of the documents prepared for his/her signature that the finished building is likely to require a period of tuning, and that a contingency amount should be in the budget to allow this tuning to take place. Perhaps a space will turn out to be the wrong size or shape once the furniture is moved in. Will the client replace the furniture or change the space? Neither are without cost! Perhaps the lighting will be insufficient for some new specialized tasks that have been instituted after the program was completed. Or the size of one department has increased while another has decreased during the construction interval, so that either people or equipment or both need to be moved. What if the very handsome paint which the designer selected for the halls or offices was much more light absorptive than the color on which the electrical engineer based his/her calculations, so that the final result is hallways or offices that are too dark? What changes, the paint tint or the illumination level? Or should the occupant simply suffer with the poor result? What if the open offices, which were expected to be quiet enough for successful operations, turn out to be too noisy for some activities? Few of the necessary changes can be accomplished without additional cost.

The client should be informed that at least one to two percent of the contingency budget must be reserved for tuning the building, and at least some portion of the programmer's commission should be oriented toward discovering and monitoring the changes that need to be made.

User's Manual

It is also possible to develop a user's manual to help the client. Is it reasonable to expect the users to know how to use a building appropriately without providing some guidance to them? Probably not, even when the users have been active in helping to develop the architectural program and design. Just as instructions are provided for the use and maintenance of a new car, washing machine, or other mass-produced object, clients would benefit from instructions as to the best use and maintenance of a new building. If provided, such a manual can help avoid both dissatisfaction with and unnecessary adjustments or alterations to the new facility. For instance, if a new food preparation system were to be proposed for a commercial kitchen, it would be important to include instructions on using the new equipment. Indeed, it would be necessary to train the cooks and kitchen help in the use of the new equipment to be certain that it would be used effectively. The same is true of many innovative systems that might be used in a new building.

Post-Occupancy Evaluation

Several books and a great number of articles have been written about post-occupancy evaluation (Marans and Spreckelmeyer 1982; Bechtel et al. 1987; Preiser et al. 1988). Therefore, there will be no effort in this text to duplicate these very thoughtful efforts. However, it is important to point out that post-occupancy evaluation (the evaluation of buildings in use) can be greatly enhanced if the values to be expressed, the goals to be accomplished, and the specific program requirements have been articulated in a program. In this case, the programmed values and goals can be posed as hypotheses about the image, function, energy efficiency, etc., that the designed and built facility should recognize and incorporate. Evaluation can consist primarily of determining if the design achieved the program stipulations, and if the intended attitudes and behaviors resulted. In other words, the program can be the beginning point for a post-occupancy evaluation.

In fact, it may be appropriate for the programmer to obtain an agreement with the client to continue in the client's employ:

1. During design, to provide guidance as the designer attempts to satisfy program requirements within the broad outlines of the value and goal statements and the constraints of site, climate, schedule, and budget.

2. During the client/user move-in, to instruct users on the intended purposes of various building, space, furnishing, and equipment elements.

3. Six months to one year after initial occupancy, to determine if the expectations of use (behavior and attitudes) are holding up, or if the building, furnishings, or equipment should be modified to permit the users to operate successfully.

It should be noted that in using the literature search and review, interviewing, observation, questionnaire/survey, and group session procedures covered in this text for architectural programming, programmers are already using most of the methods, techniques, and tools needed to conduct post-occupancy evaluation. Indeed, programmers often conduct abbreviated post-occupancy evaluations of the facilities that the client/users currently occupy. In some cases they do similar evaluations of other similar facilities. Thus, a person who is fully capable of conducting the research necessary to develop an outstanding architectural program will also be able to conduct a post-occupancy evaluation study.

If statements of original intent from a previous program are still available, it is possible for the programmer to use them as a basis for these evaluations. It may also be possible to determine whether the same problems existed when the building(s) was first occupied, or are the result of a changing and growing institution for which the original facilities are no longer adequate. Some design principles for a particular type of institution may become evident as the result of a program-oriented post-occupancy evaluations.

8.4 Body of Knowledge

Assume that programmers document not only the program, but also the changes made during design and initial building tuning. Assume also that they, or someone else, conduct a careful post-occupancy evaluation. Some important values will be found to be expressed. Others may not be expressed. Some goals will be achieved, others will not. Some building areas are likely to be found to work well as planned, others not so well, and perhaps others not to work well at all.

If the successes and failures are noted and reported in the post-occupancy evaluation, and the more generalizable findings are published in the environmental design research and architectural literature, then the next programming commission can benefit from the experience of others. In fact, all future programming and design activities can benefit from the published results.

This is an extremely important linkage that often has been missing from the environmental design research area. Not enough of our experience is transferred to other professionals, hence, we all tend to re-invent the wheel every time we take on a new commission. If only we had the knowledge of those who had tried before us, we could be so much more effective. A distinct obligation of both architectural programmers and designers is to document the values, goals, and objectives to be achieved; to insist that someone evaluate what has been accomplished; and to publish the results for the architectural community so that all can learn and advance in their ability to create architecture.

8.5 The Next Commission

If an architect learned from the last commission or the commissions of other design professionals, then he/she should be able to do a better job on the next commission. This is one reason why most clients look for architects who have done previous buildings of the same type. They hope that these architects will know more about their particular building type than architects who have not done similar buildings. At the same time, this is why some thoughtful clients avoid employing architects who have previously done similar buildings. These clients do not want to repeat the failures of the past. They want architects who have a fresh outlook—who will seek out the underlying and possibly unique values of the institution, client, and community as well as the goals that will be specific to their project. They want architects who will carefully analyze the potential of the particular site and consider the needs of the particular users.

Architectural or programming firms with the ability to do well conceived and thorough architectural programs and post-occupancy evaluations are a definite step ahead of the competition in this regard, because not only can they discover the background information that relates to the project, but they can also discover unique things about the present and future that will be appropriate for the problem at hand. And they can sell their

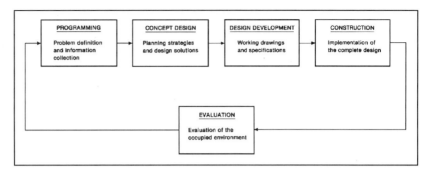

Figure 8-12 The Architectural Delivery System.

Credit: Kent Spreckelmeyer, 1986. Environmental Programming, Chapter 8. In Methods in Environmental and Behavioral Research. Robert Bechtel, Robert Marans and William Michelson (eds.). New York: Van Nostrand Reinhold. Permission: Van Nostrand Reinhold.

services to clients on this basis. If they document the insights gained from project to project and consistently share them with the entire architectural community, later projects by their firm and by other firms are likely to improve as they all repeat the good and avoid the bad. The chances are that such firms will have little trouble obtaining the next commission because of their established and documented expertise; and the entire architectural profession will benefit from their efforts. A feedback loop will have been established that allows continuing improvement of all phases of the architectural design process (Fig. 8-12).

8.6 Exercises

1. Take the program document that you have developed and evaluate it using the program evaluation procedures outlined in the text. Was the process as rigorous as required for an effective program? If not, how could it be improved?

   Use each of the simulation procedures in turn to test the information presented in the program. Was something included in the document that would make the program objectives difficult to achieve in design?

2. Take the design that you or your colleagues developed from the program and use the program as a primary means to evaluate the solution. Does the design solution work exceptionally well for all of the identified values, goals, and requirements? Does it express the important values? Does it

achieve all of the goals, especially the most important ones? Does it satisfy all of the stated requirements? If not, what is missing?

3. Imagine that one of the design solutions was actually constructed and ready for occupancy. What would you want to tell the occupants in a user's guide? Could they occupy and use the building without any guidance?

   If not, prepare a brief guide placing the use criteria in order of importance. Would the guide be effective? Would some of the guidelines be so obvious that they should not be stated? Would there still be some areas in which the user might not be able to utilize the facility properly?

4. Ask yourself and your associates if all of the careful procedures outlined throughout the text are more or less likely to help the designer in the quest for architecture. Which would be the most important procedures to follow in this regard? Which would be the least important, or would be actual impediments to the designer in developing a creative problem solution?

8.7 References

Bechtel, Robert, Robert Marans, and William Michelson. 1987. *Methods in Environmental and Behavioral Research*. New York: Van Nostrand Reinhold.

Clipson, Colin, and Joseph J. Wehrer. 1973. *Planning for Cardiac Care: a Guide to the Planning and Design of Cardiac Care Facilities*. Ann Arbor: Health Administration Press.

Kirk, Stephen J., and Kent F. Spreckelmeyer. 1988. *Creative Design Decisions: A Systematic Approach to Problem Solving in Architecture*. New York: Van Nostrand Reinhold.

Marans, Robert, and Kent Spreckelmeyer. 1981. *Evaluating Built Environments: A Behavioral Approach*. Ann Arbor: Survey Research Center, University of Michigan.

Preiser, Wolfgang F. E., Harvey Z. Rabinowitz, and Edward T. White. 1988. *Post-Occupancy Evaluation*. New York: Van Nostrand Reinhold.

Spreckelmeyer, Kent. 1982. "Architectural Programming as an Evaluation Tool." In *Knowledge for Design: Proceedings of the 13th International Conference of the Environmental Design Re-*

search Association, College Park, Maryland. Edited by Polly Bart, Alexander Chen, and Guido Francescato. Washington, D.C.: EDRA, 289-296.

_____. 1986. "Environmental Programming," Chapter 8. In *Methods in Environmental and Behavioral Research*, edited by Robert Bechtel, Robert Marans, and William Michelson. New York: Van Nostrand Reinhold.

Trites, David, Frank Galbraith Jr., Madelyne Sturdavant, and John Leckwart. 1970. "Influence of Nursing-Unit Design on the Activities and Subjective Feelings of Nursing Personnel." *Environment and Behavior*. 2(3): 303-334.

Sample Architectural Programs

A.1 The Planning Department, The University of Arizona
A.2 Mikvah for an Orthodox Jewish Congregation

A.1 The Planning Department, The University of Arizona

This program was developed in the spring semester of 1997 by 11 students in the author's course on architectural programming and in section three of the second year design studio of the College of Architecture at The University of Arizona. The program was accomplished during an intensive one-week programming charrette conducted after the content of Chapters 1 through 7 of this text had been covered in the programming class. This program was done in parallel with the other three design studio sections, which did similar programs for the Department of Landscape Architecture, the Graduate Program in Architecture, and the Undergraduate Program in Architecture. Each of the other programs were of comparable size and quality to the one presented here.

Note that the program, including covers and dividers, is shown in full in this appendix. However, the appendix to the program, which contains information uncovered using literature search, interviewing, observation, questionnaires, and site analysis, is shown only in part. The appendix contained 160 pages that were used as background information in developing the architectural program. A typical page or two from each section of the program appendix is shown in this appendix in order to give the reader an idea of the type(s) of information collected.

A combined space allocation matrix was developed after the charrette for a design studio program of five weeks' duration in which the students in all four sections prepared their individual design proposals for the expansion of the College of Architecture. The four departmental programs and their appendices are being used by the college administration to develop a definitive program for a major addition to the College of Architecture.

All four of the student programs were published on 8½" × 11" paper oriented vertically and plastic comb bound. The appendices were in matching three-ring binders for ease of assembly and use.

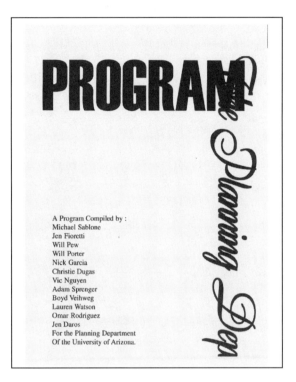

PROGRAM and Planning Dep

A Program Compiled by :
Michael Sablone
Jen Fioretti
Will Pew
Will Porter
Nick Garcia
Christie Dugas
Vic Nguyen
Adam Sprenger
Boyd Veihweg
Lauren Watson
Omar Rodriguez
Jen Daros
For the Planning Department
Of the University of Arizona.

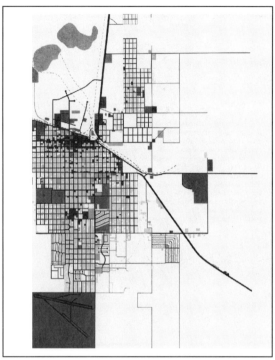

Table of Contents

METHODS

Preparation of this document began on March 24, 1997. Three days were spent gathering information by means of interviews, observation of current facilities, analysis of the proposed site, and a literature search. An interactive computerized work session was also conducted on March 27, to clarify information gathered and to increase input from the planning program members. Following the information gathering, a large matrix was produced with cards representing information and ideas gathered in a large, easy to understand format. This matrix was completed on March 28, 1997.

Using the Information displayed on the matrix, decisions were made regarding how to best provide for the needs of the planning program and achieve the goals they have expressed for the new facility. These decisions are expressed here in document format to provide information to those working on the design and implementation of this building project. Preparation of this document was completed on March 31, 1997.

ACKNOWLEDGEMENTS

We would like to extend our sincere thanks to all of those who took part in the preparation of this document. Meaningful information for a program of this type is impossible to gather without the cooperation of many people. Those of you who have given of your time to talk with us and share your thoughts, feelings, and ideas have enriched the information that will shape this project in the future.

Special thanks to Dean Richard Eribus for giving us this opportunity to be involved in this project, Kenneth Clark for taking the time to share his feelings and insights into the workings of the planning program, Dan Middleman and Alex Lakey for conducting the interactive computer work session from which we received a wealth of useful information, and to everyone else that has helped in the preparation of this document.

As students, we would also like to thank our professors, with special thanks to Professor Robert Hershberger, who has led us through each step of this process and provided us with the necessary guidance for success in this and future projects.

DIRECTORY

UNIVERSITY OF ARIZONA PLANNING, INTERDISCIPLINARY PROGRAM, COLLEGE OF ARCHITECTURE

Main Office, College of Architecture, room 214
Chairman, Kenneth Clark...621-3661
Program Coordinator, Karen Young...............................621-9597
Fax Number...621-8700
E-Mail..youngkl@ccit.arizona.edu

Faculty
Barbara Becker,.........................Drachman Institute.......623-1725
Frank Cassidy,..........................177 N. Church, #610..........621-9597
Adrian Esparza,........................Harvill 437a.........................626-7062
Lawrence Mann,.......................Harvill 439.........................621-1169
Sandra Rosenbloom,................Drachman Institute...........623-1223
Martin Yoklic,...........................Environmental Research Lab...........741-1990

Adjunct Faculty
Michael Bradley,.......................Harshbarger 324................621-3865
Art Silvers,................................McClelland 405pp.............621-4822
Brigitte Waldorf,......................Harvill 435b.......................621-7486
Robert Wortman, ...Civil Engineering..............621-2852
Stephen Yool,...........................Harvill 453c.......................621-8549

Program Staff
Karen Young,.............................Architecture 214...............621-9597
Patsy Padilla,............................Drachman Institute...........623-1223
Nancy Patsy Brown,.................Drachman Institute...........623-1223

Student Representatives
Trevor Barger, ...Architecture 214................624-6252
Bob McCrary, ...Architecture 214................628-9653

UNIVERSITY OF ARIZONA COLLEGE OF ARCHITECTURE

Main Office, College of Architecture 104
Dean, Richard Eribus...621-6754
Exec. Assistant, Claudette Barry.....................................621-6754

College Staff
Sheila Blackburn..621-6752
Linda Craig..621-6751

Eric Olson..621-3284
Mark Perry...621-4656

CAMPUS AND FACILITIES PLANNING

Main Office, ...888 N. Euclid, Suite 202.............621-1099
Director, David J. Duffy..621-1099
Fax #..621-9243

FACILITIES DESIGN AND CONSTRUCTION/FACILITIES MANAGEMENT

Main Office, 1331 E. 5ᵗʰ St...621-1805
Director, Robert R. Smith..621-9414
Fax #..621-5668

Executive Summary

The following program attempts to state the primary goals used to develop the new facilities for the Graduate Planning Department/Program. The new facilities will be further incorporated into an overall expansion including space for the undergraduate architecture program, graduate architecture program, and landscape architecture program. The space allotted for the planning department is expected to be approximately 5000 square feet.

The graduate program at the University of Arizona is a two year program resulting in a Master of Science in Planning. The program currently houses approximately forty students.

The main values/goals of the program are as follows: to establish an identity, among the University and among other planning departments; to create a sense of unity between the College of Architecture, Landscape Architecture, and the Planning Department; to provide adequate facilities for advancing technology, to stay abreast with current and future technological developments; to design a highly functional space which accommodates all necessary activities.

Some important facts include the existing facilities, which are: the Drachman Institute, the planning annex, a library and library workroom, a computer lab, and 3 class/lecture rooms in the architecture building. Most problems with these area center around the fact that all of the resources are spread out and none contain adequate space for growth.

Several needs were also uncovered: the students need a planning studio, with sufficient space for tasks; a seminar room which seat between 20-25 students; a classroom for 40; a lecture room for 150; exhibition space; offices for the Director, Executive assistant, and other administrators. Other key needs include handicap access, environmental controls, and plenty of storage space.

Important ideas include: conference room; a central outdoor area; northern views; student mailboxes; lounge space; a common pin-up area within the studio; easy interaction among students and faculty; and a dynamic entrance to the facility.

The proposed site for the new facilities will be an expansion of the existing College of Architecture at the University of Arizona in Tucson, Arizona. The expansion will extend off of the current building eastward along Speedway Blvd. This proposed area is currently a parking lot. It is surrounded by other University buildings and possibly a future fine arts library.

Space allocation for the new facilities are as follows:
    Reception 100sq ft
    Coordinator 360sq ft
    Chair 200sq ft
    Conference(sm) 200sq ft
    Faculty offices 4 @ 150sq ft ea
    2 Classrooms 850sq ft

Studio 1000sq ft
Computer Lab 250sq ft
Storage 200sq ft
Lounge 150sq ft
Conference 350sq ft

SUBTOTAL: 4260sq ft + Exhibition/Circulation @ 35%: 1491sq ft

TOTAL: 5751sq ft

TOTAL ESTIMATED PROJECT COST: $1,130,019 - $1,695,723

ESTIMATED PROJECT COMPETION BY: June, 1999

MATRIX SUMMARY

VALUES:

The most important values to the planning department in the design of the new addition are:

Functionality: The building must function well.

Technology: As a college that is heavily involved in the technologic world, the new building should provide for and plan for future advancements in technology.

Unity: In an interdisciplinary college a unity between departments, and between the college and community, is essential.

Identity: Planning department needs to be recognized as its own program within the college.

GOALS:

Main goals to be accomplished in this project include:

- A building that is comfortable to live and work in. This includes comfortable seating in all rooms.

- A G.I.S. lab in the building.

- Working relationships between the three disciplines.

- Distance learning.

FACTS:

- **Current Enrollment**
    37 graduate students currently enrolled
    Enrollment is dropping noticeably
    Enrollment could grow if planning's concerns within the new building are met.

- **Current Facilities:**
    1504 E. Helen St.:
        Approx. 1660 sq. ft.

One faculty office in building
4 drafting tables to accommodate 37 students
Medium sized conference room, 300 sq. ft.
Tackable surfaces in all rooms.

Drachman Institute:
    3 faculty offices
    New addition has recently provided 2 new faculty offices at aprox. 238 sq. ft. each.

Architecture Building:
    2 faculty offices:
        Room 214 -- Administrative Coordinator
            225 sq. ft.
            Insufficient lockable storage space for student records
            Insufficient general storage
            Insufficient work space
            Fixed office furniture offers no flexability
            Used as a planning student lounge and coordinator's office
        Room 212 -- Planning Director
            180 sq. ft.
            Ceiling leaks
            Air conditioner squeaks loudly
    Shared classroom 207:
        675 sq. ft.
        Location next to shop causes noise problems
    Shared classroom 302a:
        530 sq. ft.
        No blackout shades make projector screen unuseable
        Network connections in classroom
    Architecture computer lab 204b:
        660 sq. ft.
        No G.I.S. equipment
        17 Workstations (8 Mac & 9 IBM)
        1 printer
        2 Full size plotters
        Insufficient storage
    Architecture Library:
        1500 sq. ft.
        Stacks are already at 99% capacity
        Inaccessible to public after 5 p.m.
        Requires increase of no less then 50%

NEEDS:

Faculty Offices:
- 7-8 Offices needed in close proximity to each other
- Offices must have flexible furniture arrangements
- Privacy (closeable doors)
- Support equipment in office cluster (copiers, fax, printers)
- Planning director must have an adjacent office to his coordinator and room enough for small comfortable meetings.
- Planning coordinator must have lockable storage sufficient to hold all confidential student records.
- Archive Storage Space

Planning Studio:
- Pin-up / presentation space
- Secure storage areas for each student
- Light tables
- Large work table
- Individual work stations with writing desk, drafting table (for half the class), Ethernet, and work area.
- In-studio computers
- 15-20 drafting tables total
- Large discussion table
- Daylighting

Classroom:
- 40 persons
- New technology (Ethernet, A.V. equipment, computer assisted instruction)
- Sufficient electrical outlets
- Moveable table and chair seating

Seminar Room:
- 15-25 persons
- New technologies (see above)
- Moveable table and chair seating

Lecture Room:
- Shared between departments
- Seating for approx. 200-250
- Proper Acoustics
- Lectern controlled lighting

Technology:
- In-studio computers
- Multi-tasking
- Task lighting

- Want Ethernet connections at personal workstations
- Existing computer lab needs:
  - G.I.S. capability
  - Better security
  - Surge Protection
  - More Storage
  - Wire Management System
  - Variable Lighting (Daylighting is not a need or high priority)
  - Monitored entry - monitor would have printer control
  - Better air conditioning

Maintenance:
- Building upkeep must be provided for.

Accessibility:
- Keyed entrances for students and faculty after 5:00 p.m.
- Handicapped access to all building entrances.

Miscellaneous:
- Exhibition Space 100-200 sq. ft.; close to administration.
- Blackout shades in all rooms
- Food service area in building. (people, not vending machines)

IDEAS:

- Northern Views
- Lounge Space
  - Shared between disciplines
  - comfortable relaxed atmosphere
  - food service
- Extended hours library with all planning materials in one building
- Common pin-up area in the studio
- Flexibility – moveable seating in class/seminar rooms
- Separate office and storage space – student access to storage without interrupting offices
- Student mail boxes

- Replace outdated equipment
- Building-wide computer network
- Separate grad student computer lab
- Share software between disciplines
- Teaching capabilities in computer labs
- Individual temperature control in each room (class, lecture, seminar)
- Separate disciplines by floor
- Interaction – close relationship between grad programs
- Connect planning to arch. undergraduate studios
- Central outdoor area for relaxation
- Have one large conference room shared between departments & a smaller conference / Seminar room for planners
- Highly visible entrance with strong identity
- Make an entrance space that will serve as a welcome and introduction to the college; display space
- Borrow design ideas from other colleges with successful planning departments, such as Harvard, MIT and Berkley

Space Allocation

Reception
100 square feet

Coordinator/ Student Helper
360 Square Feet

Chair's Office
200 Square Feet

Conference Room
200 Square Feet

Faculty Offices
4 @ 150
Square Feet

Classroom (2)
1 Seating 20, 1 Seating 40
850 Square Feet

Studio
1000 Square Feet

Computer (GIS) Lab
250 Square Feet

Storage
200 Square Feet

Lounge
150 Square Feet

Large Conference Room
350 Square Feet

Exhibit/ Circulation @ 35%
1491 Square Feet

Total Area Requirement:
5751 Square Feet

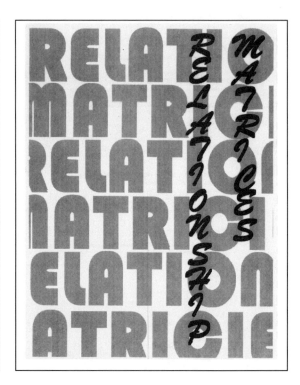

SPACE RELATIONSHIP MATRIX

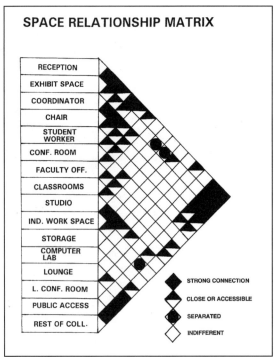

RECEPTION
EXHIBIT SPACE
COORDINATOR
CHAIR
STUDENT WORKER
CONF. ROOM
FACULTY OFF.
CLASSROOMS
STUDIO
IND. WORK SPACE
STORAGE
COMPUTER LAB
LOUNGE
L. CONF. ROOM
PUBLIC ACCESS
REST OF COLL.

STRONG CONNECTION

CLOSE OR ACCESSIBLE

SEPARATED

INDIFFERENT

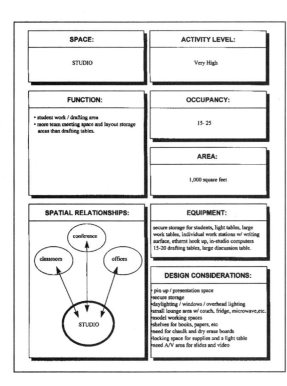

SPACE:	ACTIVITY LEVEL:
STUDIO	Very High

FUNCTION:	OCCUPANCY:
• student work / drafting area • more team meeting space and layout storage areas than drafting tables.	15- 25

	AREA:
	1,000 square feet

SPATIAL RELATIONSHIPS:

EQUIPMENT:
secure storage for students, light tables, large work tables, individual work stations w/ writing surface, ethernt hook up, in-studio computers 15-20 drafting tables, large discussion table.

DESIGN CONSIDERATIONS:
• pin-up / presentation space
• secure storage
• daylighting / windows / overhead lighting
• small lounge area w/ couch, fridge, microwave,etc.
• model working spaces
• shelves for books, papers, etc
• need for chaulk and dry erase boards
• locking space for supplies and a light table
• need A/V area for slides and video

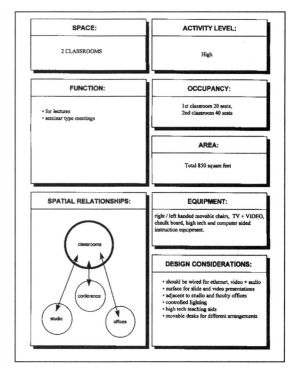

SPACE:	ACTIVITY LEVEL:
2 CLASSROOMS	High

FUNCTION:	OCCUPANCY:
• for lectures • seminar type meetings	1st classroom 20 seats, 2nd classroom 40 seats

	AREA:
	Total 850 square feet

SPATIAL RELATIONSHIPS:

EQUIPMENT:
right / left handed movable chairs, TV + VIDEO, chaulk board, high tech and computer aided instruction equipment.

DESIGN CONSIDERATIONS:
• should be wired for ethernet, video + audio
• surface for slide and video presentations
• adjacent to studio and faculty offices
• controlled lighting
• high tech teaching aids
• movable desks for different arrangements

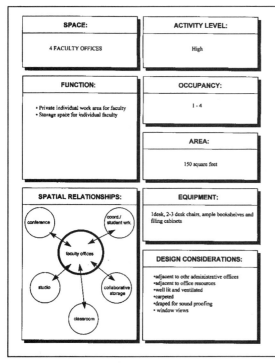

SPACE:	ACTIVITY LEVEL:
4 FACULTY OFFICES	High

FUNCTION:	OCCUPANCY:
• Private individual work area for faculty • Storage space for individual faculty	1 - 4

	AREA:
	150 square feet

SPATIAL RELATIONSHIPS:

EQUIPMENT:
1desk, 2-3 desk chairs, ample bookshelves and filing cabinets

DESIGN CONSIDERATIONS:
• adjacent to othr administrative offices
• adjacent to office resources
• well lit and ventilated
• carpeted
• draped for sound proofing
• window views

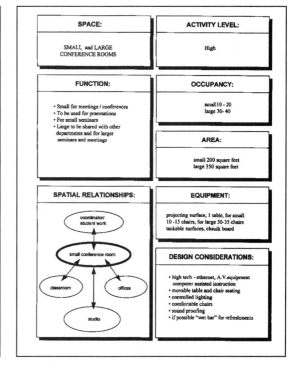

SPACE:	ACTIVITY LEVEL:
SMALL and LARGE CONFERENCE ROOMS	High

FUNCTION:	OCCUPANCY:
• Small for meetings / conferences • To be used for prsentations • For small seminars • Large to be shared with other departments and for larger seminars and meetings	small10 - 20 large 30- 40

	AREA:
	small) 200 square feet large 350 square feet

SPATIAL RELATIONSHIPS:

EQUIPMENT:
projecting surface, 1 table, for small 10 -15 chairs, for large 30-35 chairs tackable surfaces, chaulk board

DESIGN CONSIDERATIONS:
• high tech - ethernet, A.V.equipment computer assisted instruction
• movable table and chair seating
• controlled lighting
• comfortable chairs
• sound proofing
• if possible "wet bar" for refreshments

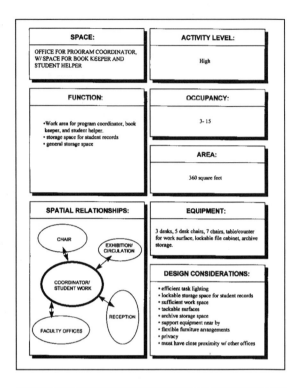

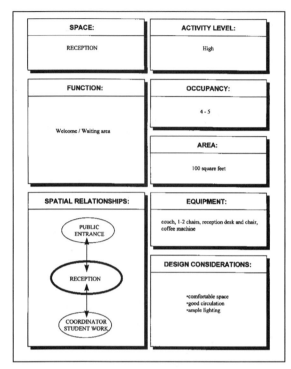

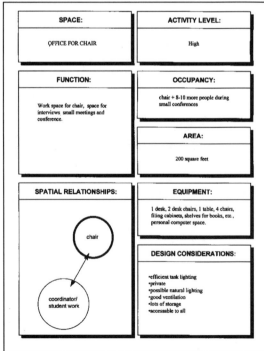

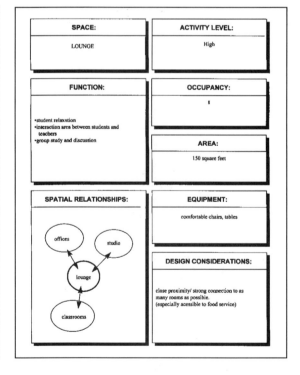

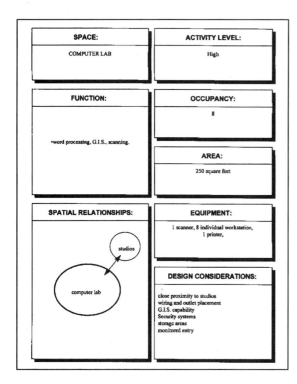

SPACE:	ACTIVITY LEVEL:
COMPUTER LAB	High

FUNCTION:	OCCUPANCY:
•word processing, G.I.S., scanning.	8

AREA:

250 square feet

SPATIAL RELATIONSHIPS:

studios

computer lab

EQUIPMENT:

1 scanner, 8 individual workstation,
1 printer,

DESIGN CONSIDERATIONS:

close proximity to studios
wiring and outlet placement
G.I.S. capability
Security systems
storage areas
monitored entry

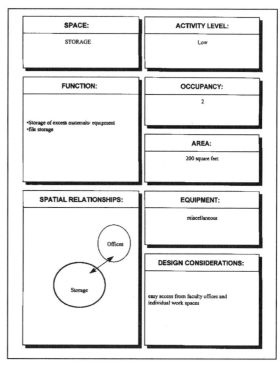

SPACE:	ACTIVITY LEVEL:
STORAGE	Low

FUNCTION:	OCCUPANCY:
•Storage of excess materials/ equipment •file storage	2

AREA:

200 square feet

SPATIAL RELATIONSHIPS:

Offices

Storage

EQUIPMENT:

miscellaneous

DESIGN CONSIDERATIONS:

easy access from faculty offices and
individual work spaces

PLANNING DEPT.
GROSS SQ./FT. = 5751SQ./FT.

	LOW AVG.	MED AVG.	HIGH AVG.
A. BUILDING COST............	$807,158	$862,650	$821,571
B. FIXED EQUIPMENT......	$ 56,501 (7%)	$ 86,265 (10%)	$115,020 (14%)
C. SITE DEVELOPMENT....	$ 40,358 (5%)	$ 86,265 (10%)	$123,236 (15%)
D. TOTAL CONST...............	$904,017	$1,035,180	$1,059,827
E. MOVABLE EQUIP..........	$ 90,402 (10%)	$124,222 (12%)	$158,974 (15%)
F. PROFESSIONAL FEES....	$ 45,200 (5%)	$103,518 (10%)	$158,974 (15%)
G. CONTINGENCIES..........	$ 45,200 (5%)	$103,518 (10%)	$158,974 (15%)
H. ADMIN COST.................	$ 45,200 (5%)	$103,518 (10%)	$158,974 (15%)

TOTAL BUDGET
REQUIRED...................$1,130,019 $1,469,956 $1,695,723

PROJECT SCHEDULE

Programming Phase — 1.5wk
Schematic Design — 3wk
Design Development — 5wk
Construction Documents — 10wk
Bid — 4wk
Approval — 12-14months
Construcion

Move In

REVIEW AND APPROVAL SESSIONS
BETWEEN PHASES APPROXIMATELY
ONE WEEK EACH

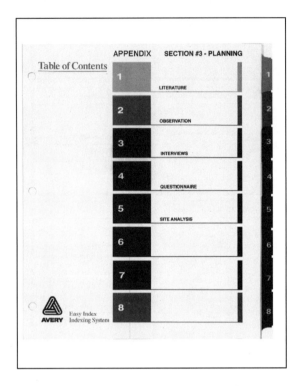

- Donovan C. Wilkin (Renewable Natural Resources)
- Robert H. Wortman (Civil Engineering)

Assistant Professors

- Frank J. Cassidy (Planning)
- D. Phillip Guertin (Watershed Managment)
- Stephen R. Yool (Geography)

The interdisciplinary Program in Planning directs a graduate professional program leading to the Master of Science degree with a major in planning.

The major consists of 52 units: 27 units of core course work, 21 units in a chosen area of concentration and a 4-unit internship. Core courses include 500, 501, 504, 514, 544, 584, 605, 611, 660 and 693. Areas of concentration include: sustainable community design, environmental resource planning, land use and transportation planning, and international/borderlands planning.

The program requires completion of a projects course. A comprehensive written examination or professional report must be completed as part of the 52 units of course work. Internship experience is required and students are exposed to field applications in other course work as well. The program is specifically designed to expose students to the interdisciplinary nature of most planning problems. The course work provides a mixture of theoretical and practical perspectives on diverse planning issues.

Interested persons should contact the program chair for further information.

Individual course descriptions may be found in The University of Arizona General Catalog.

This page last updated December 19, 1995.
For comments and/or questions about this server, please click here.

This page has been accessed 16 times since February 28, 1997. It has been accessed 0 times today.

WALK-THROUGH / SYSTEMATIC OBSERVATION
UNIVERSITY OF ARIZONA COLLEGE OF ARCH. LIBRARY
OBSERVED BY: Jennifer DaRos, Vic Nguyen

Observation	Meaning
1. 1500 sq. ft.	1. Library is smaller then necessary
2. Four 3'x7' reading tables with 4-6 chairs per table	2. 24 out of 200 students can use library reading space at the same time.
3. Library is used by students in waves, as projects are due. In the words of the librarian "It's either no one or everyone"	3. Library is either full beyond capacity, or basically empty
4. 2 SABIO computer terminals with a number of students waiting to use them	4. Not enough computer work stations for the number of students who need them.
5. Computer terminals in a very small area which serves also as the reference section. Many of the reference books are inaccessible when the computer stations are in use. • A CD-ROM computer in the back of the room is wedged behind the tables in the reading area with little or no room to sit at the station.	5. Computer stations need their own space.
6. No reading/work stations in reference or reserve area. Students read and work with the books and their notes in their laps.	6. Reference section needs to be enlarged to accommodate reading/work tables.
7. Electrical outlets are scarce and hard to find.	7. Not enough electrical access for people who bring in laptops.
8. Heavy traffic to reference and reserve sections through a very narrow area causes circulation problems.	8. Reference and reserve sections need more space.
9. Less then two feet of circulation space between reading tables and magazine racks.	9. Not enough space in library to accommodate all library functions.
10. No areas for group study sessions.	10. Students must leave library to conduct study groups.
11. No worktable by copy machine.	11. Causes difficulties with large copy jobs; difficult to staple, collate, sort copies.

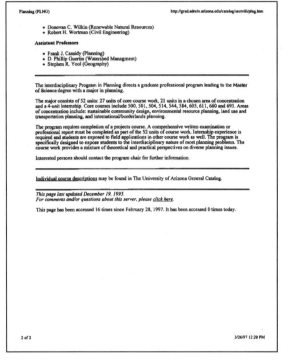

COLLEGE OF ARCHITECTURE   THE UNIVERSITY OF ARIZONA
Architecture 227: Program for Addition to and Renovation of the College

QUESTIONNAIRE: Name: KEN CLARK   Date 3/27/97

Architecture___ Landscape___ Planning ✓ Administrator ✓ Faculty ✓ Staff___

Please respond to all of the following questions for which you have an opinion.

1. A new lecture room should provide seating for approximately: (check one)
   a. 100
   b. 150
   c. 200
   d. 250 ✓
   e. More than 250 (give number)
   Explain? Room 103 holds 120 ?

2. The lecture room should have which of the following: (check the one that applies)
   a. Fixed tablet-arm seats
      Fixed tables w/ attached seats
      Fixed tables w/ moveable seats
      Moveable tablet-arm seats ✓
      Moveable tables and seats
      Other ___
      Explain?
   b. Molded plastic seats
      Padded/upholstered seats ✓
      Other ___
      Explain?
   c. Sloped floor with raised stage ✓
      Sloped floor without stage
      Level floor with raised stage
      Level floor without stage
      Other ___
      Explain?

3. The lecture room should provide which projection/presentation systems: (Rate each from 3 very important to 1 unimportant)
   a. Double Side   3
   b. Large Screen Computer/Video   3
   c. Overhead   1
   d. 16 m.m. film   1
   e. Computer hookups each seat   1
   f. Chalkboard   3
   g. Dry Erase board   3
   h. Projection booth   3
   i. Light/AV controls at lectern   3
   j. Elmo
   k. Other ___

4. New classrooms should provide seating for approximately: (check one)
   a. 30
   b. 40 ✓
   c. 50
   d. 60
   e. 70
   f. More than 70
   Explain?

5. The classrooms should have which of the following: (check the one that applies)
   a. Fixed tablet-arm seats
      Fixed table w/ attached seats
      Fixed table w/ moveable seats
      Moveable tablet-arm seats
      Moveable table, moveable seats ✓
      Other ___
      Explain?
   b. Molded plastic seats
      Padded/upholstered seats ✓
      Other ___
      Explain?

6. The classrooms should provide the following: (Rate each from 3 very important to 1 unimportant)
   a. Double side projection   1
   b. Large screen computer/video   3
   c. Overhead projection   3
   d. 16 m.m. film projection   1
   e. Computer hookup for each seat   1
   f. Chalkboard   3
   g. Dry erase board   3
   h. Windows (with blackout shades)   3
   i. Storage areas for each class   3
   k. Light/AV controls at lectern   3
   l. Carpet on the floor   3
   j. Tack-up space (one wall)   3
   k. Tack-up space (two walls)   3
   l. Tack-up space (three walls)   3
   m. Tack-up space (four walls)   3
   n. Elmo Projector
   o. Other ___

19. Studios should include the following furnishings and equipment. (Rate from 3 highly desirable, 2 desirable, to 1 undesirable)
   a. Printers
      One per floor
      One per section
      Other ___
   b. Scanners
      One per floor
      One per section
      ___ per section
      Other ___
   c. Computer hook-ups
      Five per section
      One per student station
      Other ___
   d. Cutting tables
      One per floor
      One per section
      Other ___
   e. Light tables
      One per floor
      One per section
      ___ per section
      Other ___
   f. Copy machines
      One for addition
      One per floor
      One per section
      ___ per section
      Other ___
   g. Section space
      Pin-up/discussion/review space ___
      Lounge space/furnishings ___
      Refrigerator ___
      Hot plate ___
      Other ___

20. Other suggestions:

21. Design ideas: (print, sketch below)

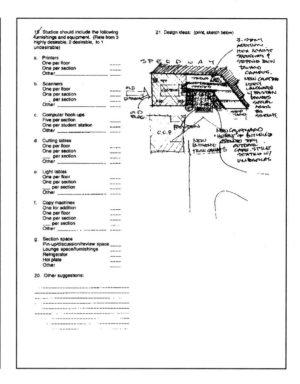

SITE ANALYSIS

- Contents:

- Views from the site
- Airborne Pollutants

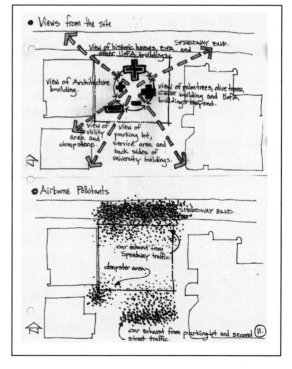

A.2 Mikvah for an Orthodox Jewish Congregation

This architectural program is typical of those done over the years by the author of this text. It was selected for presentation in this appendix both because it was formatted horizontally, in contrast to the student generated program, and because it was for a very small, but unique, facility that required nearly all of the information gathering procedures to develop an understanding of the design problem. Because of the small project size, it was possible to reproduce the entire program and its appendices in this appendix.

The reader should understand that most programs and appendix information required for unique projects will be considerably larger than shown here. But the difference will be one of size, not of kind. There will be more people to interview, more spaces to observe, a larger site to analyze, and perhaps so many occupants that questionnaires will be required to obtain the needed information.

There may also be more literature resources to find and review. And there will be many more space program sheets to develop. In other words, this is one of the smallest complete architectural programs that could be presented. The only parts of the program not included in this appendix were the very simple divider sheets used to make it easier for the reader to find the respective parts of the program.

The program was printed in the architect's office on white 8½" × 11" laser paper in order to ensure that the quality of the small photographs would not be lost. The dividers and covers were printed on the same weight gray bond paper. The program was bound on the left side with a black plastic comb binding so that it would lay flat during use. The front and back covers were covered by a clear plastic film to protect the document from heavy use during design.

MIKVAH FOR AN ORTHODOX JEWISH CONGREGATION

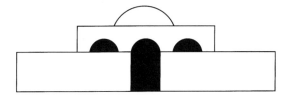

ARCHITECTURAL PROGRAM
by Robert G. Hershberger, Ph.D., FAIA, Architect   6/6/97

MIKVAH FOR AN ORTHODOX JEWISH CONGREGATION
by Robert Hershberger, Ph.D., FAIA, Architect

Contents

Acknowledgment/Directory/Methods

Executive Summary

Values, Goals, Facts, Needs Summary

Space Program Sheets

Space Allocation

Relationship Diagrams

Mikvah, Bor, Pump and Tank Relationships

Project Cost Analysis

Site Analysis

Ideas Exploration

Appendix

Literature Review

Observation of Mikvahs

MIKVAH FOR AN ORTHODOX JEWISH CONGREGATION PRELIMINARIES
by Robert Hershberger, Ph.D., FAIA, Architect

ACKNOWLEDGMENT

We are most appreciative of the desire of the clients (names withheld by request) to create a Mikvah worthy of the sacred nature of the required ritual immersion and the ancient traditions of the Orthodox Jewish faith. We especially appreciate their desire to have the Mikvah be a place of exceptional quality, serenity and beauty—a splendid opportunity for Architecture. We would also like to acknowledge (names withheld by request of the clients) for their help with appropriate material and system selection and in cost estimation. We also appreciate the help of the Rabbis and staff of the Synagogues we visited for showing us their facilities and explaining how they work both technically and functionally. Finally, we appreciate the authors of *A Hedge of Roses; Waters of Eden: The Mystery of the Mikvah*, and *Generations: The Mikvah through the Ages* , for shedding light on this sacred ritual of the Orthodox Jewish tradition.

DIRECTORY

CLIENT	ENGINEERS AND CONSULTANTS	CONTRACTOR
(names and address withheld by request)	(names and address withheld by request of client)	(names and address withheld by request of client)
	(names and address withheld by request of client)	
ARCHITECT	(names and address withheld by request of client)	
Robert Hershberger, Ph.D., FAIA, Architect	(names and address withheld by request of client)	
4001 E. Elmwood, Tucson, Arizona, 85711		
Robert Hershberger 520 320-5700		

METHODS

The work on this program began with an intensive interviewing session with the clients. This was followed by a review of the three books known to cover the subject area of the Mikvah. A trip with the clients to observe, measure and photograph existing Mikvah facilities and to interview the Rabbis and staff allowed first-hand discovery of the essential nature and character of these facilities. Sitting between the clients on the airplane allowed for intensive discussion about the visited facilities and the proposed Mikvah for the Orthodox Jewish Congregation. The information gained was developed into a draft of this document which was reviewed and edited by the clients. This final copy was then prepared for publication.

MIKVAH FOR AN ORTHODOX JEWISH CONGREGATION EXECUTIVE SUMMARY
by Robert Hershberger, Ph.D., FAIA, Architect

PURPOSE

The Mikvah for an Orthodox Jewish Congregation is intended to respond to G-d's will and Jewish Law by providing a place for the required ritual bath for married Jewish women coming seven days after the conclusion of the menses. It is intended to serve the needs of the Congregation and the general Orthodox Jewish community.

VALUES and GOALS

In addition to responding to G-d's will and Jewish Law, the immersion is intended to support family purity and love in renewing of the marriage relationship each month. It is intended to enhance the women's self esteem and the man's respect and love for his spouse. It also must provide for the women's modesty, privacy and safety. It is to be a place of spirituality—regal, serene, beautiful and elegant—a place of aesthetic pleasure. It is to be clean, safe and functional.

NEEDS

The Mikvah will be a comparatively small facility, owing to the small Orthodox Jewish population in the community. It will consist initially of a waiting room, two dressing/bath rooms, the Mikvah pool room and associated storage and equipment for a total floor area of approximately 900 sq. ft. It will have an exterior Mikvah for the ritual cleansing of food preparation containers and utensils. Expansion plans should include the addition of at least one dressing room with a shower. The Mikvah should be spacious and constructed of high quality, low maintenance materials and systems. It must provide for both the private and safe access of the participating women. It must have the capability of collecting sufficient rainfall to completely fill the bors of the Mikvah.

IDEAS

The Mikvah should be located in association with the existing courtyard, but with safe and inconspicuous access for the women. It should relate in form and materials to the existing Synagogue, but also have a character of its own, fitting within the historic traditions of the Mikvah. Consider solar water heating and an outside storage tank/filtering system.

COSTS

Depending on the quality of materials and systems, and the construction market at the time of bidding, the cost of construction could range from as low as $118, 000 to as high as $181,000, which results in an overall project cost spread of between $155,000 and $239,000.

SCHEDULE

The schedule is designed so that rain water can be collected in January and February of 1998. Programming was completed in early June, Schematic Design is scheduled to be complete by mid June, Construction Documents by late July, Bidding by mid August and Construction by mid January, 1998.

MIKVAH FOR AN ORTHODOX JEWISH CONGREGATION
by Robert Hershberger, Ph.D., FAIA, Architect

PROGRAM SUMMARY MATRIX

VALUES/ISSUES	GOALS	FACTS	NEEDS
Religious:			
Comply with G-d's Will	Provide Mikvah for community	Jewish Law requires Mikvah	New Mikvah that will attract women
Commitment to Ritual Law	Comply with all Jewish Laws	Many women not observing this	Large enough for community needs
Links to Ancestry/Tradition	Renew tradition	ritual	Traditional forms/spaces
Family:			
Family Purity/Holiness/Love	Reinforce sanctity of marriage	Abstinence reinforces love bond	Mikvah at Synagogue
Abstinence/Renewal of Marriage	Renew love/respect for spouse	Immersion sets stage for marriage	
		renewal	
Personal:			
Women's Self Esteem	Place where women want to go	The enigma of Mikvah hinders use by	Spacious, comfortable, pleasant place
Privacy/Modesty/Safety	And feel good about observance	contemporary Jewish women	Inconspicuous but safe access
		Evening use poses security problems	
Aesthetic:			
Spiritual, Regal, Serene	Instill spiritual nature of observance	Existing courtyard could provide an	Building and landscape form, light,
Order, Beauty, Elegance	Place of aesthetic pleasure	excellent setting	color, materials, textures and art that
			create the desired aesthetic qualities
Health:			
Clean/Sanitary	"So clean will not want shower after"	High humidity destroys poor surfaces	High quality, easily cleaned materials
Safe access/interior	No chance of harm to women/attendant	Integral finishes easier to maintain	Primarily self-cleaning systems
			Ready storage of cleaning supplies
Function:			
Mikvah and Bors	Ample size/easy access/observation	Typical problems include:	Two levels for short/tall women
Dressing/cleaning/preparation	2 w bath/shower, 1-2 future w shower	Inadequate counter/storage space	Dressing counter, mirror, storage, etc.
Waiting	Room for four to six women	Storage never adequate, stuff exposed	Comfortable chairs, magazines, art,
Storage	Ample for towels, robes, accessories	Slippery surfaces are safety hazard	robes, towels, accessories/sale
Washer/Dryer	As convenient as possible	Can be scary after dark	Residential side/side w/ ample storage
Access/parking	Convenient, pleasant, safe	Too often appear dirty and dingy	Close, lighted, video survey, private
Exterior Mikvah	Available for immersing utensils	Lack privacy outside and inside	Handsome, clean, garden setting
Technical:			
Rain water collection/storage	Collect enough this summer monsoon	One good rain will do, seldom renew	Make Mikvah roof the collector
Water purification/storage	Pool system ,but underground storage	Underground storage reduces humidity	Standard pool purification with tank
Temperature/humidity control	Effective, automatic, low maintenance	High quality systems will work	Standard pool air/humidity control

---

MIKVAH FOR AN ORTHODOX JEWISH CONGREGATION
by Robert G. Hershberger, Ph.D., FAIA, Architect

SPACE PROGRAM SHEET

WAITING ROOM

ISSUES

PRIVACY
SAFETY
COMFORT
CONVENIENCE
RELAXATION
BEAUTY

GOALS

1. Private and safe access to and from the exterior and waiting room.

2. Comfortable and relaxing space, possibly with meaningful art work in preparation for mikvah experience.

3. Soothing environmental quality, including lighting--appropriate for reading, conversation or meditation.

4. Convenient storage for all materials needed in the dressing room, including items for sale that may have been left at home.

4. Easy for attendant to clean and straighten up the room between uses.

5. Attractive and inviting to use--similar in quality to a fine living room.

FACTS

1. Niddah will arrive and leave after sunset by automobile or on foot. They will arrive by foot on Friday evenings, or regularly, if they are residents of the immediate neighborhood.

2. The neighborhood is currently safe, but the immediate site is not well lighted after dark and has no obvious surveillance to prevent loitering or criminal activity.

3. It would be rare to have more than two or three women waiting at any time.

NEEDS

1. Convenient and well lighted parking and walkways to entrance to waiting room, as well as a system for video surveillance and audio monitoring of these areas.

2. Adequate closet/storage space for robes, towels, wash clothes, slippers and items for sale immediately adjacent to or within the waiting room. Also closet for coats, hats and umbrellas during inclement weather.

3. At least four comfortable easy chairs and lighting suitable for conversation, reading or meditation. At least two small side tables for magazines and placing of purse/cosmetic bag while waiting for turn in dressing room.

4. Paging system for attendant to contact Niddah when Mikvah is ready to enter.

5. Handsome appointments, plants and art work to enhance the aesthetic quality of the room.

SIZE   10' x 20'   200 sq. ft

1. Large enough to accommodate all of the furniture and to leave a generous amount of space for circulation

2   10 feet wide (5' seating group, 5' circulation and plants)
20 feet long (12' mikvah width, 2 - 4' doors)

RELATIONSHIPS

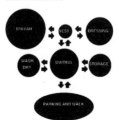

MIKVAH FOR AN ORTHODOX JEWISH CONGREGATION
by Robert G. Hershberger, Ph.D., FAIA, Architect

DRESSING ROOMS (TWO)

ISSUES

PRIVACY
CONVENIENCE
CLEANLINESS
BEAUTY

GOALS

1. Room use and entry to and from Mikvah without being seen or heard by people in waiting room.

2. Temperature must be comfortable for persons with and without clothes.

3. Light quality, surfaces and accessories must be designed for convenient use before and after the ritual bath.

4. It must be easy for attendant to clean and straighten up room between uses.

5. The room should be attractive and inviting to use—similar in quality to a fine master bath room.

FACTS

1. Niddah will be let into room by attendant, will disrobe and hang up clothes, will use toilet if necessary, remove make up and nail polish, and take bath or shower to wash body and hair before entering the Mikvah.

2. Niddah will dry off, brush hair, put on bath robe and slippers, pick up towel and inform attendant that she is ready to enter Mikvah.

3. After immersion she will return to dressing room to complete drying off, brush hair (possibly replace make-up and nail polish) and dress in preparation to return home.

4. After she leaves, attendant will inspect dressing room, pick up anything left behind, dry floor and counters in preparation for next Niddah.

NEEDS

1. Adequate closet or clothes hooks on which to hang clothes, and ample surfaces on which to place personal effects.

2. Lavatory in long counter with mirror for washing and removing and replacing makeup. A chair or stool at one end of the counter to form a dressing table would be desirable.

3. Excellent lighting so that Niddah and attendant can conduct a detailed inspection of Niddah before the immersion.

4. Convenient storage for miscellaneous supplies to use in preparing for the mikvah bath and afterwards in preparing to return home. See separate list.

5. Toilet for normal hygienic functions.

6. Bath and shower for cleaning body and washing hair.

SPACE PROGRAM SHEET

7. Ability to lock door(s) to dressing room, so that no one else may enter.

8. Private access to mikvah.

9. Paging system to inform attendant when ready to enter mikvah.

SIZE   6' x 15'   90 sq ft

1. 6 feet wide (2' counter, 4' circulation)
2. 15 feet long (2' closet, 7' counter, 3' toilet and 3' shower)

RELATIONSHIPS

MIKVAH FOR AN ORTHODOX JEWISH CONGREGATION
by Robert G. Hershberger, Ph.D., FAIA, Architect

MIKVAH POOL ROOM

ISSUES

PRIVACY
COMFORT
SAFETY
BEAUTY
SPIRITUALITY

GOALS

1. Entry to and from Mikvah without being seen or heard by people in waiting room.

2. Temperature and humidity must be comfortable for persons with and without clothes.

3. Light quality, surfaces and supports must be designed to prevent accidents.

4. Light, forms, colors and water quality must provide and feeling of beauty and spirituality.

FACTS

1. Niddah will inform attendant when they are ready to enter the Mikvah. Attendant will make certain the Mikvah is ready and open door so that niddah may enter (and lock other doors so that others may not enter).

2. Niddah will enter the Mikvah room in a bath robe and towel which they will hang up,

and disposable paper slippers which they will leave on the floor.

3. Clothed attendant will accompany Niddah into Mikvah room, inspect to be certain that she is prepared, instruct her on care in entering water and expectations for submersion and ritual statements, will watch to see that she is completely immersed, and will aid her as she emerges from the water.

4. Niddah will dry herself with towel, put on robe and slippers, and return to dressing room. Attendant will inspect Mikveh room, pick up anything left behind, dry floor area in preparation for next Niddah.

5. All water must be still during the ritual bath period.

NEEDS

1. Adequate private space for attendant to meet Niddah and to take them into Mikvah.

2. Ability to lock doors to waiting room and other dressing rooms, so that no one else may enter during ritual bath.

3. Adequate landing space, with hooks for towel and robe, bench/stool for drying feet.

4. Temperature and humidity control to keep attendant and Niddah comfortable in room.

5. Continuous handrails down into pool to assure that Niddahs will not slip or fall upon entering or leaving the pool.

SPACE ALLOCATION SHEET

6. Two levels inside pool to accommodate the needs of shorter and taller women.

7. Rail on each side of Mikvah pool to allow attendant to be near Niddah during submersion to make certain that she is fully submersed and not touching sides of pool.

8. Quality of lighting, materials, forms, colors and appointments to assure the beauty and spiritual quality of the place and experience.

SIZE   12' x 18'   216 sq ft

1. 12 feet wide (8 foot pool, 2' walk each side)
2. 18 feet long (4 foot landing, 7 - 10" treads, 2 - 3' landings at 48" and 55" depths, 3' for bor and walk way above)

RELATIONSHIPS

IDEAS

1. Masonry vault over Mikvah pool.

MIKVAH FOR AN ORTHODOX JEWISH CONGREGATION
by Robert G. Hershberger, Ph.D., FAIA, Architect

SPACE PROGRAM SHEET

LAUNDRY ALCOVE

ISSUES

HIDDEN (visual, aural)
CONVENIENCE
CLEANLINESS

GOALS

1. To store wet and soiled linen until wash day.

2. To wash and dry all of the dirty linen one or two days each week.

3. To iron and/or fold linen easily.

4. To be easy for attendant or maid to clean and straighten up room between uses.

FACTS

1. Currently have only a few women each night, so the load should be quite small and easily handled on a weekly basis, if there are two dozen sets of linen.

2. As number of Niddahs increases, it will be necessary to increase the amount of linen or to wash more often.

3. There will also be wet slippers and other disposables to store each evening and to remove daily or at least once each week

NEEDS

1. Standard residential side by side clothes washer and dryer.

2. Ventilated hamper in which to store wet and soiled linens.

3. Trash container to store disposable item.

4. Shelves, cabinets and drawers to laundry supplies.

5. Built in ironing board and folding table to prepare linens for return to storage closet.

SIZE   3' x 10'   30 sq ft

1. 5 feet for washer and dryer, 3' for folding table and ironing board, 2' for hamper.

2. 2'-6" depth for washer and dryer.

RELATIONSHIPS

IDEAS

1. Place the laundry behind louvered folding doors at one end of the waiting room so the attendant and/or cleaning service can use the waiting room as circulation and work space for ironing and folding.

2. Allow for future expansion of laundry as a separate room.

MIKVAH FOR AN ORTHODOX JEWISH CONGREGATION
by Robert G. Hershberger, Ph.D., FAIA, Architect

SPACE PROGRAM SHEET

STORAGE ALCOVE

ISSUES

HIDDEN (visual)
CONVENIENCE
CLEANLINESS

GOALS

1. To store packets of linen (robe, towels, wash cloth, slippers) to give to Niddahs.

2. To store supplies to be provided in dressing rooms, or sold for individual use by Niddahs..

3. To be control center for video and audio surveillance, sound, telephone and paging systems, as well as for receiving payments for various sales and record keeping.

4. To be easy for attendant or maid to straighten up between uses.

FACTS

1. Currently have only a few women each night, so there should only be a need for two dozen sets of linen.

2. As the number of Niddahs increases, it will be necessary to increase the amount of linen, or to wash, iron, fold and replace more often.

3. Electrical, video, sound, telephone and paging systems all require space and electrical service.

NEEDS

1. Storage shelves for sets of folded robe, towels, wash clothes, slippers.

2. Bin or drawer type storage for supplies to be sold to Niddahs.

3. Closed bin or drawer type storage for supplies for dressing rooms.

4. Desk, chair, lamp and lockable drawers and files for collections and record keeping by attendant.

5. Hanging rod and hooks for coats, hats, umbrellas of Niddahs and attendant during inclement weather.

SIZE   3' x 10'   30 sq ft

1. 3 feet for open shelves, 2' for bins, 2' for hanging clothes and 3' for video/audio equipment.

2. 8 feet of continuous counter including desk space below all but the clothes hanging area.

2. 2'-6" depth behind ventilated folding doors to allow all items to be hidden when not in use, except video monitoring screens.

RELATIONSHIPS

IDEAS

1. Place the storage behind louvered folding doors at one end of the waiting room so that the attendant can use the waiting room as circulation and work space for the desk and for placing and removing linen and supplies.

MIKVAH FOR AN ORTHODOX JEWISH CONGREGATION
by Robert G. Hershberger, Ph.D., FAIA, Architect

SPACE PROGRAM SHEET

JANITOR CLOSET

ISSUES

HIDDEN (visual, aural)
CONVENIENT

GOALS

1. To store all needed cleaning equipment and supplies.

2. To store all needed pool supplies.

3. To be easy for attendant or janitor to find supplies.

FACTS

1. Will need to spot clean dressing rooms and Mikvah between uses.

2. Will need to thoroughly clean both at end of evening or following day.

3. Will need to add chemicals and to monitor PH in pool daily.

4. Will need to monitor temperature settings of rooms and pool water.

NEEDS

1. Storage shelves for cleaning and pool supplies.

2. Hanging storage for brooms and dusting.

3. Floor level storage for vacuum cleaners, skimmers and the like.

4. Put in an easily accessible but inconspicuous location.

SIZE   2' x 3'   6 sq ft

RELATIONSHIPS

IDEAS

1. Place the janitor closet behind a solid, lockable door.

MIKVAH FOR AN ORTHODOX JEWISH CONGREGATION
by Robert G. Hershberger, Ph.D., FAIA, Architect

SPACE PROGRAM SHEET

VESTIBULES (TWO)

ISSUES

PRIVACY
CONTROL
HOUSEKEEPING

GOALS

1. To provide a completely private way for attendant to escort Niddah to and from Mikvah.

2. To store light cleaning supplies and equipment.

3. To dispose of soiled linen and supplies before use by next Niddah.

FACTS

1. Niddah should not be seen by others in waiting room when going to and from Mikvah.

2. Attendant will use vestibule space to ask Niddah if she is ready.

3. Niddah and attendant may share vestibule when going to and from Mikvah.

4. Must spot clean dressing rooms and mikvah between uses.

5. Must dispose of soiled linen and supplies between uses.

NEEDS

1. Adequate space for two people moving to and from Mikvah.

2. Storage shelves for cleaning equipment and supplies.

3. Ventilated hamper to receive wet towels, robes and wash cloths.

4. Trash receptacle to receive used paper products and other left overs.

SIZE   4' x 5'   20 sq ft

RELATIONSHIPS

IDEAS

1. Place next to janitor closet for easy access to supplies and cleaning equipment.

MIKVAH FOR AN ORTHODOX JEWISH CONGREGATION
by Robert G. Hershberger, Ph.D., FAIA, Architect

SPACE ALLOCATION

SPACE ALLOCATION

1. Mikvah Pool Room (4' landing + 11' pool + 3' bor = 18') x (2' + 8' + 2' = 12') 18' x 12' =   216 sq ft
    Mikvah Pool Length: (7 - 10" treads + 2 - 3' landings = 11')
    Mikvah Pool Width: (width of two bors + trough between = 8')
    Mikvah Deck Length: (4' at door landing, 3' over bors, 2' at sides)
    Bor Dimensions (2' x 3' x 4'-6" = 27 cu ft or approx. 200 gallons each)
    Bor Pool Length: (6" + 2' + 6" = 3')
    Bor Pool width: (3' + 2' + 3' = 8')

2. Waiting Room (10 feet deep x 8' Mikvah width + 3'-6" door width x 2)   10' x 15' =   150 sq ft

3. Dressing Rooms (15" long x 6' wide = 90 sq ft) 90 sq ft x 2 =   180 sq ft
    Length (2' closet + 7' counter + 3' toilet + 3' shower = 15')
    Width (2' counter + 4' manuvering = 6')

4. Vestibule (4' x 5' = 20 sq ft) 20 sq ft x 2=   40 sq ft

5. Washer/Dryer Alcove (7' wide x 3' deep = 21 sq ft)   21 sq ft

6. Towel/Supply Storage (7' wide x 3' deep = 21 sq. ft)   21 sq ft

7. Attendant/Janitor Storage (3' wide x 2' deep = 6 sq. ft)   6 sq ft

NET SQUARE FEET (interior)   **634 sq ft**

EFFICIENCY (approximately 70%) (halls, walls, chases)   **254 sq ft**

GROSS SQUARE FEET (net ÷ efficiency) 634 ÷ .70 =   906 sq ft

APPROXIMATE OVERALL SIZE   30' X 30' = 900 sq ft

MIKVAH FOR AN ORTHODOX JEWISH CONGREGATION
by Robert G. Hershberger, Ph.D., FAIA, Architect

PROJECT COST ESTIMATE

PROJECT COST ESTIMATE	LOW	MEDIUM	HIGH
1. BUILDING COST ($125/sq ft, $150/sq ft, $175/sq ft) (including all mechanical/plumbing/electrical equipment)	$112,500	$135,000	$157,500
2. SITE DEVELOPMENT (5%, 10%, 15% of 1)	5,625	13,500	23,625
3. TOTAL CONSTRUCTION COST (1+2)	**$118,125**	**$148,500**	**$181,125**
4. FURNISHINGS/SUPPLIES (2% of 1) (6 chairs, potted plants, towels, supplies)	2,250	2,700	3,150
5. PROFESSIONAL FEES/PERMITS (20% of 3)	23,625	29,700	36,225
6. CONTINGENCIES (10% of 3)	11,812	14,850	18,112
7. TOTAL BUDGET REQUIRED (3+4+5+6)	**$155,812**	**$195,750**	**$238,612**

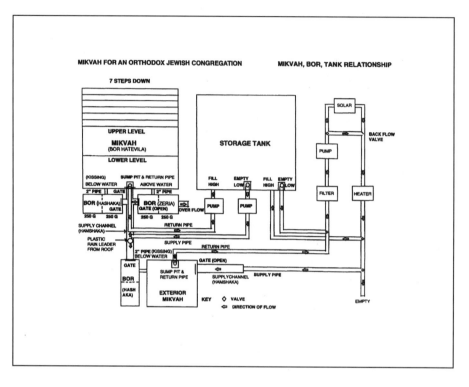

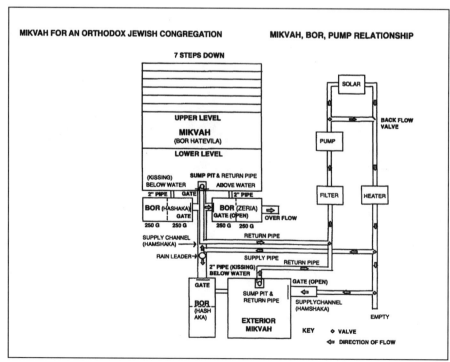

MIKVAH FOR AN ORTHODOX JEWISH CONGREGATION
by Robert Hershberger, Ph.D., FAIA, Architect

SITE ANALYSIS

[image showing site plan with labels: ALLEY, UTILITIES, PLAYGROUND, PARKING, WALL, GATE, WALL, SERVICE YARD, PLANTERS, TREE, PORCH, LAWN, WALL, COURTYARD, SYNAGOGUE, TREE, PARKING, WALL, GATE ARCH, SITE OF CHOFETZ CHAYIM-ORTHODOX, 1" = 40' NORTH DOWN, FIFTH STREET]

3. The existing parking is neither paved nor landscaped.

4. All utilities are in alley and connect with existing building at its southwest corner.

5. Alley is not paved and has a continuous wall along its south side which screens residential properties from the alley and trash stored there.

6. Existing building and courtyard wall is of a handsome yellow buff brick, probably from Texas.

7. Existing building has attractive arched windows and porch supports. Windows are of stained glass.

8. The courtyard also has a brick arch and wrought iron gate at the entry opening on the north.

9. The courtyard with lawn, planters and trees is very nice, by far the most attractive place on the site.

10. The playground is also landscaped and with generally well kept playground equipment. It is surrounded on the east, south and west and partially on the north with a six foot high chain-link fence.

11. The courtyard appears to be the obvious place on which to locate at least the ceremonial facade of the Mikvah building.

12. Issues of safe and private access must be considered in the specific location of the Mikvah.

1. Primary parking and pedestrian access is from Main Street.

2. The street is the prime generator of noise.

MIKVAH FOR AN ORTHODOX JEWISH CONGREGATION

IDEAS EXPLORATION

1. Locate the Mikvah off of the existing courtyard.

SITE LOCATION PLAN

A. SOUTH SIDE IN PLAYGROUND EAST OF OPENING
+ Open view from entrance to courtyard and synagogue porch.
+ Very close to existing utilities (power, water, sewer, gas).
+ Can hide all mechanical equipment in fenced yard east of Mikvah.
+ Can develop Mikvah for cooking utensils in garden south of Mikvah.
+ Can collect rain water off roof of existing building.
+ Can use existing roof for inconspicuous solar water heating.
+ Uses and undeveloped area of playground.
- Lack of privacy for women as must pass through courtyard.
- Difficult to assure personal safety from vehicle to and from Mikvah.
- Small buildable area, may force Mikvah to extend into courtyard.
  No visual presence from Main Street.

B. SOUTH SIDE IN PLAYGROUND WEST OF OPENING
+ View over landscaping in courtyard to entrance of Mikvah.
- Further from existing utilities (power, water, sewer, gas)
+ Can hide all mechanical equipment in fenced yard west of Mikvah.
+ Can develop Mikvah for cooking utensils in garden south of Mikvah.
- Cannot collect rain water off roof of existing building.
- Cannot use existing roof for inconspicuous solar water heating.
- Disrupts developed area of playground.
+ Can provide private access from west parking area.
+ Can develop a secure route from parking to Mikvah.
+ Larger buildable area within playground.
  No visual presence from Main Street.

C. WEST SIDE IN PARKING NORTH OF PLAYGROUND FENCE
+ View over landscaping in courtyard to entrance of Mikvah.
- Further from existing utilities (power, water, sewer, gas.)
+ Can hide all mechanical equipment in fenced yard south of Mikvah.
+ Can develop Mikvah for cooking utensils in garden west of Mikvah.
- Cannot collect rain water off roof of existing building
+ Can use south mech. yard for inconspicuous solar water heating.
+ Can provide close, private access from west parking area.
+ Can develop a secure route from parking to Mikvah.
+ Does not disrupt playground areas at all.
- May limit synagogue growth to west of courtyard.
  Strong visual presence from Main Street.

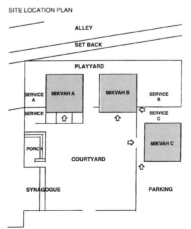

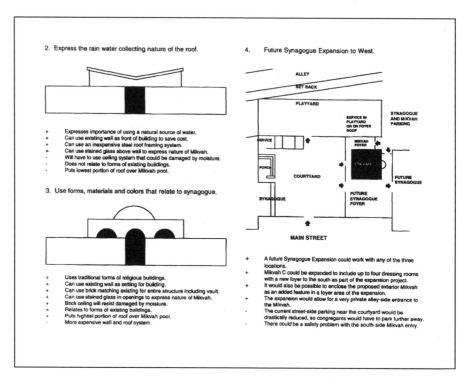

2. Express the rain water collecting nature of the roof.

+ Expresses importance of using a natural source of water.
+ Can use existing wall as front of building to save cost.
+ Can use an inexpensive steel roof framing system.
+ Can use stained glass above wall to express nature of Mikvah.
- Will have to use ceiling system that could be damaged by moisture.
- Does not relate to forms of existing buildings.
- Puts lowest portion of roof over Mikvah pool.

3. Use forms, materials and colors that relate to synagogue.

+ Uses traditional forms of religious buildings.
+ Can use existing wall as setting for building.
+ Can use brick matching existing for entire structure including vault.
+ Can use stained glass in openings to express nature of Mikvah.
+ Brick ceiling will resist damaged by moisture.
+ Relates to forms of existing buildings.
+ Puts highest portion of roof over Mikvah pool.
- More expensive wall and roof system.

4. Future Synagogue Expansion to West.

ALLEY
SET BACK
PLAYYARD
SERVICE IN PLAYYARD OR ON FOYER ROOF
SYNAGOGUE AND MIKVAH PARKING
SERVICE
MIKVAH FOYER
MIKVAH
PORCH
COURTYARD
FUTURE SYNAGOGUE
SYNAGOGUE
FUTURE SYNAGOGUE FOYER
MAIN STREET

+ A future Synagogue Expansion could work with any of the three locations.
+ Mikvah C could be expanded to include up to four dressing rooms with a new foyer to the south as part of the expansion project.
+ It would also be possible to enclose the proposed exterior Mikvah as an added feature in a foyer area of the expansion.
+ The expansion would allow for a very private alley-side entrance to the Mikvah.
- The current street-side parking near the courtyard would be drastically reduced, so congregants would have to park further away.
- There could be a safety problem with the south-side Mikvah entry.

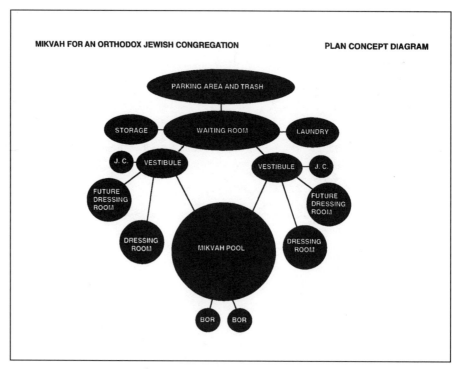

MIKVAH FOR AN ORTHODOX JEWISH CONGREGATION   PLAN CONCEPT DIAGRAM

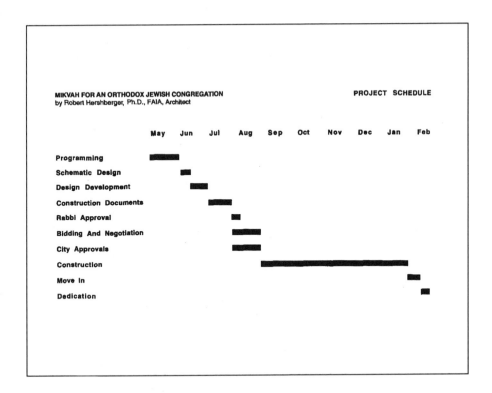

MIKVAH FOR AN ORTHODOX JEWISH CONGREGATION
by Robert Hershberger, Ph.D., FAIA, Architect

PROJECT SCHEDULE

MIKVAH FOR AN ORTHODOX JEWISH CONGREGATION

APPENDIX

ARCHITECTURAL PROGRAM
by Robert G. Hershberger, Ph.D., FAIA, Architect

MIKVAH FOR AN ORTHODOX JEWISH CONGREGATION
by Robert Hershberger, FAIA, Architect

LITERATURE REVIEW

1. Lamm, Norman. 1987. *A Hedge of Roses: Jewish Insights into Marriage and Married Life.* Sixth Edition (Revised). Jerusalem and New York: Philipp Feldheim, Inc.

    This small book contains an insightful and often poetic discussion of the sacred nature of the marriage relationship in Jewish life. It asserts "priority to Family Purity over public prayer and Torah reading; hence if a community cannot afford to erect all three communal structures, the building of the *Mikvah* takes precedence over the building of the Synagogue and the writing of the Scroll of the Torah. The purity of the Jewish family, more than worship by the community or the pursuit of scholarship, is responsible for the perpetuation of the House of Israel" (page 48).

    The book refers to Jewish Law which "forbids a husband to approach his wife during the time of her menses, generally from five to seven days, and extends the prohibition of any physical contact beyond this period for another seven days, known as the 'seven' clean days.' ... During this time husband and wife are expected to act towards each other with respect and affection but without any physical expression of love—excellent training for the time, later in their lives, when husband and wife will have to discover bonds other than sex to link them one to another (page 35). It goes on to tell how the "menstruant (known as *niddah*) must immerse herself in a body of water known as a *mikvah* and recite a special blessing in which she praises God for sanctifying us with His commandments and commanding us concerning immersion (tevilah) (Page 36)."

    "The *mikvah* itself—along with its prescribed dimensions and source of the water—is an ancient institution. Ordained by the Bible, it was in wide use during the times of the two Temples; one who had contracted any of the various kinds of "impurity" was forbidden to eat of sacrificial meat or the tithe, or to enter the precincts of the Temple. The way of effecting purification was through immersion in the *mikvah* (page 36).

    "*Mikvah* is used today not only for Family Purity, but also for the initiation of proselytes, both male and female, into Judaism, and for immersing certain kinds of new household vessels. In addition, some pious male Jews immerse themselves before prayer and before Sabbaths and Holy Days. The *mikvah* is a communal institution, generally an inconspicuous building, and administered with the utmost modesty and delicacy, often luxuriously appointed.

    There is considerably more in this 106 page volume convincingly discussing the nature and importance of Family Purity and, for example, explaining the specific measures that a women takes before her wedding, as a newly wed and throughout married life (pp. 94-99). Anyone planning or designing a *mikvah* must read this book.

2. Kaplan, Arkyeh. 1992. *Waters of Eden: The Mystery of the Mikvah.* New York: National Conference of Synagogue Youth/Union of Orthodox Jewish Congregations of America.

    Similar to *A Hedge of Roses,* this book explains the purposes and use of the Mikvah, including Niddah and use for Conversion, Pots and Dishes and associated customs including numerous historical insights. It is more explicit about the characteristics of the mikvah, itself, as follows: "At first glance a Mikvah looks like little more than a small swimming pool. The water is usually about chest high, large enough for three or four people to stand in comfortably. For easy access, there are stairs leading into the water of the Mikvah. If you look more closely, you will see a small hole, two or three inches in diameter, just below the water line of one wall of the pool. This hole may appear insignificant, but it is what actually gives this pool its status as a Mikvah. Just opposite this small hole, you will notice a removable cover over a *Bor* or "pit," which is the essential part of the Mikvah. This

Bor is a small pool by itself, and it is filled with natural rain water. The rain water must enter the *Bor* essentially in a natural manner...Under certain conditions, spring water or melted snow or ice can also be used." (page 5).

The author goes on to indicate that the *Bor* must accommodate approximately 200 gallons of rain water and must be a pit built directly into the ground. It specifically cannot be a vessel that can be disconnected and carried away, but it can be built into the upper story of a building. "The *Bor*... can be used for a Mikvah, but since it is very difficult to change its water, it is most often used as a source to give another pool connected to it the status of a Mikvah. This larger pool can be filled in any convenient manner from the ordinary city water supply, and its water can be changed as often as desirable. The only requirement is that it be connected to the water of the *Bor* by an opening at least two inches ;in diameter. By connecting the two pools and allowing ;their ;waters to mingle we give the water in the larger pool the status of the ;water in the smaller pool. The process of intermingling the waters of the two pools is known as Hashakah..." (page 6).

"There are three basic areas where immersion in the Mikvah is required by Jewish Law:
1.   After a woman has her monthly period, she may not be intimate with her husband until she immerses in the Mikvah. This involves a Biblical law of the utmost severity.
2.   Immersion in a Mikvah is an integral part of conversion to Judaism. Without immersion, conversion is not valid. This is required of men and women alike.
3.   Pots, dishes and other eating utensils manufactured by a non-Jew must also be "converted" by immersion in a Mikvah before they can be used on a Jewish table." (page 6).

3.   Reiss, C. Editor. 1995. *Generations The Mikvah Through the Ages*. Brooklyn, New York: Laine

This is an elaborately illustrated book prepared in celebration of the dedication of the Mikvah Yisroel of Flatbush, 1980 Avenue L, Brooklyn, NY. Like the others, it describes the purposes of the Mikvah. It also describes and illustrates the history of the Mikvah from Antiquity (including Masada), Europe from the Middle Ages, the Middle East and the New World. It recounts specific use during times of suppression as in Nazi Germany, China and Behind the Iron Curtain. Its illustrations show some of the amazing examples of ancient Mikvah.

Southern Wall of Masada Showing the Mikvah and the Rain Water Reservoir

Mikvah at Speyer, Germany

Diagram of the Mikvah in Tiberias

MIKVAH FOR AN ORTHODOX JEWISH CONGREGATION
by Robert G. Hershberger, Ph.D., FAIA, Architect

WALK-THROUGH OBSERVATION

1.   Mikvah Number 1

In process of enlarging to include three additional dressing rooms, a hair drying room and much more storage.

If were to do again would also have a larger mechanical room and more closet, storage and counter space in dressing rooms.

Do not like hearing other women in Mikvah. Want privacy. Object to very noisy exhaust fan. Attendant has to speak loudly to be heard.

Piped in music, but not into Mikvah. In dressing room it is nice to have relaxing music. Also like relaxing colors -- blues and greens.

Pump Room has three pumps:
1.   Circulates Water through filter, heater and solar panels
2.   Empties Mikvah to Tank
3.   Fills Mikvah through trough

Interlock to prevent more than one pump from operating at a time. Water going in and out at the same time is a problem. Must be certain through controls that pump is not on when people in Mikvah.

They have a 2000 gallon fiberglass tank, all water pumped into it at night, then pumped back into Mikvah during the day. Avoids humidity problem.

Pumped, filtered, heated all day. They add chlorine before removing water from tank. 1/4 to 1/2 cup for 20 women. Use powder. At 96° liquid breaks down. Must check the PH each time.

Can use gas pool heater. Use skimmer switched to vacuum for residual water

Exhaust Fan to room is set for humidity. Water at about 90° steams room up, so need to exhaust and to air condition. Set temperature of pool at 96°. If paint, must be very good epoxy to prevent peeling.

Fill and empty Mikvah with a timer, not a float, so must learn how long it takes and adjust. A reliable water level sensor would be better.

Two steps down before reach the water level of the Mikvah. There was no known reason why this was the case.

Grab bars must extend down into pool to prevent slipping. Sometimes another person assisting.

Attendant locks door to Mikvah, so that next person can not look or get in. She does not like going into dressing room, because of privacy. There are doors everywhere, trying to maintain privacy.

Need some shelves to place personal belongings for final preparations.

Attendant waits with people in the waiting room when no one in the Mikvah.

They have double security at the doorway, with video surveillance both directions. Seems to be a real problem to maintain privacy and security at the same time.

Counter tops around sinks are not large enough. Get very cluttered. Need more space. Drawers. Everything should be hidden.

Counter needs to be clean and dry -- not tile. Formica or a monolithic surface.

Heat lamp in dressing room is important. On a separate switch.

They use bath sheets -- very large towels. Have a set of four: 1. big bath sheet, 2. floor rug, 3. regular towel, 4. wash cloth. These are changed for each user.

A cleaning girl does the wash the next day.

Should be a rest room for the waiting women and attendant.

They change the Mikvah rain water only about once each year.

The solar water heating is very effective, and reduces water heating expenses considerably.

The storage, washing and drying facilities are completely inadequate at present.

WAITING ROOM -- STORAGE, MONITORS

WAITING ROOM -- STORAGE, SALES

Note low height of storage door and wires to all of the telephone and monitoring equipment

DRESSING ROOM COUNTER

DRESSING ROOM COUNTER/TOILET

Note all of the different required paraphernalia.

UNDER COUNTER SUPPLIES

SOLAR COLLECTOR AT ROOF

Note inefficient storage under counter and solar and water collection to rain leader at S.E. corner.

MIKVAH LANDING/STORAGE

RAILING INTO MIKVAH

Note the clutter on the landing and the sign that indicates falling hazard at mikvah.

MIKVAH LOWER POOL AND RETURN

MIKVAH CEILING

Note clutter on ceiling and messy look of multiple types of yellow/gold tile on uneven surfaces.

MIKVAH FOR CONGREGATION CHOFETZ CHAYIM-ORTHODOX
by Robert G. Hershberger, Ph.D., FAIA, Architect

WALK-THROUGH OBSERVATION

2.   Mikvah Number 2

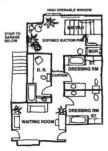

Waiting room is pleasant and nicely furnished.

Two of the dressing rooms are adequate in size, but the counters could be longer, and entry and exit lack privacy from waiting room. The other dressing room is poorly arranged.

The Mikvah room is of adequate size, but lacks privacy. Exposed pipes and conduit as afterthoughts give it a tacky look.

The washer and dryer, not shown, are adequate in size and located close enough for its purposes.

Storage seems adequate in dressing rooms, but not in waiting area.

CURTAIN AND HIGH WINDOW

Mikvah room is greatly enhanced by high operable window, because of light and ventilation. Does not have the musty smell of the windowless Mikvahs. However, high window is very difficult to open; it requires a ladder.

Curtain was an after thought when they realized that the person in the Mikvah was in complete view of the waiting room.

Artificial plants give a nice touch of color, but are also tacky.

Color of the tile at blue/green is much more successful than the yellow/gold tile at the first Mikvah.

Signs every where indicate that the selection of the tile was not carefully considered. It is obviously quite slippery when wet, and the discontinuous handrails do not help.

SLIPPERY SIGNS AND TACKY DETAILING

DISCONTINUOUS HANDRAILS

EXPOSED PIPES AT MIKVAH

EXPOSED PIPES AND CONDUIT

Exposed pipes and conduit everywhere indicate a lack of initial planning.

The small size of the lower landing and lowest section of pool up next to the pipes must make emersion quite difficult.

ADEQUATE STORAGE IN DRESSING ROOM

UNSIGHTLY UTENSIL MIKVAH

Cooking utensil Mikvah looks like a weekend project. Lid is not tight, so it collects dirt, scum and insects on the top of the water. Setting in a utility court and the lack of adequate painting makes this a sorrowful sight, and probably an undesirable activity for newlyweds setting up their household

ELECTRICAL CONTROLS IN BASEMENT

PIPES AND FILTER IN BASEMENT

Readily accessible piping and controls makes maintenance fairly easy.

Index

A

Aalto, A., 47, 77, **77,78**
abstraction in design, 50–51, **50**
acceptance of interviewee's position, 238–239
accessibility guidelines, 207, **208**
acknowledgment, in program, 371, **371**
Ackoff, R., 248, 303
acoustics, 85
active listening skills, 237, 324
administrative costs, 411
adobe, 97, **97**, 103
adversarial/reactionary relationship between architect/client, 8–10
Aerospace and Mechanical Engineering Building, Univ. of Arizona, 55, **55**
aesthetic factors, 12, 48–53, 56, 60–61, 73, 145–161, 175, 338
  color, 146
  form, 146–150
  industrial building design, 148–150, **148, 149**
  interviewing skills, 221
  meaning, 154–161
  space as form, 150–154
agreement-based programming, 17–25
  committees, 18
  context category, 23
  cost savings, 22

disadvantages, 23–24
energy category, 23–24
goals, 20
Indiana Bell as example, 23, **23**
Irwin Union Bank as example, 23, **24**
needs, 20
problem seeking programming matrix, 19–22, **19, 21, 22**
pros and cons, 25
value categories, areas, 20, 23
work sessions, 18, **18**, 20
AIA Standard Form of Agreement between Owner and Architect (AIA Document B141), 6
air pollution, 108
airport design, 78, **79**
Alexander, 426
Alleluia Lutheran Church, x, 52, **53**, 57–60, **57–60**
Altman, I., 15
American Institute of Architects (AIA), x, 201, 202
American National Standards Institute (ANSI), 206
American Pavilion, Montreal World's Fair, 124, **125**
American Society for Testing and Materials (ASTM), 207
Americans with Disabilities Act (ADA) guidelines, 208
amplification of interviewee's position, 237, 243

Note: **Boldface** numbers indicate illustrations.

487